THE HASTY GOURMET™

LOW SALT
FAVORITES

300 EASY-TO-MAKE, GREAT-TASTING RECIPES
FOR A HEALTHY LIFESTYLE

Other Low-Sodium Books by Bobbie Mostyn:

Pocket Guide to Low Sodium Foods (2003 Edition)

THE HASTY GOURMET™

LOW SALT
FAVORITES

300 Easy-to-Make, Great-Tasting Recipes
for a Healthy Lifestyle

BOBBIE MOSTYN

InData Group, Inc.

Published by InData Group, Inc.
P.O. Box 11908
Olympia, WA 98508-1908

Printed in the United States of America

Cover design: Gray Ponytail Studio
www.grayponytail.com

Visit our websites:

www.lowsaltfoods.com
www.thehastygourmet.com

All information contained in this book is provided for informational purposes only. It should not be considered as medical advice for dealing with a health problem or a substitute for the advice of a healthcare professional. The author and publisher do not endorse, warrant, or guarantee any of the products mentioned herein, nor does any omission of such imply otherwise.

Library of Congress Cataloging-in-Publication Data

Mostyn, Bobbie
   The Hasty Gourmet low salt favorites : 300 easy-to-make, great-tasting recipes for a healthy livestyle / Bobbie Mostyn. -- 1st ed. -- Olympia, WA : InData Group, 2005.

   p. ; cm.
   Includes index.

   1. Salt-free diet. 2. Salt-free diet--Recipes. I. Title. II. Low salt favorites.

RM237.8 .M67 2005
613.2/85--dc22   0509

DEDICATED TO:

My husband, Mike —
for your continued love and support . . .
you make everything so much easier!

All my friends and family —
for enduring my recipe testing . . .
even when some didn't come out very well.

CONTENTS

FOREWORD

I consider myself very health conscious—I do not eat red meat, keep fats to a minimum, and, as far as the saltshaker, I threw that out decades ago. So you can imagine my surprise when I was diagnosed with hypertension and told to cut back on salt. *How could I be eating too much salt*, I thought.

As it turns out, like most Americans, I was clueless about the amount of sodium I was consuming, particularly from the processed foods I routinely used in my cooking. When I checked my pantry, I was shocked—the lower-salt beans I regularly used had 220mg of sodium per half cup, my favorite bread had 250mg per slice, and the salad dressing I used most often had 650mg per 2 tablespoons!

Determined to lower my salt intake, I spent hours at the supermarket reading labels, searching for low-sodium products that could substitute for the higher salt foods I was using. Not only did I discover that nearly every food has a low-salt alternative, but I also noticed a large disparity within brands. Take tomato paste, for example, a 6-ounce can has anywhere from 35mg to 450mg, depending on the manufacturer. Even though there is little difference in taste, by choosing the lesser brand, you eliminate 315mg of sodium.

Unfortunately, I also learned that many low-salt products have no taste; in fact, some are downright yucky! And even worse, not only did some taste awful, but many were also unhealthy—the salt had been replaced with added fat and/or sugar.

The more I learned, the more committed I became to share my findings. It became my passion and led to my first book, *Pocket Guide to Low Sodium Foods*. In my quest to raise sodium awareness, I developed a website, **www.lowsaltfoods.com**, where I maintain a regularly updated list of low-salt products, offer dining out tips, health issues related to excess sodium, and much more.

But all was not rosy. As I began to modify my cooking to accommodate my low-salt lifestyle, many of my saltshaking friends and family rebelled. The truth is, some of these earlier dishes were not so good—they were bland and tasteless. In fact, one of my "salty" pals went so far as to sneak a saltshaker into the house and, while my back was turned, added salt to a sauce I was preparing.

Over the years, I am happy to say, my low-salt cooking has vastly improved. Not only is my friend no longer sneaking in a saltshaker, but he is now asking for my recipes. The true test, however, is my mother-in-law . . . who salts everything. If she doesn't enjoy something I've prepared, then it's back to the test kitchen until it's tasty enough for everyone. Now, not only does she find the meals I prepare pleasing, but she also is who first suggested I publish my recipes.

I hope you will enjoy these healthy, low-salt dishes as much as my family and friends. It has been a labor of love and I guarantee everyone will be asking for more . . . including your mother-in-law.

Bobbie Mostyn

LOW-SALT LIFESTYLE

*Welcome to the low-salt lifestyle, a way of eating that focuses on healthy, flavorful food with a minimum of sodium. This is not a diet, but a cuisine where the natural taste of food is at the heart of each meal. If you enjoy good cooking that does not sacrifice on flavor, and with a minimum of preparation, you will love this first cookbook in **The Hasty Gourmet™** series.*

The primary source of sodium in our diet comes from salt (also known as sodium chloride), a naturally occurring compound containing 40% sodium and 60% chlorine. (Although salt and sodium are not the same, the terms are used interchangeably throughout this book.)

Sodium is essential to the body by regulating fluids, however, too much sodium may cause fluid build up (or water retention), which puts added pressure on the heart and kidneys to work harder. Over time, this can lead to high blood pressure, or hypertension, significantly increasing an individual's risk for stroke, heart, and kidney disease.

Although the body only needs a small amount of sodium, or about 500 milligrams (mg), for fluid regulation, the average person consumes a whopping 4,000–6,000mg per day—nearly two to three times the recommended level of 2,400mg. *NOTE: At this writing, the National Academy of Sciences' Institute of Medicine is recommending that sodium guidelines be reduced to 1,500mg per day (less for older people).*

SALT IN OUR FOOD

Nearly everything we eat contains some sodium, even small amounts occur naturally in fruits and vegetables, but the vast majority comes off the grocery shelves and from restaurant meals. Surprisingly, less than 15% of the salt we consume comes from the saltshaker.

Thanks in part to our busy lifestyles, we have become accustomed to salty snacks and foods. Because we have less time to plan meals, we rely more on convenience and fast foods, which are loaded with salt. Unfortunately, excess sodium affects our health. In addition to hypertension, research suggests possible links to osteoporosis, dementia, asthma, edema, stomach cancer, and other ailments.

Nearly one-fourth of all adults—50 million—have hypertension and another 45 million are considered prehypertensive (at risk of developing high blood pressure). Even more alarming, at the rate we are going, 9 out of 10 middle-aged Americans face the threat of hypertension later in life.

So concerned, several organizations, including the American Public Health Association, are urging the food industry to reduce sodium by 50% by 2010. Manufacturers are opposed to these changes; they contend that low-sodium products often do not fare well in the marketplace. Taste is the main reason people buy a particular product and when salt is removed, consumers react negatively to the loss of flavor.

Unfortunately, food manufacturers cannot be forced to produce low-salt items. It is much easier for them to stop manufacturing a product than it is to create a new item, particularly one that probably will not be embraced by consumers.

Perhaps one day, with enough public demand, not only will the foods we purchase have less salt, but they also will not be a detriment to our health. It's already begun in England. An ongoing movement to reduce salt resulted in a large supermarket chain cutting the sodium in their store-brand products—12% the first year and 10% in subsequent years—with no decline in sales. They plan to continue with these cutbacks every few years until there is a 50% reduction.

SODIUM SENSITIVITY AND HYPERTENSION

According to researchers, there appears to be a direct correlation between sodium intake and high blood pressure. In countries where sodium consumption is high, there is a greater incidence of hypertension than in countries where sodium intake is low.

One of the reasons may be sodium sensitivity, which affects about 25% of the population and is very prevalent in hypertensive individuals, particularly blacks and the elderly.

According to the *Heart Disease Journal*, when it comes to lifestyle modifications, reducing salt intake is one of the most important changes you can make to reduce your blood pressure. Moreover, if you are taking anti-hypertensive drugs, a low-salt diet may enhance their effectiveness. (Government guidelines suggest that most people with high blood pressure should consume no more than 1,500mg sodium a day.)

THE DASH DIET

Research funded by the National Heart, Lung and Blood Institute shows that diet not only lowers blood pressure, but may also help prevent and control hypertension.

According to the Dietary Approaches to Stop Hypertension (DASH) study, sodium reduction lowers blood pressure regardless of race or sex and has the greatest effect on hypertensive individuals. Subsequent research indicates the lower the salt intake, the better the results.

The DASH diet, based on 2,000 calories a day, is low in fats and cholesterol. It is also high in fiber and plentiful in fruits, vegetables, and low-fat dairy products. What's more, following the DASH diet may also reduce your risk of cancer, heart disease, stroke, osteoporosis, and diabetes.

NOTE: Diet is only one part of the prevention and treatment of hypertension and other maladies. Other factors include exercise, maintaining a healthy weight, quitting smoking, and increasing your intake of calcium and magnesium. Before making any major changes in salt consumption or beginning an exercise program, be sure to talk with your healthcare provider.

THE DASH EATING PLAN

FOOD GROUP	DAILY SERVINGS	SERVING SIZES
Grains and grain products	7–8	1 slice bread 1 cup ready-to-eat cereal* ½ cup cooked rice, pasta, or cereal
Vegetables	4–5	1 cup raw leafy vegetable ½ cup cooked vegetable 6 oz vegetable juice
Fruits	4–5	1 medium fruit ¼ cup dried fruit ½ cup fresh, frozen, or canned fruit 6 oz fruit juice
Lowfat or fat free dairy products	2–3	8 oz milk 1 cup yogurt 1.5 oz cheese
Lean meats poultry	2 or fewer	3 oz cooked lean meat, skinless poultry, or fish
Nuts, seeds, and dried beans	4–5 per week	⅓ cup (1.5 oz) nuts 1 tbsp (0.5 oz) seeds ½ cup cooked dry beans
Fats and oils**	2–3	1 tsp soft margarine 1 tsp regular mayonnaise 1 tbsp lowfat mayonnaise 2 tbsp light salad dressing 1 tsp vegetable oil
Sweets	5 per week	1 tbsp sugar 1 tbsp jelly or jam 0.5 oz jelly beans 8 oz lemonade

* Serving sizes vary between ½ cup and 1¼ cups. Check the product's nutrition label.

** Fat content changes serving counts for fats and oils, for example:
1 tablespoon regular salad dressing = 1 serving,
1 tablespoon lowfat dressing = ½ serving, and
1 tablespoon fat-free dressing = 0 servings.

For additional info on The DASH Diet, see Resources, *page 272.*

TASTE IS IMPORTANT

Taste is the main reason most people find it difficult to stay on a low-salt diet. Clearly, when the amount of sodium is decreased, the flavor is compromised, and with no taste, there is no satisfaction in what we have eaten. Secondly, the limited availability of low-sodium convenience products makes it more difficult to stay on track. So it is understandable that even with the best intentions, we end up consuming far more salt than recommended.

Obviously, following a low-sodium lifestyle would be much easier if food manufacturers and restaurants stopped pouring on the salt. But there are several steps you can take to decrease sodium in your diet *(also see Tips to Reducing Sodium, page 23)*.

BE SODIUM CONSCIOUS

Although experts have been warning us for years to cut back on salt, most consumers are not listening. The problem is most of us are unaware of how much salt we actually take in. Consequently, we mistakenly think the amount we consume is okay. The bottom line, if you don't know how much salt is in a product, you cannot take control of your diet.

As you become more aware of the amount of sodium in grocery items, you will discover two things: (1) nearly every food has a low-salt alternative and (2) there is a large disparity among brands. For instance, some pasta sauces contain as much as 850mg sodium per serving, others have around 200mg, and no-salt added sauces have less than 50mg. Another example is teriyaki marinade—some brands have up to 3,050mg sodium per tablespoon. As a substitute, try one of the many grilling sauces with less than 140mg. Granted it won't have that wonderful teriyaki flavor, but it will still taste good, and it will be better for you.

FOODS HIGH IN SODIUM

Bakery items – bagels, breads, donuts, and pastries

Canned foods – soups, meats, fish, sauerkraut, beans, and vegetables

Convenience foods – frozen dinners, pizza, cereals and packaged mixes, such as pancakes, food "helpers," stuffing, and rice dishes

Dairy products – cheese and cottage cheese

Deli items – bacon, luncheon meats, corned beef, smoked meats or fish, sardines, anchovies and mayonnaise-based salads, like cole slaw and potato salad

Snack foods – crackers, chips, and dips

Condiments – mustard, ketchup, mayonnaise, salad dressings, pickles, olives, capers, salsas, and packaged seasoning mixes

Sauces – gravy, steak, teriyaki, soy, barbecue, and pasta sauces

Baking needs – self-rising flour, baking and biscuit mixes, bouillon cubes, batter and coating mixes, bread crumbs, corn syrup, cooking wines, meat tenderizers, monosodium glutamate (MSG), baking powder, and baking soda

Beverages – tomato and vegetable juices, Bloody Marys, and chocolate drink mixes

HIDDEN SODIUM

You may not be aware of the numerous sources of hidden sodium that are in over-the-counter health aids. For example, certain dentifrices, aspirin, and medications that contain ibuprofen (such as *Advil* and *Nuprin*) contain sodium, as do antacids, like *Rolaids* and *Alka-Seltzer* (some have as much as 761mg per dose). Check labels for low-sodium alternatives or ask your pharmacist or healthcare provider for suggestions.

Also, many households have water-softening systems that contain sodium chloride. To remedy this, potassium chloride (where potassium replaces the sodium) can be used instead. Of course, if it is still a concern you can always drink bottled water.

The Food and Drug Administration (FDA) regulates food labeling to assure consumers that the information they receive is accurate and not misleading. Labels contain a lot of useful figures and calculations to help you compare products and make healthy food choices.

Nutrition Facts	
Serving Size 1 cup (55g)	
Servings Per Container about 8	
Amount Per Serving	
Calories 170 Calories from Fat 10	
	% Daily Value*
Total Fat 4g	**6 %**
Saturated Fat 1g	**5 %**
Trans Fat 0.5g	
Cholesterol 0mg	**0 %**
Sodium 85mg	**4 %**
Total Carbohydrate 41g	**14 %**
Dietary Fiber 7g	**28 %**
Sugars 21g	
Protein 6g	
Vitamin A 0% ■ Vitamin C 0%	
Calcium 0% ■ Iron 5%	

*Percent Daily Values are based on a 2,000 calorie diet. Your daily value may be higher or lower depending on your calorie needs.

	Calories	2,000	2,500
Total Fat	Less than	65g	80g
Sat Fat	Less than	20g	25g
Cholesterol	Less than	300mg	300mg
Sodium	Less than	2,400mg	2,400mg
Total Carbohydrate		300mg	375mg
Dietary Fiber		25g	30g

WHAT THE LABEL TELLS YOU

Serving Size—Identified in familiar units (such as cups or tablespoons) followed by the metric equivalent (i.e, grams) and is determined by the amount typically eaten.

Amount per Serving—Nutritional information is based on one serving. In the example to the left, the serving size is 1 cup. If you eat 2 cups, you need to double the calories, nutrients, and *% Daily Value.*

Calories from Fat—This is the amount of fat multiplied by 9 (number of calories per gram of fat). Dietary guidelines suggest no more than 30% of daily calories come from fat. To calculate percentage, divide *Calories from Fat* by *Calories* (in this example, $10 \div 170 = 6\%$).

Nutrients—Values are listed in grams except for *Cholesterol* and *Sodium*, which are in milligrams. Use these figures to compare fat, sodium, etc. between products. (If a nutrient is not shown, there is no significant amount in the product.) *NOTE: By January 2006, all labels will show the amount of trans fat per serving. (See pages 17–18 for additional information about trans fat.)*

% Daily Value—This shows how much of the *Recommended Daily Values* (RDVs) each nutrient provides and is another way to compare similar products. Calculations are based on 2,000 calories. In this example, the total RDV for sodium (2,400mg) is divided by the amount of sodium per serving (85mg), which means this serving equals 4% of your *Recommended Daily Value* for sodium. If your caloric needs are more or less than this, adjust accordingly when determining your daily requirements.

Ingredients—Listed in order from most to least amount. Generally, if sodium is one of the first three ingredients, there is probably too much salt for a low-sodium diet.

NUTRIENT CONTENT DESCRIPTIONS

The FDA provides the guidelines for claims and descriptions manufacturers may use on food labeling. These requirements ensure that descriptive terms, such as *free, reduced,* or *healthy*, are used consistently to help consumers make informed choices about the foods they buy and eat.

Label content claims describe the level of a nutrient or dietary substance in the product, using terms such as *free*, *high*, and *low*. They can also compare the nutrient amount in a particular food to that of another food, using terms such as *more*, *reduced*, and *lite*. The following claims are used on nutritional labels and are based on one serving.

FOOD LABEL CLAIMS

	FREE	LOW	REDUCED / LESS	LITE / LIGHT
Calories	< 5 calories	40 calories or less	25% less than normal	50% less than normal
Fat	< 0.5g fat	3g or less fat	25% less than normal	50% less than normal
Saturated Fat	< 0.5g saturated fat and < 0.5g trans fatty acids	1g or less saturated fat	25% less than normal	50% less than normal
Cholesterol	< 2mg cholesterol and 2g or less saturated fat	< 20mg cholestrol and 2g or less saturated fat	25% less than normal	50% less than normal
Sugar	< 0.5g sugar		25% less than normal	50% less than normal
	FREE	**VERY LOW**	**LOW**	**UNSALTED / NSA**
Sodium	< 5mg sodium	< 35mg sodium	< 140mg sodium	No salt added to normally salted food

NOTE: *Low fat* and *fat free* do not mean low sodium or low sugar; the contrary is often true, as manufacturers frequently replace the fat with added salt and sugar.

"HEALTHY" CLAIM

A *healthy* claim means the food conforms to healthy levels of total fat, saturated fat, cholesterol, and sodium. However, the healthy limit for sodium in some foods is still rather high, such as soups (480mg) and frozen dinners (600mg). In order to bring soup products more in line with recommended sodium levels, the FDA is proposing that by 2006, soups bearing a healthy label contain no more than 360mg sodium per serving.

Initially, the FDA had proposed lowering the amount of sodium for a "healthy" claim in frozen dinners and other meals to 480mg per serving. But they decided against it when they realized this would probably limit the availability of lower sodium products. Consequently, the healthy label for these products will remain at the current 600mg level.

CALORIES

Calories measure the amount of energy contained in foods and are calculated based on the amount of carbohydrates, fat, and protein within the food. (Alcohol also provides calories.)

Once consumed and digested, food is converted to glucose which fuels everything the body does, like walking, talking, and breathing. The amount of calories needed is different for every individual, for example, the more active an individual, the greater the caloric need. However, when the body takes in more calories than it requires, the extra energy is stored as body fat.

CHOLESTEROL AND FATS

Cholesterol and fats are essential to the human body, however, too much of either can be detrimental to your health.

Cholesterol

Cholesterol is a waxy, fat-like substance produced naturally in the body and is necessary for many bodily functions. The body manufactures all the cholesterol it needs and circulates it via the bloodstream, which separates it into "good" and "bad" lipoproteins.

The bad, or low-density lipoproteins (LDL), stick to the blood vessel walls, contributing to clogged arteries and hypertension, and is the leading cause of heart disease. The good, or high-density lipoproteins (HDL), unstick LDLs and help move them through the bloodstream and out of the body. This is why the ratio of HDL to LDL is important.

Over time, the LDL deposits (along with fat) build up, causing the arteries to clog. As the arteries narrow, the flow of blood decreases and blood pressure increases. This build-up of fatty deposits is also a major factor in coronary disease and strokes.

Research indicates that saturated fats and trans fatty acids have a greater impact in raising cholesterol than from eating dietary cholesterol. It should be noted, though, that most foods high in cholesterol are also high in saturated fats, and vice versa.

Cholesterol is found mainly in animal foods (meat, poultry, fish, egg yolks, and dairy products); it is not found in plant foods. The daily recommendation for cholesterol is less than 300mg.

Fats

Not all fats are harmful and have been classified as either good or bad.

Saturated fat is considered bad, as too much of it raises LDL cholesterol levels. Monounsaturated and polyunsaturated fats help lower cholesterol and are considered good. (Although too much of any fat raises blood cholesterol levels, all fats should be used in moderation.)

> ## TYPES OF FAT
>
> **Saturated** – Usually solid at room temperature (comes mainly from animal products, such as butter, cheese, meat products, egg yolks, and whole milk dairy products.
>
> **Monounsaturated** – Liquid at room temperature, but solidifies in the refrigerator (found in plant foods, such as olive oil, canola oil, avocados, and nuts).
>
> **Polyunsaturated** – Liquid at room temperature and also in the refrigerator (examples are vegetable oils, which include corn oil, safflower oil, and sunflower oil).
>
> **Trans fatty acids** – Result of hydrogenation and used for shelf stability or solidifying a fat product (found in margarine, crackers, cookies, potato chips, and fast foods, such as French fries).

Trans fatty acids, considered saturated and classified as bad, not only raise LDLs, but also decrease HDLs. Many experts believe trans fats are as bad as, if not worse than, saturated fats.

If a product lists *hydrogenated* or *partially hydrogenated* in the ingredients, it has trans fatty acids. Be aware that many low-fat, low-cholesterol products may have trans fats. As of January 2006, in addition to total fat and saturated fat, trans fats must also be listed on food labels.

NOTE: If watching your sodium and/or sugar intake, fat-free products may not necessarily be the best choice, as the removed fat is often replaced with additional sugar and/or sodium.

The American Heart Association (AHA) suggests no more than 30% of total calories come from fat and no more than 10% from saturated fat (7% if you have heart disease, diabetes, or high LDL cholesterol). As a general rule, any food that has 5% or less fat is considered low in fat and 20% or more, is high.

Choose fats with 2g or less saturated fat per serving. If eating a food high in saturated or trans fats, balance it with foods that are low in fat at other meals during the day.

CARBOHYDRATES, FIBER AND SUGAR

Carbohydrates are the body's supplier of energy. Once consumed carbohydrates convert into two basic forms: simple carbohydrates (found in sugars) and complex carbohydrates (comprised of starches and fibers). Except for fiber (which is not digestible), all carbohydrates turn directly into sugar (or glucose) in the bloodstream and affect blood glucose in different ways:

Simple carbohydrates – generally have no nutritive value and produce a rapid rise in blood glucose followed by a rapid fall.

Complex carbohydrates – are more nutritious and produce a slower, more sustained blood glucose response.

Foods high in complex carbohydrates are usually low in calories, saturated fat, and cholesterol. They are found primarily in plant foods, such as fruits, vegetables, whole grains, beans, and legumes. They also are present in dairy products.

Daily caloric intake of carbohydrates should be between 55–60% (or 25–35 grams) with an emphasis on complex carbohydrates.

Fiber

Fiber is the part of food that is not digested. There are two types of fiber—soluble and insoluble.

Soluble – dissolves in fluids of the large intestine. Soluble fiber is found in oats, barley, rye, nuts, fruits, vegetables, psyllium seeds (used in fiber laxatives), beans and legumes. Consumed in large amounts, soluble fiber can decrease blood cholesterol, improve blood glucose levels, and appears to reduce hypertension. It also may help with weight loss by increasing the feeling of fullness.

Insoluble – instead of dissolving, it passes straight through the intestinal fluids and helps maintain regularity. It is found in whole grains, seeds, bran, fruit and vegetable skins. It also is associated with reduced risk of colon cancer.

The amount of fiber also affects blood glucose. The more fiber in a food, the slower the digestion and absorption of sugars. To help understand fiber's influence on blood glucose, the glycemic index (GI) was developed. Using glucose (the highest rated GI) as a standard, a food is ranked by how fast it is digested and how much it causes blood glucose to rise. We will not get into GI rankings in this book, but suffice to say, this new information is changing the way nutritionists and the medical society are looking at carbohydrates.

The recommended level of total soluble and insoluble fiber is 20–35 grams per day. When selecting food products, look for a minimum of 3 grams of fiber, but 5 grams or more is better.

Sugar

Sugar consumption has been on the increase and several experts believe diets high in sugar are contributing to many of today's health problems, including hypertension and heart disease. Current research indicates long-term consumption of a diet high in refined (simple) carbohydrates produces higher insulin levels. As insulin levels elevate, adrenaline production is stimulated, causing blood vessel constriction and increased sodium retention, which can contribute to hypertension. Additionally, high carbohydrate intake has been linked to increased LDL and decreased HDL cholesterol.

Even though the RDVs have no sugar guidelines, the U.S. Department of Agriculture (USDA) advises limiting sugar to 10 teaspoons or 47g a day (based on a 2,000-calorie diet).

SODIUM

Sodium is essential to the body. About 500mg a day is needed to help regulate fluids and maintain normal functioning of nerves and muscles. If excess sodium is not used, fluid builds up (water retention) increasing the work of the heart and kidneys.

Select foods that contain less than 5 percent of the daily value for sodium (or about 100mg per serving). Experts suggest limiting any food that has more than 480mg sodium per serving.

WHICH FOODS HAVE MORE SODIUM?

You might be surprised to find all the places that salt can sneak into your diet. Take the following quiz to determine your sodium IQ.

Which has more sodium?

1. A frozen dinner of sliced beef with gravy, mashed potatoes, and peas OR one cup of chicken noodle soup?
2. One-half cup instant chocolate pudding OR one-half cup regular, cooked pudding?
3. A cup of Manhattan (red) OR New England (white) clam chowder?
4. One cup of shredded wheat OR one cup bran cereal with raisins?
5. A medium serving of French fries OR 2 tablespoons ketchup?
6. A fast foods grilled chicken sandwich OR a hamburger?
7. A cup of instant oatmeal OR a cup of quick-cooking oatmeal?
8. A large bagel OR a large glazed doughnut?
9. A Pina Colada OR Bloody Mary?
10. A corn tortilla OR flour tortilla?

Answers

1. Chicken noodle soup, 1,106mg (frozen dinner has 742mg)
2. Instant, 357mg (regular pudding contains 88mg)
3. New England, 992mg (Manhattan comes in at 578mg)
4. Raisin bran, 360mg (shredded wheat only has 5mg)
5. Ketchup, 356mg (French fries amount to 265mg)
6. Chicken sandwich, 957mg (a hamburger adds up to 534mg)
7. Instant, 377mg (quick-cooking oatmeal has 1mg)
8. Large bagel, 700mg (a doughnut comes in at 257mg)
9. Bloody Mary, 1,548mg (a Pina Colada averages 130mg)
10. Flour tortilla, 234mg (one corn tortilla only has 3mg)

The most difficult time to control salt consumption is when dining out. Making good nutritional choices can be difficult, especially when we do not know what has been added to the foods we order. For example, a healthy garden salad with lowfat dressing oftentimes has more sodium than a hamburger and French fries. Hard to believe, but depending on how it is prepared, what we think is healthy may not be low sodium.

If you know you will be dining out, eat foods that are lower in salt for breakfast and lunch. Or, if you have too much salt at one meal, keep your sodium intake low for the next couple of meals. You can also place low-sodium condiments, like ketchup, mustard, and salad dressing, in small plastic containers and take them with you. The important thing: don't deprive yourself, just use moderation . . . low salt does not mean no salt.

Hopefully, one day, with enough public pressure, nutritional data will be available at all restaurants. In the meantime, follow the suggestions below in selecting healthier, low-sodium menu items.

If you eat out frequently you may want to pick up a copy of the *Pocket Guide to Low Sodium Foods*, which lists low-sodium items from 61 national restaurant chains. Use it to find the best places to get your favorite meals while staying within low-sodium guidelines.

1 Order low-sodium foods. Ask how foods are prepared; choose steamed, broiled, grilled, or roasted entrées without sauces. Find restaurants that feature "heart-healthy" meals or will accommodate your dietary restrictions. (NOTE: "Heart-healthy" usually indicates a menu item is low in fat or cholesterol and may not always be low sodium.)

2 Avoid fried foods. Most batters are salted, plus additional saturated or trans-fats in the frying liquid.

3 Stay away from soups. Most soups have way too much sodium to be included in a low-salt diet. Many will put you over your daily allotment before you eat anything else.

4 Go easy on the bread. One small piece may have several hundred milligrams of sodium, and that's before you add the margarine or butter.

5 Use oil and vinegar on salads. Stay away from salads made with mayonnaise, such as potato salad and cole slaw. (Mayo is ladened with sodium, averaging 80mg per tablespoon.)

6 Watch out for the salad bar. Many items are mayonnaise-based or pickled, which adds too much salt.

7 Order the smallest portion. Or eat half the meal and save the rest for the next day. Don't be shy about ordering kiddie meals, they have far less salt than supersized servings.

8 Request condiments be served on the side. Then you control the amount used.

9 Ask that salt not be added to your meals. Most restaurants can accommodate you, however, fast food eateries often premake many items and may not be able to handle special requests. If you like French fries, you can usually order them without the salt, but you may have to wait a few extra minutes. But hold the ketchup, it has more sodium than the fries!

BEST LOW-SODIUM FOOD CHOICES
AND WHAT TO AVOID

	BEST CHOICES	AVOID
Appetizers and Snacks	fresh fruits and vegetables, unsalted nuts, or dried fruits	crackers, chips, dips, pâtés, meatballs, and cocktail sauce
Cheeses	Swiss cheese, goat cheese, or fresh mozzarella	most cheeses, including nonfat and lower fat cheeses
Beverages	beer, wine, champagne, fruit juices, tea, or coffee	eggnog, Bloody Marys, Pina Colatas, and some soft drinks
Soups and Salads	tossed greens, carrot/raisin, and gelatin salads	all soups, three-bean, cole slaw, and mayo-based salads
Salad Dressings	vinaigrette, oil and vinegar	creamy dressings and Zesty Italian
Entrées	roasted or grilled poultry, beef, pork, or fish	ham, breaded, and dishes with sauces
Side Dishes	candied yams, glazed carrots, applesauce, sliced tomatoes, and baked potatoes (without condiments)	mashed potatoes, stuffing, rice pilaf, and cottage cheese
Breads	matzos and whole-wheat dinner rolls	biscuits, muffins, cornbread, croissants, and foccacia bread
Condiments	cranberry sauce and fruit relish	olives, pickles, and hot peppers
Desserts	meringue cookies, strudel, fruitcake, sponge cake, sherbet, sorbet, custard, and fruit tarts	pies, pastries, gingerbread, cheesecakes, angel food, and frosted cakes
Asian Restaurants	stir-fried and steamed vegetables, tofu dishes, hot and sour soup, steamed rice entrées with sauces like sweet and sour, plum, or duck – ask that no MSG be added	soy sauce, bean and oyster sauces, deep-fried or battered dishes, tempura, and pickled foods
French Bistros	dishes with wine-based sauces, vinaigrettes, sorbet, and fresh fruit desserts	creamy sauces (like hollandaise, morney, béchamel, or bernaise) and creamy soups
Italian Trattatorias	pastas with marinara sauce, pasta/fagoli dishes, primavera, marsala dishes, piccata (hold the capers), oil and vinegar dressing, and Italian ices	antipasto platters, cheese or cream sauces
Mexican Cantinas	ceviche, grilled fish or chicken, guacamole, beef or chicken tacos, corn tortillas, and fresh salsa	tortilla chips, cheese, burritos, floutas, enchiladas, flour tortillas, rice, and beans
Fast Foods	unsalted fries, veggie sandwiches, burgers (remove half the bun, hold the mayo and pickles), yogurt, and fresh fruit	breaded fish and poultry, wraps, subs, chips, condiments, cheese, pies, and cookies

Most people who enjoy my cooking, marvel at how delicious everything tastes, even though I remove the salt, fat, sugar, and anything else bad that I can eliminate. Obviously, it is much easier to prepare rich and delicious dishes when you use real butter, cream, and loads of salt. The trick is getting lots of flavor without adding the bad stuff. It doesn't take much, just a few modifications here and there, and of course, plenty of herbs, spices, and other flavorings.

When planning meals, focus on serving more fresh fruits and vegetables, which have very little sodium. Rather than making meat or poultry the center of the meal, serve it as a side dish, along with a tossed salad and two or three other side dishes. In addition to a lot of variety, your meals will be healthier and you will consume less salt.

As you become more sodium savvy, you will find that a few simple changes in your meal preparation can make a significant difference in the amount of salt you consume. It is my hope that after trying some of these recipes, you will be familiar enough with low-sodium ingredients to experiment by "desalting" some of your favorites. Listed below are some of the low-sodium ingredients and techniques I use to create many of the delicious dishes you'll find in this book.

1 Replace salt with onion and garlic powder. I use onion and garlic powder the way most people use salt. My favorite brand of garlic powder is *Lawry's Coarse Ground with Parsley*. Next to pepper, it is the ingredient I use the most. I also use several spice mills by *Drogherini Alimentari* (found in the spice section of most grocery stores). My favorites are Tuscan Herbs, Provence Herbs, Garlic, and White Pepper.

2 Add freshly ground black pepper. If you are not using freshly ground pepper in your dishes, now is the time to start. It is far superior to pre-ground and adds so much more flavor. I use black peppercorns most of the time, but when preparing white sauces, I often use the milder white peppercorn, mainly for appearance. Any size and type of grinder will work, as long as it allows you to adjust the coarseness. I like mine rather coarse, but you can set it to whatever coarseness you like.

3 Use low-sodium bouillon or soup base for added taste. This is another way to add flavor without the salt. Of the low-salt bouillons, I often use *Herb-Ox Very Low Sodium,* which has a nice flavor when added to sauces and soups (both the chicken and beef have 5mg sodium per teaspoon). When more flavor is needed, I reach for a low-salt soup base, such as *Redi-Base* (both chicken and turkey ranges from 35–140mg) or *Vogue Cuisine* Onion Soup Base (136mg sodium per teaspoon).

4 Prepare homemade stocks. Most canned broths are loaded with sodium (anywhere from 700mg to over 1,000mg per cup). There are several lower and low-salt brands, but quite frankly, their flavor is rather bland. I don't think anything beats the rich taste of a homemade stock that has simmered all day.

Freeze the strained stock into paper cups in varying amounts (¼ to 1 cup); when a recipe calls for broth, the desired amount can easily be defrosted in the microwave or under warm water.

On those occasions when I use canned low-salt broth, I add a teaspoon or two of bouillon or soup base, which adds more flavor and with very little sodium.

5 **Flavor food with herbs and spices.** When I was growing up, the only seasonings in our house were salt and pepper. In recent years with the popularity of television cooking shows, gourmet magazines, and up-scale restaurants, herbs and spices are much more common than in the past.

I use both fresh and dried herbs and spices. I usually add dried at the beginning of the cooking process and fresh at the end. Adding the dried early, for example, when cooking onions or shallots, brings out more of the flavor of the seasonings. I liken the difference to roasted nuts versus raw nuts—after roasting, the nuts are more flavorful. By adding fresh herbs and spices at the end, their full flavor and fresh fragrance is brought to the dish (the exceptions are bay leaf, rosemary, and thyme, which can be added near the beginning of the cooking process).

Dried Herbs and Spices

Dried herbs and spices are more pungent than fresh —so a little goes a long ways. As a general rule, 1 tablespoon fresh equals 1 teaspoon dried. Also, because dried herbs and spices lose their flavor quickly, do not use after 6 months. The best way to keep track is to write the purchase date on the container. Once the date

has passed, discard and purchase a new one. This is important for two reasons. First, you don't know how long it's been sitting on the shelf. Secondly, flavor comes from the freshest, most flavorful ingredients. Tired old herbs and spices without potency add little flavor to a dish.

To save time and money, you can also put together your own spice blends and keep them in an air-tight container. One of my favorite combinations is one part each tarragon, thyme, and rosemary and two parts basil.

Fresh Herbs and Spices

If you're not growing fresh herbs, now is a good time to start. Some readily available favorites are sweet basil, marjoram, rosemary, tarragon, chives, parsley, and chives.

Plant them in a sunny spot near the kitchen or in a window. (Seeds and starts are available at garden centers and nurseries.) If you need help, there are several publications available, along with vast information on the internet, to guide you in the care and feeding of your herb family.

You can also purchase fresh herbs in the produce section of most supermarkets. Look for bright green leaves without brown spots that are not limp. They usually keep for several days in the refrigerator.

TIPS TO REDUCING SODIUM

AT HOME:

Eliminate the saltshaker — Do not salt before you taste. Break the habit of automatically reaching for the saltshaker.

Use less salt in cooking — In most recipes salt can be reduced, or in many cases omitted, without compromising the flavor. Use more herbs and spices, like onion and garlic powder. Also, low-sodium bouillon can add extra flavor, as can wine, vinegar, lemon or lime juice.

Prepare low-salt recipes — There are many low-sodium cookbooks available, as well as low-salt recipes online.

Try one new low sodium product a week — There are many products available and until you try them, you won't know how delicious some of them can be.

Munch on fruits or vegetables — instead of salty snacks. Not only are they healthier, but they also have very little sodium.

AT THE SUPERMARKET:

Use less prepared foods — The less processing, the less sodium. Stay away from the center aisles which are filled with salty snacks and packaged products.

Select lower salt foods — Look for foods labeled *sodium free, low sodium, reduced sodium, unsalted,* and *no salt added.* Choose brands with less than 140mg sodium per serving (or less than 5% of the recommended daily value of sodium).

Read the label — If you don't know how much sodium is in a product, you can't take control of your diet.

Know how much sodium is in each serving — The serving size listed may be smaller than what you will actually eat. Some serving sizes may be deceptive and foods that appear low in salt, may not be. For example, clam juice has 30mg of sodium per teaspoon, but if you're using 1 cup in a recipe, it amounts to 1,450mg.

Be alert to "salty" terms — like *brine, cured, marinated, pickled,* and *smoked.*

---

6 **Use wines, vinegars, and citric juices to add another layer of flavor.** Acidic additives like wines, vinegars, lemon and lime juice, add a sweet or sour tanginess that in some recipes is pure magic. Plus, as the liquid cooks down, its flavor intensifies. Many of my recipes have one or more acidic additives.

Red and White Wines

Because I like wine, I always have several bottles around to both drink and use in my cooking. My favorite reds are Merlot, Cabernet Sauvignon, and Zinfandel. I also prefer dry whites, such as Chardonnay, Chablis, and Sauvignon Blanc. Wines used in cooking do not have to be expensive and unless you plan to drink it within a few days, don't buy a bottle just for cooking.

Fortified Wines

These wines are fortified with liquor, such as brandy, and other flavorings, which allows for a long shelf life (up to a year in some cases). They range from sweet to full-bodied and are great for cooking, adding depth and richness. The ones I use most frequently include a dry sherry, Madeira, Marsala, vermouth, and sake; all are available in the wine department. *NOTE: Avoid so-called "cooking wines" found in the condiment section of the supermarket, as they are loaded with sodium (190mg per fluid ounce versus 2mg for most fortified wines).*

Fortified wines range in color from white to red, and depending on which one you use, will change the flavor of the dish. **Dry sherry** is light, but full-bodied and adds a richness that you don't get from white wine. **Madeira** has a distinctive rich, nutty flavor and is great with mushrooms, meats, and poultry. **Marsala** is a sweeter wine and imparts a wonderful depth to fish, meats, poultry, and desserts. **Vermouth** is fruity and

perfect with lighter dishes, like fish. **Sake** has a wide-range of tastes, from sweet to dry, but most inexpensive sakes found in the supermarket have a subtle sweetness. Experiment with each of them to determine which ones you like the best.

Vinegars

There are many flavored vinegars which also affect the way a dish tastes. They range from dark and slightly sweet, like balsamic, to light and mild, like white wine vinegar. I suggest keeping at least five or six vinegars on hand. My favorites are balsamic, white balsamic, red wine, white wine, raspberry, and cider vinegar.

Lemon and Lime Juice

The sharp tanginess of lemon and lime juice mimics the taste of salt in many recipes. Although fresh lemon and lime juice is always preferable to bottled, you can usually substitute bottled in most recipes. Either of these adds a tang and brings out the flavor of the food, particularly vegetables.

7 **Add flavor with garlic.** Garlic plays an important part in low-salt cooking. It adds so much flavor and, in my opinion, makes or breaks many dishes (and I don't mean the plate you eat on). For those of you who don't care for garlic, you might try elephant garlic, which is very mild and has less of a garlic taste. Plus, there is an added bonus, research suggests garlic has many health benefits, including reducing blood pressure and lowering cholesterol.

8 **Make it hot and spicy.** When you add heat, the need for salt disappears. Try using minced hot peppers (like jalapeños or chipotles), dried red pepper flakes, cayenne pepper, hot paprika, some curry powders, or other hot sauces and spices in your dishes.

9 Pour a sauce on top. The flavor of many entrées is improved with the addition of a low-salt sauce. There are several sauces throughout the book that can be used on many different dishes. For example, a rich mushroom sauce can easily go with chicken, meat, or over mashed potatoes, rice, and pasta.

MORE LOW-SALT TIPS AND TECHNIQUES

Substitute fresh garlic for garlic salt – if a recipe calls for garlic salt, use 1 garlic clove for every ½ teaspoon garlic salt.

Don't salt the water – when cooking pasta or rice. If you want added flavor, add a teaspoon or two of low-salt chicken bouillon granules.

Instead of salt, use glazes or spice rubs on poultry, meat, and fish – rub on horseradish, preserves, or chutneys before baking or barbecuing.

Avoid ready-to-eat meat or poultry – they contain too much added salt; buy fresh or frozen that has not been precooked or has no added preparations, like spices and sauces.

Stay away from canned vegetables – use fresh or frozen instead. If you do use canned, always rinse the contents; it will not remove all the salt, but it will get rid of some of it.

Substitute sun dried tomatoes for olives or bacon – they suggest a salty taste and can be used in many recipes.

Replace milk with soy milk – it's rich and creamy and saves 40mg sodium per cup.

Instead of nonfat half-and-half, use a combination of nonfat sour cream and milk – replace half-and-half (240mg per cup) with 3 parts sour cream and 1 part milk for a total of about 115mg per cup.

In place of salty crackers or bread crumbs, use saltines – low-salt have 35mg sodium per ounce, unsalted tops have 60mg.

Try mustard powder instead of prepared mustard – in most recipes you'll get the same taste, but without the salt (some dishes may also require a little vinegar).

Use celery seed – it has a "salty" taste.

Deglaze pan drippings and reduce to concentrate flavor – brandy, wine, or vinegar work well, creating a richer, more flavorful dish.

Watch out for "less salt" or "reduced salt" items – a can of reduced sodium soup averages 450mg per serving, canned beans with 50% less salt, have about 220mg per ½ cup.

Substitute mascarpone for cream cheese – particularly in desserts (mascarpone has 16mg per ounce, cream cheese averages 86mg).

In old recipes, reduce the amount of salt by one half – in most dishes you won't notice the difference.

Experiment with low-sodium products – there are many alternatives to highly salted foods. Until you try some, you won't know what a delicious addition many of them can be.

Add sweetness – mix in a little sugar or sugar substitute to a pasta sauce or add apple juice to a gravy, and you won't miss the salt.

Use low-salt bread crumbs instead of cheese on top of pasta dishes – the added crunchiness is a great replacement to highly salted cheeses like Mozzarella, Parmesan, and Romano.

Check spice blend labels – although most don't include nutritional info, the ingredients list will let you know if there is any salt in the product. If sodium or salt is listed as the first or second ingredient, avoid it.

Use salt substitutes – they contain potassium which tastes similar to salt. *Warning: If taking hypertension drugs, check with your healthcare provider before using, as it may conflict with your medication.*

SODIUM IN COMMONLY USED INGREDIENTS

Ingredient	Sodium (mg)
SEASONINGS *(1 tsp)*	
Table salt	2,325
Sea salt	2,132
Meat tenderizer	1,680
Lite salt	1,160
MSG	50
LEAVENING AGENTS *(1 tsp)*	
Baking soda	1,259
Baking powder	488
NSA baking powder	0
FLOUR *(1 cup)*	
Self-rising	1,588
All-purpose mix (i.e. *Bisquik*)	1,532
All-purpose flour	3
COATING MIXES *(¼ cup)*	
Mix (i.e. *Shake & Bake*)	800
Seasoned bread crumbs	795
Plain bread crumbs	233
Cracker meal	8
SWEETENERS *(½ cup)*	
Corn syrup	198
Brown sugar	43
Honey	7
Granulated sugar	0
Sugar substitute (i.e. *Splenda*)	0
FATS AND OILS *(1 tbsp)*	
Butter	82
Margarine	133
Unsalted margarine	0
Oils	0
DOUGHS/PIE CRUSTS	
Puff pastry, 1 sheet	1,200
Graham pie crust, ⅛ pc	168
Flour pie crust, ⅛	104
Filo dough, 1 sheet	92
BOUILLON *(1 cube or tsp)*	
Chicken	743
Vegetable	980
Beef	611
Low-salt bouillon	15
BROTHS *(1 cup)*	
Vegetable	980
Beef	782
Chicken	763
Reduced sodium chicken	450
Low-sodium chicken	140

Ingredient	Sodium (mg)
SOUPS/CHILI *(1 cup)*	
Chili with beans	1,337
Less sodium chili	710
Chicken noodle	1,106
Onion	1,053
Clam chowder (white)	992
Clam chowder (red)	578
Cream of mushroom	918
Low sodium mushroom	49
Vegetable	791
WINE *(1 cup)*	
Cooking wine	1,452
Table wine	14
JUICES *(1 cup)*	
Tomato juice	750
Low sodium tomato juice	49
Vegetable cocktail	540
Low sodium veggie juice	140
CHEESE *(1 oz)*	
Roquefort	513
Cottage cheese, ½ cup	455
Parmesan	454
Blue	395
Feta	316
Cheddar	176
Mozzarella, part skim	150
Goat cheese	104
Swiss chese	54
Fresh mozzarella	10
Ricotta cheese, ½ cup	104
Cream cheese	84
Fat-free cream cheese	200
EGGS	
Egg substitue, ¼ cup	115
1 egg, large	70
SOUR CREAM/YOGURT *(¼ cup)*	
Sour cream	30
Fat-free sour cream	80
Yogurt, plain	29
MILK/CREAM *(¼ cup)*	
Condensed milk	97
Evaporated milk	67
Buttermilk	39
Milk, whole	26
Lowfat milk (1%)	31
Cream or Half-and-half	24
Nonfat half-and-half	88

Ingredient	Sodium (mg)
CONDIMENTS *(1 tbsp)*	
Ketchup	178
Dijon-type mustard, 1 tsp	120
Yellow mustard, 1 tsp	56
Mayonnaise	80
Fat-free mayonnaise	120
CAPERS/OLIVES *(1 tbsp)*	
Capers	255
Olives, kalamata	220
Olives, ripe (black)	115
PICKLES/RELISH *(1 oz)*	
Pickles, dill	359
Pickles, sweet	263
Pickles, bread and butter	106
Hamburger relish	328
Sweet pickle relish	244
PEANUT BUTTER/JELLY *(1 tbsp)*	
Peanut butter	75
Jam or jelly	6
SALAD DRESSINGS *(2 tbsp)*	
French	438
Blue cheese/roquefort	328
Caesar	290
Ranch	287
Fat-free ranch	350
Russian	260
Italian	231
Fat-free Italian	430
Zesty Italian	510
Thousand Island	224
Vinegar and oil	0
SAUCES *(1 tbsp)*	
Soy sauce	914
Lite	660
Teriyaki sauce	690
Hot pepper sauce	372
Steak sauce	262
Cocktail sauce	210
Bernaise sauce	210
BBQ/Grilling sauce	208
Hollandaise	170
Worcestershire sauce	165
Horseradish	150
Cheese sauce	131
Tartar sauce	130
Sweet and sour sauce	130
Salsa	70

Ingredient	Sodium (mg)
GRAVY (¼ cup)	
Chicken or Turkey	344
Mushroom	340
Beef	326
Au jus	30
PASTA/PIZZA SAUCE (½ cup)	
Alfredo	1,080
Pizza sauce	820
Pesto, ¼ cup	730
Cheese	650
Marinara	515
BEANS (½ cup)	
Canned:	
Pork and beans	557
Baked beans	504
Black beans	480
50% less salt	260
Kidney beans	444
50% less salt	220
Garbanzo beans	359
Pinto beans	353
Lima beans	312
Soybeans	204
Dried:	
Most beans (avg)	15
VEGETABLES, CANNED (½ cup)	
Tomato sauce	742
Tomato puree	598
Tomatoes, diced and chopped	290
with spices	600
Tomato paste (2 tbsp)	261
Sauerkraut	661
Asparagus	346
Green beans	311
Peas	310
Carrots	300
Corn	273
50% less sodium	176
Beets	176
Yams	30
Pumpkin	6
VEGETABLES, FRESH (½ cup)	
Artichoke (med)	120
Beets	53
Carrot, 1 med	40
Celery, 1 med stalk	35
Spinach, 1 cup	24
All other veggies	15 or less

Ingredient	Sodium (mg)
GRAINS (½ cup)	
Bulgur	24
Barley	18
Rice	0
PASTA/NOODLES (2 oz)	
Egg noodles	12
Pasta (avg)	3
BREAKFAST MEATS (1 oz)	
Bacon	208
Turkey bacon	380
Canadian-style	359
Pork sausage	187
BEEF/VEAL (4 oz)	
Corned beef brisket	1,380
Veal, shank, lean	96
Top round, lean	82
Ground beef, lean	75
T-bone, lean	66
LAMB (4 oz)	
Shoulder, blade	71
Loin, lean	67
HAM/PORK (4 oz)	
Ham steak, boneless, lean	1,440
Ham, cured, canned	1,408
Pork shoulder, lean	92
Pork ribs, lean	76
Pork loin roast, lean	52
CHICKEN/TURKEY (4 oz)	
Cornish game hen, half	102
Turkey (without skin)	
Ground, lean	105
Dark meat	96
White meat	75
Chicken (without skin)	
Leg	112
Drumstick or thigh (avg)	98
Wing	91
Breast	73
FISH/SEAFOOD, CANNED (2 oz)	
Anchovies	1,652
Herring, kippered	520
Salmon, pink	471
Crab	400
Clams, minced/chopped	320
Sardines	286
Caviar, black/red, 1 tbsp	240
Tuna	221

Ingredient	Sodium (mg)
FISH/SEAFOOD, FRESH (4 oz)	
Crab, Alaskan King	948
Blue or Dungeness	333
Lobster	336
Oysters, Eastern	201
Pacific	120
Scallops	200
Shrimp	168
Swordfish	104
Sole (flounder)	92
Snapper	72
Salmon, Atlantic	67
Smoked	888
Clams	64
Halibut or Cod	61
Tuna	41
Anchovies	39
Trout	37
HOT DOGS/SAUSAGES (1 oz)	
Turkey hot dog (1 link)	642
Beef hot dog (1 link)	462
Chorizo	350
Braunschweiger	324
Kielbasa	305
Italian sausage	207
Bratwurst	158
LUNCHEON MEATS (1 oz)	
Beef	408
Ham	405
Turkey	334
Salami	302
Bologna	289
Pastrami	255
FRUIT, FRESH (1 cup)	
Honeydew, ¼	45
Cantaloupe, ¼	11
All other fruit	3 or less
FRUIT, CANNED (1 cup)	
Applesauce	71
Plums, light syrup	50
Lychees	26
Cherries, light syrup	18
All other canned fruit	15 or less
TORTILLAS/WRAPS (1)	
Tortilla/taco shells	
Flour, 7-8 inch	559
Corn, shelf-stable	150
Corn, fresh, 6 inch	3

The low-salt pantry contains everything needed to prepare healthy, low-salt meals. I don't expect you to purchase every item on this list, but if you have a good selection, you can make a majority of *The Hasty Gourmet™* recipes *(for abbreviations, see page 34)*.

BAKING AND COOKING NEEDS

Baking powder – NSA (*such as Featherweight* SF)

Bouillon/soup base – LS (*such as Herb-Ox*, very LS beef, chicken, and vegetable)

Bread crumbs – LS

Cornmeal

Cornstarch

Extracts – vanilla • almond

Flour – any except self-rising

Grains – bulgur • couscous • rice

Herbs and Spices (dried and/or fresh)
Most used – basil (dried and fresh) • cayenne pepper • celery seed • chili powder (NSA) • chives (fresh) • cilantro (fresh) • cinnamon (ground) • crushed red pepper flakes • cumin (ground) • curry powder (hot and sweet) • garlic powder • ginger (dried and fresh gingerroot) • herbes de Provence • nutmeg (whole) • oregano (dried and fresh) • paprika (hot and sweet) • parsley (flat leaf) • rosemary (dried and fresh) • sage (dried) • tarragon (dried and fresh) • thyme (dried and fresh) • pepper mills (black and white)
Lesser used – allspice • bay leaves • cardamom • cloves • marjoram • turmeric

Molasses – dark

Nonstick cooking spray

Oil – olive • extra-virgin olive • vegetable • canola oil

Sweeteners – sugar • sugar substitute

Vinegars – balsamic • white balsamic • red wine • white wine • tarragon wine • raspberry

Wines and brandy (avoid cooking wines, purchase from liquor department) – dry sherry • Madeira • Marsala • red wine (such as merlot or zinfandel) • vermouth • white wine (such as chardonnay) • brandy

CANNED GOODS

Beans – LS (such as black, garbanzo, and kidney)

Corn – NSA (whole and creamed)

Green chiles (with 40mg or less per ounce, such as *Western Family*)

Mandarin oranges (in light syrup)

Soups and broths – LS chicken and beef broths

Tomato products – LS or NSA (paste, puree, sauce, and diced)

Tuna – very LS, water packed

Water chestnuts

CONDIMENTS AND SAUCES

Flavor enhancer – (*Kitchen Bouquet*)

Horseradish – LS prepared

Hot pepper sauce – (such as red *Tabasco*)

Jam – (fruit sweetened)

Ketchup – NSA

Lemon and lime juice – (use when out of fresh)

Mayonnaise (use brand with 70mg or less per tbsp, such as *Hain Eggless* (0mg) or *Saffola* (70mg)

Mustard – honey • LS coarse-ground • Dijon

Olives, ripe – (black)

Peanut butter – NSA

Pickle relish, sweet

Salsa (less than 40mg per tbsp) – stock several such as a tomato-based and sweet, like mango/peach)

Sauces, bottled
Alfredo sauce, LS, such as *Walden Farms*
Chocolate or fudge sauce, such as *Wax Orchards* or *Walden Farms*
Pasta Sauce (220mg or less per serving)

Soy sauce – lite

Sun-dried tomatoes – packed in oil

Worcestershire – LS

OTHER STAPLES

Breads – LS (multigrain, raisin, flatbread, pita)

Cereal – (granola and oat)

Chips – NSA (corn and potato)

Crackers – LS (such as saltines, graham, and wheat)

Egg roll wraps – (refrigerated, such as *Melissa's*)

Fruit, dried – (currants, raisins, apricots, cherries, and cranberries)

Grains
Bulgur and couscous
Rice (a variety, like brown, basmati, and arborio)

Legumes, dried – (black beans, kidney beans, lentils, and split peas)

Nuts – unsalted (such as almonds, hazelnuts, pecans, and walnuts)

Pasta – (a variety, such as spaghetti, lasagna, and elbow)

Pie crust – frozen (less than 40mg sodium per serving)

Tortilla shells – LS (corn and flour)

DAIRY PRODUCTS

Cheese
Cheddar, lowfat • Mozzarella, fresh (not packed in brine) • Parmesan, reduced fat (canned) and hard • Swiss, NSA and lowfat

Cream cheese – (mascarpone, whipped, and regular)

Eggs

Margarine or butter – NSA (if watching saturated fat, use trans-free, such as *Smart Balance*)

Milk, cream, and alternatives
Cream (light and/or half-and-half)
Milk (lowfat and/or nonfat)
Soy milk, plain

Sour cream – (lowfat and/or nonfat)

Whipped topping – (frozen, lowfat or lowfat)

Yogurt – (plain and/or fruit, lowfat and/or nonfat)

MEATS, POULTRY, FISH AND SEAFOOD

Bacon, – less salt (such as *Armour, Corn King, Gwaltney, Safeway Select, Wellshire Farms*)

Chicken and turkey – (boneless, skinless breasts, cutlets, and/or ground)

Fish and seafood – (several varieties)

Meats – (beef, pork, and/or lamb)

Sausage, meatless – (less than 170mg per oz, such as *Bocaburger, Gardenburger*, and *Gimme Lean*)

FRESH PRODUCE

Fruit
apples (sweet and tart) • berries (such as blueberries, blackberries, and strawberries) • lemons and limes • oranges (navel and tangerines) • tomatoes (plum and/or vine-ripened)

Vegetables
asparagus • broccoli • carrots • celery • leeks • onions (green, sweet and yellow) • mushrooms (several kinds and/or dried) • peppers (hot and sweet) • potatoes (red, russet, and sweet) • salad greens (several kinds) • shallots • squash (summer and winter)

FROZEN FOODS

Artichoke hearts

Berries – (when fresh is not available)

Edamame – (soy beans)

Mixed vegetables

Spinach

HERBS

Basil – has a sweet taste, similar to licorice. There are numerous varieties, ranging from sweet to pungent (Asian), and some have a hint of lemon or cinnamon. While there is a huge difference in flavor between fresh and dried, either can be used in tomato sauces, salads, vegetable dishes, soups, eggs, fish, meats, and poultry. Basil also is an ingredient in many Italian blends.

Bay leaf – has a spicy, woodsy flavor. There are two common varieties–California (larger and more potent) and Turkish (smaller and less potent). Often used in *bouquet garni* (traditionally parsley, thyme, and bay leaf), which is tied together to flavor soups, stews, and broth. Bay leaf is also used in tomato sauces.

Chervil – similar to parsley but with a slight anise (licorice) flavor. It is one of the ingredients in Fines Herbes (see below). Use in poultry, meat, vegetable, egg, and cheese dishes.

Chives – have a mild, onion-like flavor. Can use interchangeably with chopped green onions (green part). Use in eggs, salads, and as a topping for potatoes. Add chives at the last minute to hot dishes, as they don't hold up well to heat.

Cilantro – similar to parsley but has a stronger flavor; commonly used in Mexican and Asian cooking.

Dill – *Dill seed* is the dried fruit of the herb and is similar in taste to caraway (the flavor in rye bread), *dill weed* is less pungent and mild. Dried dill is very different in taste than fresh. Add fresh dill at the last minute to hot dishes, as it doesn't hold up well to heat. Use with eggs, fish, soups, salads, and veggies.

Fennel – similar to anise, but sweeter. Use with fish and in Moroccan dishes.

Fines Herbes – a French combination of herbs, usually tarragon, chervil, parsley, and chives. Use in French dishes, soups, stuffings, meats, poultry, and vegetables.

Herbes de Provence – another blend that combines French herbs and lavendar with Italian herbs and fennel. Use in French dishes, soups, meats, poultry, and vegetables.

Marjoram – comes from the oregano family and has a sweet oregano-like flavor. Use with poultry, soups, veggies, beef, and fish. Marjoram is also used in Italian blends and goes well with basil and thyme.

Mint – has a fresh minty flavor. Use with lamb, peas, or in desserts, particularly chocolate.

Oregano – more pungent, but not as sweet as marjoram. Use in Italian and Mexican dishes, soups, vegetables, meat, poultry, and pasta sauces.

Parsley – has a fresh, mildly peppery flavor. There are dozens of varieties, the two most popular are curly-leaf (used most often as a garnish) and the more flavorful flat-leaf (or Italian) parsley. Use with eggs, fish, salads, vegetables, sauces, meats, and poultry.

Rosemary – has a lemony, piney flavor, reminiscent of tea leaves. Most commonly used in Italian cooking. Add to poultry, meats, fish, and vegetables (especially roasted root veggies).

Sage – originally used for medicinal purposes, it is one of the most popular herbs. It is slightly bitter with an undertone of musty mint. It is used in stuffings and savory breads, poultry, soup, vegetables, and fish.

Savory – similar in taste to thyme, but with peppery, minty undertones There are two varieties—winter and summer—the latter is milder than winter, but both have a strong taste, so use sparingly. Add to soups, meat, and fish.

Tarragon – has a distinctive anise-like flavor. Most frequently used in French dishes and sauces. It is one of the ingredients in Fines Herbes. Use with eggs, fish (particularly salmon), poultry, meats, and vegetables.

Thyme – has a minty flavor with lemony undertones. Frequently used in Mediterranean cooking. Use with fish, chicken, salads, vegetables, and eggs.

SPICES

Allspice – contrary to what most people think, is not a blend of several spices, but comes from the myrtle tree family. Its taste is similar to cloves, cinnamon, and nutmeg. It comes in whole and ground varieties and is most frequently used in savory and sweet foods, from salads to desserts.

Cardamom – has a sweet, spicy flavor and is used in many curry blends. On its own, it makes a nice addition to many desserts. Use sparingly, a little goes a long way.

Cayenne Pepper also called *red pepper*, is very hot. Use sparingly in eggs, soups, potatoes, and other hot and spicy dishes.

Celery Seed – tastes similar to celery and lends a "salty" taste to many dishes. Use in soups and sauces.

Chili Powder spicy flavor, ranging from mild to hot depending on the pepper(s) used. Use in Mexican cooking, chili, and other spicy dishes.

Cinnamon – has a sweet flavor and is sold either ground or in sticks. Use in sweet or savory dishes, curries, soups, stews, and desserts.

Cloves – have a strong, aromatic flavor. Use in sweet dishes.

Cumin – has a distinctive peppery flavor and is used most frequently in Mexican dishes. Add to eggs, soups, chili, vegetables, meats, and poultry.

Ginger – fresh ginger (gingerroot) has a slightly sweet, pungent flavor and is used in Asian dishes; the powdered form has a different flavor than the root and is used most often with vegetables, soups, and desserts.

Mace – has a pungent nutmeg taste. Use in custards and spicy desserts.

Nutmeg – has a sweet, spicy flavor. Although sold whole or ground, the whole is superior in flavor when freshly ground. Use in desserts, Italian dishes, soups, and vegetable dishes.

Paprika – comes from sweet red peppers and range from sweet and mild to hot and pungent. Most supermarkets carry the mild variety, ethnic markets carry the more pungent. Hungarian paprika is considered the best and is stronger than American. Use in most savory dishes, poultry, eggs, and as a topping on potatoes.

Turmeric – has a pungent flavor with a hint of ginger and is a main ingredient in curry. It is bright-orange in color and can be substituted for saffron in many dishes. It is primarily used in Indian cooking, but can also be added to soups, stews, and vegetables.

YIELDS AND EQUIVALENTS

This is a listing of many common ingredients and how much it makes or yields. For example, a pound of fresh spinach yields about 1½ cups cooked. Also, listed are a few substitutions, such as substituting red wine with a little sweetener for recipes calling for Madeira wine. Keep this handy as a quick reference.

BAKING AND COOKING NEEDS

Baking powder – NSA baking powder (use twice as much as called for in the recipe)

Baking soda – 1½ tablespoons NSA baking powder, plus replace acidic liquid in recipe with non-acidic liquid

Bouillon/Broths – 1 tsp bouillon = 1 envelope or cube

Brandy or Rum – ¼ cup = 1 tsp extract + liquid to make ¼ cup

Bread crumbs
1 cup soft = 1–2 slices bread
1 cup dry = 4–5 slices bread

Chocolate – *semisweet*, add 4 tsp sugar or sugar substitute to 1 oz unsweetened chocolate

Cornstarch – 1 tbsp = 2 tbsp all-purpose flour or 1 tbsp arrowroot

Crumbs (cookie/graham)
1 cup cookie crumbs = 22 vanilla wafers
1 cup graham crumbs = 14 squares
1 cup saltines = 28 crackers

Grains (

Herbs and Spices (1 tbsp fresh = 1 tsp dried)
Allspice – ½ tsp = ¼ tsp cinnamon and ¼ tsp ground cloves
Ginger – 1 tsp fresh = ¼ tsp ground
Saffron – turmeric

Nuts – 1 cup nuts = 4 oz unshelled (approx)

Sweeteners (sugar or sugar substitute)
Brown sugar – granulated or sugar substitute
Powdered sugar – pulse equal amounts sugar or sugar substitute in blender until fine

Honey – ¾ cup maple syrup, corn syrup, or light molasses plus ½ cup granulated or sugar substitute

Vanilla – 1 tbsp extract = ½ bean

Vinegar – 1 tsp = 1 tsp lemon juice or wine
Balsamic – 1 tbsp cider or red wine vinegar plus ½ tsp sugar or sugar substitute

Wines
Madeira – 1 tbsp red wine plus ½ tsp sugar substitute or sugar
Red – substitute Marsala or port
White – substitute sake, vermouth, dry sherry, LS chicken or vegetable broth

CONDIMENTS AND SAUCES

Chili oil – 1 tbsp oil plus 2–3 drops hot pepper sauce (such as *Tabasco*)

Horseradish – 1 tbsp fresh = 2 tsp bottled

Hot pepper sauce (such as *Tabasco*) – cayenne pepper or crushed red pepper flakes

Mayonnaise – use half mayonnaise and half plain yogurt

Mustard – 1 tbsp prepared = 1 tsp powdered

Pimento – 2 tbsp = 3 tbsp chopped red bell pepper

Soy sauce – 1 tbsp = 2 tsp tamari

Worcetershire sauce – steak sauce

GRAINS AND RICE

Barley – 1 cup uncooked = 4 cups cooked

Bulgur/Couscous – 1 cup dried = 3 cups cooked

Pasta – 8 oz = 4 cups cooked

Rice – 1 cup uncooked = 3 cups cooked

DAIRY PRODUCTS

Butter/Margarine – ½ cup = 1 stick or ¼ lb

Buttermilk – 1 cup milk plus ½ tsp lemon juice (let stand 5 minutes)

Cheese – 1 oz firm (i.e. Swiss) = ¼ cup shredded
1 oz hard (i.e. Parmesan) = ⅓ cup grated (approx)

Cream – 1 cup = 2 cups whipped

Eggs – 2 large = 3 small, 1 egg = 2 whites

Milk – soy or almond milk
Evaporated – half-and-half or light cream

Sour cream – plain yogurt

FRUITS, VEGETABLES AND LEGUMES

Apples – 1 medium = 1 cup sliced

Apricots – 3 apricots = ¼ lb

Avocado – 1 avocado = 1 cup mashed

Beans – 1 cup dry = 2½ cups cooked

Cabbage – 1 med head = 1½ lb = 6 cups shredded (approx)
1 lb pkg = 6 cups

Carrots – 1 lb = 3 cups shredded or 3½ cups diced
1½ med = 1 cup shredded
2 med = 1 cup sliced

Cauliflower – 1 lb = 3 cups florets

Celery – 2 stalks = 1 cup sliced or chopped

Corn – 2 ears = 1 cup kernels

Cranberries – 4 oz fresh or dried = 1 cup

Cucumber – 3/4 med = 1 cup chopped

Eggplant – 1 med = ½ lb = 2 cups chopped

Garlic – 1 clove = ½ tsp finely chopped = ⅛ tsp powder or ½ tsp bottled

Gingerroot – 1 tbsp = 1½ tsp dried ginger, plus ½ tsp fresh lemon juice

Greens – 1 lb = 6 cups fresh or 1½ cups cooked
10 oz pkg = 6 cups (approx)

Lemon – 1 med = 2–3 tbsp juice or 2 tsp grated peel or 1 tsp lemon extract
Lemon juice – 1 tsp = ½ tsp vinegar

Lime – 1 lime = 1–2 tbsp juice

Melon – 1 lb = 2 cups chunks, 1 med – 3 lbs

Mushrooms – 1 lb fresh = 6 cups sliced or 3 oz dried or 2 cups cooked
8 oz = 2½ cups chopped

Onion – 1 small = ¼ cup chopped or 1–2 tbsp instant minced or 1 tsp onion powder
Green onions – 2 med = 2 Tbsp

Orange – 1 med = 6–8 tbsp juice or 2 tbsp grated peel

Peaches – 1 lb = 3 peaches = 2 cups sliced

Peas – 1 lb in pods = 1 c shelled

Peppers (sweet) – 1 med = 1 cup chopped

Potatoes – 1 med = 1 cup chopped
1 lb = 3½ cups diced or 1½ cup mashed
Red (small) – 10–12 = 1½ lb

Pumpkin – 1 lb uncooked = 1 cup canned

Spinach – 1 lb = about 10 cups fresh or 1 cup cooked

Squash
Summer – 1 med = 2 cups chopped
Winter – 1 med = 2 lbs

Strawberries – 1 lb = 2 cups sliced

Tomato – 3 med = 1 lb or 6 oz sauce or ¼ cup paste
1 large = 1 cup chopped
2 cups chopped = 16-oz can

MEASUREMENTS AND ABBREVIATIONS

MEASUREMENTS / EQUIVALENTS

Dash	=	<⅛ teaspoon	=	0.02 oz	=	0.58 grams
1½ teaspoons	=	½ tablespoon	=	0.25 oz	=	7 grams
3 teaspoons	=	1 tablespoon	=	0.5 oz	=	14 grams
2 tablespoons	=	⅛ cup	=	1 oz	=	28 grams
4 tablespoons	=	¼ cup	=	2 oz	=	56 grams
8 tablespoons	=	½ cup	=	4 oz	=	112 grams
12 tablespoons	=	¾ cup	=	6 oz	=	168 grams
16 tablespoons	=	1 cup	=	8 oz	=	224 grams

LIQUID

Dash	=	0.625 mil	=	2–3 drops
½ fl oz	=	15 ml	=	1 tablespoon
1 fl oz	=	30 ml	=	⅛ cup
2 fl oz	=	60 ml	=	¼ cup
4 fl oz	=	120 ml	=	½ cup
8 fl oz	=	240 ml	=	1 cup
16 fl oz	=	480 ml	=	1 pint
2 cups	=	1 pint	=	½ quart
4 cups	=	2 pints	=	1 quart
4 pints	=	2 quarts	=	½ gallon
8 pints	=	4 quarts	=	1 gallon

ABBREVIATIONS

approx	approximately	**N/A**	not applicable
cal	calories	**NF**	nonfat
carb	carbohydrates	**NSA**	no salt added
chol	cholesterol	**oz**	ounce(s)
envl	envelope	**pkg**	package(s)
fl oz	fluid ounce(s)	**sat**	saturated fat
lb	pound(s)	**sl**	slice(s)
LF	low fat	**sm**	small
lrg	large	**sod**	sodium
LS	low salt	**tbsp**	tablespoon
med	medium-sized	**TF**	trans fat free
mg	milligram(s)	**tsp**	teaspoon

ABOUT THE RECIPES

The following recipes focus on healthy, flavorful food with a minimum of sodium. Even though low in salt, you can be assured that the whole family, including heavy-handed salt shakers, will be satisfied with these great-tasting recipes. Most dishes are also low in fat and cholesterol, and all have passed the "taste test" with family and friends.

As you browse through the recipes you will find a wide variety of dishes, including Asian, Mediterranean, Hispanic, and good old comfort food. Many are perfect for entertaining or special occasions, but the emphasis is on everyday family meals that are easy to make.

Although some of the recipes are more complex than others, most can be prepared in 30 minutes or less. Like most of you, I usually don't have much time to prepare a meal and rely on many low-salt convenience products. However, for those of you who have lots of time and enjoy cooking from scratch, I've included several recipes for pie crusts, mayonnaise, breads, and many other basics.

If you are trying to watch your salt for health reasons, your healthcare provider will probably suggest you stay well below the 2,400mg recommendation—probably closer to 1,200mg. This means you'll need to aim for about 400mg per meal (3 meals x 400mg = 1,200mg). A majority of the recipes have less than 100mg per serving, giving you a wide variety of dishes from which to choose.

For the most part, all ingredients used are readily available. For those that are harder to find, alternatives are suggested, and ordering information from manufacturers and other sources can be found in the **Resources** (pages 272–274).

Although the recipes are delicious as printed, the final outcome depends on you and the products you use. For example, you may prefer a different bouillon than I or choose a variety of vegetable or fruit that, depending on the season, may or may not be as flavorful. Plus, the spices that you use may have a difference in potency or flavor than what I use. You might, also, need to make substitutions based on other dietary needs. For instance, if you are lactose intolerant, you probably will use soy products instead of dairy. Any of these variables can change the flavor of the dish.

Consequently, you should taste before you serve anything. As you become familiar with spices and herbs, and which combinations work well together, you can make subtle adjustments. Sometimes just a little more lemon juice, an added teaspoon of low-salt bouillon, or a sprinkling of freshly chopped parsley may be all that is needed. And finally, make notes about what works and what doesn't. Most recipes have enough blank space on the page where you can jot down your comments and additions.

THE RECIPES

Recipes are divided into chapters based on courses—from appetizers to desserts. For easy reference, each recipe in a particular category, along with its page number, is listed at the start of each chapter.

Every recipe includes the number of servings, ingredients, step-by-step instructions, nutritional data, notes on ingredients and alternatives, and the total sodium and fats per ingredient. Some recipes also have helpful information on choosing, storing, and preparing certain foods.

The following is an explanation of some of these features:

Yield – Most of the recipes serve four people, but many one-pot meals and salads are sized for eight or more. This will give you several days of leftovers, some of which you can freeze and save for another day.

Nutritional info – Each recipe includes a per-serving analysis, and is broken down into calories, fat, saturated fat, cholesterol, carbohydrates, fiber, sugar, and sodium. (The sodium per serving is also shown below the recipe name for quick reference.) All values are rounded off to the nearest whole number. Nutrients with less than 0.05 are shown as 0, those with 0.05 or greater are listed as 1.

Optional ingredients are included in the analysis, but substitutions are not. Nutritional values are based on the USDA National Nutritonal Database, food manufacturer labels, and author calculations.

Comments – This gives added information about ingredients and substitutions, for example specific brands, handling instructions, etc.

Cooking Tips and *Food Notes* – Some recipes feature helpful hints on preparing certain dishes; others offer useful information on choosing, storing, and preparing specific foods, particularly items you may not be familiar with.

Total Sodium and Fat Per Ingredient – This is a listing of recipe ingredients (including alternative ingredients) that contain sodium or fat and shows the total amount per recipe. For example, if a recipe calls for 2 tablespoons lowfat or nonfat sour cream, the following is shown:

> *Sodium:*
>   2 T LF sour cream - 15mg or
>   NF sour cream - 20mg
> *Fat (Sat Fat):*
>   2 T LF sour cream - 3mg (1mg) or
>   NF sour cream - 0mg

This is useful for comparing ingredients you use versus ingredients I use, and then adjusting the nutritional data. In this case, if you use a brand of sour cream that has 25mg sodium per tablespoon, the total sodium is 50mg (or 35mg more). If the recipe serves 4, this equates to an additional 9mg per serving.

This also will help familiarize you with the amount of sodium in frequently used ingredients.

THE INGREDIENTS

In addition to specific alternatives which you will find in the COMMENTS column of each recipe, the following ingredient information may be helpful.

Fats, Oils and Cooking Sprays

To keep fats and oils to a minimum, I suggest using a nonstick skillet when cooking. If you don't have one, coat the pan with a nonstick cooking spray. Not only does this keep food from sticking, but also less oil, margarine, and/or butter is needed.

Olive Oil

I use olive oil in most of my dishes, not only for the "healthy heart" benefits of polunsaturated fats, but also because I prefer its subtle flavor. Even though you can substitute vegetable oil, the taste you get may not be the same as mine.

As far as salad dressings, I highly recommend extra-virgin olive oil. Although olive oil is more expensive than vegetable oils, to save money, use plain olive oil for cooking and the more expensive extra-virgin for salad dressings. If you don't anticipate using all the oil within a month, keep it in the refrigerator. *NOTE: This will cause the oil to solidify, when ready to use, run under warm water or place in the microwave for 30 to 60 seconds.*

Margarine and Butter

Unsalted margarine or butter is specified in many recipes. If you are concerned with saturated fat, use trans-free margarine. *Smart Balance* is what I usually use, as it tastes, cooks, and bakes just like butter. *NOTE: There are smany trans-free margarines, but are not recommended for cooking or baking.* (Unfortunately, they contain significant amounts of sodium, most have 90mg or more per tablespoon.)

To keep both fat and sodium to a minimum, use a combination of both. For those who prefer using trans-free margarines, the amount of sodium per serving is indicated in the COMMENTS section.

Butter Spray

Another option to butter or margarine in some dishes is using a butter-like spray; it adds a butter taste but without the fat and salt. Spray it on top of potatoes, vegetables, and pastry doughs (it works really well on phyllo sheets).

Eggs and Egg Substitute

Recent research indicates that eating eggs may not be as bad as we once thought. According to two Harvard University studies, eating one egg a day or more posed no more risk for developing heart disease than consuming one egg a week or less. Of more concern is the amount of saturated fat consumed, which has a greater impact on raising cholesterol.

To keep fat and cholesterol to a minimum, an egg substitute may be used. Although some brands have no fat, they all have significant amounts of sodium (100mg or more to 70mg for a large egg).

Many people use 2 egg whites instead of a whole egg, however, if you are watching your sodium intake, the whites is where the sodium resides (a large egg white has 55mg). I've found that when more than one egg is needed, a combination of eggs, egg whites, and egg substitute helps keep both fat and sodium to a minimum. Below is a comparison of a recipe calling for 2 large eggs:

FAT AND SODIUM COMPARISON OF EGGS AND EGG SUBSTITUTES	Fat	Sat Fat	Sodium
2 eggs	10mg	4mg	140mg
1 egg and ¼ cup egg substitute	5mg	2mg	170mg
½ cup substitute	0mg	0mg	200mg
4 egg whites	0mg	0mg	220mg

NOTE: Although the AHA is no longer making recommendations on the number of egg yolks one should eat in a day, they do suggest keeping saturated fat intake lower on the days you consume eggs.

Unless specified, when a recipes calls for an egg, it is of large size.

Sweeteners

As previously mentioned (page 19), sugar also affects blood pressure. In fact some cardiologists think heart problems are associated with high serum triglycerides, which they attribute to increased sugar consumption.

The two sweeteners I use most often are fructose and sucralose (also know as *Splenda*). Fructose has no sodium and is low on the glycemic index, meaning it releases slowly in the body instead of spiking. Fructose, however, does contain calories and carbohydrates. *Splenda*, on the other hand, has no calories or carbs, however, one of its main ingredients, Maltodextrin, ranks high on the glycemic index. According to research, Maltodextrin reacts the same way as sugar in the body and raises blood sugars.

Because sugar substitutes differ from sugar in sweetness, the amount needed is determined by the sweetener used. While *Splenda* is equal to sugar in sweetness (1 cup *Splenda* equals 1 cup sugar), fructose is sweeter, so less is used. In all recipes where a sweetener is called for, the amount of sugar, *Splenda*, and fructose is listed in the COMMENTS.

NOTE: If using Splenda, you may notice some differences in how things cook. For example, cookies do not spread as well (flattening the cookies before baking helps this problem) and baked items cook quicker (start checking several minutes earlier than directed). You may also find some items do not have as much volume as you are accustomed and baked goods don't last as long as items made with sugar (store in the refrigerator for longer life).

Although there are many other sugar substitutes available, tI cannot guarantee the recipes will come out the same, as only *Splenda*, fructose, and sugar have been tested.

Dairy Products

In most of my cooking, I try to keep the fat to a minimum and use many lowfat and nonfat dairy products. Not only do most dairy products have significant amounts of sodium, but there also is a wide range within brands. For instance, one brand of nonfat sour cream may have 40mg sodium per 2 tablespoons and another, 15mg. It may not sound like much, but if you're using ½ cup, that's a difference of 200mg. So it behooves you to familarize yourself with the different brands and the amount of sodium in each. The following is a generic comparison of a variety of dairy products.

I realize that using nonfat products is not to everyone's liking, so most of my recipes use lowfat ingredients. I have tested many of the dishes with nonfat products without much loss of flavor, but in others there is a loss of richness. Feel free to experiment. Since I know the dish tastes good using lowfat ingredients, if you use a higher fat product, it will taste even richer and creamier.

Adding creaminess: There are many ways to add creaminess without a lot of fat and sodium. When a recipe calls for cream, one option is substituting a combination of sour cream and milk (use 2 to 3 times as much milk as sour cream, for example if a recipe calls for 1 cup cream, use ⅔ cup milk and ⅓ cup sour cream).

Other suggestions are using half-and-half, milk, or soy milk. Although fat-free half-and-half may be used, it has 352mg sodium per cup verus 96 for regular half-and-half (see chart below for comparisons).

And finally, another way to add creaminess in many dishes is using tofu and milk. If a recipe calls for 1 cup cream, use 5 ounces silken tofu, plus ½ cup nonfat milk or soy milk (for a total of 56mg and 69mg sodium, respectively).

DAIRY PRODUCTS COMPARISON
Sodium per ¼ cup (or 2 ounces)

Cream, light	20 mg
Soy milk	21mg
Half and half	24 mg
Fat free	88 mg
Milk (avg all)	28 mg
Yogurt (whole and lowfat)	28 mg
Fat free	47 mg
Sour cream	30 mg
Lowfat	50 mg
Fat free	80 mg
Ricotta cheese	52 mg
Part skim	78 mg
Buttermilk	64 mg
Cream cheese	172 mg
Whipped	118 mg
Fat free	328 mg
Cottage cheese	215 mg

Well, that's about all the space I can devote to the recipes and ingredients, now it's time to get started with the low-salt lifestyle. Hope you enjoy!

APPETIZERS

COMMENTS:

1 *Canned garbanzo beans (chickpeas) average 359mg sodium per ½ cup, 50% less salt varieties have 220mg, and no-salt-added (NSA), 10mg. (See RESOURCES, page 272, for brand information.) If NSA beans are unavailable, you can cook them from scratch using dried garbanzo beans (see COOKING TIP below).*

2 *Tahini (or sesame paste) is made from ground sesame seeds. It is available in most grocery stores. Before using, stir thoroughly to incorporate the oil on the top.*

3 *If you like a lot of heat, leave the seeds in the jalapeño.*

4 *I add a little salt to bring out the flavors, but the hummus tastes equally good without it (2 tablespoons without salt is 4mg).*

SPICY ROASTED RED PEPPER HUMMUS

Sodium Per Serving – 13mg   Makes 2 cups (16 servings)

Hummus is a thick and delicious Middle Eastern sauce made from garbanzo beans and sesame paste that whips up quickly in a blender or food processor. This version gets added zip from roasted red peppers and cayenne pepper. There is a lot of room for variation, depending on how you like your hummus. Start with the minimum ingredient amounts, then add more garlic, tahini, lemon juice, or cayenne. Serve wtih pita bread pieces and crackers or use as a dip with veggies. This also makes a yummy spread on sandwiches and wraps.

1 (15-ounce) can no-salt-added garbanzo beans, drained and liquid reserved[1]

1 roasted red pepper, chopped *(see COOKING TIP, Roasting Peppers, page 141)*

2 garlic cloves, minced

3–4 tablespoons tahini[2]

1–2 tablespoons lemon juice

1 tablespoon olive oil

1 teaspoon ground cumin

¼ teaspoon garlic powder

1 jalapeño, seeded and chopped, or ⅛–¼ teaspoon cayenne pepper[3]

Pinch salt (optional)[4]

1 tablespoon chopped fresh flat-leaf (Italian) parsley, or 1 teaspoon dried (optional)

▸ Combine all ingredients in a food processor or blender; pulse until smooth and the consistency of peanut butter. If hummus is grainy, add ½ tablespoon olive oil, or if too thick, thin with reserved bean liquid, a tablespoon at a time.

▸ Serve with pita bread pieces and crackers or use as a dip with veggies.

NUTRITIONAL INFO PER 2 TABLESPOONS: Calories 50mg, Fat 3mg (Saturated Fat 0mg), Cholesterol 0mg, Carbohydrates 5mg (Fiber 1mg, Sugar 0mg), Sodium 13mg

TOTAL SODIUM AND FAT PER INGREDIENT
Sodium:
   15 oz NSA garbanzo beans - 30mg
   1 red pepper - 2mg
   2 garlic cloves - 2mg
   3 T tahini - 16mg
   1 t cumin - 4mg
   Pinch salt - 155mg
   1 T parsley - 2mg
Fat (Sat Fat):
   15 oz NSA garbanzos - 6mg (0mg)
   1 T olive oil - 14mg (2mg)
   3 T tahini - 24mg (3mg)

COOKING TIP

COOKING DRIED BEANS

Wash and pick through 1 cup dried beans, discarding any foreign particles or flawed beans. Place in a heavy pot and add enough water to cover the beans; cover and soak 6 to 8 hours or overnight. Drain and rinse.

Return beans to the same pot and cover with 2 inches of water; stir in 1 tablespoon (or 3 envelopes) low-salt chicken bouillon granules. Bring to a boil over high heat; decrease heat to low and simmer, partially covered, until tender, about 1 hour. Drain.

Makes enough to equal one can of beans.

CARAMELIZED ONION DIP

Sodium Per Serving – 12mg   Makes 2 cups (16 servings)

If the only onion dip you've tasted is made with dried soup mix, just wait until you try this delicious dip made with caramelized onions. Allow at least 2 hours before serving (overnight is even better), as the longer this sits, the stronger the onion flavor.

- 1 tablespoon olive oil
- 1 tablespoon unsalted margarine or butter[1]
- 1 large yellow onion, finely chopped[2]
- 1½ cups (12 ounces) lowfat sour cream or lowfat sour cream[3]
- 2 tablespoons finely chopped fresh chives or green onions (green part only)

- 2 tablespoons chopped fresh basil (optional)[4]
- 1 garlic clove, finely minced
- ½ teaspoon lemon juice or vinegar
- ¼ teaspoon garlic powder
- ¼ teaspoon onion powder
- ⅛ teaspoon ground black pepper
- Pinch cayenne pepper

▷ Heat oil and margarine in a skillet over medium-high heat; add onions. Cook, stirring constantly, until onions begin to brown, 3 to 4 minutes. Decrease heat to medium-low; continue to cook, stirring occasionally, until onions are golden brown and caramelized, about 30 minutes. Remove from heat and let cool slightly.

▷ In a bowl, mix the caramelized onions with the sour cream, chives, basil, garlic, lemon juice, garlic powder, onion powder, black pepper, and cayenne. Cover and refrigerate at least 2 hours or overnight. Serve with vegetables, low-salt chips, or crackers.

NUTRITIONAL INFO PER 2 TABLESPOONS: Calories 62mg, Fat 6mg (Saturated Fat 3mg), Cholesterol 10mg, Carbohydrates 2mg (Fiber 0mg, Sugar 1mg), Sodium 12mg

COOKING TIP

CARAMELIZING ONIONS

Caramelizing brings out the natural sugars of a food and onions benefit greatly from caramelization. Use them to add richness to soups, entrées, and side dishes; as a topping on pizzas; and anywhere else cooked onions are specified. Make up extra and freeze (up to 3 months) for later use.

To caramelize onions, a combination of butter (or margarine) and oil is used to cook sliced onions until they turn a rich caramel color. Yellow onions are most often used, as they have less water than other onions, allowing for better caramelization. In some dishes where additional sweetness is desired, stir in 1–2 teaspoons sugar or sugar substitute. Three common ways to caramelize onions:

Stove-top slow-cook: Cook onions in butter (or margarine) and oil in a skillet over low heat for 30 to 45 minutes, stirring frequently, until caramelized.

Quick caramelization: Some chefs speed up the process by cooking over high heat, but unless it is done properly, the onions can easily burn. Cook onions in butter (or margarine) and oil in a skillet over medium-high heat, stirring constantly. Scrap up onions and any browned bits that stick to the bottom of the pan, adding 1 to 2 tablespoons water, while stirring constantly (this is called deglazing). Continue stirring and deglazing until onions are caramelized.

Slow-cooker method: Place onions and butter or margarine (1–2 teaspoons per onion) in the cooker, cover, and cook on LOW for 10 to 12 hours, or until onions are dark brown in color.

COMMENTS:

1 *To reduce saturated fat, use trans-free margarine. Since it contains sodium (90mg per tablespoon), it will increase the sodium per serving to 17mg.*

2 *Yellow onions are preferred, as they have less water than other onions, allowing for better caramelization (see COOKING TIP below).*

3 *Although this tastes best with regular sour cream, lowfat, nonfat, or a combination of these, may be used.*

4 *The basil compliments the sweetness of the onions and adds another layer of flavor to this dip, but tastes equally good without it.*

TOTAL SODIUM AND FAT PER INGREDIENT

Sodium:
- 1 onion - 3mg
- 1½ c sour cream - 183mg
  or LF sour cream - 240mg
- 1 garlic clove - 1mg

Fat (Sat Fat):
- 1 T olive oil - 14mg (2mg)
- 1 T NSA margarine - 8mg (2mg)
  or NSA butter - 12mg (8mg)
- 1½ c sour cream - 74mg (45mg)
  or LF sour cream - 49mg (30mg)

1 *Canned refried beans average 530mg sodium per ½ cup, reduced salt varieties have about 320mg, and no-salt-added (NSA) brands, 5mg.* **Bearitos** *offers an NSA variety, available at many health food stores, online grocers, and from the manufacturer (see RESOURCES, page 272).*

2 *The optional salsa in the bean dip adds more flavor, but is equally good without it. Most bottled salsas average 139mg sodium per 2 tablespoons, but there are many delicious low-salt varieties with less than 80mg. See RESOURCES, page 272, for low-salt brands.*

3 *The optional lime juice adds a bit of zip, but is also good without it.*

WARM BEAN DIP

Sodium Per Serving – 33mg   Makes 2½ cups (20 servings)

This crowd-pleasing dip is creamy and delicious. It also is great as a spread in tacos, sandwiches, and wraps.

2 cups QUICK REFRIED BEANS (page 192), **or 1 (15-ounce) can no-salt-added lowfat refried beans**[1]

½ (4-ounce) can diced green chiles

2 ounces no-salt-added Swiss cheese, shredded (about ½ cup)

2 ounces lowfat Cheddar cheese, shredded (about ½ cup)

¼ cup lowfat sour cream

2 tablespoons low-salt salsa (optional)[2]

▷ In a saucepan over medium-low heat, combine beans, green chiles, Swiss and Cheddar cheeses. Cook, stirring frequently, until cheese melts, about 5 minutes.

▷ Mix in sour cream and salsa; heat through.

▷ Serve with low-salt tortilla chips. *NOTE: Dip thickens as it cools; reheat to return to original consistency, if desired.*

NUTRITIONAL INFO PER 2 TABLESPOONS: Calories 48mg, Fat 2mg (Saturated Fat 1mg), Cholesterol 4mg, Carbohydrates 4mg (Fiber 2mg, Sugar 0mg), Sodium 33mg

TOTAL SODIUM AND FAT PER INGREDIENT

Warm Bean Dip:
Sodium:
2 c QUICK REFRIED BEANS - 82mg
   or 15 oz NSA beans - 18mg
2 oz green chiles - 140mg
2 oz NSA Swiss cheese - 20mg
2 oz LF Cheddar cheese - 348mg
¼ c NF sour cream - 30mg
   or LF sour cream - 40mg
2 T LS salsa - 40mg
Fat (Sat Fat):
2 c QUICK BEANS - 22mg (4mg)
   or 15 oz NSA beans - 11mg (0mg)
2 oz NSA Swiss - 16mg (10mg)
2 oz LF Cheddar - 4mg (2mg)
¼ c NF sour cream - 0mg
   or LF sour cream - 8mg (5mg)

Guacamole:
Sodium:
1 avocado - 14mg
2 t LS salsa - 13mg
Fat (Sat Fat):
1 avocado - 30mg (4mg)

GUACAMOLE

Sodium Per Serving – 3mg   Makes 1 cup (8 servings)

This guacamole is simple to make and full of flavor. Serve it as a dip with chips or as a spread in tacos, sandwiches, and wraps. Using a ripe avocado is essential, not only for taste, but also consistency. If making ahead of time, cover with plastic wrap, leaving the avocado pit in the guacamole until ready to serve (this helps prevent the avocado from turning brown).

1 ripe avocado, preferably Hass

1 tablespoon finely chopped sweet onion, such as Vidalia

2–3 teaspoons low-salt salsa[2]

½ teaspoon lime juice (optional)[3]

▷ Halve avocado, remove pit, and scoop out flesh. Mash flesh with a fork; mix in the onion, salsa, and lime juice. Serve with low-salt tortilla chips.

NUTRITIONAL INFO PER 2 TABLESPOONS: Calories 41mg, Fat 4mg (Saturated Fat 1mg), Cholesterol 0mg, Carbohydrates 2mg (Fiber 2mg, Sugar 0mg), Sodium 3mg

CHERVIL CHEESE DIP

Sodium Per Serving – 55mg   Makes 2½ cups (24 servings)

My long-time friend, Geraldine Scully, brought this dip to a gathering and it was devoured in a matter of minutes. The garlic, combined with the subtle anise flavor of the fresh chervil is scrumptous. The original had lots of fat, which I've lowered by using lite mayonnaise and whipped cream cheese. Make this several hours ahead of time to let the flavors intensify. NOTE: While dried chervil may be substituted, fresh chervil really makes this dip.

8 ounces (1 cup) cream cheese[1]

8 ounces (1 cup) whipped cream cheese[2]

2 tablespoons lite mayonnaise or mayonnaise-type dressing

2 garlic cloves, finely minced

2 tablespoons chopped fresh chervil, or 2 teaspoons dried[3]

2 tablespoons chopped fresh flat-leaf (Italian) parsley

▸ Mix all ingredients together until well blended. Serve with low-salt crackers or assorted fresh vegetables.

NUTRITIONAL INFO PER 2 TABLESPOONS: Calories 60mg, Fat 6mg (Saturated Fat 4mg), Cholesterol 17mg, Carbohydrates 1mg (Fiber 0mg, Sugar 0mg), Sodium 55mg

COMMENTS:

1 *Instead of cream cheese, substitute ½ cup lowfat ricotta cheese and ½ cup nonfat or lowfat plain yogurt. This will decrease the sodium to 37mg per serving (see FOOD NOTE below for a cream cheese comparison).*

2 *Whipped cream cheese is simply cheese that has been whipped with air. Its texture is less firm than regular cream cheese and it has less volume.*

3 *Chervil is one of the components of fines herbes and is similar in taste to parsley, but with a hint of licorice. Fresh chervil is often hard to find, but if you do locate it, you're in for a treat.*

FOOD NOTE

CREAM CHEESE COMPARISON

Cream cheese has a lot of sodium, particularly lower fat and nonfat varieties, and is a good example of how manufacturers increase the salt when fat is removed. Below is a comparison of varieties from a leading manufacturer of cream cheese (per 1-ounce serving):

	Fat	Sat Fat	Sodium
Regular	10mg	6mg	90mg
Whipped	6mg	3.5mg	90mg
Neufchatel (⅓ less fat)	6mg	4mg	120mg
Lite	4.5mg	3mg	150mg
Fat free	0mg	0mg	200mg

Several manufacturers, such as *Lucerne, Nancy's,* and *Morning Select,* have lower sodium versions of some varieties. Look for brands with less than 65mg per ounce. To keep fat and sodium to a minimum, combine regular or whipped cream cheese with lower fat brands:

	Fat	Sat Fat	Sodium
½ regular and ½ lite	7mg	4.5mg	120mg
½ regular and ½ fat free	5mg	3mg	145mg
½ whipped and ½ lite	5mg	3mg	120mg
½ whipped and ½ fat free	3mg	2mg	145mg

Other alternatives that may be used in many recipes calling for cream cheese:

	Fat	Sat Fat	Sodium
½ LF ricotta and ½ LF plain yogurt	1mg	1mg	27mg
Mascarpone (sweet, cream-cheese like)	13mg	7mg	16mg

TOTAL SODIUM AND FAT PER INGREDIENT

Sodium:
8 oz cream cheese - 671mg
8 oz whipped cream cheese - 520mg
2 T lite mayonnaise - 120mg
2 garlic cloves - 2mg
2 T chervil - 3mg
2 T parsley - 4mg
Fat (Sat Fat):
8 oz cream cheese - 79mg (50mg)
8 oz whipped cheese - 56mg (36mg)
2 T lite mayonnaise - 6mg (0mg)

1 *To reduce saturated fat, use trans-free margarine. Since it contains sodium (90mg per tablespoon), it will increase the sodium per serving to 10mg.*

2 *Crimini and button mushrooms are similar, but criminis have more flavor (see FOOD NOTE below).*

3 *Toasting brings out the flavor of the nuts (see FOOD NOTE, page 90 for toasting methods.*

MUSHROOM PATE WITH PORT AND ALMONDS

Sodium Per Serving – 1mg   Makes 2½ cups (20 servings)

My neighbor, Susie Gaines, brought this delicious spread to one of our summer barbecues. Serve with low-salt crackers or baguette-size bread slices. This also makes a great pita sandwich with cream cheese and sliced apple.

2 tablespoons all-purpose flour

¼ cup port or Marsala wine

2 tablespoons unsalted margarine or butter[1]

8 ounces crimini or button mushrooms, finely chopped (about 3 cups)[2]

¼ cup finely chopped sweet onion, such as Vidalia

1 garlic clove, finely chopped

¼ teaspoon garlic powder

⅛ teaspoon ground black pepper

⅛ teaspoon freshly ground nutmeg

⅓ cup sliced almonds, toasted[2]

1 tablespoon chopped fresh chives

▸ Mix together the flour and port until smooth; set aside.

▸ Melt margarine in a skillet over medium-high heat; add mushrooms, onion, garlic, garlic powder, pepper, and nutmeg. Cook, stirring frequently, until mushrooms and onions are soft, 2 to 3 minutes. Mix in port mixture, stirring constantly, until liquid begins to thicken, 1 to 2 minutes.

▸ Place one-half of the mushroom mixture in a blender or food processor and pulse until a smooth paste. Combine the purée with the remaining mushroom mixture; stir in the almonds and chives. Cover and chill several hours. Serve with low-salt crackers or bread slices.

NUTRITIONAL INFO PER 2 TABLESPOONS: Calories 39mg, Fat 3mg (Saturated Fat 0mg), Cholesterol 0mg, Carbohydrates 2mg (Fiber 0mg, Sugar 0mg), Sodium 1mg

TOTAL SODIUM AND FAT PER INGREDIENT
Sodium:
¼ c port or Marsala wine - 5mg
1½ c mushrooms - 3mg
2 T onion - 1mg
1 garlic clove - 1mg
⅓ c almonds - 1mg
Fat (Sat Fat):
2 T NSA margarine - 16mg (3mg)
  or NSA butter - 24mg (16mg)
⅓ c almonds - 40mg (3mg)

FOOD NOTE

ABOUT MUSHROOMS

Mushrooms not only have a wide-range of textures and taste, but they also add an earthy quality to dishes. They are low in calories and nearly fat and sodium free. There are thousands of varieties, but the most commonly available in supermarkets are:

Button – range in color from white to light brown and come in many sizes from small to large. They have a mild flavor that is enhanced by cooking. *Criminis* – related to button mushrooms, but are brown in color. Their taste is similar to buttons, but more flavorful. *Portobellos* – larger relatives of the button and crimini, reaching up to 4 or 5 inches in diameter. They have a meaty flavor, a firm texture, and are often used in place of meat in vegetarian dishes.

Wild varieties include *shiitake* (rich, woodsy flavor with a spongy texture), *oyster* (mild flavor with a soft, chewy texture), *enoki* (sweet taste and crisp in texture), and *porcini* (one of the best tasting, usually sold dried and have a meaty, buttery flavor). Other wild varieties include *maitakes*, *chanterelles*, and *morels*.

Selection and Preparation: Select firm, evenly-colored mushrooms that are tightly closed on the underside. To prepare, trim off the stem bottom and wipe clean. If you must rinse them, do so quickly, as they absorb water.

Storage: Keep refrigerated in a paper bag 5 to 7 days (up to 2 weeks for shiitake).

CELERY WITH PIMENTO-WALNUT CHEESE

Sodium Per Serving – 43mg   Makes about 20 appetizers

Stuffed celery is easy to make and is a great munchie. This yummy spread was passed on to me from a close friend. Arrange on a platter and serve at your next gathering, or keep a few handy for a tasty lowfat, low-carb snack. The cheese spread is also good on crackers, finger sandwiches, and burgers.

Cheese Spread:

1 cup (8 ounces) whipped cream cheese[1]

2 tablespoons lowfat sour cream

2 tablespoons finely chopped walnuts or pecans

2 tablespoons chopped pimento

2–3 drops hot pepper sauce (such as *Tabasco*)

1 bunch celery (about 10 medium stalks), cut into 3 or 4-inch lengths

▷ *For the Cheese Spread:* Combine cream cheese, sour cream, walnuts, pimento, and hot pepper sauce; mix well.

▷ Spread onto celery and serve.

NUTRITIONAL INFO PER APPETIZER: Calories 38mg, Fat 3mg (Saturated Fat 2mg), Cholesterol 8mg, Carbohydrates 1mg (Fiber 0mg, Sugar 1mg), Sodium 43mg

CHIVE-CHEESE STUFFED CELERY

Sodium Per Serving – 42mg   Makes about 20 appetizers

Make the filling several hours ahead of time to allow the flavor of the chives to permeate the cream cheese.

Cheese Spread:

1 cup (8 ounces) whipped cream cheese[1]

1 tablespoon chopped fresh chives

½ teaspoon garlic powder

½ teaspoon paprika[2]

1 bunch celery (about 10 medium stalks), cut into 3 or 4-inch lengths

▷ *For the Cheese Spread:* Combine cream cheese, chives, garlic powder, and paprika; mix well.

▷ Spread onto celery and serve.

NUTRITIONAL INFO PER APPETIZER: Calories 31mg, Fat 3mg (Saturated Fat 2mg), Cholesterol 8mg, Carbohydrates 1mg (Fiber 0mg, Sugar 1mg), Sodium 42mg

COMMENTS:

1 *Whipped cream cheese is simply cheese that has been whipped with air. Its texture is less firm than regular cream cheese and it has less volume. For a comparison of cream cheese varieties, see* FOOD NOTE, *page 43.*

2 *Paprika comes in sweet or hot varieties. Most American paprika is sweet, while Hungarian paprika is more pungent. Hungarian is available in ethnic or gourmet shops and some large supermarkets. Either may be used in this dish, but if you like a little heat, use the hot variety.*

OTHER VEGGIE STUFFERS:

In addition to celery, other favorite stuffers are cherry tomatoes, mushrooms, and zucchini. Scoop out the centers and stuff with the filling of your choice.

TOTAL SODIUM AND FAT PER INGREDIENT

Celery with Pimento-Walnut:
Sodium:
8 oz whipped cheese - 520mg
2 T LF sour cream - 17mg
2 T pimento - 4mg
2 drops hot pepper sauce - 4mg
10 celery stalks - 320mg
Fat (Sat Fat):
8 oz whipped cheese - 56mg (36mg)
2 T walnuts - 10mg (1mg)
10 celery stalks - 1mg (0mg)
2 T LF sour cream - 3mg (2mg)

Chive-Cheese Stuffed Celery:
Sodium:
8 oz whipped cheese - 520mg
10 celery stalks - 320mg
Fat (Sat Fat):
8 oz whipped cheese - 56mg (36mg)
10 celery stalks - 1mg (0mg)

COMMENTS:

1 For info on mushroom varieties, cleaning, and storage, see FOOD NOTE, page 44.

2 Seasoned bread crumbs may be used instead of plain. If so, reduce sage, thyme, and rosemary to ¼ teaspoon each. You can also make fresh bread crumbs by tearing 1 slice of dried low-salt bread into pieces. Place in blender or food processor and pulse until desired coarseness (see COOKING TIP below).

3 To reduce saturated fat, use trans-free margarine. Since it contains sodium (90mg per tablespoon), it will increase the sodium per serving to 6mg.

STUFFED MUSHROOMS

Sodium Per Serving – 2mg | Makes 24 appetizers

These mushrooms, stuffed with seasoned bread crumbs and topped with melted cheese, are the perfect party finger food.

- **1 cup chopped mushrooms, any type or combination, such as button, crimini, or wild varieties[1]**
- **¾ cup salt-free plain bread crumbs[2]**
- **⅓ cup chopped fresh flat-leaf (Italian) parsley**
- **1 tablespoon olive oil**
- **1 tablespoon unsalted margarine or butter, melted[3]**
- **½ teaspoon garlic powder**
- **½ teaspoon dried rosemary, crushed**
- **½ teaspoon dried sage**
- **½ teaspoon dried thyme**
- **¼ teaspoon ground black pepper**
- **24 large (2–3 inch) button or crimini mushrooms, stemmed[1]**
- **2 ounces no-salt-added Swiss cheese, shredded (about ½ cup)**

▷ Preheat oven to 400°F (200°C).

▷ In a large bowl, combine the chopped mushrooms, bread crumbs, parsley, olive oil, margarine, garlic powder, rosemary, sage, thyme, and pepper; mix well.

▷ Fill mushroom caps with bread crumb mixture; arrange in a large oven-proof dish and bake in a preheated oven for 20 minutes. Remove and sprinkle cheese on top of mushrooms; return to oven and bake another 4 to 5 minutes, until cheese melts.

NUTRITIONAL INFO PER MUSHROOM: Calories 36mg, Fat 2mg (Saturated Fat 1mg), Cholesterol 2mg, Carbohydrates 5mg (Fiber 0mg, Sugar 1mg), Sodium 2mg

TOTAL SODIUM AND FAT PER INGREDIENT

Sodium:
1 c + 24 mushrooms - 24mg
⅓ c parsley - 12mg
2 oz NSA Swiss cheese - 20mg
Fat (Sat Fat):
1 c + 24 mushrooms - 2mg (0mg)
¾ cup NSA crumbs - 9mg (0mg)
1 T olive oil - 14mg (2mg)
1 T NSA margarine - 8mg (2mg)
  or NSA butter - 12mg (8mg)
2 oz NSA Swiss - 16mg (10mg)

COOKING TIP

BREAD CRUMBS

Preparation: Homemade bread crumbs are easy to make and the taste is far superior to any store-bought brand. Use dry bread crumbs for breading and as a topping on pasta (instead of cheese); add soft bread crumbs to meatloafs (for a moister loaf) and as a topping on casseroles.

Dry bread crumbs: For 1 cup bread crumbs, use 3–4 slices stale bread. If bread is not at least one day old, dry it in the oven. (Arrange slices in a single layer on a baking sheet; bake in a preheated oven at 250°F (300°C) until dry and crisp, 20 to 30 minutes.) Break into small pieces and place in a food processor or blender; pulse until desired coarseness. You can also make coarse crumbs with a knife or use a grater for very fine crumbs.

Soft bread crumbs: For 1 cup fresh crumbs, use 1–2 slices fresh bread. Break into small pieces and place in a food processor or blender; pulse until the desired coarseness.

Storage: Store crumbs in an airtight container in the refrigerator for several weeks or in the freezer indefinitely.

TOASTED BREAD CRUMBS: Heat 1 tablespoon oil in a skillet over medium heat, add ½ cup dry crumbs. Cook, stirring frequently, until golden brown, about 2 minutes.

SPICY CRAB STUFFED MUSHROOMS

Sodium Per Serving – 49mg   Makes 24 appetizers

These spicy mushrooms were inspired by my neighbor, Bill Gaines. Although his original recipe was loaded with sodium, I think you'll agree that they are downright yummy even with a few low-salt modifications. If you like it hot and spicy, add more hot pepper sauce and cayenne pepper, or crushed red pepper flakes.

1 (6.5-ounce) can crabmeat, drained

8 ounces (1 cup) cream cheese, at room temperature[1]

1 tablespoon chopped fresh flat-leaf (Italian) parsley (optional)

2 teaspoons finely minced celery

2 garlic cloves, minced

1 teaspoon low-salt Worcestershire sauce

4–5 drops hot pepper sauce, such as *Tabasco*

⅛ teaspoon garlic powder

⅛ teaspoon ground white pepper

24 large (2–3 inch) crimini or button mushrooms, stemmed[2]

2 ounces no-salt-added Swiss cheese, shredded (about ½ cup)

Pinch cayenne pepper or hot paprika (optional)

▷ Preheat oven to 350°F (175°C). Spray a large oven-proof dish with nonstick cooking spray.

▷ In a large bowl, combine crab, cream cheese, parsley, celery, garlic, Worcestershire, hot pepper sauce, garlic powder, and white pepper; mix well.

▷ Fill mushroom caps with crab mixture and arrange in prepared baking dish; bake in a preheated oven for 15 minutes. Remove and sprinkle with cheese and cayenne; return to oven and bake another 5 minutes, or until cheese melts. Serve immediately.

NUTRITIONAL INFO PER MUSHROOM: Calories 52mg, Fat 4mg (Saturated Fat 3mg), Cholesterol 12mg, Carbohydrates 1mg (Fiber 0mg, Sugar 0mg), Sodium 49mg

1 *To reduce fat and keep sodium to a minimum, combine regular cream cheese with lower fat brands. For a comparison of cream cheese varieties, see* FOOD NOTE, *page 43.*

2 *Crimini and button mushrooms are similar, but criminis have more flavor. For additional info on mushroom varieties, cleaning, and storage, see* FOOD NOTE, *page 44.*

TOTAL SODIUM AND FAT PER INGREDIENT

Sodium:
6.5 oz crab - 416mg
8 oz cream cheese - 671mg
1 T parsley - 2mg
2 t celery - 4mg
2 garlic cloves - 2mg
1 t Worcestershire - 20mg
1 t hot pepper sauce - 8mg
24 mushrooms - 22mg
2 oz NSA Swiss cheese - 20mg
Fat (Sat Fat):
6.5 oz crab - 2mg (0mg)
8 oz cream cheese - 79mg (50mg)
24 mushrooms - 2mg (0mg
2 oz NSA Swiss - 16mg (10mg)

1 *To reduce fat and keep sodium to a minimum, combine whipped cream cheese with lower fat brands. For a comparison of cream cheese varieties, see* FOOD NOTE, *page 43.*

2 *Canned salmon averages 620mg sodium (per 4 oz), reduced salt varieties have 120mg, and fresh, 67mg (see* RESOURCES, *page 272, for more info).*

3 *The original recipe used smoked salmon, which is loaded with sodium (888mg per 4 oz).* **Liquid Smoke** *(available at grocers in the sauces and marinades aisle) is added for a smoked flavor.*

4 *Most 10-inch flour tortillas average 335mg sodium, but a few manufacturers, such as* **Adios Carbs** *and* **Tumaro's**, *offer low-sodium shells. See* RESOURCES, *page 272, for additional information.*

TOTAL SODIUM AND FAT PER INGREDIENT

Salmon Tortilla Roll-Ups:
Sodium:
  8 oz whipped cheese - 520mg
  4 oz salmon - 120mg
  1 T green onion - 1mg
  1 T celery - 6mg
  10 LS flour tortillas - 820mg
Fat (Sat Fat):
  8 oz whipped cheese - 56mg (36mg)
  4 oz salmon - 10mg (2mg)
  10 LS flour tortillas - 40mg (0mg)

Spicy & Cheesy Tortilla Swirls:
Sodium:
  8 oz whipped cheese - 520mg
  2 T pimento - 4mg
  2 T green chiles - 25mg
  1 green onion - 4mg
  2 T LS Salsa - 40mg
  10 LS flour tortillas - 820mg
Fat (Sat Fat):
  8 oz whipped cheese - 56mg (36mg)
  10 LS flour tortillas - 40mg (0mg)

SALMON TORTILLA ROLL-UPS

Sodium Per Serving – 24mg   Makes 60 appetizers

Prepare salmon filling the day before; cover and refrigerate to let the flavors intensify. This filling is also delicious as a spread on crackers.

Salmon Spread:

8 ounces (1 cup) whipped cream cheese[1]

4 ounces reduced salt canned salmon, or 4 ounces cooked salmon[2]

1 tablespoon finely minced celery

1 tablespoon finely chopped green onion (green part only) or fresh chives

¼ teaspoon garlic powder

1–2 drops *Liquid Smoke* (optional)[3]

10 (10-inch) low-salt flour tortillas[4]

▶ *For the Salmon Spread:* Combine cream cheese, salmon, celery, green onion, garlic powder, and *Liquid Smoke*.

▶ Evenly divide salmon mixture; spread onto each tortilla and roll up. Cover with plastic wrap and refrigerate at least one hour. Slice each roll into 6 pieces and serve cut-side up to display the filling.

NUTRITIONAL INFO PER APPETIZER: Calories 30mg, Fat 2mg (Saturated Fat 1mg), Cholesterol 4mg, Carbohydrates 2mg (Fiber 1mg, Sugar 0mg), Sodium 24mg

SPICY AND CHEESY TORTILLA SWIRLS

Sodium Per Serving – 24mg   Makes 60 appetizers

These tasty appetizers are simple to prepare and add color to the buffet table. The optional salsa and cilantro add even more flavor. The cheese spread is also good on crackers and in sandwiches.

Cheese Spread:

8 ounces (1 cup) whipped cream cheese[1]

2 tablespoons chopped pimento

2 tablespoons diced green chiles

1 green onion, minced

1 jalapeño, seeded and chopped

¼ teaspoon onion powder or garlic powder

2–3 tablespoons low-salt salsa (optional)

1–2 tablespoons chopped fresh cilantro (optional)

10 (10-inch) low-salt flour tortillas[4]

▶ *For the Cheese Spread:* In a bowl, mix together all Cheese Spread ingredients,.

▶ Evenly divide cheese mixture; spread onto each tortilla and roll up. Cover with plastic wrap and refrigerate at least one hour. Slice each roll into 6 pieces and serve cut-side up to display the colorful swirls.

NUTRITIONAL INFO PER APPETIZER: Calories 28mg, Fat 2mg (Saturated Fat 1mg), Cholesterol 3mg, Carbohydrates 2mg (Fiber 1mg, Sugar 0mg), Sodium 24mg

SPINACH AND GOAT CHEESE ROLLS

Sodium Per Serving – 30mg   Makes 24 appetizers

Normally made with phyllo dough, these mouth-watering treats, reminiscent of spanakopita, use low-sodium egg roll wrappers.

1 tablespoon olive oil	1 egg, beaten, or ¼ cup egg substitute[2]
4 garlic cloves, finely minced	
1 shallot, finely minced	¼ teaspoon paprika
1 (10-ounce) package frozen chopped spinach, thawed and squeezed dry, or 1 pound fresh spinach, cooked	⅛ teaspoon freshly ground nutmeg[3]
	6 EGG ROLL WRAPS *(page 229)* or low-salt egg roll wrappers[4]
4 ounces goat cheese[1]	Canola or vegetable oil, for frying
3 tablespoons chopped fresh flat-leaf (Italian) parsley	

▶ Heat oil in a skillet over medium heat; add garlic and shallots. Cook, stirring constantly, until shallots begin to soften, about 2 minutes. Transfer to a bowl and combine with spinach, goat cheese, parsley, and egg. Season with paprika and nutmeg.

▶ Spread one-sixth filling on one side of the wrapper to within one-quarter inch of the edges; roll up like a jelly-roll, folding in sides one-quarter inch (this keeps filling from oozing out when frying). Repeat with remaining filling and wrappers.

▶ Heat several tablespoons oil in a skillet over medium-high heat; fry rolls until golden on all sides. Remove and drain on paper towel. Slice into 4 pieces and serve.

NUTRITIONAL INFO PER APPETIZER*: Calories 66mg, Fat 2mg (Saturated Fat 0mg), Cholesterol 19mg, Carbohydrates 9mg (Fiber 1mg, Sugar 0mg), Sodium 30mg (25mg with LS packaged wrappers)

* Does not include oil for frying.

VARIATION

CHEESY SPINACH ROLLS

Instead of goat cheese, substitute 4 ounces no-salt-added Swiss or fresh mozzarella. *NOTE: Fresh mozzarella, packaged in water, averages 30mg sodium per ounce, and is available in most supermarkets. Check label, as some brands have added sodium.*

NUTRITIONAL INFO PER APPETIZER: Calories 82mg, Fat 3mg (Saturated Fat 1mg), Cholesterol 23mg, Carbohydrates 9mg (Fiber 1mg, Sugar 0mg), Sodium 31mg (26mg with store-bought LS egg roll wrappers)

COMMENTS:

1 *Goat cheese can range from sweet and mild to tangy and sharp. Two of the better-known are Chèvre and Montrachet. Chèvre usually has the least sodium (about 50mg per ounce), other varieties average 146mg.*

2 See Eggs and Egg Substitutes, *page 38, for a comparison of fat and sodium in eggs and egg substitutes.*

3 *Freshly grated nutmeg is far superior in taste to the pre-ground variety.*

4 *Most packaged egg roll wrappers have up to 450mg sodium per wrap, but a few manufacturers offer low-salt wrappers (see FOOD NOTE, page 50, for more info).*

TOTAL SODIUM AND FAT PER INGREDIENT

Sodium:
- 4 garlic cloves - 4mg
- 1 shallot - 2mg
- 10 oz spinach - 210mg
- 4 oz goat cheese - 200mg
- 3 T parsley - 6mg
- 1 egg - 70mg
  - or ¼ cup egg substitute - 100mg
- 6 EGG ROLL WRAPS - 223mg
  - or LS egg roll wrappers - 102mg

Fat (Sat Fat):
- 1 T olive oil - 14mg (2mg)
- 10 oz spinach - 2mg (1mg)
- 4 oz goat cheese - 24mg (0mg)
- 1 egg - 5mg (2mg)
  - or ¼ cup egg substitute - 0mg
- 6 EGG ROLL WRAPS - 6mg (0mg)
  - or LS wrappers - 6mg (6mg)

1 *To reduce fat and keep sodium to a minimum, use a combination of regular cream cheese with lower fat brands. For a comparison of cream cheese varieties, see* FOOD NOTE, *page 43.*

2 *Pimento may be substituted for the roasted red peppers.*

3 *On a scale of 1 to 5, jalapeños are a 3, with most of the heat contained in the seeds and veins.*

   CAUTION: When handling hot chiles, wear rubber gloves, as the oils of the pepper can be very potent. A piece of plastic wrap or a sandwich bag also works to hold the pepper. If you should touch the pepper with your bare fingers, wash your hands thoroughly and be sure to keep your fingers away from your eyes or you'll be in sheer agony!

4 *Most packaged egg roll wraps have up to 450mg per wrap, but a few manufacturers offer low-salt wrappers (see* FOOD NOTE *below).*

JALAPENO-CHEESE ROLLS

Sodium Per Serving – 37mg   Makes 24 appetizers

These hot and spicy treats are a big hit at social gatherings. Make ahead of time and warm in the microwave or oven before serving. The spicy spread is also good on crackers, sandwiches, and wraps.

Cheese Spread:

8 ounces (1 cup) cream cheese[1]

2 tablespoons chopped roasted red peppers[2]

1 jalapeño, seeded and chopped[3]

6 EGG ROLL WRAPS *(page 229)* **or low-salt egg roll wrappers[4]**

Canola or vegetable oil, for frying

▸ *For the Cheese Spread:* Mix cream cheese with pimento and jalapeños.

▸ Spread one-sixth filling on one side of the wrapper to within one-quarter inch of the edges; roll up like a jelly-roll, folding in sides one-quarter inch (this keeps filling from oozing out when frying). Repeat with remaining filling and wrappers.

▸ Heat several tablespoons oil in a skillet over medium-high heat; fry rolls until golden on all sides. Remove and drain on a paper towel. Slice into 4 pieces and serve warm.

*NUTRITIONAL INFO PER APPETIZER: Calories 74mg, Fat 4mg (Saturated Fat 2mg), Cholesterol 18mg, Carbohydrates 8mg (Fiber 0mg, Sugar 0mg), Sodium 37mg (32mg with LS packaged wrappers)

* Does not include oil for frying.

TOTAL SODIUM AND FAT PER INGREDIENT

Sodium:
 8 oz cream cheese - 671mg
 2 T pimento - 4mg
 6 EGG ROLL WRAPS - 223mg
   or LS egg roll wrappers - 102mg
Fat (Sat Fat):
 8 oz cream cheese - 79mg (50mg)
 6 EGG ROLL WRAPS - 6mg (0mg)
   or LS wrappers - 6mg (6mg)

FOOD NOTE

EGG ROLL WRAPPERS

Egg roll wraps are a great substitute for puff pastry or pie dough in many recipes. Just spread your favorite filling on the wrapper, either fold in half on the diagonal or roll up; then fry or bake until golden brown.

Although most egg roll wrappers have up to 450mg sodium, there are several low-salt brands, such as *Melissa's* (17mg per wrap) and *Dynasty* (60mg). Wraps are available in the produce section of many supermarkets and health food stores; *Melissa's* also offers direct sales through their online store (*see* RESOURCES, *page 272*).

If unable to find low-salt wrappers, they are easy to make from scratch (*see* EGG ROLL WRAPS, *page 229*).

SPINACH AND FETA WONTONS

Sodium Per Serving – 21mg · Makes about 60 wontons

These wontons are reminiscent of spanakopita and are delicious by themselves or dipped in hot mustard sauce.

- **1 (10-ounce) package frozen chopped spinach, thawed and squeezed dry**
- **2 ounces herbed feta or goat cheese[1]**
- **1 egg white, beaten**
- **½ teaspoon finely minced garlic**
- **⅛ teaspoon garlic powder**
- **⅛ teaspoon freshly ground nutmeg**
- **⅛ teaspoon ground white pepper**
- **15 EGG ROLL WRAPS** *(page 229)* **or packaged low-salt egg roll wrappers, each square cut into 4 equal pieces[2]**
- **Canola or vegetable oil, for frying**
- **CHINESE HOT MUSTARD** *(recipe follows)* **for dipping**

▷ In a bowl, mix together spinach, feta, egg substitute, garlic, garlic powder, nutmeg, and pepper.

▷ Place 1 tablespoon filling in center of each wonton wrapper, wet two adjacent edges with water, and fold per instructions *(see COOKING TIP, page 52)*. Place on a platter, dividing each layer with waxed paper or aluminum foil. NOTE: If not cooking immediately, cover and refrigerate until ready to cook.

▷ Heat several tablespoons oil in a skillet over medium-high heat; fry wontons, turning once, until golden brown on both sides, about 4 minutes. Drain on paper towels. Serve with hot mustard sauce.

NUTRITIONAL INFO PER WONTON*: Calories 45mg, Fat 1mg (Saturated Fat 0mg), Cholesterol 8mg, Carbohydrates 8mg (Fiber 1mg, Sugar 0mg), Sodium 21mg (16mg with LS packaged wrappers)

* Does not include oil for frying.

CHINESE HOT MUSTARD

Sodium Per Serving – 0mg · Makes about 3 tablespoons

This hot mustard is the perfect accompaniment to wontons. Although this does not make a lot of sauce, it's hot enough that a little goes a long way.

- **1 tablespoon dry mustard, such as *Coleman's***
- **2 tablespoons water**
- **4 drops lite soy sauce**

▷ Mix all ingredients together and serve.

NUTRITIONAL INFO PER WONTON: Calories 1mg, Fat 0mg (Saturated Fat 0mg), Cholesterol 0mg, Carbohydrates 0mg (Fiber 0mg, Sugar 0mg), Sodium 0mg

COMMENTS:

1 *Most feta cheese is high in sodium, averaging 316mg per ounce.* **Athenos** *offers a lower-salt basil and tomato feta (220mg) or use* HERBED GOAT CHEESE *(page 100).*

2 *Most packaged egg roll wrappers have up to 450mg sodium per wrap, but a few manufacturers (such as* **Melissa's** *and* **Dynasty**) *offer low-salt wraps (see* FOOD NOTE, *page 50, for additional info).*

TOTAL SODIUM AND FAT PER INGREDIENT

Spinach and Feta Wontons:

Sodium:
- 10 oz spinach - 210mg
- 2 oz herbed feta - 440mg
- or goat cheese - 200mg
- 1 egg white - 55mg
- 15 EGG ROLL WRAPS - 558mg
- or LS wrappers - 255mg

Fat (Sat Fat):
- 10 oz spinach - 2mg (1mg)
- 2 oz herbed feta - 12mg (8mg)
- or goat cheese - 12mg (0mg)
- 15 EGG ROLL WRAPS - 16mg (4mg)
- or LS wrappers - 15mg (15mg)

Chinese Hot Mustard:

Sodium:
- 1 T dry mustard - 1mg
- 4 drops lite soy sauce - 24mg

Fat (Sat Fat):
- 1 T dry mustard - 3mg (0mg)

1 *Avoid imitation shrimp (200mg per ounce), which has nearly four times as much sodium as fresh or canned.*

2 *Most packaged egg roll wrappers have up to 450mg sodium per wrap, but a few manufacturers (such as **Melissa's** and **Dynasty**) offer low-salt wraps (see FOOD NOTE, page 50, for additional info).*

3 *Most prepared sweet and sour sauces average 130mg sodium per tablespoon, but there are many brands with 50mg or less (see RESOURCES, page 272, for additional information).*

CRISPY PORK AND SHRIMP WONTONS

Sodium Per Serving – 11mg   Makes about 60 wontons

One of many recipes acquired while living in Hawaii. Not only do the wontons go together quickly, but they also are onolicious!

8 ounces ground pork

4 ounces small shrimp (fresh, frozen, or canned)[1]

½ (7-ounce) can water chestnuts, chopped (about ½ cup)

2 green onions, chopped (green and light green parts)

1 teaspoon lite soy sauce

⅛ teaspoon onion powder

⅛ teaspoon ground black pepper

15 EGG ROLL WRAPS (page 229) or packaged low-salt egg roll wrappers, each square cut into 4 equal pieces[2]

Canola or vegetable oil, for frying

Dipping Sauces:

CHINESE HOT MUSTARD (page 51) for dipping

Low-salt sweet-and-sour sauce for dipping[3]

▸ In a bowl, mix pork, shrimp, water chestnuts, green onions, soy sauce, onion powder, and pepper together.

▸ Place 1 tablespoon filling in center of each wonton wrapper. Fold per instructions (*see* COOKING TIP *below*) and place on platter, dividing each layer with waxed paper or aluminum foil. NOTE: If not cooking immediately, cover and refrigerate until ready to cook.

▸ Heat several tablespoons oil in a skillet over medium heat; fry wontons until golden brown on both sides, 5 to 6 minutes. NOTE: Because these contain pork, it is important to thoroughly cook the pork. Drain on paper towels. Serve with CHINESE HOT MUSTARD or sweet-and-sour sauce.

NUTRITIONAL INFO PER WONTON*: Calories 53mg, Fat 1mg (Saturated Fat 0mg), Cholesterol 13mg, Carbohydrates 8mg (Fiber 0mg, Sugar 0mg), Sodium 11mg (12mg with LS packaged wrappers)

* Does not include oil for frying.

TOTAL SODIUM AND FAT PER INGREDIENT

Sodium:
  8 oz ground pork - 127mg
  4 oz shrimp - 168mg
  ½ c water chestnuts - 10mg
  2 green onions - 8mg
  1 t lite soy sauce - 163mg
  15 EGG ROLL WRAPS - 558mg
    or LS wrappers - 255mg
  Dipping sauces (per tsp):
    Hot mustard - 0mg
    LS sweet and sour - 17mg
Fat (Sat Fat):
  8 oz ground pork - 48mg (18mg)
  4 oz shrimp - 2mg (1mg)
  15 EGG ROLL WRAPS - 16mg (4mg)
    or LS wrappers - 15mg (15mg)

COOKING TIP

FOLDING WONTONS

Dip finger in water and rub onto two adjacent edges of wrapper. Fold in half on the diagonal to form a triangle; pinch together edges to seal. Finish by folding two opposite points under to make a packet. *NOTE: While making wontons, cover wrappers with a damp towel to keep from drying out.*

SOUPS AND CHILI

COMMENTS:

1 *Cut off 1–2 inches from the spear ends and remove lower 3 inches of outer skin with a vegetable peeler. (If using thin-stalked spears, this step is not necessary.) For additional info, see* FOOD NOTE, *About Asparagus, page 170.*

2 *To reduce saturated fat, use trans-free margarine. Since it contains sodium (90mg per tablespoon), it will increase the sodium per serving to 72mg (or 155mg with low-salt canned broth).*

3 *Shallots look like small onions and have a mild garlic flavor (see* FOOD NOTE, *page 171, for more info).*

A chopped leek (white and light green parts) may also be used (see FOOD NOTE, *About Leeks, page 176).*

4 *Coulis (prounounced COO-lee) is a roasted red pepper purée that takes this soup from everyday to gourmet faire.*

CREAMY ASPARAGUS SOUP

Sodium Per Serving – 50mg   Serves 4

This luscious recipe, given to me by my long-time friend, Sally Pearce, is the perfect first course for a special dinner. To keep fat to a minimum, I use lowfat sour cream and milk instead of cream.

2 pounds asparagus spears, trimmed and cut in 1-inch pieces (about 20 spears)[1]

3 cups CHICKEN STOCK (page 232) or canned low-salt chicken broth

2 teaspoons (or 2 envelopes) low-salt chicken bouillon granules

1 tablespoon unsalted margarine or butter[2]

1 tablespoon olive oil

3 large shallots, chopped (about ½ cup)[3]

2 garlic cloves, minced

3 tablespoons all-purpose flour

½ teaspoon lemon juice

¾ teaspoon dried thyme or tarragon

½ teaspoon garlic powder

¼ teaspoon ground black pepper

⅓ cup lowfat milk

½ cup lowfat sour cream

RED PEPPER COULIS (page 141) (optional)[4]

Hot pepper sauce, such as *Tabasco* (optional)

 In a large saucepan over high heat, combine asparagus, chicken stock, and bouillon. Bring to a boil; decrease heat to medium-low and simmer, covered, until asparagus is bright green and tender, 8 to 10 minutes. Do not overcook *(see* FOOD NOTE, *About Asparagus, page 170).*

 Meanwhile, heat margarine and oil in a skillet over medium heat; add shallots and garlic. Cook, stirring frequently, until shallots are soft, 3 to 4 minutes.

 Add flour, lemon juice, thyme, garlic powder, and pepper; cook, stirring constantly, until mixture begins to turn golden, about 2 minutes. Add to asparagus/stock mixture and mix thoroughly; remove from heat and cool slightly.

 Place one-half of asparagus mixture in a blender or food processor and pulse until smooth; repeat with remaining mixture.

 Return purée to pan and simmer over low heat, 5 minutes. Stir in milk and sour cream; heat through. (If soup is too thick, add a little more milk.) Ladle into soup bowls and serve with a dollop of **RED PEPPER COULIS** on top. If not using coulis, grate freshly ground nutmeg on top, if desired.

NUTRITIONAL INFO PER SERVING: Calories 202mg, Fat 10mg (Saturated Fat 3mg), Cholesterol 21mg, Carbohydrates 20mg (Fiber 5mg, Sugar 5mg), Sodium 50mg (132 with LS canned broth)

TOTAL SODIUM AND FAT
PER INGREDIENT

Sodium:
2 lb asparagus spears - 14mg
3 c CHICKEN STOCK - 60mg
 or LS canned broth - 390mg
2 t LS chicken bouillon - 10mg
3 shallots - 6mg
2 garlic cloves - 2mg
⅓ c LF milk - 38mg
½ c LF sour cream - 68mg
Fat (Sat Fat):
2 lb asparagus spears - 1mg (0mg)
3 c CHICKEN STOCK - 3mg (0mg)
 or LS canned broth - 6mg (3mg)
1 T NSA margarine - 8mg (2mg)
 or NSA butter - 12mg (8mg)
1 T olive oil - 14mg (2mg)
⅓ c LF milk - 2mg (0mg)
½ c LF sour cream - 14mg (8mg)

CURRIED YAM AND APPLE BISQUE

Sodium Per Serving – 45mg   Serves 8

Friends and family rave about this soup (another favorite from my dear friend, Sally), which I've desalted and perked up with hot curry powder and hot pepper sauce. The combination of sweetness and heat creates a delicious accompaniment to any meal.

- 1 tablespoon olive oil
- 1 tablespoon unsalted or trans-free margarine[1]
- 1 yellow onion, chopped
- 2 sweet apples, chopped, such as Braeburn, Fuji, or Gala
- 1 tablespoon hot curry powder[2]
- ½ teaspoon ground coriander
- ¼ teaspoon garlic powder
- ⅛ teaspoon ground black pepper
- 1 garlic clove, minced
- 1 cup dry sherry[3]

- 7 cups CHICKEN STOCK (*page 232*) or canned low-salt chicken broth
- 1 tablespoon (or 3 envelopes) low-salt chicken bouillon granules
- 2 large yams or dark-skinned sweet potatoes, cubed (about 2 pounds)[4]
- 2–3 drops hot pepper sauce, such as *Tabasco*
- 1 cup lowfat sour cream or plain yogurt

▸ Heat oil and margarine in a large saucepan over medium heat; add onion, apples, curry, coriander, garlic, and pepper. Cook, stirring frequently, until onions are translucent, 3 to 4 minutes. Add garlic; cook, stirring constantly, until you smell the garlic, about 1 minute.

▸ Add sherry, chicken stock, bouillon, yams, and hot pepper sauce; bring to boil. Decrease heat to low, cover, and simmer until potatoes are done, about 20 minutes. Remove from heat and cool slightly.

▸ Place one-third of the apple-yam mixture in a blender or food processor and pulse until smooth; repeat with remaining mixture.

▸ Return purée to pan and heat through. Serve with a dollop of yogurt.

NUTRITIONAL INFO PER SERVING: Calories 199mg, Fat 7mg (Saturated Fat 2mg), Cholesterol 21mg, Carbohydrates 19mg (Fiber 2mg, Sugar 7mg), Sodium 45mg (141mg with LS canned broth)

COMMENTS:

1 *To reduce saturated fat, use trans-free margarine. Since it contains sodium (90mg per tablespoon), it will increase the sodium per serving to 56mg (or 152mg with low-salt canned broth).*

2 *I like a lot of heat and use hot curry powder, however, any variety of curry may be used. For additional curry info, see FOOD NOTE, page 198.*

3 *Madeira or brandy may be substituted for the sherry.*

4 *Although similar, sweet potatoes and yams are from different species. In the U.S. there are two common sweet potatoes: a pale skinned and a darker orange variety. Although the latter is called a yam, to the rest of the world, it's a sweet potato.*

TOTAL SODIUM AND FAT PER INGREDIENT

Sodium:
- 1 onion - 3mg
- 2 apples - 2mg
- 1 garlic clove - 1mg
- 1 T curry powder - 3mg
- 1 c sherry - 20mg
- 7 c CHICKEN STOCK - 140mg
  - or LS canned broth - 910mg
- 1 T LS chicken bouillon - 15mg
- 2 lb yams - 34mg
- 2 drops hot pepper sauce - 4mg
- 1 c LF sour cream - 136mg
  - or LF yogurt - 172mg

Fat (Sat Fat):
- 1 T NSA margarine - 8mg (2mg)
  - or NSA butter - 12mg (8mg)
- 1 T olive oil - 14mg (2mg)
- 1 T curry powder - 1mg (0mg)
- 7 c CHICKEN STOCK - 7mg (0mg)
  - or LS canned broth - 14mg (7mg)
- 1 c LF sour cream - 27mg (16mg)
  - or LF yogurt - 4mg (2mg)

ARTICHOKE AND LEEK SOUP

Sodium Per Serving – 79mg   Serves 4

This pleasing soup gets additional flavor from the cumin and cayenne. Using frozen artichokes instead of canned, saves 180mg sodium per serving.

1 tablespoon olive oil

1 tablespoon unsalted margarine or butter[1]

3 leeks, cleaned and thinly sliced (white and light green parts)[2]

2 garlic cloves, finely minced

2 tablespoons uncooked white rice

1 russet potato, peeled and chopped

1 (9-ounce) package frozen artichoke hearts, defrosted and halved[3]

4 cups CHICKEN STOCK (page 232) or canned low-salt chicken broth

1 teaspoon (or 1 envelope) low-salt chicken bouillon granules

1 teaspoon low-salt Worchester-shire sauce

½ teaspoon ground cumin

¼ teaspoon garlic powder

¼ teaspoon ground black pepper

¼ teaspoon dried thyme

Pinch cayenne pepper

1 tablespoon lemon juice

1 tablespoon chopped fresh flat-leaf (Italian) parsley

▷ Heat oil and margarine in a large saucepan over medium heat; add leeks and garlic. Cook, stirring frequently, until leeks are soft, 3 to 4 minutes.

▷ Stir in rice and cook, stirring frequently, 3 minutes. Add potato, artichokes, chicken stock, bouillon, Worcestershire, cumin, garlic powder, black pepper, thyme, and cayenne; bring to boil. Reduce heat to low, cover, and simmer until potatoes are done, about 30 minutes. Remove from heat and cool slightly.

▷ Place one-half of the artichoke-leek mixture in a blender or food processor and pulse until smooth; repeat with remaining mixutre. Return purée to pan, add lemon juice and heat through. Sprinkle with parsley and serve.

NUTRITIONAL INFO PER SERVING (WITH STOCK): Calories 245mg, Fat 7mg (Saturated Fat 1mg), Cholesterol 15mg, Carbohydrates 36mg (Fiber 6mg, Sugar 4mg), Sodium 79mg (189mg with LS canned broth)

CREAMED BROCCOLI WITH MANDARIN ORANGES

Sodium Per Serving – 83mg   Serves 4

Cream soups are notoriously high in fat and salt. This luscious low-sodium soup has been lightened up using fat-free half-and-half, milk, and sour cream. In addition to its rich flavor, the mandarin oranges lend an unexpected twist.

1 tablespoon unsalted margarine or butter[1]

3–4 small red potatoes, quartered (about 1¼ pounds)[2]

½ teaspoon ground cumin

¼ teaspoon garlic powder

¼ teaspoon ground black pepper

1 small sweet onion, thinly sliced, such as Vidalia

4 cups or 1 (16-ounce) package broccoli florets

2 cups CHICKEN STOCK *(page 232)* or canned low-salt chicken broth

2 teaspoons (or 2 envelopes) low-salt chicken bouillon granules

½ cup half-and-half[3]

½ cup lowfat milk[3]

2 tablespoons lowfat sour cream

⅛ teaspoon ground nutmeg

1 (10-ounce) can mandarin oranges in light syrup, drained

▶ Melt margarine in a large saucepan over medium heat; add potatoes, cumin, garlic powder, and pepper, stirring until potatoes are well coated. Mix in onions and broccoli; cook, stirring frequently, until onions are soft, 2 to 3 minutes.

▶ Add chicken stock and bouillon; bring to a boil. Decrease heat to medium-low; cover, and simmer until vegetables are tender, 10 to 15 minutes.

▶ Stir in the half-and-half, milk, and sour cream. Remove from heat and cool slightly.

▶ Place one-half broccoli mixutre in a blender or food processor and pulse until smooth; repeat with remaining mixutre.

▶ Return purée to pan, add nutmeg and mandarin oranges; heat through.

NUTRITIONAL INFO PER SERVING: Calories 284mg, Fat 11mg (Saturated Fat 4mg), Cholesterol 23mg, Carbohydrates 36mg (Fiber 4mg, Sugar 9mg), Sodium 83mg (138mg with LS canned broth)

VARIATION

CHEESY BROCCOLI SOUP

Omit the mandarin oranges and add 2 ounces shredded lowfat Cheddar cheese (about ½ cup) to the puréed soup; stir until melted.

NUTRITIONAL INFO PER APPETIZER: Calories 271mg, Fat 12mg (Saturated Fat 4mg), Cholesterol 25mg, Carbohydrates 31mg (Fiber 3mg, Sugar 6mg), Sodium 113mg (171mg with LS canned broth)

COMMENTS:

1 *To reduce saturated fat, use trans-free margarine. Since it contains sodium (90mg per tablespoon), it will increase the sodium per serving to 123mg (178mg with low-salt canned broth).*

2 *Other potato choices are Yukon gold or white potatoes. For additional variety info, see* FOOD NOTE, *page 77.*

3 *Another alternative to adding creaminess to the soup without much salt is to eliminate the half-and-half and increase the milk to ⅔ cup and the sour cream to ¼ cup.*

TOTAL SODIUM AND FAT PER INGREDIENT

Sodium:
 3 red potatoes - 30mg
 ½ t cumin - 2mg
 1 sweet onion - 9mg
 4 c broccoli - 76mg
 2 c CHICKEN STOCK - 40mg
   or LS canned broth - 260mg
 2 t LS chicken bouillon - 10mg
 ½ c half-and-half - 50mg
 ½ c LF milk - 58mg
 2 T LF sour cream - 17mg
 10 oz mandarin oranges - 40mg
Fat (Sat Fat):
 1 T NSA margarine - 8mg (2mg)
   or NSA butter - 12mg (8mg)
 3 red potatoes - 1mg (0mg)
 4 c broccoli - 1mg (0mg)
 2 c CHICKEN STOCK - 2mg (0mg)
   or LS canned broth - 4mg (2mg)
 ½ c half-and-half - 14mg (9mg)
 ½ c LF milk - 3mg (1mg)
 2 T LF sour cream - 3mg (2mg)

MIGHTY FINE BORSCHT

Sodium Per Serving – 171mg   Serves 12

Originally from Russia, this beet soup is prepared in a variety of ways—with or without meat and with a combination of vegetables. It also can be thick and stew-like or light and brothy. Serve it hot or cold and always with a dollop of sour cream or yogurt on top. My borscht is very thick and the longer it cooks, the better it gets, so allow 1 to 2 hours of simmering time. For a meatless version, the beef may be omitted without much loss of flavor.

8 ounces round steak, sliced in thin strips[1]

½ teaspoon garlic powder

⅛ teaspoon ground black pepper

1 tablespoon olive oil

1 onion, sliced

2 shallots, minced[2]

2–3 garlic cloves, minced

1 (28-ounce) can crushed tomatoes in puree[3]

1 cup (8 ounces) no-salt-added tomato puree[4]

1 (6-ounce) can no-salt-added tomato paste

5 cups water

1 tablespoon cider vinegar

1 tablespoon low-salt beef bouillon granules

1 tablespoon sugar substitute or sugar

2 bay leaves

4–5 large beets, peeled and grated (about 8 cups)[5]

1 small head cabbage, finely shredded (about 4 cups), or 1 (10-ounce) package coleslaw mix

2 carrots, diced

1 (10-ounce) package frozen no-salt-added peas

1 cup (8 ounces) lowfat sour cream[6]

▸ Season meat with garlic powder and pepper.

▸ Heat oil in a large pot or Dutch oven over medium-high heat; add meat and brown on all sides, stirring frequently, 3 to 4 minutes.

▸ Add onions, shallots, and garlic; cook, stirring constantly, until onions are soft, 2 to 3 minutes.

▸ Stir in crushed tomatoes, tomato puree, tomato paste, water, vinegar, bouillon, sweetener, bay leaves, beets, cabbage, and carrots. Decrease heat to medium-low; cover, and simmer 1 to 2 hours. *NOTE: The longer this simmers, the better it tastes.*

▸ Stir in peas and continue simmering 30 minutes more.

▸ Remove bay leaves and serve in individual bowls with a dollop of sour cream. *NOTE: Do not omit the sour cream, as stirring it into the soup makes it rich and creamy.*

NUTRITIONAL INFO PER SERVING: Calories 146mg, Fat 5mg (Saturated Fat 2mg), Cholesterol 18mg, Carbohydrates 18mg (Fiber 5mg, Sugar 9mg), Sodium 171mg

NUTRITIONAL INFO PER SERVING (WITHOUT MEAT): Calories 120mg, Fat 4mg (Saturated Fat 2mg), Cholesterol 5mg, Carbohydrates 18mg (Fiber 5mg, Sugar 9mg), Sodium 160mg

MUSHROOM BISQUE WITH BRANDY

Sodium Per Serving – 62mg   **Serves 4**

This rich and creamy soup is ready in less than 30 minutes. The addition of brandy enhances the subtle flavors. For added taste, stir in 1 tablespoon fresh thyme (or 1 teaspoon dried) to the mushrooms while they saute.

- 1 tablespoon olive oil
- 1 tablespoon unsalted margarine or butter[1]
- 1 medium onion, diced
- 1 shallot, minced[2]
- 2 garlic cloves, finely minced
- 8 ounces portobello mushrooms, stemmed and sliced[3]
- ¼ teaspoon garlic powder
- ¼ teaspoon ground white pepper
- ¼ cup brandy[4]
- 1 small russet potato, peeled and diced

- 3 cups CHICKEN STOCK *(page 232)* or canned low-salt chicken broth
- 2 teaspoons (or 2 envelopes) low-salt chicken bouillon granules
- ½ cup half-and-half or light cream
- ½ cup lowfat milk
- 2 tablespoons lowfat sour cream
- 2 tablespoons chopped fresh chives (optional)

▶ Heat oil and margarine in large saucepan over medium heat; add onions and shallots. Cook, stirring frequently, until onions are translucent, about 3 to 4 minutes. Add mushrooms, garlic powder, and white pepper; cook, stirring occasionally, 5 minutes more.

▶ Stir in brandy, potatoes, chicken stock, and bouillon; simmer until potatoes are done, about 15 minutes. Remove from heat and cool slightly.

▶ Place one-half the mushroom mixture in a blender or food processor and pulse until smooth; repeat with remaining mixture. Return purée to pan; stir in the half-and-half, milk, and sour cream. If soup is too thick, thin with additional chicken broth or milk. Heat through and serve with chopped chives.

NUTRITIONAL INFO PER SERVING: Calories 300mg, Fat 12mg (Saturated Fat 4mg), Cholesterol 27mg, Carbohydrates 31mg (Fiber 3mg, Sugar 6mg), Sodium 62mg (144mg with LS canned broth)

COMMENTS:

1 *To reduce saturated fat, use trans-free margarine. Since it contains sodium (90mg per tablespoon), it will increase the sodium per serving to 102mg (or 184mg with low-salt canned broth).*

2 *Shallots look like small onions, but have a mild flavor like garlic. For additional information on choosing and storing shallots, see* FOOD NOTE, *page 171.*

3 *Portobellos are mature criminis, reaching up to 6 inches in diameter and are very flavorful and meaty. Criminis or porcinis may be used instead of the portabellos. For additional info, on mushroom varieties, see* FOOD NOTE, *page 44.*

4 *Dry sherry or Madeira may be substituted for the brandy.*

TOTAL SODIUM AND FAT PER INGREDIENT

Sodium:
- 1 onion - 3mg
- 1 shallot - 2mg
- 2 garlic cloves - 2mg
- 8 oz portobellos - 27mg
- 1 russet potato - 18mg
- 3 c CHICKEN STOCK - 60mg
  - or LS canned broth - 390mg
- 2 t LS chicken bouillon - 10mg
- ½ c half-and-half - 50mg
- ½ c LF milk - 58mg
- 2 T LF sour cream - 17mg

Fat (Sat Fat):
- 1 T olive oil - 14mg (2mg)
- 1 T NSA margarine - 8mg (2mg)
  - or NSA butter - 12mg (8mg)
- 8 oz portobellos - 1mg (0mg)
- 3 c CHICKEN STOCK - 3mg (0mg)
  - or LS canned broth - 6mg (3mg)
- ½ c half-and-half - 14mg (9mg)
- ½ c LF milk - 3mg (1mg)
- 2 T LF sour cream - 3mg (2mg)

1 *To reduce saturated fat, use trans-free margarine. Since it contains sodium (90mg per tablespoon), it will increase the sodium per serving to 145mg (or 214mg with low-salt canned broth).*

2 *Parsnips or a combination of parsnips and carrots may be substituted. Parsnips have a sweetness, similar to carrots, but with much less sodium (7mg versus 50mg for a medium carrot).*

FRESH CARROT POTAGE

Sodium Per Serving – 123mg   Serves 4

This creamy soup with a hint of basil and dill is one of my favorites. Not only is it ready in 30 minutes, but it contains ingredients usually on hand.

1 tablespoon olive oil

1 tablespoon unsalted margarine or butter[1]

1 small sweet onion, chopped

1–2 garlic cloves, minced

½ teaspoon garlic powder

¼ teaspoon ground black pepper

5 large carrots, sliced (about 3 cups)[2]

2½ cups CHICKEN STOCK (page 232) or canned low-salt chicken broth

½ cup Madeira wine or dry sherry

½ cup uncooked medium-grain rice

1 teaspoon (or 1 envelope) low-salt chicken bouillon granules

1 teaspoon dried basil

¼ teaspoon dried dill weed

2–3 drops hot pepper sauce, such as *Tabasco*

½ cup lowfat sour cream

¾ cup lowfat milk

Freshly grated nutmeg

2 tablespoons chopped fresh flat-leaf (Italian) parsley (optional)

▸ Heat oil and margarine in a large saucepan over medium heat; add onions. Cook, stirring frequently, until onions are soft, 3 to 4 minutes. Add garlic, garlic powder, and pepper; cook, stirring constantly, until you smell the garlic, about1 minute.

▸ Add carrots, chicken stock, Madeira, rice, bouillon, basil, dill weed, and hot pepper sauce; bring to boil. Decrease heat to low; cover, and cook, stirring occasionally, until rice is cooked, 20 to 25 minutes. Remove from heat and cool slightly.

▸ Place one-half the carrot mixture in a blender or processor and pulse until smooth; repeat with remaining mixture.

▸ Return purée to pan and bring to simmer over low heat. Stir in sour cream and milk; heat through. Top with nutmeg and parsley; serve.

NUTRITIONAL INFO PER SERVING: Calories 319mg, Fat 11mg (Saturated Fat 3mg), Cholesterol 21mg, Carbohydrates 38mg (Fiber 3mg, Sugar 5mg), Sodium 123mg (191mg with LS canned broth)

TOTAL SODIUM AND FAT PER INGREDIENT

Sodium:
  1 sweet onion - 9mg
  1 garlic clove - 1mg
  5 carrots - 248mg
  2½ c CHICKEN STOCK - 50mg
    or LS canned broth - 325mg
  ½ c Madeira wine - 10mg
  ½ c rice - 5mg
  1 t LS chicken bouillon - 5mg
  2 drops hot pepper sauce - 4mg
  ½ c LF sour cream - 68mg
  ¾ c LF milk - 86mg
  2 T parsley - 4mg
Fat (Sat Fat):
  1 T olive oil - 14mg (2mg)
  1 T NSA margarine - 8mg (2mg)
    or NSA butter - 12mg (8mg)
  5 carrots - 1mg (0mg)
  2½ c CHICKEN STOCK - 3mg (0mg)
    or LS canned broth - 5mg (3mg)
  ½ c rice - 1mg (0mg)
  ½ c LF sour cream - 14mg (8mg)
  ¾ c LF milk - 4mg (2mg)

VARIATION

CURRIED CARROT SOUP

Instead of the basil and dill, add 1 tablespoon curry powder, ½ teaspoon dried coriander, and ¼ teaspoon dried cardamom.

NUTRITIONAL INFO PER SERVING: Calories 325mg, Fat 11mg (Saturated Fat 3mg), Cholesterol 21mg, Carbohydrates 39mg (Fiber 4mg, Sugar 5mg), Sodium 123mg (192mg with LS canned broth)

CREAM OF LEEK SOUP

Sodium Per Serving – 81mg   Serves 4

This mild soup gets added flavor from the caramelization of the vegetables. Make this the day before to let the flavors intensify, as it only gets better the next day.

1 tablespoon olive oil

1 tablespoon unsalted margarine or butter[1]

4–5 leeks, sliced (white and light green parts)

1 sweet onion, chopped

1 celery stalk, chopped

2 medium red potatoes, diced (about 3 cups)

¼ teaspoon garlic powder

⅛ teaspoon celery seed

⅛ teaspoon ground black pepper

1–3 garlic cloves, minced

¼ cup Madeira wine or dry sherry

3 cups CHICKEN STOCK (page 232) or canned low-salt chicken broth

2 teaspoons (or 2 envelopes) low-salt chicken bouillon granules

¼ cup chopped fresh flat-leaf (Italian) parsley[2]

4–5 drops hot pepper sauce, such as *Tabasco*

½ cup lowfat milk

¼ cup lowfat sour cream

Freshly grated nutmeg

▸ Heat oil and margarine in a large pan over medium-low heat; add leeks, onion, celery, potato, garlic powder, celery seed, and pepper. Cook, stirring occasionally, until potatoes are tender and golden brown, about 20 minutes.

▸ Add garlic and cook, stirring frequently, until you smell the garlic, 1 to 2 minutes; stir in Madeira, chicken stock, bouillon, and parsley. Cover and simmer 1 hour. Remove from heat and cool slightly.

▸ Place one-half leek mixture in a blender or food processor and pulse until smooth; repeat with remaining mixture.

▸ Return purée to pan and stir in hot pepper sauce, milk, and sour cream; heat through. Top with nutmeg and serve.

NUTRITIONAL INFO PER SERVING: Calories 286mg, Fat 9mg (Saturated Fat 3mg), Cholesterol 17mg, Carbohydrates 38mg (Fiber 4mg, Sugar 8mg), Sodium 81mg (163mg with LS canned broth)

VARIATION

MUSHROOM-LEEK SOUP

For a heartier soup, add 8 ounces (about 2 cups) sliced mushrooms (such as crimini, button, and/or shiitake) and increase the margarine to 2 tablespoons; proceed as directed.

NUTRITIONAL INFO PER SERVING: Calories 294mg, Fat 9mg (Saturated Fat 3mg), Cholesterol 17mg, Carbohydrates 39mg (Fiber 5mg, Sugar 9mg), Sodium 82mg (164mg with LS canned broth)

COMMENTS:

1 *To reduce saturated fat, use trans-free margarine. Since it contains sodium (90mg per tablespoon), it will increase the sodium per serving to 103mg (186 with low-salt canned broth).*

2 *For herbal variety, replace half the parsley with minced fresh basil or tarragon (or 2 teaspoons dried).*

TOTAL SODIUM AND FAT PER INGREDIENT

Sodium:
 4 leeks - 72mg
 1 sweet onion - 9mg
 1 celery stalk - 32mg
 2 red potatoes- 26mg
 1 garlic clove - 1mg
 ¼ c Madeira - 5mg
 3 c Chicken Stock - 60mg
  or LS canned broth - 390mg
 2 t LS chicken bouillon - 10mg
 ¼ c parsley - 8mg
 4 drops hot pepper sauce - 8mg
 ½ c LF milk - 58
 ¼ c LF sour cream - 34mg
Fat (Sat Fat):
 1 T olive oil - 14mg (2mg)
 1 T NSA margarine - 8mg (2mg)
  or NSA butter - 12mg (8mg)
 3 c Chicken Stock - 3mg (0mg)
  or LS canned broth - 0mg
 ½ c LF milk - 3mg (1mg)
 ¼ c LF sour cream - 7mg (4mg)

1 *To reduce saturated fat, use trans-free margarine. Since trans-free contains sodium (90mg per tablespoon), it will increase the sodium per serving to 130mg (or 205mg with low-salt canned broth).*

2 *Yellow onions are preferred, as they have less water than other onions, allowing for better caramelization. For additional info, see* COOKING TIP, *Caramelizing Onions, page 41.*

3 *I use* **Vogue Cuisine** *Onion Base (available from the manufacturer, see* RESOURCES, *page 272). It takes this soup from good to outstanding.*

4 *Madeira gives a rich creamy taste to the soup, but you may substitute brandy or sherry. There will be a subtle change in taste depending on which is used.*

TOTAL SODIUM AND FAT PER INGREDIENT

Sodium:
4 onions - 18mg
3 garlic cloves - 3mg
6 c BEEF STOCK - 120mg
  or LS canned broth - 720mg
4 t LS beef bouillon - 20mg
1 t onion soup base - 136mg
2 c Madeira wine - 44mg
8 sl EVERYDAY BREAD - 200mg
  or LS bread - 320mg
8 sl LF Swiss cheese - 320mg

Fat (Sat Fat):
2 T olive oil - 28mg (3mg)
2 T NSA margarine - 16mg (6mg)
  or NSA butter - 24mg (16mg)
6 c BEEF STOCK - 6mg (0mg)
  or LS canned broth - 0mg
8 sl EVERYDAY BREAD - 21mg (4mg)
  or LS bread - 8mg (8mg)
8 sl LF Swiss - 32mg (16mg)

FRENCH ONION SOUP

Sodium Per Serving – 108mg   Serves 8

My friend, Jeannette Phillips, prepared this delicious soup during a "girls only weekend." Although onion soup is normally high in sodium (about 1,053mg per cup), my low-salt adaptation is rich and creamy and I think, just as good. The slow caramelizing of the onions and the crunchiness of the multigrain bread adds to the taste and richness. NOTE: The amount of sodium per serving will vary depending on the brand of bread and cheese used. The nutritional values listed below are based on 27mg sodium per slice of bread and 40mg per ounce of cheese.

2 tablespoons olive oil

2 tablespoons unsalted margarine or butter[1]

4 large yellow onions, thinly sliced[2]

½ teaspoon garlic powder

¼ teaspoon ground black pepper

3 cloves garlic, minced

1 teaspoon sugar substitute or sugar

6 cups BEEF STOCK *(page 233)* **or canned low-salt beef broth**

1 cup water

4 teaspoons (or 4 envelopes) low-salt beef bouillon granules

1 teaspoon onion soup base (optional)[3]

2 cups Madeira wine[4]

2 tablespoons flour, mixed with 4 tablespoons water to form a paste

8 slices EVERYDAY MULTIGRAIN BREAD *(page 218)* **or low-salt multigrain bread**

8 slices lowfat Swiss cheese

▸ Heat oil and margarine in a large skillet over medium heat; add onions. Cook, stirring frequently, until they start to brown, 4 to 5 minutes; sprinkle with garlic powder and pepper. Decrease heat to medium-low; cook, stirring frequently, until onions are a deep brown color and caramelized, 30 to 45 minutes.

▸ Stir in garlic and sugar; add beef stock, water, bouillon, soup base, Madeira, and flour paste. Continue stirring until flour is mixed in well; cover and cook 30 minutes. Remove lid and simmer, uncovered, 15 minutes longer.

▸ Ladle into oven-proof bowls; place a piece of bread on soup and top with 1 slice cheese. Broil until cheese melts and edges of bread start to brown, about 2 minutes.

NUTRITIONAL INFO PER SERVING: Calories 443mg, Fat 13mg (Saturated Fat 4mg), Cholesterol 27mg, Carbohydrates 56mg (Fiber 3mg, Sugar 8mg), Sodium 108mg (183mg with LS canned broth)

PUMPKIN JALAPENO SOUP

Sodium Per Serving – 54mg   Serves 4

This deliciously light and aromatic soup recipe was given to me by my friend, Sally Pearce, who truly is a "soup queen." After a few low-salt substitutions, I think you'll love the sweet taste of pumpkin combined with the heat of the jalapeños, not to mention the wonderful aroma that fills the house as it's cooking.

- 2 tablespoons unsalted margarine or butter[1]
- 1 small onion, chopped
- 2–4 jalapeños, seeded and chopped[2]
- 1 russet potato, cubed
- 1 clove garlic, minced
- ½ teaspoon curry powder
- ½ teaspoon garlic powder
- ½ teaspoon ground white pepper
- 2 carrots, chopped
- ⅓ cup chopped fresh flat-leaf (Italian) parsley

- 4 cups CHICKEN STOCK (page 232) or canned low-salt chicken broth, divided
- 1 tablespoon (or 3 envelopes) low-salt chicken bouillon granules
- 1 (15-ounce) can pumpkin puree
- ¼ cup Madeira wine or dry sherry
- 2–3 drops hot pepper sauce, such as *Tabasco*
- Freshly ground nutmeg
- ½ cup lowfat sour cream (optional)

▷ Melt margarine in a large pot over medium heat; add onion and jalapeños. Cook, stirring frequently, until onions are translucent, about 4 minutes. Mix in potatoes, curry, garlic, garlic powder, and white pepper; cook 1 minute longer.

▷ Add carrots, parsley, 2 cups chicken stock, and bouillon; bring to boil. Decrease heat to low; cover and simmer until vegetables are cooked, about 20 minutes. Remove from heat and cool slightly.

▷ Place one-half pumpkin mixture in a blender or food processor and pulse until smooth; repeat with remaining mixture.

▷ Return purée to pan; add remaining 2 cups chicken broth, pumpkin, Madeira, and hot pepper sauce. Heat through and serve, topped with nutmeg and a dollop of sour cream.

NUTRITIONAL INFO PER SERVING: Calories 189mg, Fat 6mg (Saturated Fat 2mg), Cholesterol 15mg, Carbohydrates 25mg (Fiber 5mg, Sugar 6mg), Sodium 54mg (128mg with LS canned broth)

COMMENTS:

1 *To reduce saturated fat, use trans-free margarine. Since it contains sodium (90mg per tablespoon), it will increase the sodium per serving to 84mg (or 158mg with low-salt canned broth).*

2 *Two jalapeños give this soup a hint of heat, but if you like it hot . . . add all four! For information on handling jalapeños, see COMMENTS #2, page 50.*

TOTAL SODIUM AND FAT PER INGREDIENT

Sodium:
- 1 onion - 2mg
- 1 russet potato - 30mg
- 1 garlic clove - 1mg
- ½ t curry - 1mg
- 2 carrots - 84mg
- ⅓ c parsley - 12mg
- 4 c CHICKEN STOCK - 80mg
  - or LS canned broth - 520mg
- 1 T LS chicken bouillon - 15mg
- 15 oz pumpkin - 25mg
- ¼ c Madeira - 5mg
- 2 drops hot pepper sauce - 4mg
- ½ c LF sour cream - 68mg

Fat (Sat Fat):
- 2 T NSA margarine - 16mg (3mg)
  - or NSA butter - 24mg (16mg)
- 4 c CHICKEN STOCK - 4mg (0mg)
  - or LS canned broth - 8mg (4mg)
- 15 oz pumpkin - 1mg (0mg)
- ½ c LF sour cream - 14mg (8mg)

SPLIT PEA SOUP

Sodium Per Serving – 41mg — Serves 8

I've always been fond of split pea soup and as a young child, going to "Pea Soup Andersen's" just north of Santa Barbara, California, for a bowl of their famous pea soup was a big event. Here is an equally good version that is both thick and luscious.

1 tablespoon olive oil
1 small sweet onion, chopped
2 celery stalks, chopped
2 medium carrots, chopped
2 garlic cloves, minced
¼ teaspoon dried basil
¼ teaspoon celery seed
¼ teaspoon garlic powder
¼ teaspoon ground black pepper
¼ teaspoon dried thyme
2 cups dried split peas, rinsed

1 medium russet potato, peeled and cubed, or 2 red potatoes, cubed[1]
½ cup barley, uncooked
4 cups CHICKEN STOCK (page 232) or canned low-salt chicken broth
3½ cups water
½ cup brandy (optional)[2]
1 tablespoon (or 3 envelopes) low-salt chicken bouillon granules
1 bay leaf

▸ Heat oil in a large pot over medium heat; add onion, celery, and carrots. Cook, stirring frequently, until onion is translucent, 4 to 5 minutes. Stir in garlic, basil, garlic powder, pepper, and thyme; continue cooking and stirring until you smell the garlic, about 1 minute.

▸ Add split peas, potato, barley, chicken stock, water, brandy, bouillon, and bay leaf; bring to boil. Decrease heat to low; cover and simmer, stirring occasionally, until most of the water has been absorbed and soup has thickened, 2 to 3 hours. Remove and let cool slightly.

▸ Remove bay leaf and place one-third of the split pea mixture in a blender or food processor and pulse until smooth; repeat with remaining mixture. (If you like it chunky, skip this step.)

▸ Return purée to pot and heat through; serve.

NUTRITIONAL INFO PER SERVING: Calories 272mg, Fat 3mg (Saturated Fat 0mg), Cholesterol 8mg, Carbohydrates 38mg (Fiber 14mg, Sugar 6mg), Sodium 41mg (96mg with LS canned broth)

VARIATION

SPICY SPLIT PEA SOUP

For a spicy flavor, instead of the basil and thyme, substitute 2 teaspoons no-salt-added chili powder, 1 teaspoon ground cumin, ½ teaspoon ground coriander, ½ teaspoon ground turmeric, and ¼ teaspoon ground ginger.

NUTRITIONAL INFO PER SERVING: Calories 278mg, Fat 7mg (Saturated Fat 1mg), Cholesterol 12mg, Carbohydrates 39mg (Fiber 5mg, Sugar 9mg), Sodium 80mg (162mg with LS canned broth)

MINESTRONE

Sodium Per Serving – 66mg   Serves 12

My Italian grandmother made the best vegetable soup. Although I haven't captured the exact flavor, my desalted version is pretty close. It makes a load of soup and can easily be cut in half. Better yet, freeze some and save for another day. This also is a great way to clean out the refrigerator.

- 1 tablespoon olive oil
- 1 onion, diced
- 2 celery stalks, chopped
- 2 carrots, chopped
- 2 garlic cloves, minced
- 1/2 teaspoon garlic powder
- 1/2 teaspoon ground black pepper
- 4 cups CHICKEN STOCK *(page 232)* or canned low-salt chicken broth
- 2 cups BEEF STOCK *(page 233)* or canned low-salt beef broth
- 1 (28-ounce) can crushed tomatoes in puree[1]
- 1 tablespoon (or 3 envelopes) low-salt beef or chicken bouillon granules
- 3 cups fresh or frozen vegetables, sliced or cut into bite-sized chunks[2]

- 1 medium potato, diced
- 1/2 (10-ounce) package no-salt-added frozen peas
- 1 (15-ounce) can no-salt-added red kidney beans, undrained
- 1 (11-ounce) can no-salt-added whole corn, or 1 1/2 cups frozen or fresh corn kernels
- 2 cups shredded cabbage
- 4 ounces uncooked pasta, such as elbow, penne, or ziti
- 1 tablespoon cider vinegar
- 1 tablespoon sugar substitute or sugar
- 1/2 teaspoon dried basil
- 1/2 teaspoon dried oregano
- 1/2 teaspoon dried rosemary, crumbled

▷ Heat oil in a large pot over medium heat; add onion, celery, carrots, garlic, garlic powder, and pepper. Cook, stirring frequently, until onion is translucent, 3 to 4 minutes.

▷ Add remaining ingredients and bring to boil. Decrease heat to medium-low; cover, and simmer until veggies and macaroni are tender, about 40 minutes. Serve with Parmesan cheese, if desired.

NUTRITIONAL INFO PER SERVING: Calories 153mg, Fat 2mg (Saturated Fat 0mg), Cholesterol 15mg, Carbohydrates 21mg (Fiber 6mg, Sugar 6mg), Sodium 66mg

COMMENTS:

1 *Although most of the sodium in this soup comes from the crushed tomatoes in puree (1,235mg per 28-ounce can), I think the added salt is necessary for a flavorful soup.*

2 *Use any combination of veggies that you like, such as broccoli, cauliflower, green beans, or zucchini.*

TOTAL SODIUM AND FAT PER INGREDIENT

Sodium:
- 1 onion - 3mg
- 2 celery - 64mg
- 2 carrots - 84mg
- 2 garlic cloves - 2mg
- 4 c CHICKEN STOCK - 80mg
  - or LS canned broth - 520mg
- 2 c CHICKEN STOCK - 40mg
  - or LS canned broth - 240mg
- 28 oz crushed tomatoes - 280mg
- 1 T bouillon - 15mg
- 3 c mixed veggies - 43mg
- 1 potato - 13mg
- 5 oz peas - 7mg
- 15 oz NSA kidney beans - 45mg
- 15 oz NSA whole corn - 30mg
- 2 c cabbage - 25mg
- 4 oz macaroni - 4mg

Fat (Sat Fat):
- 1 T olive oil - 14mg (2mg)
- 4 c CHICKEN STOCK - 4mg (4mg)
  - or LS canned broth - 8mg (4mg)
- 2 c BEEF STOCK - 2mg (0mg)
  - or LS canned broth - 0mg
- 15 oz NSA corn - 3mg (0mg)
- 4 oz macaroni - 1mg (0mg)

GRANDMA'S LENTIL SOUP

Sodium Per Serving – 96mg   Serves 6

This is one of the wonderful dishes my Italian grandmother prepared for family gatherings. Filled with many vegetables, this thick and yummy soup is one of my favorites.

2 tablespoons olive oil

3 carrots, chopped

2 celery stalks, chopped

1 onion, chopped

2 garlic cloves, minced

1 teaspoon dried basil

½ teaspoon garlic powder

½ teaspoon dried oregano

½ teaspoon ground black pepper

½ teaspoon dried thyme

5 cups CHICKEN STOCK (page 232) or canned low-salt chicken broth

1 tablespoon (or 3 envelopes) low-salt chicken bouillon granules

1 (15-ounce) can no-salt-added crushed tomatoes[1]

2 cups dry red lentils[2]

1 potato, peeled and chopped

2 bay leaves

1–2 teaspoons hot pepper sauce, such as *Tabasco*

¼ cup chopped fresh flat-leaf (Italian) parsley

▸ Heat oil in a large pot over medium heat; add carrots, celery, and onions. Cook, stirring frequently, until onions are transparent, 4 to 5 minutes; add garlic and cook, stirring frequently, until you smell the garlic, about 1 minute.

▸ Decrease heat to medium-low; stir in basil, garlic powder, oregano, pepper, and thyme. Add lentils, chicken stock, bouillon, tomatoes, potato, and bay leaves; cover and simmer until lentils are tender and soup has thickened, about 45 minutes to an hour. Remove from heat and cool slightly.

▸ Remove bay leaves and place one-half of lentil mixture in a blender or food processor; pulse until smooth. Return purée to pot and stir in hot pepper sauce, and parsley; serve.

NUTRITIONAL INFO PER SERVING: Calories 390mg, Fat 6mg (Saturated Fat 1mg), Cholesterol 13mg, Carbohydrates 58mg (Fiber 23mg, Sugar 10mg), Sodium 96mg

TOTAL SODIUM AND FAT PER INGREDIENT

Sodium:
3 carrots - 126mg
2 celery stalks - 64mg
1 onion - 3mg
5 c CHICKEN STOCK - 100mg
  or LS canned broth - 650mg
3 t LS chicken bouillon - 15mg
15 oz NSA tomatoes - 160mg
2 c dried lentils - 38mg
1 potato - 30mg
1 t hot pepper sauce - 30mg
¼ c parsley - 8mg
Fat (Sat Fat):
2 c lentils - 4mg (1mg)
2 T olive oil - 28mg (4mg)
5 c CHICKEN STOCK - 5mg (0mg)
  or LS canned broth - 10mg (5mg)

FOOD NOTE

ABOUT LENTILS

There are several kinds of lentils and all are high in protein and fiber, and have very little sodium.

Preparation: Place lentils in a pot and cover lentils with water (no need to soak before cooking); bring to boil over high heat. Decrease heat to medium-low, cover, and simmer until tender (see below for cooking times). One cup dried beans equals 3 cups cooked.

Brown – Ready in 30 to 40 minutes.

French – Cooks up quickly, less than 30 minutes, and stays frim and nutty after cooking. Don't cook them in an iron pot or they will turn black.

Red – Turns a yellowish-beige when cooked, takes 15 to 20 minutes cooking time until tender.

SIMPLY WHITE CLAM CHOWDER

Sodium Per Serving – 200mg   Serves 4

Clam chowder, particularly the white or New England variety, is loaded with sodium, averaging 992mg per cup. This yummy version is thick and creamy with substantially less salt. The hot pepper sauce is a must, adding a little heat and spiciness that goes perfectly with the chowder.

1 tablespoon olive oil

1 tablespoon unsalted margarine or butter[1]

½ sweet onion, chopped, such as Vidalia

1 carrot, chopped

1 celery stalk, chopped

1 red potato, diced (about 1 cup)

¼ teaspoon herbes de Provence[2]

¼ teaspoon garlic powder

¼ teaspoon dried marjoram

¼ teaspoon dried thyme

⅛ teaspoon celery seed

⅛ teaspoon white pepper

1 (15-ounce) can no-salt-added cream corn

½ CHICKEN STOCK *(page 232)* or canned low-salt chicken broth

1 teaspoon (or 1 envelope) low sodium chicken bouillon granules

1 (6.5-ounce) can minced baby clams, drained and juice reserved

1½ cups lowfat milk[3]

4 5 drops hot pepper sauce, such as *Tabasco*

⅛ teaspoon *Liquid Smoke*[4]

2 tablespoons cornstarch, mixed with ¼ cup water to make a paste

Chopped chopped fresh flat-leaf (Italian) parsley (optional)

▸ Heat oil and margarine in a large pan over medium heat; add onion, carrot, celery, potato, herbes de Provence, garlic powder, marjoram, thyme, celery seed, and white pepper. Cook, stirring frequently, until onion is translucent, about 4 minutes.

▸ Stir in corn, chicken stock, bouillon, and reserved clam juice; decrease heat to low, cover, and simmer until vegetables are tender, 20 to 30 minutes.

▸ Add clams, milk, hot pepper sauce, and *Liquid Smoke*; increase heat to medium and heat through.

▸ Slowly mix in cornstarch paste, stirring constantly until thickened to desired consistency. Serve with parsley and additional hot pepper sauce.

NUTRITIONAL INFO PER SERVING: Calories 293mg, Fat 9mg (Saturated Fat 1mg), Cholesterol 37mg, Carbohydrates 37mg (Fiber 4mg, Sugar 10mg), Sodium 200mg (216 with LS canned broth)

COMMENTS:

1 *To reduce saturated fat, use trans-free margarine. Since it contains sodium (90mg per tablespoon), it will increase the sodium per serving to 222mg.*

2 *Herbes de Provence is a blend of herbs commonly used in French cooking— most often a mix of basil, chervil, fennel, lavendar, marjoram, rosemary, sage, savory, and/or thyme. The combination and portions vary depending on the manufacturer.*

3 *For a richer soup, instead of milk, use light cream or half-and-half.*

4 *Liquid Smoke gives a smokey flavor to foods and is available in most supermarkets in the grilling sauces and marinades section.*

TOTAL SODIUM AND FAT PER INGREDIENT

Sodium:
½ sweet onion - 6mg
1 carrot - 42mg
1 celery stalk - 32mg
1 red potato - 13mg
15 oz NSA cream corn - 30mg
½ c CHICKEN STOCK - 10mg
  or LS canned broth - 65mg
1 t LS chicken bouillon - 5mg
6.5 oz clams w/juice - 460mg
1½ c LF milk - 183mg
½ t hot pepper sauce - 16mg
2 T cornstarch - 2mg
Fat (Sat Fat):
1 T olive oil - 14mg (2mg)
1 T NSA margarine - 8mg (2mg)
  or NSA butter - 12mg (8mg)
15 oz NSA cream corn - 3mg (0mg)
½ c CHICKEN STOCK - 1mg (0mg)
  or LS canned broth - 1mg (1mg)
6.5 oz clams w/juice - 4mg (0mg)
1½ c LF milk - 4mg (2mg)

COMMENTS:

1 See FOOD NOTE, *page 73, for info on no-salt-added (NSA) beans.*

2 **Health Valley** *also makes a no-salt-added chili. Although I prefer the lightly salted variety, the NSA version decreases the sodium per serving to 133mg.*

3 Choose salsas with less than 45mg sodium per 2 tablespoons.

4 Chipotle peppers in adobo is nothing more than smoked jalapeños in a spicy tomato sauce. They are very hot and are found in Hispanic markets and some larger grocery stores.

EASY 4-BEAN SOUP

Sodium Per Serving – 214mg   Serves 8

This delicious chili-like soup is ideal for spur-of-the-moment gatherings; just open a few cans, pour in a pot and heat it up. Add a tossed salad, CORNBREAD *(page 222), and you have a great crowd pleaser.*

2 (15-ounce) cans no-salt-added kidney beans, undrained[1]

1 (15-ounce) can no-salt-added black beans, undrained[1]

1 15-ounce) can no-salt-added pinto beans, undrained[1]

1 15-ounce) can no-salt-added garbanzo beans, undrained[1]

1 (15-ounce) can *Health Valley* Spicy Vegetarian Chili[2]

1 (4-ounce) can diced green chiles

1 (16-ounce) jar low-salt salsa[3]

2 tablespoons minced chipotle peppers in adobo sauce[4]

Garnishes:

2 ounces shredded lowfat Cheddar cheese (about ½ cup)

4 ounces shredded no-salt-added Swiss cheese (about 1 cup)

½ cup chopped sweet onions (such as Vidalia) or green onions (white and light green parts)

▸ Combine all ingredients, except garnishes, in a pot over medium heat; cook, stirring occasionally, until heated through, 10 to15 minutes.

▸ Mix Cheddar and Swiss cheeses together. Serve soup with cheese and onions on top.

NUTRITIONAL INFO PER SERVING: Calories 258mg, Fat 1mg (Saturated Fat 0mg), Cholesterol 0mg, Carbohydrates 46mg (Fiber 20mg, Sugar 3mg), Sodium 214mg

---

TOTAL SODIUM AND FAT PER INGREDIENT

Sodium:
  30 oz NSA kidney beans - 90mg
  15 oz NSAblack beans - 45mg
  15 oz NSA pinto beans - 45mg
  15 oz NSA garbanzoss - 30mg
  15 oz HV Vegetarian Chili - 780mg
  4 oz green chiles - 100mg
  16 oz LS salsa - 480mg
  2 T chipotle in adobo - 140mg
Fat (Sat Fat):
  15 oz NSA garbanzos - 6mg (0mg)
  15 oz HV Veg Chili - 2mg (0mg)
  2 T chipotle in adobo - 1mg (0mg)

VARIATION

MEATY BEAN SOUP

Heat 1 tablespoon olive oil in a large pot over medium heat; brown ½ pound ground beef or turkey. Add 1 teaspoon no-salt-added chili powder[5], ½ teaspoon spicy seasoning[6], ¼ teaspoon ground cumin, ¼ teaspoon garlic powder, ⅛ teaspoon ground black pepper, and ¼ cup low-salt salsa. Stir in beans and remainingr ingredients; proceed as directed.

NUTRITIONAL INFO PER SERVING: Calories 314mg, Fat 5mg (Saturated Fat 1mg), Cholesterol 16mg, Carbohydrates 47mg (Fiber 20mg, Sugar 3mg), Sodium 217mg

HEARTY BLACK BEAN SOUP

Sodium Per Serving – 67mg   Serves 4

This filling soup with a hint of orange goes together quickly. Use a large skillet, so the liquid cooks down quickly to a rich and tasty broth. This serves 4 as a first course or 2 as a main dish.

1 tablespoon olive oil

½ sweet onion, chopped

1 carrot, diced

1 celery stalk, diced

1 garlic clove, minced

1 (15-ounce) can no-salt-added black beans, drained and rinsed[1]

4 cups CHICKEN STOCK (page 232) or canned low-salt chicken broth

1 (15-ounce) can no-salt-added whole corn, drained

½ (6-ounce) can no-salt-added tomato paste, or 1 cup no-salt-added tomato puree

2 teaspoons (or 2 envelopes) low-salt chicken bouillon granules

1–2 teaspoons no-salt-added chili powder[2]

½ teaspoon dried cumin

¼ teaspoon ground black pepper

Pinch cayenne pepper

½ teaspoon finely grated orange rind

Optional Garnishes:

Nonfat or lowfat sour cream

No-salt-added Swiss cheese, shredded

▶ Heat oil in a large skillet over medium heat; add onions, carrots, and celery. Cook, stirring frequently, until onions are translucent, 4 to 5 minutes. Add garlic; cook, stirring constantly, until you smell the garlic, 1 to 2 minutes.

▶ Stir in the beans, chicken stock, corn, tomato paste, bouillon, chili powder, cumin, black pepper, cayenne, and orange rind; cook, uncovered, until vegetables are tender, 40 to 45 minutes. *NOTE: Liquid will reduce to about 2 cups, creating a deep-colored, rich-tasting broth.*

▶ Serve, topped with sour cream and cheese.

NUTRITIONAL INFO PER SERVING: Calories 231mg, Fat 5mg (Saturated Fat 1mg), Cholesterol 15mg, Carbohydrates 31mg (Fiber 12mg, Sugar 9mg), Sodium 67mg (133mg with LS canned broth)

COMMENTS:

1 *There are several brands of no-salt-added black beans. See* FOOD NOTE, *page 73, for additional info.*

2 *Surprisingly, chili powder contains sodium (26mg per teaspoon). Look for no-salt-add brands, like* **The Spice Hunter,** *available at many supermarkets or from online grocers (see* RESOURCES, *page 272, for more info).*

For a spicy soup, use 2 teaspoons chili powder. For a less spicy version, 1 teaspoon is probably enough.

TOTAL SODIUM AND FAT PER INGREDIENT

Sodium:
½ sweet onion - 6mg
1 garlic clove - 1mg
1 carrot - 42mg
1 celery stalk - 32mg
15 NSA black beans - 45mg
2 c CHICKEN STOCK - 80mg
  or LS canned broth - 520mg
2 t LS chicken bouillon - 10mg
15 oz NSA corn - 30mg
8 oz NSA tomato sauce - 60mg
½ t cumin - 2 mg
Fat (Sat Fat):
1 T olive oil - 14mg (2mg)
2 c CHICKEN STOCK - 4mg (0mg)
  or LS canned broth - 8mg (4mg)
15 oz NSA corn - 3mg (0mg)

COMMENTS:

1 See COMMENTS #2, page 69, for info on no-salt-added chili powder brands.

2 **Eden, Pomi,** and **S&W** offer NSA diced tomatoes with 30mg or less sodium per ½ cup serving. See RESOURCES, page 272, for more information.

3 Most canned kidney beans have up to 480mg sodium per ½ cup. There are several brands of no-salt-added beans, such as **Eden** and **American Prairie,** which have less than 40mg per serving. See FOOD NOTE, About Canned Beans, page 73, for additional info and RESOURCES, page 272, for manufacturers and online sources.

TEXAS-STYLE TURKEY CHILI

Sodium Per Serving – 104mg   Serves 8–10

This is a very hearty and spicy chili that goes together quickly using canned beans. Allow the chili to cook at least an hour or more. If you like it spicy, add more dried red pepper flakes and/or cayenne pepper.

1 tablespoon olive oil

1 onion, chopped

2 bell peppers, chopped

4 garlic cloves, minced

1½ pounds lean ground turkey

2 tablespoons no-salt-added chili powder[1]

1½ teaspoons ground cumin

1 teaspoon dried basil

1 teaspoon dried oregano

1 teaspoon dried red pepper flakes, or ½ teaspoon hot pepper sauce, such as *Tabasco*

½ teaspoon cayenne pepper

½ teaspoon ground cinnamon

½ teaspoon ground black pepper

2 (15-ounce) cans no-salt-added diced tomatoes[2]

2 (15-ounce) cans no-salt-added kidney beans, drained[3]

1 (15-ounce) can no-salt-added tomato puree

1 (4-ounce) can diced green chiles

▶ Heat oil in a large pot over medium heat; add onion and bell peppers. Cook, stirring frequently, until onions are translucent, 4 to 5 minutes; add garlic and cook, stirring frequently, until you smell the garlic, about 1 minute.

▶ Add turkey; cook, stirring frequently and breaking up any large pieces, until no longer pink, about 5 minutes. Add the chili powder, cumin, basil, oregano, red pepper flakes, cayenne, cinnamon, and black pepper; thoroughly mix with turkey mixture.

▶ Stir in undrained tomatoes, beans, tomato puree, and green chiles. Bring to a boil; decrease heat to medium-low. Cover and simmer, stirring occasionally, for 1 to 2 hours. *NOTE: The longer this cooks, the more the flavors intensify and the richer the soup becomes.*

NUTRITIONAL INFO PER SERVING: Calories 212mg, Fat 6mg (Saturated Fat 1mg), Cholesterol 39mg, Carbohydrates 21mg (Fiber 9mg, Sugar 5mg), Sodium 104mg

TOTAL SODIUM AND FAT PER INGREDIENT

Sodium:
 1 onion - 3mg
 2 bell peppers - 8mg
 4 garlic cloves - 4mg
 1½ lb ground turkey - 640mg
 1½ t cumin - 6mg
 ½ t hot pepper sauce - 15mg
 30 oz NSA diced tomatoes - 210mg
 30 oz NSA kidney beans - 90mg
 15 oz NSA tomato puree - 120mg
 4 oz green chiles - 100mg
Fat (Sat Fat):
 1 T olive oil - 14mg (2mg)
 1½ lb ground turkey - 56mg (15mg)
 2 T NSA chili powder - 3mg (0mg)

SALADS AND SALAD DRESSINGS

COMMENTS:

1 *Most canned beans have up to 480mg sodium per ½ cup. There are several brands of no-salt-added beans, such as* **Eden** *and* **American Prairie,** *which have less than 40mg per serving. See* FOOD NOTE, *page 73, for additional info and* RESOURCES, *page 272, for manufacturers and online sources.*

2 *Instead of frozen corn, use 1½ cups fresh (about 3 ears).*

BLACK BEAN AND PEPPER SALAD

Sodium Per Serving – 27mg   Serves 10–12

This salad is a personal favorite. Not only colorful, but it is quick and easy to make. Perfect for a picnic or potluck – make lots as everyone will come back for more!

Salad:

2 (15-ounce) cans no-salt-added black beans, drained and rinsed[1]

2 green bell peppers, diced

1 red bell pepper, diced

1 yellow bell pepper, diced

1 sweet onion, diced

1 (15-ounce) can no-salt-added whole kernel corn, drained[2]

Dressing:

¼ cup balsamic vinegar

¼ cup extra-virgin olive oil

¼ teaspoon finely minced garlic

1 teaspoon Dijon-style mustard

2 teaspoons sugar substitute or sugar

2 tablespoons chopped fresh flat-leaf (Italian) parsley (optional)

▸ *For the salad:* In a large bowl, combine beans, peppers, onion, and corn.

▸ *For the dressing:* Blend together the vinegar, oil, garlic, mustard, and sweetener, either by whisking in a small bowl or by shaking well in a screw-top jar. Pour over bean mixture and mix thoroughly; cover and refrigerate several hours.

▸ Before serving, mix in parsley and stir well.

NUTRITIONAL INFO PER SERVING: Calories 145mg, Fat 6mg (Saturated Fat 1mg), Cholesterol 0mg, Carbohydrates 17mg (Fiber 8mg, Sugar 4mg), Sodium 27mg

TOTAL SODIUM AND FAT PER INGREDIENT

Sodium:
30 oz NSA black beans - 90mg
2 green bell pepper - 8mg
1 red bell pepper - 2mg
1 yellow bell pepper - 2mg
1 sweet onion - 12mg
15 oz NSA whole corn - 30mg
1 t dijon mustard - 120mg
2 T parsley - 4mg
Fat (Sat Fat):
15 oz NSA whole corn - 3mg (0mg)
¼ c olive oil - 56mg (8mg)

VARIATIONS

BEAN, PEPPER AND CHEVRE SALAD

Before serving, stir in 2 ounces crumbled chèvre cheese (*see* COMMENTS #1, *page 49, for more info on chèvre cheese*).

NUTRITIONAL INFO PER SERVING: Calories 159mg, Fat 7mg (Saturated Fat 1mg), Cholesterol 3mg, Carbohydrates 18mg (Fiber 8mg, Sugar 4mg), Sodium 37mg

BEAN, PEPPER AND FETA SALAD

Before serving, stir in 2 ounces *Athenos* Basil and Tomato Feta (or other flavored feta with 220mg sodium or less per ounce).

NUTRITIONAL INFO PER SERVING: Calories 160mg, Fat 7mg (Saturated Fat 2mg), Cholesterol 4mg, Carbohydrates 18mg (Fiber 8mg, Sugar 4mg), Sodium 71mg

FOUR BEAN SALAD

Sodium Per Serving – 15mg   Serves 12–14

I have been making this delicious salad for more than 25 years, except now I use no-salt-added beans. Make it at least 6 hours ahead of time or the day before to let the flavors marinate.

Salad:

- 1 (15-ounce) can no-salt-added red kidney beans, drained[1]
- 2 (15-ounce) cans no-salt-added whole green beans, drained[1]
- 2 (15-ounce) cans no-salt-added yellow (wax) beans, drained[1]
- 1 (15-ounce) can no-salt-added garbanzo beans, drained[1]
- 1 red or green bell pepper, chopped
- 1 sweet onion, chopped (such as Vidalia)

Dressing:

- ½ cup cider vinegar
- 5–8 tablespoons sugar substitute or sugar[2]
- 2 tablespoons extra-virgin olive oil
- ¼ teaspoon onion or garlic powder
- ¼ teaspoon ground black pepper

▸ *For the salad:* In a large bowl, combine beans, bell pepper, and onion.

▸ *For the dressing:* Blend together the vinegar, sweetener, oil, garlic powder, and black pepper, either by whisking in a small bowl or by shaking well in a screw-top jar.

▸ Pour dressing over beans, mixing well. Cover and refrigerate at least 6 hours or overnight.

NUTRITIONAL INFO PER SERVING: Calories 112mg, Fat 3mg (Saturated Fat 0mg), Cholesterol 0mg, Carbohydrates 17mg (Fiber 4mg, Sugar 2mg), Sodium 15mg

---

FOOD NOTE

ABOUT CANNED BEANS

Most canned beans have large amounts of salt added–averaging anywhere from 350mg to 480mg per ½ cup serving. There are several brands of no-salt-added beans, such as *Eden* or *American Prairie* (with 35mg or less sodium per ½ cup serving). There also are low-salt varieties, like *Westbrae Natural* (which contains 140mg), and less salt products, such as "50% less salt," that have 260mg or more per serving.

No-salt-added beans do not need rinsing, but all others should be rinsed. NOTE: Although rinsing removes some salt, it is not a significant amount. If unable to find unsalted beans, there are several online sources (*see* RESOURCES, *page 272*) or you can cook up a pot of dried beans (*see* COOKING TIP, Cooking Dried Beans, *page 40*).

TOTAL SODIUM AND FAT PER INGREDIENT

Sodium:
- 15 oz NSA kidney beans - 45mg
- 30 oz NSA green beans - 30mg
- 30 oz NSA yellow beans - 60mg
- 15 oz NSA garbanzos - 30mg
- 1 red bell pepper - 2mg
- 1 sweet onion - 9mg
- ½ c vinegar - 1mg

Fat (Sat Fat):
- 15 oz NSA garbanzos - 6mg (0mg)
- ½ c olive oil - 28mg (4mg)

COMMENTS:

[1] *Balsamic adds a robust flavor, while the red wine vinegar is more subtle.*

[2] *Stilton is milder and firmer than other blue cheeses, plus it has much less sodium. Listed below are several popular blue cheese varieties and the sodium per ounce:*

Stilton	*220mg*
Gorgonzola	*350mg*
Blue	*395mg*
Roquefort	*513mg*

Sodium Per Serving – 95mg   Serves 10

If you like beets, you'll love this wonderfully rich salad. The deep maroon color of the beets makes a beautiful presentation, especially on buffet tables. Save time and prepare this the day before, adding the nuts and cheese just before serving.

2 tablespoons balsamic vinegar or red wine vinegar[1]

2 tablespooons extra virgin olive oil

1 teaspoon Dijon-style mustard

1 teaspoon sugar substitute or sugar

6–8 beets, roasted (see COOKING TIP *below***) and cubed (about 5–6 cups)**

½ cup chopped walnuts

2 ounces Stilton cheese or other blue cheese, crumbled[2]

▸ Blend together the vinegar, oil, mustard, and sweetener either by whisking in a small bowl or by shaking well in a screw-top jar.

▸ In a large bowl, combine beets and dressing: chill at least 30 minutes. Before serving, mix in walnuts and cheese.

NUTRITIONAL INFO PER SERVING: Calories 106mg, Fat 9mg (Saturated Fat 2mg), Cholesterol 6mg, Carbohydrates 6mg (Fiber 2mg, Sugar 3mg), Sodium 95mg

TOTAL SODIUM AND FAT PER INGREDIENT

Sodium:
- 1 t Dijon mustard - 120mg
- 6 beets - 384mg
- ½ c walnuts - 1mg
- 2 oz Stilton cheese - 440mg

Fat (Sat Fat):
- 1 T olive oil - 28mg (4mg)
- 6 beets - 1mg (0mg)
- ½ c walnuts - 38mg (4mg)
- 2 oz Stilton cheese - 18mg (10mg)

COOKING TIP

ROASTING BEETS

Roasting beets brings out their richness and intensifies the flavor. To roast: Wash and trim beets (do not peel) and either wrap each in aluminum foil or place in a baking dish with 2 cups water and cover. Bake in a preheated oven at 425ºF (220ºC) for 45 minutes to 1 hour (depending on size).

When cool enough to handle, remove skin and prepare according to recipe instructions.

SWEET AND SOUR COLE SLAW

Sodium Per Serving – 26mg   Serves 8

This tangy, sweet slaw is a great alternative to the heavy, mayo-based salads in the supermarket. Allow several hours for the flavors to blend or make a day ahead of time.

Dressing:
3 tablespoons extra-virgin olive oil

2 tablespoons cider vinegar

1 tablespoon lemon or lime juice

1/4–1/3 cup sugar substitute or sugar[1]

1 garlic clove, minced

1/2 teaspoon hot pepper sauce, such as *Tabasco*, or 1/4 teaspoon crushed red pepper flakes

1/2 teaspoon garlic or onion powder

1/4 teaspoon ground black pepper

Salad:
6–8 cups (1 medium head) green cabbage, shredded, or 1 (16-ounce) package cole slaw mix

1 small sweet onion, chopped, such as Vidalia

1 large carrot, grated

2 celery stalks, chopped

▸ *For the dressing:* Blend together the oil, vinegar, lemon juice, sweetener, garlic, hot pepper sauce, garlic powder, and black pepper, either by whisking in a small bowl or by shaking well in a screw-top jar.

▸ *For the salad:* In a large bowl, combine cabbage, onion, carrot, and celery; add dressing and toss. Season with additional pepper to taste.

▸ Cover and refrigerate 2 to 3 hours to allow flavors to blend. Toss before serving.

NUTRITIONAL INFO PER SERVING: Calories 69mg, Fat 5mg (Saturated Fat 1mg), Cholesterol 0mg, Carbohydrates 5mg (Fiber 2mg, Sugar 3mg), Sodium 26mg

COMMENTS:

1 *Because sugar substitutes differ from sugar in sweetness, the amount needed depends on the sweetener used:*

  Splenda or sugar - 1/3 cup
  Fructose - 1/4 cup

  For additional information, see **Sweeteners**, *page 37.*

VARIATION

Spicy Cole Slaw

For a spicy taste, add 1/2 teaspoon ground cumin to the dressing and to the salad add 1/4 cup chopped cilantro.

NUTRITIONAL INFO PER SERVING: Calories 70mg, Fat 5mg (Saturated Fat 1mg), Cholesterol 0mg, Carbohydrates 5mg (Fiber 2mg, Sugar 3mg), Sodium 27mg

TOTAL SODIUM AND FAT PER INGREDIENT
Sodium:
  1 garlic clove - 1mg
  1/2 t hot pepper sauce - 15mg
  6 cups cabbage - 76mg
  1 sweet onion - 9mg
  1 carrot - 42mg
  2 celery stalks - 64mg
Fat (Sat Fat):
  3 T olive oil - 42mg (6mg)
  6 cups cabbage - 1mg (0mg)

COMMENTS:

1 *Water chestnuts are a wonderful low-salt food that adds crunchiness to dishes.*

2 *See* FOOD NOTE *below for lower-salt bacon brands.*

PEA SALAD WITH BACON AND CASHEWS

Sodium Per Serving – 56mg   Serves 8

This simple and "crunchy" salad is perfect for a potluck or barbecue. Although bacon is very salty, using a small amount of a lower-sodium brand allows this "no-no" to fit into a low-salt diet. This salad is best if made the day before to allow the flavors to blend.

1 (16-ounce) package frozen no-salt-added peas, do not thaw

1 small sweet onion, chopped, such as Vidalia

2 celery stalks, chopped

1 (8-ounce) can water chestnuts, drained and chopped[1]

⅔ cup lowfat sour cream

¼ teaspoon onion or garlic powder

⅛ teaspoon ground black pepper

4 slices lower-sodium bacon, cooked and crumbled[2]

⅓ cup chopped unsalted cashews or peanuts

▸ Combine peas, onion, celery, water chestnuts, sour cream, onion powder, and pepper; cover and refrigerate overnight.

▸ Before serving, fold in bacon and cashews. Let stand at room temperature 30 minutes before serving.

NUTRITIONAL INFO PER SERVING: Calories 133mg, Fat 9mg (Saturated Fat 3mg), Cholesterol 8mg, Carbohydrates 10mg (Fiber 2mg, Sugar 3mg), Sodium 56mg

TOTAL SODIUM AND FAT PER INGREDIENT

Sodium:
  16 oz NSA peas - 10mg
  1 sweet onion - 9mg
  2 celery stalks - 64mg
  8 oz water chestnuts - 20mg
  ⅔ c LF sour cream - 91mg
  4 sl LS bacon - 240mg
  ⅓ c NSA cashews - 10mg

Fat (Sat Fat):
  ⅔ c LF sour cream - 18mg (10mg)
  4 sl LS bacon - 12mg (4mg)
  ⅓ c NSA cashews - 40mg (7mg)

FOOD NOTE

LOW-SODIUM BACON

There are several brands of low-salt bacon, such as *Wellshire Farms*, *Gwaltney*, and *Safeway Select*, which have 120mg or less per 2 slices. Other lower salt varieties with 230mg or less odium per ounce, include *Bar-S*, *Corn King*, *Farmland*, *Oscar Meyer*, and *Smithfield's*. Many supermarkets carry one or more of these brands.

BAKED POTATO SALAD

Sodium Per Serving – 95mg   Serves 10

This is a crowd favorite; the addition of the mustard and pickle relish imparts enough flavor that no one misses the salt. Because potatoes are very absorbant, marinating them in the pickle relish adds a lot of flavor. Allow several hours for the flavors to blend.

4 russet potatoes (about 2½ pounds), baked and cooled slightly[1]

2 tablespoons sweet pickle relish

½ cup sweet onion, chopped

2 celery stalks, chopped

2 tablespoons ripe olives, chopped

1 tablespoon prepared mustard

⅓ cup lite mayonnaise or mayonnaise-like dressing

½ teaspoon garlic or onion powder

½ teaspoon ground black pepper

⅛ teaspoon ground cumin (optional)

▸ While potatoes are still warm, cut into cubes and place in a large bowl. Mix in pickle relish; cover and refrigerate 15 minutes to allow the flavor of the relish to permeate the potatoes.

▸ Add remaining ingredients to the potato mixture. If salad seems a little dry and needs a little extra dressing, add several tablespoons of plain yogurt. Cover and refrigerate 2 to 3 hours to allow flavors to blend.

NUTRITIONAL INFO PER SERVING: Calories 121mg, Fat 2mg (Saturated Fat 0mg), Cholesterol 0mg, Carbohydrates 23mg (Fiber 2mg, Sugar 2mg), Sodium 95mg

COMMENTS:

1 *To bake potatoes, prick in several places, wrap in aluminum foil and bake in a preheated oven at 425ºF (220ºC) for 60 minutes. Let cool completely before cutting into cubes. For added flavor and color, do not remove the skins.*

FOOD NOTE

ABOUT POTATOES

Potatoes are one of the most versatile and popular vegetables. They are high in potassium (nearly twice as much as a banana), have no fat, and very little sodium.

Varieties: There are more than 100 kinds of potatoes, the most common supermarket varieties are:

Russet – the most popular potato; high in starch and cooks up light and fluffly; best for baking, mashing, roasting, and frying

White – good all-purpose potato, available in both round and long varieties, has medium starch and creamy flavor; hold their shape when cooked; use in most potato dishes

Red – low-starch potato; has a firm texture; best in salads, roasting, steaming, or boiling (not recommended for mashing, may become sticky and gummy)

Yellow-fleshed – good all-purpose potato; most common variety is Yukon Gold; creamy texture; use in most potato dishes

Blue or purple – medium starch potato with a nutty taste that is not as flavorful as other varieties; adds color to any potato dish

Storage: Will keep for several weeks in a cool (45ºF to 50ºF), dark place. Do not store below 40ºF (such as the refrigerator) or the starch will turn into sugar, changing the flavor. Avoid prolonged exposure to light, as potatoes will turn green and can be toxic. *NOTE: Green potatoes can be eaten, just cut away the green areas.*

TOTAL SODIUM AND FAT PER INGREDIENT

Sodium:
4 russet potatoes - 55mg
1 sweet onion - 9mg
2 celery stalks - 64mg
2 T ripe olives - 146mg
2 T pickle relish - 150mg
1 T mustard - 168mg
⅓ c lite mayonnaise - 360mg

Fat (Sat Fat):
4 russet potatoes - 1mg (0mg)
2 T ripe olives - 2mg (0mg)
⅓ c lite mayonnaise - 18mg (0mg)

GERMAN POTATO SALAD

Sodium Per Serving – 44mg   Serves 10

This classic is a nice alternative to mayo-based potato salads. It gets even better over time, so make it a day ahead and let the flavors blend.

6 slices lower-sodium bacon, cooked, reserving 1 tablespoon drippings[1]

Salad:

6–8 red potatoes (about 2½ pounds), cooked and cubed, do not remove skins[2]

½ cup chopped sweet onion

½ red bell pepper, chopped

2 tablespoons chopped fresh flat-leaf (Italian) parsley

Dressing:

⅓ cup red wine or cider vinegar

2 tablespoons sugar substitute or sugar

¼ teaspoon garlic or onion powder

¼ teaspoon ground marjoram

¼ teaspoon mustard powder

⅛ teaspoon ground black pepper

⅛ teaspoon ground thyme

▸ *For the salad:* In a large bowl, combine bacon, potatoes, onion, bell pepper, and parsley.

▸ *For the Dressing:* Blend together 1 tablespoon reserved bacon drippings, vinegar, sweetener, garlic powder, marjoram, mustard powder, pepper, and thyme, either by whisking in a small bowl or by shaking well in a screw-top jar.

▸ Pour dressing over potatoes, mixing well. Cover and refrigerate at least 2 to 3 hours or overnight to let flavors blend.

NUTRITIONAL INFO PER SERVING: Calories 121mg, Fat 2mg (Saturated Fat 1mg), Cholesterol 3mg, Carbohydrates 22mg (Fiber 3mg, Sugar 3mg), Sodium 44mg

---

VARIATION

WARM POTATO SALAD

Remove all but 1 tablespoon bacon drippings from the skillet, add dressing ingredients (vinegar through thyme). Cook over medium heat until hot; pour over potato mixture and mix carefully. Serve at once.

NUTRITIONAL INFO PER SERVING: Calories 121mg, Fat 2mg (Saturated Fat 1mg), Cholesterol 3mg, Carbohydrates 22mg (Fiber 3mg, Sugar 3mg), Sodium 44mg

THREE-LAYER MOLDED SALAD

Sodium Per Serving – 65mg   Serves 10–12

This festive red, white, and green salad is perfect during the holidays. Substitute other flavors for a change of pace and instead of cranberries, use berries or other fruit. The cream cheese layer is rich-tasting, making this an extra special salad. Allow plenty of preparation time, as each gelatin layer needs several hours of refrigeration in order to set up.

1 (3-ounce) package lime-flavored gelatin mix	2 cups cranberries, chopped
1 cup chopped celery	1 orange, peeled and cut into bite-sized pieces
½ cup (4 ounces) whipped cream cheese[1]	3–4 tablespoons sugar substitute or sugar[2]
½ cup frozen lowfat whipped topping, thawed	¼ cup unsalted walnuts (optional)[3]
1 teaspoon vanilla extract	
1 (3-ounce) package raspberry or cherry-flavored gelatin mix	

▷ Prepare lime gelatin per package directions; stir in celery and pour into a gelatin mold. Cover and refrigerate until gelatin has set.

▷ Mix together cream cheese, whipped topping, and vanilla. Spread over the set-up lime gelatin. Cover and refrigerate until cream cheese has set.

▷ Prepare raspberry gelatin per package directions; stir in cranberries, orange, sweetener, and walnuts. Cover and refrigerate 30 minutes; pour onto cream cheese layer. Cover and refrigerate for several hours until set; unmold and serve.

NUTRITIONAL INFO PER SERVING: Calories 98mg, Fat 6mg (Saturated Fat 3mg), Cholesterol 8mg, Carbohydrates 7mg (Fiber 2mg, Sugar 3mg), Sodium 65mg

COMMENTS:

1 *Whipped cream cheese is simply cheese that has been whipped with air. Its texture is less firm and has less volume than regular cream cheese.*

2 *Because sugar substitutes differ from sugar in sweetness, the amount needed depends on the sweetener used:*

Splenda or sugar - ¼ cup
Fructose - 3 tablespoons
For additional information, see Sweeteners, *page 37.*

3 *Eliminating the walnuts reduces the fat per serving to 3mg and the saturated fat to 2mg.*

TOTAL SODIUM AND FAT PER INGREDIENT

Sodium:
3 oz lime gelatin - 150mg
1 c celery - 96mg
4 oz whipped cream cheese - 260mg
3 oz raspberry gelatin - 138mg
2 c cranberries - 4mg
1 orange - 1mg
¼ c NSA walnuts - 2mg

Fat (Sat Fat):
½ c LF whipped topping - 4mg (4mg)
4 oz whipped cream cheese - 28mg (18mg)
¼ c NSA walnuts - 32mg (3mg)

FRUIT SALAD WITH VANILLA YOGURT

Sodium Per Serving – 17mg   Serves 8

This is a favorite fruit salad; any mixture of fresh fruit works well. We love to eat it the next day for breakfast with warm muffins . . . yum!

- 2 apples, cubed
- 1 small bunch (1 cup) red seedless grapes
- 1 orange, peeled and cut into bite-sized chunks
- 2 plums, cut into bite-sized chunks
- 1 pear, cubed
- 1 cup fresh blueberries or strawberries
- 1 (10-ounce) can mandarin oranges, drained
- ½ cup nonfat or lowfat vanilla yogurt
- ¼ cup unsalted walnuts (optional)[1]

▸ In a large bowl, combine apples, grapes, orange, plums, pear, blueberries, and mandarin oranges. Stir in yogurt until fruit is well coated. Add walnuts and serve.

NUTRITIONAL INFO PER SERVING: Calories 145mg, Fat 5mg (Saturated Fat 1mg), Cholesterol 1mg, Carbohydrates 24mg (Fiber 4mg, Sugar 16mg), Sodium 17mg

---

VARIATION

GRAND MARNIER FRUIT SALAD

Instead of vanilla yogurt, combine 2–3 tablespoons Grand Marnier or Triple Sec, 1 tablespoon sugar substitute (or sugar), and 4 tablespoons orange juice; blend into the fruit and refrigerate an hour or more before serving.

NUTRITIONAL INFO PER SERVING: Calories 152mg, Fat 5mg (Saturated Fat 0mg), Cholesterol 0mg, Carbohydrates 25mg (Fiber 4mg, Sugar 17mg), Sodium 7mg

---

TOTAL SODIUM AND FAT PER INGREDIENT
Sodium:
2 apples - 2mg
1 c grapes - 3mg
1 orange - 1mg
1 pear - 2mg
1 c blueberries - 1mg
10 oz mandarin oranges - 40mg
½ c LF vanilla yogurt - 86mg
¼ c walnuts - 2mg
Fat (Sat Fat):
2 plums - 1mg (0mg)
½ c LF vanilla yogurt - 2mg (1mg)
¼ c walnuts - 37mg (3mg)

MEDITERRANEAN PASTA SALAD

Sodium Per Serving – 56mg   Serves 8

For a healthier version, use whole wheat pasta. The flavor gets even better after marinating in the dressing for several hours.

12 ounces (about 3 cups) macaroni or penne pasta, cooked per package directions[1]

1 red bell pepper, chopped

½ cup oil-packed sun-dried tomatoes, drained and chopped

1 (15-ounce) can no-salt-added whole corn, drained[2]

2 tablespoons chopped black olives

1 carrot, chopped

½ sweet onion, chopped

4 ounces no-salt-added Swiss cheese, cubed

Dressing:

3 tablespoons extra virgin olive oil

3 tablespoons red wine vinegar

2 tablespoons reduced fat grated parmesan cheese

2 tablespoons chopped fresh basil

½ teaspoons garlic powder or onion powder

½ teaspoon dried oregano

¼ teaspoon ground black pepper

▸ Mix together cooked pasta with the bell pepper, tomato, corn, olives, carrot, onion and Swiss cheese.

▸ Blend together dressing ingredients either by processing in a blender or shaking well in a screw-top jar. Pour over pasta and mix well. Cover and refrigerate an hour or more; serve chilled or at room temperature.

NUTRITIONAL INFO PER SERVING: Calories 310mg, Fat 12mg (Saturated Fat 4mg), Cholesterol 13mg, Carbohydrates 41mg (Fiber 3mg, Sugar 6mg), Sodium 65mg

NOTES:

1 *When cooking pasta, there is no need to add salt to the water. If you want additional flavor, stir 1–2 teaspoons low-salt chicken bouillon granules into the cooking water.*

2 *Frozen corn (1 cup) or fresh kernels cut from from 2 ears of corn may be substituted.*

TOTAL SODIUM AND FAT PER INGREDIENT

Sodium:
12 oz macaroni - 24mg
1 red pepper - 2mg
½ c sun-dried tomato - 80mg
15 oz NSA whole corn - 30mg
2 T ripe olives - 146mg
1 carrot - 42mg
½ onion - 6mg
4 oz NSA Swiss cheese - 40mg
2 T Parmesan cheese - 150mg

Fat (Sat Fat):
12 oz macaroni - 5mg (1mg)
½ c dried tomato - 8mg (1mg)
15 oz NSA corn - 3mg (0mg)
2 T ripe olives - 2mg (0mg)
4 oz NSA Swiss - 32mg (20mg)
3 T olive oil - 42mg (6mg)
2 T Parmesan - 2mg (0mg)

COMMENTS:

1 For variety, instead of or in addition to the corn, add half of a chopped apple or red seedless grapes.

2 Although high in sodium, the strong flavor of blue cheese allows a little to go a long way. There are many blue cheese varieties and the amount of sodium varies with the type and brand of cheese. Stilton has the least, averaging 220mg per ounce and Roquefort, the most at 513mg. See COMMENTS #3, page 74, for other varieties and sodium amounts.

FAVORITE TOSSED SALAD

Sodium Per Serving – 71mg   Serves 6

This is the tossed salad we serve most often in our family. For the dressing, I particularly like using a slightly sweet vinaigrette, but any dressing of your choice may be used.

1 head romaine lettuce, torn into bite-sized pieces, or 5 cups mixed greens

½ small sweet onion, thinly sliced

½ red bell pepper, sliced

½ cucumber, sliced

½ cup no-salt added corn[1]

1 large tomato, cut into bite-sized pieces

1 ounce Stilton cheese, crumbled (about ¼ cup) (optional)[2]

THE BEST VINAIGRETTE *(page 92)*

▸   In a large bowl, mix together all ingredients, tossing well. Add freshly ground black pepper to taste and serve.

NUTRITIONAL INFO PER SERVING (WITHOUT DRESSING): Calories 79mg, Fat 3mg (Saturated Fat 1mg), Cholesterol 8mg, Carbohydrates 10mg (Fiber 3mg, Sugar 6mg), Sodium 71mg

---

VARIATION

CHICKEN, ROMAINE AND STILTON SALAD

For a main course salad for 4, add 12 ounces cooked chicken (cut into bite-size pieces) and increase the romaine to 1½ heads (or about 8 cups).

NUTRITIONAL INFO PER SERVING (WITHOUT DRESSING): Calories 173mg, Fat 3mg (Saturated Fat 2mg), Cholesterol 57mg, Carbohydrates 12mg (Fiber 4mg, Sugar 7mg), Sodium 121mg

---

TOTAL SODIUM AND FAT PER INGREDIENT

Sodium:
  1 head romaine - 22mg
    or 5 c mixed greens - 25mg
  ½ sweet onion - 5mg
  ½ red bell pepper - 1mg
  ½ cucumber - 2mg
  ½ 15-oz can NSA corn - 15mg
  1 tomato - 6mg
  1 oz Stilton cheese - 220mg
Fat (Sat Fat):
  1 head romaine - 1mg (0mg)
    or 5 c mixed greens - 0mg
  ½ 15-oz can NSA corn - 1mg (0mg)
  1 oz Stilton cheese - 9mg (5mg)

MACHE, PEAR AND TOASTED WALNUT SALAD

Sodium Per Serving – 85mg
Serves 6

The combination of flavors in this traditional dish is lovely. If unable to find mâche, substitute mixed greens. This also makes a nice luncheon salad, serving 3 or 4.

- 1 (5-ounce) package mâche or mixed greens (about 8 cups)[1]
- 2 pears (such as Anjou, Bartlett, or Bosc), cored and sliced lengthwise
- 2 ounces Stilton cheese, crumbled (about ½ cup)[2]
- ¼ sweet onion, thinly sliced
- ½ cup walnuts, toasted and chopped[3]
- ½ cup FRENCH DRESSING (page 92)

▷ Toss mâche with the onions and half the vinaigrette; place on individual plates. Equally divide pear slices and place on top; sprinkle with Stilton and walnuts. Drizzle remaining vinaigrette on top and serve.

NUTRITIONAL INFO PER SERVING (WITHOUT DRESSING): Calories 112mg, Fat 6mg (Saturated Fat 2mg), Cholesterol 10mg, Carbohydrates 11mg (Fiber 3mg, Sugar 7mg), Sodium 85mg

---

VARIATION

SPINACH, PEAR AND WALNUT SALAD

Substitute a 6-ounce package baby spinach (about 8 cups) for the mâche.

NUTRITIONAL INFO PER SERVING (WITHOUT DRESSING): Calories 112mg, Fat 9mg (Saturated Fat 4mg), Cholesterol 20mg, Carbohydrates 10mg (Fiber 2mg, Sugar 6mg), Sodium 148mg

---

COMMENTS:

1 *Mâche (pronounced MOSH), also known as lamb's lettuce, field salad, or corn salad, has a mild buttery flavor and is available in many larger supermarkets.*

2 *See* COMMENTS #2, *page 74, for amount of sodium in blue cheese varieties.*

3 *Chopped, toasted pecans are also nice with this salad.*

TOTAL SODIUM AND FAT PER INGREDIENT

Sodium:
  8 c mâche - 60mg
    or 8 cups mixed greens - 40mg
  2 c peas - 3mg
  2 oz Stilton - 440mg
  ¼ onion - 4mg
Fat (Sat Fat):
  2 oz Stilton - 18mg (10mg)
  ½ c walnuts - 19mg (2mg)

MIXED GREENS WITH AVOCADO AND ORANGE

Sodium Per Serving – 20mg   Serves 6

This colorful tossed salad with avocado, mandarin oranges, and dried cranberries is not only festive, but also very tasty.

1 (10-ounce) package mixed greens, or ½ head red-leaf and ½ head green-leaf lettuce (about 9 cups)[1]

1 large avocado (preferably Hass), peeled and sliced

½ sweet onion (such as Vidalia), sliced

1 (12-ounce) can mandarin oranges, drained[2]

2 tablespoons dried cranberries or cherries

ORANGE VINAIGRETTE *(page 91)*

▸ In a large bowl, mix together all ingredients, tossing well. Add freshly ground black pepper to taste and serve.

NUTRITIONAL INFO PER SERVING (WITHOUT DRESSING): Calories 134mg, Fat 8mg (Saturated Fat 1mg), Cholesterol 0mg, Carbohydrates 17mg (Fiber 6mg, Sugar 7mg), Sodium 20mg

---

FOOD NOTE

VARIETIES OF LETTUCE AND OTHER SALAD GREENS

There are dozens of lettuce varieties and most supermarkets carry anywhere from 4 to 12 different kinds. As far as nutrition, iceberg is the least nutritious; just about any other lettuce, particularly varieties with darker green leaves, is a better choice. There are 4 basic types of lettuce:

Butterhead – includes *Boston* and *Bibb* lettuces, both have a mild, buttery flavor, but Bibb is more flavorful

Iceberg – the crispest of all lettuces, keeps well in the refrigerator (up to 2 weeks)

Looseleaf (such as Oakleaf, red and green leaf) – mild flavored with smooth or ruffled, green or red-edged leaves

Romaine (cos) – crunchy and flavorful, used most often in Caesar salads

Other salad greens, each with their own distinct flavor, also provide added color and texture:

Arugula – has a peppery, slightly bitter taste

Belgian endive (French endive) – has a slightly bitter taste, turns bitter when exposed to light

Curly endive (chicory) – generally has a slightly bitter flavor (use young inner leaves for salads)

Escarole – has a slightly bitter flavor, but milder than Belgian or curly endive (use young inner leaves for salads)

Mâche (prounounced mosh, also known as lamb's lettuce, field salad, corn salad) – has a mild buttery flavor

Radicchio – has a slightly bitter taste, similar to Belgian endive; the purplish red and white leaves add lots of color to salads

Spinach – has a slightly bitter flavor, baby spinach is particularly good in salads

Watercress – has a peppery, mustard-like flavor

NOTE: Mesclun is not a type of lettuce, but a mixture of baby greens. There are many different combinations and often include arugula, fresee, mâche, mizuni, oakleaf, radicchio, and baby spinach.

MESCLUN WITH STILTON AND SUGARED PECANS

Sodium Per Serving – 85mg   Serves 6

Mesclun is nothing more than a mixture of baby greens, add sugared pecans and you have a restaurant quality salad. This also is a great luncheon main course, serving 3 or 4.

1 (10-ounce) package mesclun or mixed field greens (about 8 cups)[1]

¼ small sweet onion, thinly sliced

2 cups red, seedless grapes

THE BEST VINAIGRETTE *(page 92)*

2 ounces Stilton blue cheese, crumbled (about ½ cup)[2]

¼ cup sugared chopped pecans *(see FOOD NOTE, page 88)*

▸ In a large bowl, mix together the mesclun, onion, grapes, and vinaigrette, tossing well. Divide and place on individual plates. Sprinkle with cheese and pecans; add freshly ground black pepper to taste and serve.

NUTRITIONAL INFO PER SERVING (WITHOUT DRESSING): Calories 116mg, Fat 6mg (Saturated Fat 2mg), Cholesterol 10mg, Carbohydrates 12mg (Fiber 2mg, Sugar 9mg), Sodium 85mg

SPINACH, DRIED CRANBERRIES AND CHEVRE

Sodium Per Serving – 49mg   Serves 6

The sweetness of the cranberries and the tart cheese go together beautifully in this tasty salad.

1 (10-ounce) packaged baby spinach (about 8 cups)

¼ small sweet onion, thinly sliced

½ cup dried cranberries

RASPBERRY VINAIGRETTE *(page 92)*

2 ounces Chèvre (goat cheese) (about ½ cup)[3]

¼ cup walnuts, chopped and toasted[4]

▸ In a large bowl, mix together the spinach, onion, cranberries, and vinaigrette, tossing well. Divide and place on individual plates. Sprinkle with cheese and walnuts; add freshly ground black pepper to taste and serve.

NUTRITIONAL INFO PER SERVING (WITHOUT DRESSING): Calories 116mg, Fat 6mg (Saturated Fat 0mg), Cholesterol 4mg, Carbohydrates 12mg (Fiber 2mg, Sugar 7mg), Sodium 49mg

---

COMMENTS:

1 *Mesclun is a mixture of baby greens. Use any lettuce combination of your choice, see FOOD NOTE, page 84, for info on lettuce varieties.*

2 *Although high in sodium, the strong flavor of blue cheese allows a little to go a long way. There are many blue cheese varieties and the amount of sodium varies with the type and brand of cheese. Stilton has the least, averaging 220mg per ounce and Roquefort, the most at 513mg. See COMMENTS #3, page 74, for varieties and sodium amounts.*

3 *Chèvre has a tart flavor with about 50mg sodium per ounce. It will keep up to 2 weeks in the refrigerator, after that it becomes sour.*
    Stilton blue cheese may be used instead.

4 *See COOKING TIP, page 90, for several ways of toasting nuts.*

TOTAL SODIUM AND FAT PER INGREDIENT

Mesclun w/Stilton and Pecans:
Sodium:
  8 c mixed greens - 60mg
  ¼ sweet onion - 2mg
  2 c grapes - 6mg
  2 oz stilton cheese - 440mg
Fat (Sat Fat):
  ¼ c pecans - 26mg (2mg)
  2 oz stilton cheese - 18mg (10mg)

Spinach, Cranberries and Chèvre:
Sodium:
  8 c spinach - 190mg
  ¼ sweet onion - 2mg
  ½ c dried cranberries - 1mg
  2 oz Chèvre cheese - 100mg
Fat (Sat Fat):
  8 c spinach - 1mg (0mg)
  ½ c dried cranberries - 1mg (0mg)
  2 oz Chèvre cheese - 12mg (0mg)
  ¼ c walnuts - 19mg (2mg)

CAESAR SALAD

Sodium Per Serving – 102mg   Serves 6 (2 as a main dish)

This classic salad has been lightened up in both fat and sodium. Add cooked chicken or shrimp for a scrumptous main course.

1 head romaine (about 1 pound), torn into bite-size pieces

2 cups HERBED GARLIC CROUTONS (page 228)

CAESAR DRESSING *(recipe follows)*

¼ cup reduced-fat Parmesan cheese[1]

Freshly ground pepper

▶ Mix lettuce and CAESAR DRESSING together in a large bowl; add croutons and toss until well mixed. Divide onto six plates, sprinkle with Parmesan and top with freshly ground pepper.

NUTRITIONAL INFO PER SERVING: Calories 256mg, Fat 20mg (Saturated Fat 4mg), Cholesterol 1mg, Carbohydrates 12mg (Fiber 2mg, Sugar 1mg), Sodium 102mg

VARIATION

CHICKEN CAESAR

For a main course for 4, add 12 ounces cooked and sliced chicken breast (such as grilled chicken or **FRIED CHICKEN** *(page 96)* to the salad above.

NUTRITIONAL INFO PER SERVING: Calories 381mg, Fat 21mg (Saturated Fat 4mg), Cholesterol 50mg, Carbohydrates 17mg (Fiber 2mg, Sugar 2mg), Sodium 192mg

CAESAR DRESSING

Sodium Per Serving – 11mg   Makes ⅓ cup (6 servings)

This classic dressing is made without raw eggs and anchovies. It is delicious on most any tossed salad.

3 tablespoons extra-virgin olive oil

1 tablespoon red or white wine vinegar

1 tablespoon fresh lemon juice

½ teaspoon Dijon-style mustard

Dash low-salt Worcestershire sauce[2]

1 garlic clove, finely minced

1 tablespoon finely minced shallot (optional)[3]

▶ Blend together all ingredients, either by whisking in a small bowl or by shaking well in a screw-top jar. Pour over salad and toss.

NUTRITIONAL INFO PER SERVING: Calories 64mg, Fat 7mg (Saturated Fat 1mg), Cholesterol 0mg, Carbohydrates 1mg (Fiber 0mg, Sugar 0mg), Sodium 11mg

SPINACH SALAD WITH WARM BACON DRESSING

Sodium Per Serving – 140mg   Serves 4

The delicious salad is ready in less than 15 minutes. Using lower-sodium bacon creates a reduced-salt dish that is a perfect starter for that special dinner.

1 (6-ounce) package baby spinach (about 8 cups)

½ sweet onion (such as Vidalia), thinly sliced

WARM BACON DRESSING *(recipe follows)*

⅛ teaspoon ground black pepper

2 medium hard-boiled eggs, chopped

▶ In a large bowl, gently toss the spinach with the onion and **WARM BACON DRESSING** until the spinach begins to wilt. Season with pepper and sprinkle with egg and reserved bacon from **WARM BACON DRESSING.**

NUTRITIONAL INFO PER SERVING: Calories 88mg, Fat 5mg (Saturated Fat 2mg), Cholesterol 98mg, Carbohydrates 3mg (Fiber 1mg, Sugar 1mg), Sodium 140mg

COMMENTS:

1 *There are several lower-sodium bacon brands available. See* FOOD NOTE, *page 76, for more information.*

WARM BACON DRESSING

Sodium Per Serving – 60mg   Serves 4

In addition to spinach salad, serve this tasty dressing over asparagus or green beans.

4 slices lower-sodium bacon[1]

3 tablespoons apple cider vinegar

1 teaspoon sugar substitute or sugar

▶ In a large skillet over medium-high heat, fry bacon until crisp on both sides, about 5 minutes. Remove bacon and drain on paper towels; let cool until able to handle. Crumble and set aside.

▶ Remove all but 3 tablespoons bacon fat from skillet (if necessary, add enough olive oil to equal 3 tablespoons). Mix in vinegar and sugar; stirring constantly, scrape up any browned bits of bacon. While still warm, pour over spinach or vegetables; sprinkle with bacon.

NUTRITIONAL INFO PER SERVING: Calories 37mg, Fat 3mg (Saturated Fat 1mg), Cholesterol 5mg, Carbohydrates 0mg (Fiber 0mg, Sugar 0mg), Sodium 60mg

TOTAL SODIUM AND FAT PER INGREDIENT

Spinach Salad:
Sodium:
 6 oz spinach - 190mg
 2 med eggs - 124mg
 ¼ sweet onion - 4mg
Fat (Sat Fat):
 6 oz spinach - 1mg (0mg)
 2 med eggs - 8mg (2mg)

Warm Bacon Dressing:
Sodium:
 4 sl LS bacon - 240mg
Fat (Sat Fat):
 2 sl LS bacon - 12mg (4mg)

COMMENTS:

1 Jicama is a large brown-skinned tuber that can weigh up to 5 pounds. The white meat has a mildly sweet flavor and is very crisp and crunchy, much like water chestnuts. It is good both raw and cooked and should be peeled before using. Available most of the year in many supermarkets; it will keep up to 2 weeks in the refrigerator.

2 Toasting the nuts intensifies their flavor (see FOOD NOTE, page 90, for toasting methods).

3 For a delicious chicken, see FRIED CHICKEN, *page 96.*

4 Use tart or semi-tart apples, such as Granny Smith or Braeburn.

AVOCADO, APPLE, DATES AND JICAMA SALAD

Sodium Per Serving – 36mg   Serves 4

My pal, Sally, loves this delicious salad. Although high in fat, the majority comes from the avocados and almonds, which contain monounsaturated fats (considered "good" fats, as they lower LDL, which is the bad cholesterol).

4 avocados, cubed

4 apples, diced

2 celery stalks, sliced

1 medium jicama, peeled and cubed (about 2 cups)[1]

12 date halves, pitted and chopped

½ cup sliced almonds, toasted[2]

12 lettuce leaves, such as romaine

ORANGE VINAIGRETTE *(page 91)*

▷ In a large bowl, gently mix the avocados, apples, celery, dates, jicama, and almonds; mix in ORANGE VINAIGRETTE.

▷ Place several lettuce leaves on a plate and top with one-fourth salad.

NUTRITIONAL INFO PER SERVING (WITHOUT DRESSING): Calories 625mg, Fat 44mg (Saturated Fat 5mg), Cholesterol 0mg, Carbohydrates 58mg (Fiber 26mg, Sugar 26mg), Sodium 36mg

---

TOTAL SODIUM AND FAT PER INGREDIENT

Avocado, Apple, Dates & Jicama:
Sodium:
4 avocados - 56mg
4 apples - 4mg
2 celery stalks - 64mg
1 jicama - 10mg
12 lettuce leaves - 10mg
Fat (Sat Fat):
4 avocados - 118mg (17mg)
½ c almonds - 58mg (4mg)

Chicken, Apple & Pecan Salad:
Sodium:
12 oz chicken breasts - 219mg
1 head romaine - 22mg
2 apples - 2mg
4 oz NSA Swiss cheese - 40mg
Fat (Sat Fat):
12 oz chicken - 3mg (0mg)
1 head romaine - 1mg (0mg)
4 oz NSA Swiss - 32mg (20mg)
½ c pecans - 40mg (4mg)

CHICKEN, APPLE AND PECAN TOSSED SALAD

Sodium Per Serving – 47mg   **Serves 4**

Add a freshly-baked LEMON CURRANT SCONE *(page 224) and you have a delicious main course meal.*

12 ounces cooked chicken breast, cubed (about 3 cups)[3]

1 head romaine lettuce, torn into bite-size pieces (about 8 cups)

2 apples, cored and cut into bite-size pieces[4]

½ cup POPPY SEED DRESSING *(page 91)*

4 ounces no-salt-added Swiss cheese, shredded (about 1 cup)

½ cup chopped pecans, toasted[2]

Freshly ground black pepper

▷ In a large bowl, combine chicken, romaine, and apples. Mix in dressing; tossing well. Divide salad onto 6 plates and sprinkle with cheese, pecans, and freshly ground black pepper; serve.

NUTRITIONAL INFO PER SERVING (WITHOUT DRESSING): Calories 223mg, Fat 13mg (Saturated Fat 4mg), Cholesterol 49mg, Carbohydrates 10mg (Fiber 3mg, Sugar 6mg), Sodium 47mg

COBB SALAD

Sodium Per Serving – 186mg   Serves 4

The Cobb Salad, created in the 1930's by Bob Cobb, then owner of the Brown Derby in Hollywood, is arguably one of the most famous American dishes. Many chefs still abide by the original ingredients, although just about anything works. To be a true cobb, however, it must contain several veggies (such as avocado and tomatoes), cheese, and a protein (like poultry, fish, beef, or eggs). Generally, the presentation is what makes a cobb salad unique—all ingredients are placed in single rows on the plate (it also is quite acceptable to toss the salad and then serve it). Prepare and chill the cooked ingredients before making the salad.

6–8 cups mixed greens[1]

12 ounces cooked chicken breast, cubed (about 3 cups)[2]

16 cherry tomatoes, cut in half, or 2 large tomatoes, chopped

16 cooked asparagus spears

1 avocado, cubed or sliced

4 ounces no-salt-added Swiss cheese, cubed (about ¾ cup)[3]

4 slices lower-salt bacon, crispy-cooked and crumbled[4]

2 medium hard-boiled eggs, chopped

2 tablespoons chopped chives, or 2 green onions, chopped (green part only)

½ cup THE BEST VINAIGRETTE (*page 92*) or FRENCH DRESSING (*page 92*)

▶ Evenly divide all ingredients, beginning with the mixed greens. Starting in the middle, place chicken in a row on top of the greens; working out to both sides, arrange the tomato and asparagus on one side, and the avocado and cheese on the other.

▶ Sprinkle each salad with bacon, eggs, and chives; drizzle with dressing (or serve the dressing on the side, so each guest can add their own.)

NUTRITIONAL INFO PER SERVING (WITHOUT DRESSING): Calories 381mg, Fat 22mg (Saturated Fat 8mg), Cholesterol 172mg, Carbohydrates 13mg (Fiber 7mg, Sugar 4mg), Sodium 186mg

COMMENTS:

1 *The original cobb had a mixture of romaine, bibb lettuce, watercress, and chicory; however, any combination of greens may be used.*

2 *For a delicious cooked chicken, see* FRIED CHICKEN, *page 96.*

3 *A lower-salt goat cheese, such as Chèvre and Montrachet, may also be substituted. Select brands with 50mg or less per ounce.*

4 *See* FOOD NOTE, *page76, for low-salt manufacturers or* RESOURCES, *page 272, for online grocers carrying low-salt bacon.*

TOTAL SODIUM AND FAT PER INGREDIENT

Sodium:
6 c mixed greens - 60mg
12 oz chicken breast - 219mg
16 cherry tomatoes - 14mg
  or 2 lrg tomatoes - 18mg
16 asparagus - 34mg
1 avocado - 14mg
4 oz NSA Swiss cheese - 40mg
4 sl LS bacon - 240mg
2 med eggs - 124mg

Fat (Sat Fat):
12 oz chicken breast - 4mg (1mg)
16 cherry tomatoes - 1mg (0mg)
  or 2 lrg tomatoes - 1mg (0mg)
16 asparagus - 1mg (0mg)
1 avocado - 30mg (4mg)
4 oz NSA Swiss -32mg (20mg)
4 sl LS bacon - 12mg (4mg)
2 med eggs - 8mg (2mg)

CURRIED TURKEY WALDORF

Sodium Per Serving – 131mg   **Serves 4**

Here's a salad that's full of flavor and combines turkey with fruit, nuts, and curry. This also makes a delicious filling for pita sandwiches or wraps. Allow 2 hours for the flavors to intensify before serving.

Dressing:
- ⅔ **cup lowfat plain yogurt**
- ¼ **cup lite mayonnaise or mayonnaise-like dressing**
- **1 tablespoon curry powder**
- **1 tablespoon fresh lime juice**
- **1 teaspoon sugar substitute or sugar**
- ½ **teaspoon grated gingerroot**
- ¼ **teaspoon onion powder**
- ⅛ **teaspoon ground black pepper**

Salad:
- **4 cups cubed cooked turkey (about 21 ounces)[1]**
- **2 apples (such as Braeburn, Fuji, or Gala), cubed**
- **4–5 green onions, chopped (about 1 cup)**
- **1 celery stalk, chopped**
- ½ **cup raisins**
- ½ **cup almonds, toasted and chopped[2]**
- **Lettuce leaves**

▶ *For the dressing:* Mix together yogurt, mayonnaise, curry, lime juice, sweetener, gingerroot, onion powder, and black pepper.

▶ *For the salad:* In a large bowl, mix together turkey, apples, onions, celery, and raisins; pour dressing over and mix well. Cover and refrigerate 2 hours or overnight. Add almonds and serve on lettuce leaves.

NUTRITIONAL INFO PER SERVING: Calories 374mg, Fat 16mg (Saturated Fat 2mg), Cholesterol 66mg, Carbohydrates 20mg (Fiber 5mg, Sugar 16mg), Sodium 131mg

TOTAL SODIUM AND FAT PER INGREDIENT

Sodium:
⅔ c LF yogurt - 115mg
¼ c lite mayonnaise - 240mg
1 T curry - 3mg
4 c turkey - 358mg
2 apples - 3mg
1 c green onions - 16mg
1 celery stalk - 32mg
½ c raisins - 8mg
Fat (Sat Fat):
⅔ c LF yogurt - 3mg (1mg)
¼ c lite mayo - 12mg (0mg)
1 T curry - 1mg (0mg)
4 c turkey - 18mg (6mg)
½ c almonds - 60mg (4mg)

COOKING TIP

TOASTING NUTS

Toasting intensifies the flavor of nuts; the amount of time it takes varies with the type and size of nuts. For instance, chopped nuts cook faster than whole. There are three common ways to toast nuts:

Oven/toaster oven – spread nuts on a baking sheet and bake in a preheated oven at 350ºF (180ºC) until they start to brown, 5 to 10 minutes. Watch carefully, as they can quickly burn—once you smell them, take them out.

Stove-top – spread nuts in a dry skillet. Cook over medium-low heat, stirring or shaking frequently, until they start to turn golden, 5 to 7 minutes.

Microwave – Spread nuts in one layer on microwave-safe plate. Microwave on high 1 minute; stir. Continue microwaving in 30 second intervals, until nuts are fragrant and golden. *NOTE: Nuts will continue to darken after they are removed.*

Sugared Nuts: Follow stove-top method above. Remove from heat and sprinkle with sugar (1 teaspoon per ¼ cup nuts) and a dash of cayenne pepper (if desired); mix well. Remove from skillet and let cool.

SALAD DRESSINGS

NOTES:
1 *I like to vary this salad by sometimes adding either hot or sweet curry powder, see* FOOD NOTE, *page 198, for curry varieties).*
2 *Because sugar substitutes differ from sugar in sweetness, the amount needed depends on the sweetener used:*
   Splenda or sugar - 1/3 *cup*
   Fructose - 1/4 *cup*
   For additional info, see Sweeteners, *page 37.*

ORANGE VINAIGRETTE

Sodium Per Serving – 12mg   Makes about 1/2 cup

This tangy dressing is a wonderful accompaniment to any salad.

1/4 cup extra-virgin olive oil

2 tablespoons orange juice

2 teaspoons sugar substitute or sugar

1 tablespoon lemon or lime juice

1/2 teaspoon Dijon-style mustard

1/2 teaspoon curry powder[1]

1/4 teaspoon paprika

1–2 garlic cloves, finely minced, or 1 teaspoon finely minced shallot

▶ Blend together the oil, orange juice, sweetener, lemon juice, mustard, cumin, paprika, and garlic, either by whisking in a small bowl or by shaking well in a screw-top jar. Will keep for up to a week in a covered container in the refrigerator.

NUTRITIONAL INFO PER 2 TABLESPOONS: Calories 53mg, Fat 5mg (Saturated Fat 1mg), Cholesterol 0mg, Carbohydrates 3mg (Fiber 0mg, Sugar 2mg), Sodium 12mg

POPPY SEED DRESSING

Sodium Per Serving – 0mg   Makes about 1 cup

This sweet dressing is delicious on most salads or mixed with fresh fruit.

1/4–1/3 cup sugar substitute or sugar[2]

3 tablespoons apple cider or red wine vinegar

1 tablespoon lemon juice

1 teaspoon mustard powder

1/4 teaspoon garlic powder

2 tablespoons finely minced onion

1 1/2 teaspoons poppy seeds

1/2 cup extra-virgin olive oil

▶ Place sweetener, vinegar, lemon juice, mustard powder, garlic powder, and onion in a blender. With blender running, slowly add oil until well mixed; stir in poppy seeds. (If mixing by hand, either whisk together ingredients in a small bowl or shake well in a screw-top jar.) Will keep for up to a week in a covered container in the refrigerator.

NUTRITIONAL INFO PER 2 TABLESPOONS: Calories 124mg, Fat 14mg (Saturated Fat 2mg), Cholesterol 0mg, Carbohydrates 1mg (Fiber 0mg, Sugar 0mg), Sodium 0mg

TOTAL SODIUM AND FAT PER INGREDIENT
Orange Vinaigrette:
Sodium:
  1/2 t Dijon mustard - 60mg
Fat (Sat Fat):
  2 T olive oil - 28mg (4mg)

Poppy Seed Dressing:
Sodium:
  2 t onion - 1mg
Fat (Sat Fat):
  1 t dry mustard - 1mg (0mg)
  1/2 c olive oil - 112mg (16mg)

1 White balsamic vinegar is made from white grapes and is combined with white wine vinegar. Although milder and sweeter, it also is not as overpowering in salads as the darker balsamic vinegar.

2 Dijon mustard averages 120mg sodium per teaspoon. There are several brands with less than 70mg per teaspoon, such as Temeraine (7mg) and Westbrae Natural (65mg). See RESOURCES, page 272, for additional information.

3 Bottled roasted minced garlic may also be used and is found in the produce section of most supermarkets.

THE BEST VINAIGRETTE

Sodium Per Serving – 30mg   Serves 6

Everyone loves this easy-to-make dressing. The addition of roasted garlic is the secret ingredient. You can use it on just about any tossed salad.

2 tablespoons white balsamic or red wine vinegar[1]

2 tablespoons extra-virgin olive oil

1 teaspoon Dijon-style mustard[2]

1 teaspoon sugar substitute or sugar

1 garlic clove, finely minced[3]

⅛ teaspoon dried basil or tarragon

▸ Blend together all ingredients, either by whisking in a small bowl or by shaking well in a screw-top jar. Pour over salad and toss.

NUTRITIONAL INFO PER 2 TABLESPOONS: Calories 63mg, Fat 7mg (Saturated Fat 1mg), Cholesterol 0mg, Carbohydrates 0mg (Fiber 0mg, Sugar 0mg), Sodium 30mg

VARIATIONS

FRENCH DRESSING

Omit the sweetener and increase the Dijon-style mustard to 1½ teaspoons.

NUTRITIONAL INFO PER 2 TABLESPOONS: Calories 65mg, Fat 7mg (Saturated Fat 1mg), Cholesterol 0mg, Carbohydrates 0mg (Fiber 0mg, Sugar 0mg), Sodium 75mg

RASPBERRY VINAIGRETTE

Substitute 2 tablespoons raspberry vinegar for the balsamic and ½ teaspoon finely grated orange peel for the garlic; reduce the sweetener to ½ teaspoon.

NUTRITIONAL INFO PER 2 TABLESPOONS: Calories 62mg, Fat 7mg (Saturated Fat 1mg), Cholesterol 0mg, Carbohydrates 0mg (Fiber 0mg, Sugar 0mg), Sodium 30mg

SHALLOT VINAIGRETTE

Omit the garlic and sweetener, add 2 tablespoons finely minced shallots.

NUTRITIONAL INFO PER 2 TABLESPOONS: Calories 66mg, Fat 7mg (Saturated Fat 1mg), Cholesterol 0mg, Carbohydrates 1mg (Fiber 0mg, Sugar 0mg), Sodium 31mg

ROASTED GARLIC DRESSING

Add 1 tablespoon roasted garlic *(see* COOKING TIP, *page 185).*

NUTRITIONAL INFO PER 2 TABLESPOONS: Calories 80mg, Fat 7mg (Saturated Fat 1mg), Cholesterol 0mg, Carbohydrates 4mg (Fiber 0mg, Sugar 0mg), Sodium 32mg

TOTAL SODIUM AND FAT PER INGREDIENT
Sodium:
1 t Dijon mustard - 120mg
½ t roasted garlic - 1mg
Fat (Sat Fat):
2 T olive oil - 28mg (4mg)

RANCH DRESSING

Sodium Per Serving – 39mg   Makes about 1 cup

Once you try this low-fat dressing, you won't use the bottled variety again. Keep refrigerated in a covered container for up to a week. This also makes a great addition to wraps.

⅔ cup lowfat buttermilk

2 tablespoons lite mayonnaise or mayonnaise-type dressing

2 tablespoons lowfat sour cream

1 tablespoon finely chopped fresh flat-leaf (Italian) parsley[1]

1 tablespoon finely chopped basil, or 1 teaspoon dried[1]

1 teaspoon finely minced garlic

1 teaspoon mustard powder

½ teaspoon onion powder

⅛ teaspoon celery seed

⅛ teaspoon ground black pepper

Dash dried thyme or dill weed

▸ Blend together all ingredients, either by whisking in a small bowl or by shaking well in a screw-top jar. Pour desired amount of dressing over salad and toss

NUTRITIONAL INFO PER 2 TABLESPOONS: Calories 25mg, Fat 1mg (Saturated Fat 0mg), Cholesterol 2mg, Carbohydrates 2mg (Fiber 0mg, Sugar 1mg), Sodium 39mg

GREEN GODDESS DRESSING

Sodium Per Serving – 57mg   Makes about 1 cup

This is my low-salt version of this classic dressing. Usually made with anchovies, I've substituted Dijon mustard instead and added an avocado for creaminess.

1 ripe avocado (preferably Hass), peeled, pitted, and quartered

½ cup lowfat sour cream

2 garlic cloves, chopped

1 green onion, chopped

1 tablespoon fresh tarragon, or ½ teaspoon dried

2 tablespoons olive oil

1 tablespoon lemon juice or white balsamic vinegar[2]

1 teaspoon Dijon-style mustard

½ teaspoon low-salt Worcestershire sauce

¼ teaspoon hot pepper sauce, such as *Tabasco*

½ teaspoon garlic powder

⅛ teaspoon ground black pepper

▸ Place all ingredients in a blender or food processor and purée until smooth. Let sit 30 minutes in the refrigerator before serving. Will keep up to 3 days in a covered container in the refrigerator.

NUTRITIONAL INFO PER 2 TABLESPOONS: Calories 193mg, Fat 18mg (Saturated Fat 4mg), Cholesterol 8mg, Carbohydrates 8mg (Fiber 4mg, Sugar 2mg), Sodium 57mg

COMMENTS:

1 *For a change of pace, use fresh dill in place of the parsley and basil.*

2 *For info on white balsamic, see COMMENTS #1, page 92. White wine vinegar may be substituted for the lemon juice or white balsamic.*

TOTAL SODIUM AND FAT PER INGREDIENT

Ranch Dressing:
Sodium:
⅔ c LF buttermilk - 170mg
2 T lite mayonnaise - 120mg
2 T LF sour cream - 17mg
1 T parsley - 2mg
½ t garlic - 1mg
½ t onion powder - 1mg
Fat (Sat Fat):
⅔ c LF buttermilk - 1mg (1mg)
2 T lite mayonnaise - 6mg (0mg)
2 T LF sour cream - 3mg (2mg)
1 t mustard powder - 1mg (0mg)

Green Goddess Dressing:
Sodium:
1 avocado - 14mg
½ c LF sour cream - 68mg
2 garlic cloves - 2mg
1 green onion - 4mg
1 t Dijon mustard - 120mg
½ t LS Worcestershire - 10mg
¼ t hot pepper sauce - 8mg
Fat (Sat Fat):
1 avocado - 30mg (4mg)
2 T olive oil - 28mg (4mg)
½ c LF sour cream - 14mg (8mg)

MAIN COURSES

FRIED CHICKEN

Sodium Per Serving – 77mg   Serves 4

The secret to this delicious chicken is the combination of spices, which I often use as a basic seasoning in many of my recipes.

2 tablespoons all-purpose flour

½ teaspoon dried basil

½ teaspoon garlic powder

¼ teaspoon ground black pepper

¼ teaspoon dried rosemary, crushed

¼ teaspoon dried tarragon

¼ teaspoon dried thyme

4 boneless, skinless chicken breasts or thighs (about 1 pound)[1]

1–2 tablespoons olive oil

▶ Mix together flour, basil, garlic powder, pepper, rosemary, tarragon, and thyme; dredge chicken in flour mixture, shaking off any excess.

▶ Heat oil in a large skillet over medium-high heat; add chicken. Cook until brown on one side, 4 to 5 minutes; turn. Decrease heat to medium-low; cover and cook until chicken is no longer pink, but still moist inside, 15 to 20 minutes.

NUTRITIONAL INFO PER SERVING: Calories 176mg, Fat 5mg (Saturated Fat 1mg), Cholesterol 69mg, Carbohydrates 3mg (Fiber 0mg, Sugar 0mg), Sodium 77mg

---

VARIATION

OVEN-BAKED CHICKEN

Beat together 2 eggs and place in a dish. Instead of flour, substitute ½ cup unsalted or low-salt bread crumbs (*see* COMMENTS #2 *above*) and mix with spices in recipe above. Dip chicken in eggs, then coat with bread crumb mixture. Bake in a preheated oven at 350°F (180°C) for about 20 minutes, or until chicken is no longer pink, but still moist inside.

NUTRITIONAL INFO PER SERVING: Calories 216mg, Fat 6mg (Saturated Fat 1mg), Cholesterol 69mg, Carbohydrates 10mg (Fiber 0mg, Sugar 0mg), Sodium 77mg

FRIED CHICKEN WITH COUNTRY GRAVY

Sodium Per Serving – 78mg   Serves 4

This yummy gravy gets its richness and flavor from sake. Make extra gravy and serve over HERBED BUTTERMILK BISCUITS *(page 223).*

4 servings FRIED CHICKEN *(page 96)*

1–2 tablespoons all-purpose flour

½ cup sake or fortified wine (such as a dry sherry or Madeira)[1]

1 teaspoon low-salt chicken bouillon granules

½ cup water

2 tablespoons lowfat milk

2–3 drops *Kitchen Bouquet* **(optional)**[2]

Optional spices:

⅛ teaspoon dried basil

⅛ teaspoon garlic powder

Pinch ground black pepper

Pinch dried rosemary, crumbled

Pinch dried tarragon

Pinch dried thyme

▷ Cook FRIED CHICKEN per directions, reserving any excess flour for the gravy.

▷ In a small bowl, combine reserved flour and enough additional flour to equal 2 tablespoons. (If there is little reserved flour from dredging the chicken, add the optional spices to the combined flours; mix with sake, stirring until smooth.

▷ In same skillet chicken was cooked, increase heat to medium-high; stir in sake/flour mixture, scraping up any browned bits of chicken.

▷ Mix in bouillon and water; cook, stirring constantly, until sauce thickens to a gravy consistency, 2 to 3 minutes. Stir in 2 tablespoons milk and *Kitchen Bouquet*; serve over chicken.

NUTRITIONAL INFO PER SERVING: Calories 229mg, Fat 5mg (Saturated Fat 1mg), Cholesterol 69mg, Carbohydrates 7mg (Fiber 0mg, Sugar 1mg), Sodium 82mg

(GRAVY ONLY): Calories 53mg, Fat 0mg (Saturated Fat 0mg), Cholesterol 1mg, Carbohydrates 4mg (Fiber 0mg, Sugar 1mg), Sodium 5mg

COMMENTS:

1 *Sake adds a light, rich flavor to this gravy (inexpensive sake is found in most supermarkets). A dry white or fortified wine (see* Fortified Wines, *page 24) may also be used—depending on what you use, imparts a slightly different flavor to the gravy.*

2 Kitchen Bouquet *is a browning and seasoning sauce that was popular in the 1960s and 70s. It is used to lightly brown gravies and add a little punch to bland or mellow sauces. A drop or two goes a long way. It is found with the steak sauces in most supermarkets.*

TOTAL SODIUM AND FAT PER INGREDIENT
Sodium:
 4 FRIED CHICKEN - 307mg
 ½ c sake - 2mg
  or sherry - 6mg
 1 t LS chicken bouillon - 5mg
 2 T LF milk - 14mg
Fat (Sat Fat):
 4 FRIED CHICKEN - 20mg (4mg)
 2 T LF milk - 1mg (0mg)

CHICKEN DIANE

Sodium Per Serving – 143mg   Serves 4

This is my poultry version of Steak Diane, an elegant dish usually served tableside in finer rstaurants. It's so quick and easy, you'll want to serve it often, not just on special occasions.

4 boneless, skinless chicken breasts (about 1 pound), flattened to ¼-inch thick[1]

½ teaspoon garlic or onion powder

¼ teaspoon ground black pepper

1 tablespoon olive oil

Sauce:

1 tablespoon unsalted margarine or butter[2]

2 garlic cloves, minced

1 large shallot, finely chopped[3]

4 ounces sliced mushrooms (about 1 cup)

1 teaspoon (or 1 envelope) low-salt chicken bouillon granules

¼ cup dry white wine[4]

2 tablespoons brandy

1 tablespoon lemon juice

2 teaspoons Dijon-style mustard

2–3 drops hot pepper sauce, such as *Tabasco* (optional)

¼ teaspoon low-salt Worcestershire sauce

1 tablespoon chopped fresh flat-leaf (Italian) parsley (optional)

▸ Season chicken with garlic powder and pepper.

▸ Heat oil in a large skillet over medium-high heat; add chicken. Cook until lightly browned on both sides, 3 to 4 minutes per side. (Chicken is done when it is no longer pink, but still moist inside.)

▸ Transfer chicken to a platter and keep warm while preparing the sauce.

▸ *For the sauce:* In the same skillet, melt margarine; decrease heat to medium and add garlic and shallots. Cook, stirring constantly, until you smell the garlic, about 1 minute. Add mushrooms and cook, stirring frequently, until mushrooms soften, 4 to 5 minutes. Stir in bouillon, wine, brandy, lemon juice, mustard, hot pepper sauce, and Worcestershire; bring to boil. Cook, stirring frequently, until liquid is reduced to a gravy consistency, 3 to 4 minutes.

▸ Serve chicken with sauce on top; sprinkle with parsley.

NUTRITIONAL INFO PER SERVING: Calories 222mg, Fat 7mg (Saturated Fat 1mg), Cholesterol 69mg, Carbohydrates 3mg (Fiber 0mg, Sugar 1mg), Sodium 143mg

CHICKEN PICCATA

Sodium Per Serving – 97mg   Serves 4

You won't believe how easy it is to make this delcious dish, which is served in many upscale restaurants. Although chicken piccata is often prepared with capers (which are high in sodium), this version, without the capers, is just as tasty. This is an impressive dinner party entrée and takes less than 15 minutes to prepare, so have everything ready before cooking the chicken. Serve with CARAMELIZED SHALLOTS AND ASPARAGUS *(page 171) and* BASIC STEAMED RICE *(page 195).*

2 tablespoons all-purpose flour

1 teaspoon dried tarragon

½ teaspoon dried basil

½ teaspoon garlic powder

½ teaspoon dried rosemary, crushed

½ teaspoon dried thyme

¼ teaspoon ground black pepper

4 boneless, skinless chicken breasts (about 1 pound), flattened to ¼-inch thick[1]

1 tablespoon olive oil

Sauce:

1 tablespoon unsalted margarine or butter[2]

1 large shallot, minced[3]

2–3 tablespoons lemon juice

½ cup Madeira or dry white wine

¼ teaspoon low-salt Worcestershire sauce

4–5 drops hot pepper sauce, such as *Tabasco*

2–3 tablespoons lowfat milk[4]

1 tablespoon chopped fresh flat-leaf (Italian) parsley (optional)

▷ Mix flour, tarragon, basil, garlic powder, rosemary, thyme, and pepper together; dredge chicken in flour mixture, shaking off any excess.

▷ Heat oil in a large skillet over medium-high heat; add chicken. Cook until lightly browned on both sides, 3 to 4 minutes per side. (Chicken is done when it is no longer pink, but still moist inside.)

▷ Transfer chicken to a platter and keep warm while preparing the sauce.

▷ *For the sauce:* In the same skillet, melt margarine; add shallots. Cook, stirring frequently, until shallots are soft, 1 to 2 minutes. Add lemon juice, Madeira, Worcestershire, and hot pepper sauce; cook, stirring frequently, for 2 minutes. Mix one tablespoon of the pan sauce into the milk (to prevent milk from curdling); stir into shallot mixture. Cook, stirring constantly, until sauce has thickened to a gravy consistency, 2 to 3 minutes.

▷ Pour sauce over chicken and serve with parsley sprinkled on top.

NUTRITIONAL INFO PER SERVING: Calories 239mg, Fat 7mg (Saturated Fat 1mg), Cholesterol 69mg, Carbohydrates 8mg (Fiber 0mg, Sugar 1mg), Sodium 87mg

COMMENTS:

1 *See* COMMENTS #1, *page 98, for flattening instructions.*

Turkey cutlets may be used instead of chicken, but decrease cooking time to 2 to 3 minutes on each side.

2 *To reduce saturated fats, use trans-free margarine. Since it contains sodium (90mg per tablespoon), it will increase the sodium per serving to 109mg.*

3 *For information on selecting and storing shallots, see* FOOD NOTE, *page 171.*

4 *For a creamier sauce, use a light cream or half-and-half.*

TOTAL SODIUM AND FAT PER INGREDIENT

Sodium:
1 lb chicken breasts - 307mg
1 shallot - 2mg
⅓ cup Madeira wine - 9mg
¼ t LS Worcestershire - 5mg
4 drops red pepper sauce - 8mg
2 T LF milk - 15mg
1 T parsley - 2mg
Fat (Sat Fat):
1 lb chicken breasts - 6mg (2mg)
1 T olive oil - 14mg (2mg)
1 T NSA margarine - 8mg (2mg)
 or NSA butter - 12mg (8mg)
2 T LF milk - 1mg (0mg)

HERBED GOAT CHEESE STUFFED CHICKEN

Sodium Per Serving – 104mg   Serves 4

Don't be fooled by the simplicity of this delightful dish. Filled with a sun-dried tomato and herb goat cheese, it's elegant enough for company.

4 boneless, skinless chicken breasts (about 1 pound), flattened to ¼-inch thick[1]

2 tablespoons all-purpose flour

½ teaspoon dried basil

½ teaspoon garlic powder

¼ teaspoon ground black pepper

¼ teaspoon dried rosemary, crushed

¼ teaspoon dried tarragon

¼ teaspoon dried thyme

1–2 tablespoons olive oil

HERBED GOAT CHEESE (recipe follows)

▶ Place one-fourth of the **HERBED GOAT CHEESE** in the center of each breast and roll up; secure with a toothpick, if necessary, to hold together.

▶ Mix flour, basil, garlic powder, pepper, rosemary, tarragon, and thyme together; dredge chicken rolls in flour mixture, shaking off any excess.

▶ Heat oil in a large skillet over medium-high heat; add chicken. Cook until lightly browned on one side, 4 to 5 minutes; turn. Decrease heat to medium-low; cover and cook until chicken is no longer pink, but still moist inside, about 15 minutes.

NUTRITIONAL INFO PER SERVING: Calories 216mg, Fat 8mg (Saturated Fat 1mg), Cholesterol 75mg, Carbohydrates 5mg (Fiber 0mg, Sugar 0mg), Sodium 104mg

HERBED GOAT CHEESE

Sodium Per Serving – 27mg   Serves 4

This cheese mixture is also good as a spread on crackers and served as an appetizer.

2 ounces goat cheese[2]

1 tablespoon oil-packed sun-dried tomatoes, drained and minced[3]

1 tablespoon chopped fresh flat-leaf (Italian) parsley

1½ teaspoons chopped fresh basil, or ½ teaspoon dried

½ teaspoon finely minced roasted garlic (see COOKING TIP, *page, 185)*[3]

¼ teaspoon onion powder

⅛ teaspoon ground black pepper

▶ Mix together goat cheese, tomatoes, parsley, basil, and onion powder. Refrigerate until ready to use.

NUTRITIONAL INFO PER SERVING: Calories 40mg, Fat 3mg (Saturated Fat 0mg), Cholesterol 7mg, Carbohydrates 1mg (Fiber 0mg, Sugar 0mg), Sodium 27mg

FETA-STUFFED CHICKEN

Instead of the **HERBED GOAT CHEESE**, use 2 ounces basil and tomato-flavored feta.[1]

NUTRITIONAL INFO PER SERVING: Calories 216mg, Fat 8mg (Saturated Fat 3mg), Cholesterol 79mg, Carbohydrates 4mg (Fiber 0mg, Sugar 1mg), Sodium 187mg

CREAMY CHEESY CHICKEN

Sodium Per Serving – 160mg   Serves 6

This is a quick and delicious way to prepare chicken. Similar to the previous dish except some of the cheese oozes out and creates a yummy cheese sauce. Serve over a bed of pasta and garnish with chopped green onions.

- **6 boneless, skinless chicken breasts (about 1½ pounds), flattened to ¼-inch thick[2]**
- **1 (6.5-ounce) container garlic and herbs spreadable cheese, such as *Alouette*, divided[3]**
- **2 tablespoons all-purpose flour**
- **½ teaspoon dried basil**
- **½ teaspoon garlic powder**
- **¼ teaspoon ground black pepper**
- **¼ teaspoon dried rosemary, crushed**
- **¼ teaspoon dried tarragon**
- **¼ teaspoon dried thyme**
- **1 tablespoon olive oil**
- **½ cup dry white wine**
- **6 ounces sliced mushrooms (about 2½ cups)[4]**
- **1 teaspoon (or 1 envelope) low-salt chicken bouillon granules**
- **1 tablespoon cornstarch, mixed with 2 tablespoons water to form a paste (optional)**

▷ Spread 1–2 tablespoons cheese over the top of each breast and roll up, jelly-roll style.

▷ Mix flour, basil, garlic powder, pepper, rosemary, tarragon, and thyme together; dredge chicken rolls in flour mixture, shaking off any excess.

▷ Heat oil in a large skillet over medium-high heat; add chicken. Cook until lightly browned on one side, 4 to 5 minutes; turn. Decrease heat to medium-low; add wine, mushrooms, and bouillon. Cover and cook until chicken is no longer pink, but still moist inside, about 15 minutes. Transfer chicken to a platter and keep warm.

▷ Stir remaining cheese spread into sauce; if sauce is not thick and creamy, increase heat to medium and slowly add cornstarch paste, stirring constantly, until thickened to a gravy consistency. Serve over chicken and top with green onions, if desired.

NUTRITIONAL INFO PER SERVING: Calories 321mg, Fat 9mg (Saturated Fat 4mg), Cholesterol 89mg, Carbohydrates 8mg (Fiber 0mg, Sugar 4mg), Sodium 160mg

COMMENTS:

1 **Athenos** *(available in many large supermarkets) makes a basil and tomato feta that has 220mg sodium per ounce.*

2 *See* COMMENTS #1, *page 98, for flattening instructions.*

3 *Spreadable cheeses range anywhere from 60mg to 450mg per 2 tablespoons. To keep fat to a minimum, I use* **Alouette** *Garlic & Herbs Light (available in many supermarkets).* **Alouette** *also has several other low-salt varieties that range from 60mg to 110mg.*

4 *Any variety or combination of mushrooms may be used. For info on mushroom varieties, see* FOOD NOTE, *page 11.*

TOTAL SODIUM AND FAT PER INGREDIENT

Sodium:
1½ lbs chicken breasts - 460mg
6.5 oz spreadable cheese - 480mg
½ c white wine - 6mg
6 oz mushrooms - 5mg
1 t LS chicken bouillon - 5mg
1 T cornstarch - 1mg

Fat (Sat Fat):
1½ lbs chicken - 9mg (2mg)
6.5 oz cheese - 32mg (20mg)
1 T olive oil - 14mg (2mg)
6 oz mushrooms - 1mg (0mg)

SUN-DRIED TOMATO CHICKEN

Sodium Per Serving – 148mg   Serves 4

So quick and so-o-o good. The sun-dried tomatoes lend an intense, tangy flavor. Serve over a bed of rice and garnish with chopped chives.

4 boneless, skinless chicken breasts (about 1 pound)[1]
2 tablespoons all-purpose flour
½ teaspoon garlic powder
½ teaspoon ground black pepper
⅛ teaspoon cayenne pepper
1 tablespoon olive oil

Sauce:

1 tablespoon unsalted margarine or butter[2]
1 onion, chopped[3]
2 garlic cloves, minced
¼ cup oil-packed sun-dried tomatoes, drained and chopped[4]
2 tablespoons chopped ripe olives (optional)[5]
½ teaspoon dried basil
1 cup dry white wine
⅔ cup lowfat sour cream

▷ Place chicken, smooth side down, between two sheets of waxed paper or aluminum foil; pound gently with a meat mallet, rolling pin, or hammer until flattened to ¼-inch thick.

▷ Mix flour with garlic powder, black pepper, and cayenne; dredge chicken in flour mixture, shaking off any excess.

▷ Heat oil in a large skillet over medium-high heat; add chicken. Cook until lightly browned on both sides, 3 to 4 minutes per side. (Chicken is done when it is no longer pink, but still moist inside.)

▷ Transfer chicken to a platter and keep warm while preparing the sauce.

▷ *For the sauce:* Melt margarine in the same skillet chicken was cooked; add onion and garlic. Cook, stirring frequently, until onions are translucent, 2 to 3 minutes. Decrease heat to medium; stir in tomatoes, olives, basil, wine, and sour cream. Cook, uncovered, until sauce thickens and is reduced by one-half, 3 to 5 minutes.

▷ Return chicken to the skillet; simmer until chicken is heated through, 2 to 3 minutes.

NUTRITIONAL INFO PER SERVING: Calories 362mg, Fat 16mg (Saturated Fat 5mg), Cholesterol 79mg, Carbohydrates 14mg (Fiber 1mg, Sugar 5mg), Sodium 148mg

CHICKEN PAPRIKA WITH TOMATO CREAM SAUCE

Sodium Per Serving – 94mg   Serves 6

This creamy paprika-flavored chicken is served in Hungary for Christmas dinner, but you don't have to wait until then to try this classic. Serve over noodles or rice.

2 tablespoons all-purpose flour

1 tablespoon paprika[1]

½ teaspoon garlic powder

¼ teaspoon ground black pepper

6 boneless, skinless chicken breasts (about 1½ pounds)

1 tablespoon olive oil

1 tablespoon unsalted margarine or butter[2]

1 onion, sliced

1 garlic clove, minced

1 green bell pepper, seeded and chopped

1 cup water

½ cup dry white wine[3]

2 large tomatoes, chopped (about 2 cups)

1 teaspoon (or 1 envelope) low-salt chicken bouillon granules

1 teaspoon mustard powder

¼ teaspoon cayenne pepper

2 tablespoons cornstarch, mixed with ¼ cup water to make a paste

½ cup lowfat sour cream

▶ Place flour, paprika, garlic powder, and black pepper in a small paper bag; add chicken one piece at a time and shake until well coated. Set aside.

▶ Heat oil and margarine in a large skillet over medium heat; add onions, garlic, and bell pepper. Cook, stirring frequently, until onions are translucent, 3 to 4 minutes. Transfer onion mixture to a bowl, reserve.

▶ Add floured chicken to same skillet; increase heat to medium-high and cook chicken until lightly browned on both sides, 3 to 4 minutes per side. Stir in a few tablespoons of water, scraping up any browned bits of chicken. Add remaining water, wine, tomatoes, bouillon, mustard, cayenne, and reserved onion mixture; stir well. Decrease heat to medium-low; cover and cook until chicken is no longer pink, but still moist inside, about 20 minutes.

▶ Just before serving, slowly add cornstarch paste, stirring until sauce has thickened to a gravy consistency. Mix in sour cream and serve over noodles or rice, if desired.

NUTRITIONAL INFO PER SERVING: Calories 257mg, Fat 8mg (Saturated Fat 2mg), Cholesterol 74mg, Carbohydrates 12mg (Fiber 2mg, Sugar 4mg), Sodium 94mg

VARIATION

MUSHROOM CHICKEN PAPRIKASH

Cook 1 cup sliced mushrooms with the onions and peppers; proceed as directed.

NUTRITIONAL INFO PER SERVING: Calories 259mg, Fat 8mg (Saturated Fat 2mg), Cholesterol 74mg, Carbohydrates 13mg (Fiber 2mg, Sugar 4mg), Sodium 95mg

COMMENTS:

1 *Paprika comes in sweet or hot varieties. Most American paprika is sweet, while Hungarian paprika is more pungent. Hungarian is available in ethnic or gourmet shops and some supermarkets. If using a hot paprika, omit the cayenne pepper.*

2 *To reduce saturated fat, use trans-free margarine. Since it contains sodium (90mg per tablespoon), it will increase the sodium per serving to 109mg.*

3 *A dry sherry, Madeira, or Marsala may be substituted for the white wine.*

TOTAL SODIUM AND FAT PER INGREDIENT

Sodium:
1 onion - 3mg
1 garlic clove - 1mg
1 bell pepper - 4mg
1½ lbs chicken breasts - 460mg
½ c white wine - 6mg
2 tomatoes - 18mg
1 t LS chicken bouillon - 5mg
1 T cornstarch - 1mg
½ c LF sour cream - 68mg

Fat (Sat Fat):
1 T olive oil - 14mg (2mg)
1 T NSA margarine - 8mg (2mg)
  or NSA butter - 12mg (8mg)
1½ lbs chicken - 9mg (2mg)
2 tomatoes - 1mg (0mg)
1 T mustard powder - 1mg (0mg)
½ c LF sour cream - 14mg (8mg)

1 *See* COMMENTS #1, *page 98, for flattening instructions.*

2 *Tuscan spice blends are found in most supermarkets. To make your own, use equal amounts of dried rosemary, sage, thyme, and basil.*

3 *For shallot selection and storage, see* FOOD NOTE, *page 171. If shallots are un-available, substitute 2 table-spoons minced onion or leek.*

4 *For a richer flavor, soak 2 ounces dried porcini mush-rooms in 1 cup warm water for 30 minutes. Pat dry with paper towel and coarsely chop; pro-ceed as directed.*

5 *To reduce saturated fat, use trans-free margarine. Since it contains sodium (90mg per tablespoon), it will increase the sodium per serving to 107mg.*

VARIATION:

For a tangy sauce, stir in the juice of half a lemon (about 1 tablespoon) before serving.

TOTAL SODIUM AND FAT
PER INGREDIENT
Sodium:
1 lb chicken breasts - 307mg
1 shallot - 2mg
2 garlic cloves - 2mg
8 oz mushrooms - 4mg
1 t LS chicken bouillon - 5mg
½ c marsala wine - 10mg
¼ c sherry - 5mg
2 T parsley - 4mg
Fat (Sat Fat):
1 lb chicken breasts - 6mg (2mg)
2 T olive oil - 28mg (4mg)
1 T NSA margarine - 8mg (2mg)
  or NSA butter - 12mg (8mg)

MARSALA CHICKEN

Sodium Per Serving – 85mg   Serves 4

This classic Italian dish is so quick and easy to make, yet elegant enough to serve when company comes.

4 boneless, skinless chicken breasts (about 1 pound), flattened to ¼-inch thick[1]

2 tablespoons all-purpose flour

½ teaspoon garlic or onion powder

½ teaspoon Tuscan spice blend[2]

¼ teaspoon ground black pepper

1 tablespoon olive oil

Sauce:

1 tablespoon olive oil

1 shallot, minced[3]

2–3 garlic cloves, minced

8 ounces sliced mushrooms (about 2 cups)[4]

½ cup Marsala wine

¼ cup dry sherry

1 teaspoon (or 1 envelope) low-salt chicken bouillon granules

½ teaspoon sugar substitute or sugar

1 tablespoon unsalted margarine or butter[5]

2 tablespoons chopped fresh flat-leaf (Italian) parsley (optional)

▷ Mix flour with garlic powder, Tuscan spice blend, and pepper; dredge chicken in flour mixture, shaking off any excess.

▷ Heat oil in a large skillet over medium-high heat; add chicken. Cook until lightly browned on both sides, 3 to 4 minutes per side. (Chicken is done when it is no longer pink, but still moist inside.)

▷ Transfer chicken to a platter and keep warm while preparing the sauce.

▷ *For the sauce:* Heat oil in the same skillet over medium heat; add shallots and garlic. Cook, stirring frequently, until you smell the garlic, 2 to 3 minutes. Add mushrooms and cook, stirring frequently, until the mushrooms soften, 2 to 3 minutes. Stir in Marsala, sherry, bouillon, and sweetener; reduce heat to medium-low, cover and simmer 10 to 15 minutes. The sauce should be the consistency of gravy; if not, raise heat to medium-high and cook a few minutes longer until reduced. Stir in margarine.

▷ Peturn chicken to skillet; simmer, covered, until chicken is heated through, 2 to 3 minutes. Serve chicken with mushroom sauce on top; sprinkle with parsley.

NUTRITIONAL INFO PER SERVING: Calories 307mg, Fat 11mg (Saturated Fat 2mg), Cholesterol 69mg, Carbohydrates 12mg (Fiber 0mg, Sugar 2mg), Sodium 85mg

CHICKEN IN MUSHROOM-ASPARAGUS-TARRAGON SAUCE

Sodium Per Serving – 88mg   Serves 4

This pleasing dish has a rich, creamy sauce. The caramelized onions and mushrooms add a bit of sweetness, while the asparagus adds another element of flavor.

2 tablespoons olive oil, divided

1 tablespoon unsalted margarine or butter[1]

1 medium onion, sliced

1 shallot, chopped[2]

1 teaspoon sugar substitute or sugar

2 tablespoons all-purpose flour

1 teaspoon dried tarragon

1/2 teaspoon garlic powder

1/2 teaspoon dried rosemary, crushed

1/2 teaspoon dried thyme

4 boneless, skinless chicken breasts (about 1 pound), flattened to 1/4-inch thick[3]

Sauce:

4 ounces mushrooms, sliced (about 1 cup)[4]

1/2 cup dry white wine[5]

1 cup asparagus pieces (about 6 spears, cut in 1-inch pieces)

1 teaspoon (or 1 envelope) low-salt chicken bouillon granules, mixed with 1/2 cup water

1/4 cup half-and-half or light cream

1/4 teaspoon ground black pepper

3 tablespoons chopped fresh tarragon, or 1 tablespoon dried

▶ Heat 1 tablespoon oil and margarine in a large skillet over medium heat; add onions and shallots. Cook, stirring frequently, until onions are translucent, 3 to 4 minutes. Decrease heat to medium-low; cook, uncovered, stirring frequently, until onions are caramelized and a deep golden brown, about 20 minutes. Stir in sweetener and set aside.

▶ Meanwhile, mix flour with dried tarragon, onion powder, rosemary, and thyme; dredge chicken in flour mixture, shaking off any excess.

▶ Heat remaining 1 tablespoon oil in another skillet over medium-high heat; add chicken. Cook until lightly browned on both sides, 3 to 5 minutes on each side; add mushrooms and cook, stirring occasionally, until mushrooms have softened, 3 to 5 minutes.

▶ Stir in wine, asparagus, and bouillon; reduce heat to medium. Cover and simmer until chicken is no longer pink, but still moist inside, about 10 minutes. Transfer chicken to a platter and keep warm while preparing the sauce.

▶ *For the sauce:* Add caramelized onion mixture, half-and-half, pepper, and fresh tarragon to the mushrooms; stir until well mixed and slightly thickened. NOTE: If sauce is not thick enough, mix together 1 tablespoon cornstarch with 1 tablespoon water; gradually add to sauce, stirring constantly, until desired consistency.

▶ Slice chicken on the diagonal and serve with sauce on top.

NUTRITIONAL INFO PER SERVING: Calories 292mg, Fat 12mg (Saturated Fat 3mg), Cholesterol 74mg, Carbohydrates 10mg (Fiber 1mg, Sugar 3mg), Sodium 88mg

COMMENTS:

1 *To reduce saturated fat, use trans-free margarine. Since it contains sodium (90mg per tablespoon), it will increase the sodium per serving to 119mg.*

2 *For shallot selection and storage info, see FOOD NOTE, page 171. If shallots are unavailable, substitute 1 tablespoon minced garlic.*

3 *Place chicken, smooth side down, between two sheets of waxed paper, plastic wrap, or aluminum foil; pound gently with a meat mallet, rolling pin, or rubber hammer until flattened to desired thickness.*

4 *Any variety or combination of mushrooms may be used. For a more intense, woodsy flavor, use several varieties of wild mushrooms, both dried and fresh. (If using dried mushrooms, reconstitute in water, wine, or chicken broth for 30 minutes.) For info on mushroom varieties, see FOOD NOTE, page 44.*

5 *A dry sherry or Madeira may used instead of the white wine.*

TOTAL SODIUM AND FAT PER INGREDIENT

Sodium:
1 onion - 3mg
1 shallot - 2mg
1 lb chicken - 307mg
1 c mushrooms - 2mg
1/2 c white wine - 6mg
6 asparagus spears - 2mg
1 t LS chicken bouillon - 5mg
1/4 c half-and-half - 25mg
  or light cream - 24mg
Fat (Sat Fat):
2 T olive oil - 28mg (4mg)
1 T NSA margarine - 8mg (2mg)
  or NSA butter - 12mg (8mg)
1 lb chicken - 6mg (2mg)
1/4 c half-and-half - 7mg (4mg)
  or light cream - 12mg (8mg)

CHICKEN BREASTS WITH SHALLOT SAUCE

Sodium Per Serving – 85mg   Serves 4

Rosemary and chicken blend together nicely in this simple yet flavorful dish. Serve over a bed of rice to soak up the savory sauce.

4 boneless, skinless chicken breasts (about 1 pound), flattened to ¼-inch thick[1]

1 tablespoon olive oil

1 tablespoon lemon juice[2]

¼ teaspoon garlic or onion powder

¼ teaspoon ground black pepper

1 tablespoon fresh rosemary, minced, or 1 teaspoon dried

SHALLOT SAUCE *(recipe follows)*

3 cups cooked rice *(see BASIC STEAMED RICE, page 195)*

1 tablespoon chopped fresh flat-leaf (Italian) parsley (optional)

▸ Place chicken in a baking dish. Mix oil, lemon juice, garlic powder, pepper, and rosemary together and rub into chicken, coating both sides. Cover and let marinate 30 minutes or more in refrigerator, turning chicken a couple of times.

▸ Bake in a preheated oven at 350°F (180°C) for 30 to 35 minutes, until chicken is no longer pink, but still moist inside.

▸ Slice chicken on the diagonal and place on a bed of rice; pour SHALLOT SAUCE over the chicken and top with chopped parsley.

NUTRITIONAL INFO PER SERVING: Calories 457mg, Fat 10mg (Saturated Fat 2mg), Cholesterol 69mg, Carbohydrates 50mg (Fiber 1mg, Sugar 1mg), Sodium 85mg

SHALLOT SAUCE

Sodium Per Serving – 9mg   Serves 4

This sauce is also good on burgers or mashed potatoes.

2 teaspoons olive oil

1 shallot, minced[3]

1 teaspoon fresh rosemary, minced, or ¼ teaspoon dried

1 teaspoon (or 1 envelope) low-salt chicken bouillon granules

½ cup water

½ cup Madeira wine or dry sherry

4–5 drops hot pepper sauce, such as *Tabasco*

¼ teaspoon low-salt Worcestershire sauce

1 tablespoon unsalted margarine or butter[4]

▸ Heat 2 teaspoons oil in a skillet over medium heat; add shallots and rosemary. Cook, stirring frequently, until shallots are translucent, 4 to 5 minutes. Add bouillon, water, wine, hot pepper sauce, and Worcestershire; cook until liquid is slightly thickened, 4 to 5 minutes. Stir in margarine just before serving.

NUTRITIONAL INFO PER SERVING: Calories 89mg, Fat 4mg (Saturated Fat 1mg), Cholesterol 0mg, Carbohydrates 5mg (Fiber 0mg, Sugar 1mg), Sodium 6mg

VARIATION

MUSHROOM-SHALLOT SAUCE

Cook 1 cup thinly sliced crimini mushrooms with the shallots; proceed as directed.

NUTRITIONAL INFO PER SERVING: Calories 93mg, Fat 4mg (Saturated Fat 1mg), Cholesterol 0mg, Carbohydrates 5mg (Fiber 0mg, Sugar 1mg), Sodium 8mg

COMMENTS:

1 *Tuscan spice blends are found in most supermarkets. To make your own, mix together equal amounts of dried rosemary, sage, thyme, and basil.*

COQ AU VIN

Sodium Per Serving – 111mg   Serves 4

Coq Au Vin is a classic French dish that is usually made with chicken, vegetables, bacon, and red wine. My quick and easy version is without bacon and uses white wine.

4 boneless, skinless chicken breasts

¼ teaspoon garlic powder

⅛ teaspoon ground black pepper

1 tablespoon olive oil

1 small sweet onion, sliced, such as Vidalia

2 carrots, sliced

8 ounces mushrooms, sliced (about 2 cups)

2 medium red potatoes, cubed

1–2 garlic cloves, minced

½ cup white wine (such as Chardonnay)

1 teaspoon (or 1 envelope) low-salt chicken bouillon granules

1 teaspoon dried Tuscan spice blend[1]

1 tablespoon cornstarch, mixed with 2 tablespoons water to make a paste

1 tablespoon chopped fresh flat-leaf (Italian) parsley

▸ Season chicken with garlic powder and pepper. Heat oil in a large skillet over medium-high heat; add chicken. Cook until lightly browned on both sides, 3 to 4 minutes per side; decrease heat to medium-low.

▸ Add onions, carrots, mushrooms, potatoes, garlic, wine, bouillon, and Tuscan herbs; cover and simmer 30 minutes or until vegetables are cooked.

▸ Increase heat to medium, slowly add cornstarch paste, stirring constantly, until sauce has thickened to the consistency of gravy. Sprinkle with parsley and serve.

NUTRITIONAL INFO PER SERVING: Calories 297mg, Fat 5mg (Saturated Fat 1mg), Cholesterol 69mg, Carbohydrates 26mg (Fiber 4mg, Sugar 5mg), Sodium 111mg

TOTAL SODIUM AND FAT PER INGREDIENT

Sodium:
1 lb chicken breasts - 307mg
1 sm sweet onion - 9mg
2 carrots - 84mg
2 c mushrooms - 4mg
2 red potatoes - 26mg
1 garlic clove - 1mg
½ c white wine - 6mg
1 t LS chicken bouillon - 5mg
1 T parsley - 2mg
Fat (Sat Fat):
1 lb chicken breasts - 6mg (2mg)
1 T olive oil - 14mg (2mg)

CHICKEN PIRI PIRI

Sodium Per Serving – 86mg   Serves 6

This wonderfully hot and spicy dish (shown on the cover) is Portuguese in origin, but also has links to Africa (piri piri is Swahili for the fiery hot peppers of Africa). Make the sauce several days before to allow the peppers to intensify. Allow 3 hours for marinating.

1½ pounds boneless, skinless chicken breasts and/or thighs, cut into 2-inch pieces

1½ cups PIRI PIRI SAUCE *(recipe follows)*, **divided**[1]

1 tablespoon olive oil

1 sweet onion, diced

1 red bell pepper, thinly sliced[2]

2–3 garlic cloves, finely minced

½ cup brandy[3]

1 (10-ounce) package frozen pearl onions

▸ Place chicken in a baking dish and pour over 1 cup PIRI PIRI SAUCE; cover with aluminum foil or plastic wrap and marinate in the refrigerator at least 3 hours.

▸ Preheat oven to 350°F (180°C); bake chicken with marinade for 20 to 25 minutes, until chicken is no longer pink, but still moist inside.

▸ Meanwhile, heat oil in a large skillet over medium heat; add onions and bell peppers. Cook, stirring frequently, until onions are translucent, 3 to 4 minutes; add garlic. Cook, stirring constantly, until you smell the garlic, about 1 minute; add brandy, onions, and reserved ½ cup PIRI PIRI SAUCE. Cook, stirring frequently, until sauce has thickened to a gravy consistency, about 5 minutes; add baked chicken and serve.

NUTRITIONAL INFO PER SERVING: Calories 466mg, Fat 32mg (Saturated Fat 5mg), Cholesterol 91mg, Carbohydrates 10mg (Fiber 2mg, Sugar 4mg), Sodium 86mg

PIRI PIRI SAUCE

Sodium Per Serving – 4mg   Makes about 2 cups

Traditionally this sauce steeps for a week before using, but this version is ready in 24 hours (however, the longer this sits, the hotter it gets). The sauce will keep for a month at room temperature and is great on grilled chicken and fish.

1 cup olive oil

¼ cup fresh lemon juice or red wine vinegar

2–4 jalapeno and/or serrano peppers, stems removed[4]

2 garlic cloves

1 red bell pepper, seeded and quartered

1 teaspoon crushed red pepper flakes

½ teaspoon dried cumin

½ teaspoon dried oregano

½ teaspoon paprika

½ teaspoon ground black pepper

½ teaspoon dried thyme

¼ teaspoon garlic powder

¼ teaspoon onion powder

> Place all ingredients in a saucepan and simmer over medium-low heat for 10 minutes; remove and let cool completely.

> Place in a blender or food processor and pulse until smooth; place purée in a covered container and let sit at room temperature for 24 hours or longer to allow peppers to intensify.

NUTRITIONAL INFO PER 2 TABLESPOONS: Calories 125mg, Fat 14mg (Saturated Fat 2mg), Cholesterol 0mg, Carbohydrates 22mg (Fiber 6mg, Sugar 7mg), Sodium 17mg

ASPARAGUS TURKEY WITH CREAM SAUCE

Sodium Per Serving – 112mg   Serves 4

This is a great dish for leftover turkey or chicken. Mix in a few items from the pantry and serve this thick and creamy delight over rice or pasta. Although high in fat, much of it comes from the almonds which have monounsaturated fats (considered "good" fats, as they lower LDLs, the "bad" cholesterol).

1 tablespoon olive oil	¼ cup dry sherry
1 small sweet onion, chopped	1 tablespoon lemon juice
2 cloves garlic, minced	½ teaspoon onion or garlic powder
4 ounces sliced mushrooms (about 1 cup)	½ teaspoon ground black pepper
2 cups asparagus, cut in 2-inch lengths	½ teaspoon herbes de Provence[1]
1 (8-ounce) can sliced water chestnuts, drained	⅓ cup sliced unsalted almonds, toasted[2]
1½ cups cooked turkey, cubed	4 ounces (½ cup) garlic and herbs spreadable cheese, such as *Alouette*[3]
2 teaspoons (or 2 envelopes) low-salt chicken bouillon granules	4 cups cooked rice (*see* BASIC STEAMED RICE, *page 195*) **or pasta**
½ cup water	

> Heat oil in a large skillet over medium-high heat; add onions. Cook, stirring frequently, until onions are translucent, 2 to 3 minutes; add garlic and cook, stirring constantly, until you smell the garlic, about 1 minute.

> Stir in mushrooms, asparagus, water chestnuts, turkey, bouillon, water, sherry, lemon juice, onion powder, pepper, and herbes de Provence; cook until asparagus is fork tender, about 5 minutes.

> Stir in almonds and cream cheese; mix until cheese is melted, forming a thick sauce. Serve over rice or pasta; sprinkle with Parmesan cheese, if desired.

NUTRITIONAL INFO PER SERVING: Calories 560mg, Fat 21mg (Saturated Fat 4mg), Cholesterol 55mg, Carbohydrates 62mg (Fiber 5mg, Sugar 7mg), Sodium 112mg

COMMENTS:

1 *Herbes de Provence is a blend of herbs commonly used in French cooking, most often a mix of basil, chervil, fennel, lavendar, marjoram, rosemary, sage, savory, and/or thyme. The combination and portions vary depending on the manufacturer.*

2 *To toast almonds, spread nuts in a dry skillet. Cook over medium-low heat, stirring or shaking frequently, until they start to turn golden, 5 to 7 minutes. See COOKING TIP, page 90, for additional toasting methods.*

3 *Spreadable cheeses range anywhere from 60mg to 450mg per 2 tablespoons. To keep fat to a minimum, I use* **Alouette** *Garlic & Herbs Light (available in many supermarkets).* **Alouette** *also has several other low-salt varieties that range from 60mg to 110mg.*

TOTAL SODIUM AND FAT PER INGREDIENT

Sodium:
1 sweet onion - 9mg
2 garlic cloves - 2mg
4 oz mushrooms - 3mg
2 c asparagus - 6mg
8 oz water chestnuts - 20mg
1½ c cooked turkey - 147mg
2 t LS chicken bouillon - 10mg
¼ c sherry - 5mg
¼ t onion powder - 1mg
4 oz cheese spread - 240mg
 or cream cheese - 260mg
4 c cooked rice - 6mg
Fat (Sat Fat):
1 T olive oil - 14mg (2mg)
1½ c cooked turkey - 10mg (2mg)
⅓ c NSA almonds - 43mg (3mg)
4 oz cheese spread - 16m (10mg)
 or cream cheese - 40mg (25mg)
4 c cooked rice - 2mg (0mg)

CREAMY ARTICHOKES, MUSHROOMS, PEAS AND CHICKEN

Sodium Per Serving – 110mg   Serves 4

Another quick and delicious way to prepare leftover turkey or chicken. Served over noodles or rice, it's a family favorite.

1 tablespoon olive oil

1 onion, chopped

1 garlic clove, minced

8 ounces sliced mushrooms (about 2 cups)

½ cup Madeira wine

1 teaspoon (or 1 envelope) low-salt chicken bouillon granules

1 cup water

2–3 drops hot pepper sauce, such as *Tabasco*

¼ teaspoon low-salt Worcestershire sauce

1 tablespoon fresh lemon juice

1 (10-ounce) package frozen no-salt-added peas

1 (9-ounce) package frozen no-salt-added artichoke hearts, thawed and halved[1]

2 cups cooked chicken or turkey breast, cubed[2]

½ cup lowfat sour cream

1 tablespoon cornstarch, mixed with 2 tablespoons water to make a paste

4 cups cooked rice *(see* BASIC STEAMED RICE, *page 195),* **noodles, or pasta**

▷ Heat oil in a large skillet over medium-high heat; add onions. Cook, stirring frequently, until onions are translucent, 2 to 3 minutes; add garlic. Cook, stirring constantly, until you smell the garlic, about 1 minute; add mushrooms and cook until softened, 3 to 4 minutes.

▷ Mix in Madeira, bouillon, water, hot pepper sauce, Worcestershire, lemon juice, peas, artichoke hearts, and chicken. Reduce heat to medium-low; cover and simmer 10 minutes, until peas and artichoke hearts are cooked.

▷ Stir in sour cream. The sauce should be thick and creamy, if not, slowly stir in cornstarch paste until thickened. Serve over rice.

NUTRITIONAL INFO PER SERVING (WITH RICE): Calories 528mg, Fat 11mg (Saturated Fat 3mg), Cholesterol 68mg, Carbohydrates 67mg (Fiber 6mg, Sugar 6mg), Sodium 112mg

TURKEY SAUSAGE WITH ARTICHOKES

Sodium Per Serving – 282mg   Serves 4

This dish shows that you can have high-sodium foods, like sausage, and still remain within sodium guidelines, particularly if you add low-salt side dishes.

1 tablespoon olive oil

2 links sweet turkey sausage (about 6 ources)[1]

½ sweet onion, chopped

3 garlic cloves, minced

½ teaspoon herbes de Provence[2]

¼ teaspoon garlic powder

¼ teaspoon ground black pepper

1 (9-ounce) package frozen artichoke hearts, thawed and halved[3]

2 large tomatoes, chopped (about 2 cups)

½ cup dry white wine

1 teaspoon (or 1 envelope) low-salt chicken bouillon granules

1 tablespoon unsalted margarine or butter[4]

4 cups cooked pasta, noodles, or rice

2 tablespoons chopped fresh flat-leaf (Italian) parsley (optional)

▸ Heat oil in a large skillet over medium-high heat; add sausage. Cook until slightly browned on all sides, about 5 minutes. Remove sausage and let cool slightly; slice into bite-sized pieces. Set aside.

▸ In same skillet, cook onion, stirring frequently, until translucent; add garlic. Cook, stirring constantly, until you smell the garlic, 1 to 2 minutes; mix in herbes de Provence, garlic powder, pepper, and sliced sausage. Add artichokes, tomatoes, wine, and bouillon; decrease heat to medium-low. Cover and cook until artichokes are soft, 10 to 15 minutes.

▸ Stir in margarine and heat through. Serve over pasta and top with parsley.

NUTRITIONAL INFO PER SERVING: Calories 382mg, Fat 10mg (Saturated Fat 2mg), Cholesterol 13mg, Carbohydrates 52mg (Fiber 6mg, Sugar 6mg), Sodium 282mg

COMMENTS:

1 *Although there are no low-sodium sausages, there are several brands of sweet turkey sausages which have 350mg to 500mg sodium per link, such as* **Gerhard's** *and* **Johnson-ville** *(see RESOURCES, page 272).*

2 *Herbes de Provence is a blend of herbs commonly used in French cooking, most often a mix of basil, chervil, fennel, lavendar, marjoram, rosemary, sage, savory and/or thyme. The combination and portions vary depending on the manufacturer.*

3 *Instead o frozen artichokes, cook 5 fresh artichokes; remove and cut up the hearts. Add to the tomato-wine mixture during the last 5 minutes, stirring frequently, until heated through; proceed as directed.*

4 *To reduce saturated fat, use trans-free margarine. Since it contains sodium (90mg per tablespoon), increase the sodium per serving to 304mg.*

TOTAL SODIUM AND FAT PER INGREDIENT

Sodium:
  2 turkey sausage links - 958mg
  ½ sweet onion - 6mg
  3 garlic cloves - 3mg
  9 oz artichoke hearts - 120mg
  2 tomatoes - 18mg
  ½ c white wine - 6mg
  1 t LS chicken bouillon - 5mg
  4 c cooked pasta - 6mg
  2 T parsley - 4mg
Fat (Sat Fat):
  1 T olive oil - 14mg (2mg)
  2 turkey sausage - 14mg (5mg)
  9 oz artichokes - 1mg (0mg)
  2 tomatoes - 1mg (0mg)
  1 T NSA margarine - 8mg (2mg)
    or NSA butter - 12mg (8mg)
  4 c cooked pasta - 4mg (1mg)

1 *Herbes de Provence is a blend of herbs commonly used in French cooking, most often a mix of basil, chervil, fennel, lavendar, marjoram, rosemary, sage, savory, and/or thyme. The combination and portions vary depending on the manufacturer.*

2 *A dry sherry or Madeira wine may be substituted for the brandy.*

3 *To toast almonds, spread nuts in a dry skillet. Cook over medium-low heat, stirring or shaking frequently, until they start to turn golden, 5 to 7 minutes. See* COOKING TIP, *page 90, for additional toasting methods.*

TURKEY STROGANOFF

Sodium Per Serving – 91mg   Serves 4

This is another yummy variation of the classic Stroganoff. I'm sure your family will love it as much as mine.

12 ounces cooked turkey, cubed (about 2 cups)

1 tablespoon olive oil

1 sweet onion, sliced

2 garlic cloves, minced

4 ounces sliced mushrooms (about 1 cup)

½ teaspoon herbes de Provence[1]

¼ teaspoon ground black pepper

1 cup broccoli florets

1 cup snap peas, broken in half

1 cup CHICKEN STOCK *(page 232)* **or canned low-salt chicken broth**

1 teaspoon (or 1 envelope) low-salt chicken bouillon granules

¼ cup brandy[2]

6 ounces (¾ cup) lowfat sour cream

¼ cup slivered almonds, toasted (optional)[3]

4 cups cooked pasta, noodles, or rice

▷ Heat oil in a large skillet over medium heat; add onions. Cook, stirring frequently, until onions are translucent, 3 to 4 minutes; add garlic. Cook, stirring constantly, until you smell the garlic, 1 to 2 minutes.

▷ Add mushrooms, herbes de Provence, and pepper; cook, stirring frequently, until mushrooms soften, about 3 minutes. Stir in broccoli, peas, chicken stock, bouillon, and brandy; cover and cook until veggies are soft, 10 to 15 minutes.

▷ Stir in sour cream and almonds; heat through. Serve over pasta.

NUTRITIONAL INFO PER SERVING: Calories 562mg, Fat 18mg (Saturated Fat 4mg), Cholesterol 86mg, Carbohydrates 55mg (Fiber 5mg, Sugar 6mg), Sodium 91mg (119 with canned broth)

TOTAL SODIUM AND FAT PER INGREDIENT

Sodium:
12 oz cooked turkey - 175mg
1 sweet onion - 12mg
2 garlic cloves - 2mg
4 oz mushrooms - 4mg
1 c broccoli - 29mg
1c snap peas - 7mg
1 c CHICKEN STOCK - 20mg
 or LS canned broth - 130mg
1 t LS chicken bouillon - 5mg
¼ c brandy - 5mg
6 oz LF sour cream - 102mg
4 c cooked pasta - 6mg
Fat (Sat Fat):
12 oz cooked turkey - 2mg (1mg)
1 T olive oil - 14mg (2mg)
1 c CHICKEN STOCK - 1mg (0mg)
 or LS canned broth - 2mg (1mg)
¼ c NSA almonds - 30mg (2mg)
4 c cooked pasta - 4mg (1mg)
6 oz LF sour cream - 20mg (12mg)

VARIATION

RICH AND CREAMY TURKEY STROGANOFF

For a richer and creamier version, instead of ¾ cup sour cream, use ¼ cup lowfat cream cheese, ¼ cup lowfat milk, and ¼ cup lowfat sour cream.

NUTRITIONAL INFO PER SERVING: Calories 561mg, Fat 18mg (Saturated Fat 4mg), Cholesterol 89mg, Carbohydrates 54mg (Fiber 5mg, Sugar 7mg), Sodium 138mg (165mg with LS canned broth)

TUSCAN CHICKEN STEW

Sodium Per Serving – 146mg   Serves 4

This excellent one-pot meal is ready in less than one hour. Serve as is or over a bed of rice or pasta.

3 tablespoons all-purpose flour, divided

1 teaspoon garlic powder

1 teaspoon dried rosemary, crumbled

½ teaspoon ground black pepper

½ teaspoon dried thyme

4 boneless, skinless chicken breasts and/or thighs (about 1 pound)[1]

1 tablespoon olive oil

1 small sweet onion, sliced, such as Vidalia

1 red bell pepper, sliced

4 garlic cloves, minced

4 small red potatoes, quartered

2 carrots, sliced

4 ounces sliced mushrooms (about 1 cup)

2 teaspoons (or 2 envelopes) low-salt chicken bouillon granules

½ cup Madeira wine or dry sherry

2 tablespoons chopped ripe olives (optional)

1 tablespoon cornstarch, mixed with 2 tablespoons water to make a paste

▸ Mix 2 tablespoons flour with garlic powder, rosemary, pepper, and thyme; dredge chicken in flour mixture, shaking off excess.

▸ Heat oil in a large skillet or pot over medium heat; add chicken. Lightly brown on each side, about 5 minutes per side; remove chicken.

▸ In same skillet, add onion and bell pepper; cook, stirring frequently, until onions are translucent, about 5 minutes. Add garlic; cook, stirring constantly, until you smell the garlic, about 1 minute.

▸ Return chicken to skillet. Add potatoes, carrots, mushrooms, bouillon, and Madeira; bring to boil. Decrease heat to medium-low, cover, and simmer until potatoes are tender, about 30 minutes.

▸ Mix in olives; increase heat to medium. Gradually add cornstarch paste, stirring constantly, until sauce has thickened to a gravy consistency.

NUTRITIONAL INFO PER SERVING: Calories 408mg, Fat 6mg (Saturated Fat 1mg), Cholesterol 69mg, Carbohydrates 47mg (Fiber 5mg, Sugar 7mg), Sodium 146mg

COMMENTS:

[1] *Different chicken parts have a varying amount of fat and sodium. The following breakdown is for 4 ounces skinless, boneless meat.*

	Fat	SatFat	Sod
Breast	1	0	73
with skin	10	3	73
Wing	5	2	91
Thigh	4	1	96
Drumstick	4	1	99

TOTAL SODIUM AND FAT PER INGREDIENT

Sodium:
1 lb chicken breasts - 292mg
1 t garlic powder - 1mg
1 sm sweet onion - 9mg
1 bell pepper - 2mg
4 garlic cloves - 4mg
4 sm red potatoes - 7mg
2 carrots - 84mg
4 oz mushrooms - 2mg
2 t LS chicken bouillon - 10mg
½ c Madeira wine - 11mg
2 T ripe olives - 146mg
1 T cornstarch - 1mg
Fat (Sat Fat):
1 lb chicken breasts - 6mg (2mg)
1 T olive oil - 14mg (2mg)
4 sm red potatoes - 1mg (0mg)
2 T ripe olives - 2mg (0mg)

COMMENTS:

1 *To reduce saturated fat, use trans-free margarine (or a combination of both). Since it contains sodium (90mg per tablespoon), it will increase the sodium per serving to 109mg.*

2 *For poaching info, see* COOKING TIP, *page 115.*

3 *Criminis, similar to button mushrooms, are brown in color, but have more flavor. A combination of criminis and buttons may also be used.*

4 *If using store-bought shells, look for brands with 55mg or less per serving (see* RESOURCES, *page 272). If frozen, thaw completely before removing from pie pan.*

TOTAL SODIUM AND FAT PER INGREDIENT

Sodium:
1 sweet onion - 12mg
2 garlic cloves - 2mg
½ c flour - 2mg
2 c CHICKEN STOCK - 40mg
  or LS canned broth - 260mg
1 T LS chicken bouillon - 15mg
½ c LF sour cream - 68mg
1 T mustard - 168mg
1 lb chicken breasts - 307mg
2 carrots - 84mg
1 celery stalk - 32mg
4 oz mushrooms - 2mg
10 oz NSA peas - 13mg
10 oz pearl onions - 28mg
2 T parsley - 4mg
2 BASIC PIE CRUSTS - 318mg
  or store-bought - 800mg
Fat (Sat Fat):
2 T NSA margarine - 16mg (3mg)
  or NSA butter - 24mg (16mg)
½ c flour - 1mg (0mg)
2 c CHICKEN STOCK - 3mg (0mg)
  or LS canned broth - 4mg (2mg)
½ c LF sour cream - 14mg (8mg)
1 lb chicken breasts - 6mg (2mg)
10 oz NSA peas - 1mg (0mg)
2 BASIC PIE CRUSTS - 132mg (12mg)
  or store-bought - 112mg (32mg)

CHICKEN POT PIE

Sodium Per Serving – 94mg   Makes 2 pies, serves 12

This is the ultimate in comfort food. It may look like a time-consuming recipe, but it takes less than 30 minutes to prepare and 45 minutes to bake. To cut down on salt, fat, and calories, only one crust per pie is used. To save time, make the filling the day before.

2 tablespoons unsalted margarine or butter[1]

1 sweet onion, chopped

½ teaspoon dried basil

½ teaspoon dried rosemary, crushed

½ teaspoon dried tarragon

½ teaspoon dried thyme

¼ teaspoon garlic powder

¼ teaspoon ground black pepper

2 medium red potatoes, diced

2 carrots, diced

1 celery stalk, diced

2 garlic cloves, minced

½ cup all-purpose flour

2 cups CHICKEN STOCK (page 232) or canned low-salt chicken broth

½ cup white wine

1 tablespoon (or 3 envelopes) low-salt chicken bouillon granules

1 teaspoon mustard powder

½ cup lowfat sour cream

1 tablespoon coarse-grain mustard

4 (4-ounce) boneless, skinless chicken breasts, poached and cubed, or 2½ cups cubed cooked chicken[2]

4 ounces crimini mushrooms, thickly sliced (about 1 cup)[3]

1 (10-ounce) package frozen no-salt-added peas (about 2 cups)

1 (10-ounce) package frozen pearl onions

2 tablespoons chopped fresh flat-leaf (Italian) parsley (optional)

2 BASIC PIE CRUSTS (page 229) or unbaked pie shells[4]

▶ Preheat oven to 350°F (180°C). Coat two 9-inch round, 2-inch deep pans (such as deep-dish or quiche pans) or casserole dishes with nonstick cooking spray.

▶ Melt margarine in a large pot over medium heat; add onions, basil, rosemary, tarragon, thyme, garlic powder, and pepper. Cook, stirring frequently, until onions are translucent, about 5 minutes. Add potatoes, carrots, celery, and garlic; cook, stirring frequently, until you smell the garlic, 2 to 3 minutes.

▶ Mix flour and ½ cup chicken stock together; add to veggies and cook, stirring constantly, for 2 minutes.

▶ Stir in the remaining 1½ cups stock, wine, bouillon, and dmustard powder; increase heat to medium-high and bring to a boil. Decrease heat to medium and continue cooking, stirring frequently, until sauce has thickened enough to coat the back of a spoon, 3 to 4 minutes.

▶ Mix sour cream with coarse-grain mustard and add to broth mixture; stir in chicken, mushrooms, peas, pearl onions, and parsley.

▷ Divide chicken/vegetable mixture equally and pour into prepared pans; top each with a pie crust. Trim any dough overhang and tuck edges inside the pan; cut several slits in the crust to allow steam to escape.

▷ Place pies on a baking sheet (to catch any spilled juices) and bake in a preheated oven for 45 minutes, or until crust is golden brown.

NOTE: The filling can be made the day before, covered, and refrigerated until ready to bake.

NUTRITIONAL INFO PER SERVING: Calories 367mg, Fat 14mg (Saturated Fat 3mg), Cholesterol 28mg, Carbohydrates 40mg (Fiber 4mg, Sugar 4mg), Sodium 94mg (112mg with LS canned broth)

NUTRITIONAL INFO PER SERVING (WITH STORE-BOUGHT SHELL): Calories 293mg, Fat 13mg (Saturated Fat 4mg), Cholesterol 28mg, Carbohydrates 29mg (Fiber 3mg, Sugar 4mg), Sodium 134mg (153mg with LS canned broth)

COOKING TIP

POACHING CHICKEN

There are several ways to poach chicken:

Stove-top: In a large pot over medium-high heat, place chicken breasts, 1 onion (peeled and quartered), 1 celery stalk (cut into large chunks, including leaves), 1 carrot (cut into large chunks), 4–5 parsley sprigs, 6 peppercorns, 1 tablespoon fresh thyme or tarragon (or 1½ teaspoons dried), and 1 bay leaf. Add 2 cups low-salt chicken stock or canned broth and ½ cup white wine; bring to a boil. Decrease heat; cover, and simmer until chicken is tender and no longer pink inside, about 20 minutes.

Oven: Place chicken, 1 onion (peeled and quartered), 1 celery stalk (cut into large chunks, including leaves), 1 carrot (cut into large chunks), 4–5 parsley sprigs, 6 peppercorns, 1 tablespoon fresh thyme or tarragon (or 1½ teaspoons dried), 1 bay leaf, 2 cups low-salt chicken stock (or canned broth), and ½ cup white wine into a baking dish; cover and bake in a preheated oven at 425ºF (220ºC) for 20 minutes.

Microwave: Arrange chicken in a microwave-safe dish with the thickest portions toward the outside of the dish. Add 1 cup low-salt chicken broth, ½ cup white wine, 1 tablespoon fresh thyme or tarragon (or 1 ½ teaspoons dried), and 1 teaspoon (or 1 envelope) low-salt chicken bouillon granules. Cover with a microwave-safe lid or plastic wrap. Microwave at 50% for 20 minutes.

Remove chicken and let cool slightly; prepare chicken per recipe directions. Strain the broth and freeze for other uses.

Sweet and Sour Turkey Meatloaf

Sodium Per Serving – 91mg   **Serves 8**

This spicy meatloaf is balanced with a tangy sweet and sour sauce. If you think meatloafs are too bland, this will change your mind. Everyone loves this one! Plus, there's plenty left over for a day or two of meatloaf sandwiches . . . yum!

- 1½ pounds ground lean turkey or chicken or a combination of turkey and chicken[1]
- ¾ cup unsalted or low-salt plain bread crumbs[2]
- 1 bell pepper, diced
- ½ sweet onion, diced (about 1 cup)
- 2–3 tablespoons chopped fresh flat-leaf (Italian) parsley
- ½ teaspoon dried basil
- ½ teaspoon garlic powder
- ½ teaspoon dried rosemary, crumbled
- ½ teaspoon dried thyme
- ¼ teaspoon ground black pepper
- 2 eggs, lightly beaten, or ½ cup egg substitute[3]
- ⅓ cup lowfat milk

Sweet and Sour Sauce:
- ½ cup no-salt-added ketchup
- 1 tablespoon cider vinegar
- 1 teaspoon low-salt coarse-grain mustard
- 1 teaspoon sugar substitute or sugar (optional)

▸ Preheat oven to 350ºF (180ºC). Coat a 9x5x3-inch baking dish or loaf pan with nonstick cooking spray.

▸ In a large bowl, combine turkey, bell pepper, onions, parlsey, bread crumbs, basil, garlic powder, rosemary, thyme, and black pepper. Add eggs and milk; mix well and form into a loaf. Place in prepared baking dish and bake, uncovered, in preheated oven for 30 minutes.

▸ Meanwhile, mix together ketchup, vinegar, and mustard; pour over meatloaf. Continue baking for 30 to 45 minutes longer, until no longer pink in the center and internal temperature registers 160ºF (71ºC).

NUTRITIONAL INFO PER SERVING: Calories 205mg, Fat 8mg (Saturated Fat 2mg), Cholesterol 103mg, Carbohydrates 14mg (Fiber 1mg, Sugar 6mg), Sodium 91mg

TOTAL SODIUM AND FAT PER INGREDIENT

Sodium:
1½ lb ground turkey - 480mg
½ c sweet onion - 9mg
1 bell pepper - 4mg
2 eggs - 140mg
 or ½ c egg substitute - 200mg
⅓ c LF milk - 38mg
½ c NSA ketchup - 48mg
1 t mustard - 10mg

Fat (Sat Fat):
1½ lb turkey - 42mg (12mg)
⅔ c NSA crumbs - 6mg (0mg)
2 eggs - 10mg (3mg)
 or ½ c egg substitute - 0mg
⅓ c LF milk - 2mg (1mg)

VARIATION

Beef, Pork and Veal Meatloaf

Instead of turkey or chicken, substitute 12 ounces lean ground beef, 6 ounces ground pork, and 6 ounces ground veal; proceed as directed.

NUTRITIONAL INFO PER SERVING: Calories 303mg, Fat 19mg (Saturated Fat 7mg), Cholesterol 118mg, Carbohydrates 14mg (Fiber 1mg, Sugar 6mg), Sodium 89mg

CHICKEN TAGINE WITH EGGPLANT

Sodium Per Serving – 94mg   Serves 10

Tagine (pronounced ta-zheen) is from Morocco and refers both to a slow-cooked stew or the conical-shaped pot used to cook the stew. Moroccan cuisine uses a variety of intense spices and flavors. This throw-it-in-the-pot-and-forget-about dish is my adaptation of a recipe from **Bon Appetit** *and is both delicious and colorful. The longer this cooks the better it is; allow 2 to 3 hours cooking time. This recipe makes a lot of sauce; freeze leftovers and use again later. Reheat with cooked chicken, cut into bite-size pieces.*

¼ cup all-purpose flour

1½ tablespoons paprika[1]

1½ teaspoons ground black pepper, divided

1 teaspoon garlic powder

2½ pounds chicken, skin removed and larger pieces cut in half[2]

3 tablespoons olive oil, divided

1 large sweet onion, sliced

6 garlic cloves, minced

1½ tablespoons ground coriander

1½ tablespoons ground fennel seeds

1½ tablespoons turmeric

1½ teaspoons ground cumin

1½ teaspoons ground ginger

2 (15-ounce) cans no-salt-added diced tomatoes, drained[3]

4 cups CHICKEN STOCK (page 232) or 2 (15-ounce) cans low-salt chicken broth

2 teaspoons (or 1 envelope) low-salt chicken bouillon granules

2 tablespoons lemon juice

1 large eggplant, unpeeled and cubed[4]

1½ teaspoons dried marjoram

Chopped cilantro (optional)

Slivered almonds (optional)

▷ Place flour, paprika, pepper, and garlic powder in a small paper bag; add chicken, a few pieces at a time, and shake until well coated.

▷ Heat 1 tablespoon oil in a Dutch oven or large heavy pot over medium-high heat; add chicken. Cook until lightly browned on all sides, 4 to 5 minutes.

▷ Add 1 tablespoon oil to same pot; add onions. Cook, stirring frequently, until onions are translucent, 4 to 5 minutes; add garlic. Cook, stirring constantly, until you smell the garlic, 1 to 2 minutes.

▷ Mix in coriander, fennel, turmeric, cumin, ginger, tomatoes, chicken stock, bouillon, and lemon juice; bring to boil. Decrease heat to medium-low; cover and simmer, stirring occasionally, until chicken is tender and falls away from the bone, about 2 hours.

▷ Meanwhile, preheat oven to 400°F (200°C); coat a baking sheet with nonstick cooking spray. In a bowl, mix eggplant and remaining 1 tablespoon oil until coated thoroughly. Place on baking sheet and bake until soft and brown, 20 to 25 minutes.

▷ Ten minutes before serving, stir eggplant and marjoram into the stew; simmer uncovered 10 minutes. Serve topped with cilantro and/or almonds.

NUTRITIONAL INFO PER SERVING: Calories 229mg, Fat 7mg (Saturated Fat 1mg), Cholesterol 70mg, Carbohydrates 15mg (Fiber 4mg, Sugar 6mg), Sodium 94mg (145mg with LS canned broth)

COMMENTS:

1 *I use sweet paprika, but if you like it spicy, add a hotter variety, like Hungarian.*

2 *A good combination to use is 1½ pounds boneless breasts and 1 pound thighs (with bones—the bones will add more flavor to the dish).*

3 *See* COMMENTS #1, *page 151, for additional information on NSA tomatoes.*

4 *Choose smooth skinned eggplants that are 3 to 6-inches in diameter and free of tan spots, scars, or wrinkles. They should feel heavy, have a bright green stem, and quickly return to normal when pressed with the thumb.*

Many recipes suggest salting before cooking to draw out moisture and eliminate any bitter taste, however, it is not necessary if you choose smaller, tender eggplants. Prick the skin in several places before baking to allow the steam to escape.

TOTAL SODIUM AND FAT PER INGREDIENT

Sodium:
1½ T paprika - 4mg
2½ lb chicken - 697mg
1 sweet onion - 12mg
6 garlic cloves - 6mg
1½ T coriander - 3mg
1½ t cumin - 6mg
1½ T fennel - 8mg
1½ T turmeric - 4mg
30 oz NSA diced tomatoes - 100mg
4 c CHICKEN STOCK - 80mg or
LS canned broth - 520mg
1 t LS chicken bouillon - 10mg
1 eggplant - 9mg
Fat (Sat Fat):
1½ T paprika - 1mg (0mg)
2½ lb chicken - 20mg (5mg)
3 T olive oil - 42mg (6mg)
4 c CHICKEN STOCK - 4mg (0mg) or
LS canned broth - 8mg (4mg)
1 eggplant - 1mg (0mg)

1 *Game hens are usually purchased frozen. Once defrosted, remove the giblets and rinse the hen cavity with water before halving.*

2 *Use fresh herbs if possible, the flavor is far superior to dried.*

HERB ROASTED GAME HENS

Sodium Per Serving – 84mg   **Serves 4**

This is an elegant meal that takes very little time to prepare. For added flavor, refrigerate the hens overnight in the herbal marinade. The perfect accompaniment is RICE STUFFING WITH ALMONDS AND OLIVES *(page 199).*

2 Cornish game hens (about 1½ pounds each), defrosted and halved lengthwise[1]

Marinade:

¼ cup dry sherry

1 tablespoon olive oil

6 garlic cloves, minced (about 2 tablespoons)

2 tablespoons chopped fresh basil, or 2 teaspoons dried[2]

2 tablespoons chopped fresh rosemary, or 2 teaspoons dried[2]

2 tablespoons chopped fresh tarragon, or 2 teaspoons dried[2]

▶ *For the marinade*: Mix together the sherry, oil, garlic, basil, rosemary, and tarragon.

▶ Place hens in a plastic bag; add marinade and refrigerate at least 4 hours or overnight, turning bag several times.

▶ Preheat oven to 350°F (180°C). Position rack in bottom third of the oven.

▶ *If using fresh herbs:* Strain marinade, reserving liquid. Place the strained solids (herbs and garlic) and 1–2 tablespoons reserved liquid in a blender, pulse until a smooth paste (add more reserved liquid, if necessary). *If using dried herbs:* Measure 2 tablespoons marinade and set aside; reserve remaining marinade.

▶ Gently slide fingertips under the skin to loosen; rub one-fourth of the herb paste (or marinade) onto each hen. Place skin side up in a roasting pan; drizzle reserved marinade over hens. Bake in preheated oven for 30 minutes, or until golden brown and juices run clear when pierced with a fork. Baste with pan juices every 10 minutes.

NUTRITIONAL INFO PER SERVING (WITHOUT THE SKIN): Calories 200mg, Fat 8mg (Saturated Fat 2mg), Cholesterol 109mg, Carbohydrates 4mg (Fiber 0mg, Sugar 0mg), Sodium 84mg

---

VARIATION

ROASTED GAME HENS WITH ORANGE-HERB SAUCE

Add 1 tablespoon finely grated orange peel to the marinade; proceed as directed. Transfer cooked hens to a platter and keep warm.

For the sauce: Place roasting pan (with juices) on stove over medium-high heat; stir in ½ cup orange juice, ½ cup CHICKEN STOCK *(page 232)* or low-salt canned broth, and ½ teaspoon low-salt chicken bouillon granules, scraping up any browned bits. Bring to a boil; continue cooking until reduced to a gravy consistency, 2 to 3 minutes. Spoon sauce over hens and serve.

NUTRITIONAL INFO PER SERVING: Calories 221mg, Fat 8mg (Saturated Fat 2mg), Cholesterol 111mg, Carbohydrates 8mg (Fiber 0mg, Sugar 3mg), Sodium 88mg

TOTAL SODIUM AND FAT PER INGREDIENT
Sodium:
2 game hens - 325mg
¼ c sherry - 5mg
6 garlic cloves - 6mg
Fat (Sat Fat):
2 game hens - 16mg (4mg)
1 T olive oil - 14mg (2mg)

PAN-SEARED STEAKS WITH TARRAGON SHALLOT SAUCE

Sodium Per Serving – 71mg   Serves 4

This outstanding dish could not be any simpler and is an excellent entrée for entertaining. The tarragon sauce makes this a "restaurant quality" steak.

4 (¾-inch thick) top loin (or New York strip) steaks (about 1 pound)[1]

¼ teaspoon garlic powder

¼ teaspoon ground black pepper

Tarragon Shallot Sauce:

2 shallots, finely chopped

2 tablespoons balsamic vinegar

2 tablespoons white wine vinegar or a dry white wine[2]

⅔ cup BEEF STOCK *(page 233)* or canned low-salt beef broth

½ teaspoon (or ½ envelope) low-salt beef bouillon granules

2 tablespoons unsalted margarine or butter[3]

½ teaspoon dried tarragon

1 tablespoon chopped fresh flat-leaf (Italian) parsley (optional)

▷ Sprinkle steaks with garlic powder and pepper. To cook steaks:

Stove-top cooked steaks: Place a large skillet on medium-high heat; when hot, cook steaks for 4 to 5 minutes per side (medium rare); transfer to a platter and keep warm while preparing sauce.

Oven cooked steaks: Preheat oven to 400°F (200°C). Place an oven-proof skillet over medium-high heat; when hot, quickly brown steaks on all sides. Add 2 tablespoons beef broth; place skillet with steaks in the oven for 10 minutes (for medium rare), or until desired doneness. Transfer steaks to a platter and keep warm while preparing the sauce.

▷ *For the sauce:* Place the same skillet the steaks were cooked on medium-high heat; add shallots. *CAUTION: I can't tell you the number of times I've forgotten that the skillet is extremely hot. Place a pot holder over the handle to remind you not to touch the bare metal.* Ccook, stirring constantly, for 1 minute. Stir in balsamic and white wine vinegars, beef stock, bouillon, margarine, and tarragon, scraping up any browned bits. Bring to a boil; cook, stirring frequently, until sauce has thickened to a gravy consistency. Spoon over steaks and top with parsley.

NUTRITIONAL INFO PER SERVING: Calories 225mg, Fat 12mg (Saturated Fat 4mg), Cholesterol 77mg, Carbohydrates 2mg (Fiber 0mg, Sugar 0mg), Sodium 71mg (88mg with LS canned broth)

COMMENTS:

1 *Use loin cuts for this dish; they are the most tender and flavorful and are best for pan-searing or broiling. See FOOD NOTE, page 120, for info on cuts of beef.*

2 *May also substitute red wine vinegar, a dry sherry, or Marsala wine for the white wine vinegar.*

3 *To reduce saturated fat, use trans-free margarine. Since it contains sodium (90mg per tablespoon), it will increase the sodium per serving to 16mg.*

To keep fat and sodium to a minimum, use a combination of trans-free and unsalted.

TOTAL SODIUM AND FAT PER INGREDIENT

Sodium:
1 lb top loin - 263mg
2 shallot - 2mg
⅔ c BEEF STOCK - 14mg
  or LS canned broth - 80mg
½ t LS beef bouillon - 3mg
1 T parlsey - 2mg
Fat (Sat Fat):
1 lb top loin - 29mg (11mg)
2 T NSA margarine - 16mg (3mg)
  or NSA butter - 24mg (16mg)

1 Rib cuts are very tender and flavorful and are best for pan searing or broiling. Other less expensive cuts that may be substituted, include round steak and top sirloin.

2 To reduce saturated fat, use trans-free margarine. Since it contains sodium (90mg per tablespoon), it will increase the sodium per serving to 74mg.

RIB-EYE STEAK WITH BRANDIED MUSHROOMS

Sodium Per Serving – 66mg   Serves 4

Another excellent and easy-to-prepare dish that will win raves from family and friends.

1 pound rib-eye (or Delmonico), club, or strip steak, cut into 4 pieces[1]	**2–3 garlic cloves, minced**
¼ teaspoon garlic or onion powder	**2 tablespoons chopped fresh flat-leaf (Italian) parsley**
⅛ teaspoon ground black pepper	**½ cup BEEF STOCK (page 233) or canned low-salt beef broth**
1 tablespoon olive oil	**½ teaspoon (or ½ envelope) low-salt beef bouillon granules**
¼ cup sliced sweet onion	**2 tablespoons brandy**
2 ounces sliced mushrooms (about ½ cup)	**1 tablespoon unsalted margarine or butter**[2]

▹ Season meat with garlic powder and pepper.

▹ Heat oil in a heavy skillet over medium-high heat; add meat and brown on both sides, 4 to 5 minutes per side (medium rare). Transfer steaks to a platter and keep warm while preparing sauce.

▹ *For the sauce:* Decrease heat to medium; add onion, mushrooms, garlic, and parsley. Cook, stirring frequently, until onions and mushrooms are soft, 3 to 4 minutes. Add beef stock, bouillon, and brandy; bring to boil and cook until sauce is reduced to a thick, gravy consistency, about 5 minutes. Stir in margarine and serve over steaks. Top with additional chopped parsley.

NUTRITIONAL INFO PER SERVING: Calories 328mg, Fat 23mg (Saturated Fat 8mg), Cholesterol 67mg, Carbohydrates 3mg (Fiber 0mg, Sugar 1mg), Sodium 66mg (78mg with LS canned broth)

TOTAL SODIUM AND FAT PER INGREDIENT

Sodium:
1 lb rib-eye steaks - 236mg
¼ c sweet onion - 2mg
3 garlic cloves - 3mg
½ c mushrooms - 2mg
2 T parsley - 4mg
½ cup BEEF STOCK - 10mg
  or LS canned broth - 60mg
½ t LS beef bouillon - 3mg
2 T brandy - 3mg
Fat (Sat Fat):
1 lb rib-eye steaks - 70mg (28mg)
1 T olive oil - 14mg (2mg)
½ cup BEEF STOCK - 1mg (0mg)
  or LS canned broth - 0mg
1 T NSA margarine - 8mg (2mg)
  or NSA butter - 12mg (8mg)

FOOD NOTE

CUTS OF BEEF

There are five main cuts of beef: chuck, rib, loin, round, and breast/flank. The best beef is marbled with very thin lines of fat; lower grades of beef have lots of marbling or none at all. The cut of beef determines the way it should be cooked and whether or not it needs marinating:

Chuck – tough with lots of gristle, but most flavorful and economical. Perfect for slow cooking, such as pot roasts. Popular cuts are arm, chuck, shoulder, and blade roasts or steaks.

Rib – tender, juicy, and flavorful. Does not need marinating, perfect for grilling or roasting. Popular cuts are rib and rib-eye steaks and roasts.

Loin – the most tender and expensive. Does not need marinating and is ideal for grilling or broiling. Popular cuts are tenderloin, Porterhouse, T-bone, top loin (or New York strip), filet mignon, top sirloin, and roast beef.

Round – tough, but lean. Best if marinated or slow cooked with liquid. Popular cuts are bottom round, London broil, round, top round, round tip, and rump roast.

Breast or Flank – tough and fatty. Best if marinated, then grilled or slow cooked. Popular cuts are brisket, short ribs, hanger, flank, or skirt steaks.

TOP SIRLOIN WITH MUSTARD SAUCE

Sodium Per Serving – 83mg   Serves 4

This dish is simple to prepare, just pan fry the steaks, add a sauce, and "wow" everyone with a restaurant-quality meal.

1 pound top sirloin, cut into 4 pieces[1]

½ teaspoon garlic or onion powder

¼ teaspoon ground black pepper

1 teaspoon olive oil

Mustard Sauce:

3 tablespoons brandy

1 cup BEEF STOCK *(page 233)* **or canned low-salt beef broth**

½ teaspoon (or ½ envelope) low-salt beef bouillon granules

2 tablespoons coarse-grain mustard[2]

1 tablespoon unsalted margarine or butter[3]

▸ Season meat with garlic powder and pepper.

▸ Heat oil in a large skillet over medium-high heat; add meat and brown on both sides, 4 to 5 minutes per side (medium rare). Transfer steaks to a platter and keep warm while preparing sauce.

▸ *For the Mustard Sauce:* Decrease heat to medium; stir in brandy and deglaze by scraping up any brown bits of meat. Add beef stock and bouillon; bring to a boil and cook, uncovered, until the sauce is reduced to about ½ cup and has thickened to a gravy consistency. Stir in mustard and margarine.

▸ Pour on top of steaks and serve.

NUTRITIONAL INFO PER SERVING: Calories 248mg, Fat 10mg (Saturated Fat 2mg), Cholesterol 52mg, Carbohydrates 2mg (Fiber 0mg, Sugar 0mg), Sodium 85mg (115mg with LS canned broth)

COMMENTS:

1 *Substitute any lean and flavorful cut of your choice, like Porterhouse, rib-eye, beef tenderloin, or filet mignon.*

2 *Most coarse-grained mustard has 65mg sodium per teaspoon, look for no-salt-added brands with 10mg or less (see RESOURCES, page 272).*

3 *To reduce saturated fat, use trans-free margarine. Since it contains sodium (90mg per tablespoon), it will increase the sodium per serving to 108mg.*

VARIATION

STEAKS WITH WILD MUSHROOM-MUSTARD SAUCE

After deglazing the pan, add 1 minced shallot and 1 cup sliced wild mushrooms (such as oyster and shiitake). Cook, stirring frequently, until shallots are translucent, 2 to 3 minutes.

When you add the beef stock, also add 1 tablespoon chopped fresh tarragon (or 1 teaspoon dried) and ½ cup white wine; proceed are directed. Before serving, stir in ¼ cup lowfat milk, half-and-half, or light cream.

NUTRITIONAL INFO PER SERVING: Calories 284mg, Fat 10mg (Saturated Fat 2mg), Cholesterol 53mg, Carbohydrates 4mg (Fiber 0mg, Sugar 2mg), Sodium 95mg

TOTAL SODIUM AND FAT PER INGREDIENT

Sodium:
  1 lb top sirloin - 254mg
  3 T brandy - 4mg
  1 c BEEF STOCK - 20mg
    or LS canned broth - 120mg
  ½ t bouillon - 3mg
  2 T NSA mustard - 60mg

Fat (Sat Fat):
  1 lb top sirloin - 19mg (7mg)
  1 t olive oil - 5mg (1mg)
  1 c BEEF STOCK - 1mg (0mg)
    or LS canned broth - 0mg
  2 T coarse mustard - 6mg (0mg)
  1 T NSA margarine - 8mg (2mg)
    or NSA butter - 12mg (8mg)

COMMENTS:

1 CHICKEN STOCK *(page 232) or canned low-salt chicken broth may be substituted for the beef stock or broth.*

POT ROAST

Sodium Per Serving – 162mg   Serves 8–10

The secret to a tender and succulent pot roast is the long, slow cooking (about 3 hours).

3½ pounds chuck roast

1 teaspoon garlic powder

1 teaspoon sweet paprika

1 teaspoon dried rosemary, crushed

1 teaspoon dried thyme

1 teaspoon ground black pepper

1 tablespoon olive oil

¾ cup BEEF STOCK *(page 233)* or canned low-salt beef broth[1]

1 teaspoon (or 1 envelope) low-salt beef bouillon granules

2 yellow onions, cut into wedges

4 garlic cloves, minced

3 large carrots, cut in 1" pieces

3 large red potatoes, cut in 1" pieces

½ cup red wine

2 tablespoons cornstarch, mixed with 2 tablespoons water to make a paste

▹ Preheat oven to 350°F (180°C).

▹ Combine garlic powder, paprika, pepper, rosemary, thyme, and pepper; rub onto roast.

▹ Heat oil in a large oven-proof pan over medium-high heat; brown roast on all sides. Remove and set aside.

▹ Stir in beef stock and deglaze by scraping up any browned bits of meat; mix in bouillon. Return roast to pan; arrange onions and garlic on top; cover and bake in a preheated oven for 2 hours. Remove from oven.

▹ Lift out roast and place onions underneath; add potatoes, carrots, and enough liquid (stock and/or water) to nearly cover veggies. Place roast on top of veggies (roast should be out of the liquid). Cook, covered, for 1 hour more; remove roast and let sit 10 minutes before slicing.

▹ Remove vegetables to a platter and keep warm while preparing the gravy.

▹ *For the gravy:* Place roasting pan (with juices) over medium-high heat; add wine, scraping up any browned bits of meat. Bring to a boil; gradually add cornstarch paste, stirring constantly, until thickened to a gravy consistency.

▹ Slice meat and place on a platter with vegetables; serve with gravy poured on

NUTRITIONAL INFO PER SERVING: Calories 576mg, Fat 36mg (Saturated Fat 14mg), Cholesterol 142mg, Carbohydrates 21mg (Fiber 3mg, Sugar 3mg), Sodium 162mg (172mg with LS canned broth)

TOTAL SODIUM AND FAT PER INGREDIENT

Sodium:
 3½ lb chuck roast - 1095mg
 ¾ c BEEF STOCK - 15mg
  or LS canned broth - 90mg
 1 t LS beef bouillon - 5mg
 2 onions - 6mg
 4 garlic cloves - 4mg
 3 carrots - 126mg
 3 red potatoes - 38mg
 ½ c red wine - 6mg
 1 T cornstarch - 1mg

Fat (Sat Fat):
 3½ lb chuck roast - 197mg (80mg)
 1 T olive oil - 14mg (2mg)
 ¾ c BEEF STOCK - 1mg (0mg)
  or LS canned broth - 0mg

Beef Stroganoff

Sodium Per Serving – 134mg   Serves 4

Beef, mushrooms, and brandy simmered in a thick sour cream sauce that is laced with dill. Serve this family favorite over pasta.

COMMENTS:

1 tablespoon all-purpose flour

½ teaspoon garlic or onion powder

½ teaspoon ground black pepper

⅛ teaspoon paprika[1]

1 pound top sirloin, cut into strips[2]

1 tablespoon olive oil

1 large sweet onion, sliced

2 garlic cloves, minced

1 pound crimini mushrooms, sliced (about 8 cups)[3]

2 cups BEEF STOCK *(page 233)* or canned low-salt beef broth

¼ cup brandy or cognac[4]

2 teaspoons (or 2 envelopes) low-salt beef bouillon granules

1 teaspoon low-salt Worcestershire sauce

1½ tablespoons prepared horseradish

2 teaspoons fresh dill, snipped (optional)[5]

½ cup lowfat sour cream

8 ounces linguine or pasta (such as farfalle or fusilli)

▸ Mix together the flour, garlic powder, pepper, and paprika; place in a paper bag. Add meat and shake until well coated.

▸ Heat oil in a large skillet over medium-high heat; add meat. Cook, stirring frequently, until browned on all sides, 2 to 3 minutes; remove meat and set aside.

▸ Add onions and cook, stirring frequently, until onions are translucent, 2 to 3 minutes; add garlic and mushrooms and cook, stirring frequently, until the mushrooms soften, 3 to 4 minutes.

▸ Stir in 2 tablespoons brandy and deglaze skillet by scraping up any browned bits. Add broth, bouillon, Worcestershire, and remaining 2 tablespoons brandy; decrease heat to medium-low and simmer, uncovered, until liquid is reduced by half, about 10 minutes. Stir in meat, horseradish, dill, and sour cream; cook until meat is heated through, about 3 minutes. Serve over cooked linguine or pasta; sprinkle with paprika.

NUTRITIONAL INFO PER SERVING: Calories 548mg, Fat 15mg (Saturated Fat 5mg), Cholesterol 63mg, Carbohydrates 56mg (Fiber 3mg, Sugar 7mg), Sodium 134mg (184mg with LS canned broth)

COMMENTS:

1 I like a little zip in this dish, so I add Hungarian hot paprika, but sweet paprika works well, too. If you use sweet paprik, and want a little heat, add a pinch of cayenne pepper or dash of hot pepper sauce before serving.

2 Because the meat is not cooked for very long, the more tender the beef, the better it will be. Other comparable cuts to use, include beef tenderloin (or filet mignon) and Porterhouse steaks.

3 Criminis are similar to button mushrooms, but have more flavor. Buttons, criminis, or a combination of both, may be used. For other mushroom varieties, see FOOD NOTE, page 44.

4 Marsala or red wine may be substituted.

5 Use kitchen shears to snip the dill into small pieces.

TOTAL SODIUM AND FAT PER INGREDIENT

Sodium:
1 lb top sirloin - 254mg
1 sweet onion - 12mg
2 garlic cloves - 2mg
1 lb mushrooms - 22mg
2 c BEEF STOCK - 40mg
  or LS canned broth - 240mg
2 t LS beef bouillon - 10mg
1 t LS Worcestershire - 20mg
1½ T horseradish - 90mg
2 t dill - 1mg
½ c LF sour cream - 68mg
8 oz linguine or pasta - 16mg
Fat (Sat Fat):
1 lb top sirloin - 19mg (7mg)
1 T olive oil - 14mg (2mg)
1 lb mushrooms - 2mg (0mg)
2 c BEEF STOCK - 2mg (0mg)
  or LS canned broth - 0mg
1½ T horseradish - 4mg (0mg)
½ c LF sour cream - 14mg (8mg)
8 oz linguini or pasta - 4mg (1mg)

1 *Pork, chicken, or turkey breasts, pounded thin, may be substituted for more costly veal.*

2 *To reduce saturated fat, use trans-free margarine. Since it contains sodium (90mg per tablespoon), it will increase the sodium per serving to 108mg.*

3 *Criminis are similar to button mushrooms, but have more flavor. Any mushroom or combination of mushrooms may be used. See* FOOD NOTE, *page 44, for mushroom varieties.*

VEAL MARSALA

Sodium Per Serving – 78mg   Serves 4

This classic Italian dish is sure to impress any guest, especially if you use a nice cut of veal. (Although veal can be a bit pricey, this is well worth the extra cost.) Veal Marsala is often made with demi-glace, a rich brown concentrate that is the basis for many delicious sauces. Even though making demi-glace is very time consuming, bottled demi-glace is available in many supermarkets. Unfortunately, it is very high in sodium. This version does not use demi-glace, but achieves a similar taste and richness (and without the salt) by cooking down the liquids to a syrup consistency.

1½ pounds sliced veal cutlets[1]
2 tablespoons all-purpose flour
¼ teaspoon garlic powder
¼ teaspoon dried oregano
¼ teaspoon dried thyme
⅛ teaspoon ground black pepper
1 tablespoon olive oil

Sauce:

2 tablespoons unsalted margarine or butter, divided[2]
6 ounces sliced mushrooms, such as crimini or button (about 3 cups)[3]
1 garlic clove, minced
½ cup Marsala wine
½ cup BEEF STOCK *(page 233)* **or canned low-salt beef broth**
1 teaspoon (or 1 envelope) low-salt beef bouillon granules

▸ Mix flour with garlic powder, oregano, thyme, and pepper; dredge veal in flour mixture, shaking off any excess.

▸ Heat oil in skillet over medium-high heat; add veal and brown on both sides, 2 to 3 minutes per side. Transfer veal to a platter and keep warm while making the sauce.

▸ *For the sauce:* Decrease heat to medium; melt 1 tablespoon margarine in the same skillet. Add mushrooms and cook, stirring frequently, until soft, 3 to 4 minutes; add garlic and cook, stirring constantly, until you smell the garlic, about 1 minute. Stir in Marsala and deglaze the pan by scraping up any brown bits; add beef stock and bring to a boil. Continue cooking until sauce thickens to a syrup consistency; stir in remaining 1 tablespoon margarine.

▸ Return veal to skillet and heat through. Transfer veal to a platter, pour sauce over meat and serve with parsley sprinkled on top.

NUTRITIONAL INFO PER SERVING: Calories 216mg, Fat 7mg (Saturated Fat 2mg), Cholesterol 90mg, Carbohydrates 6mg (Fiber 0mg, Sugar 1mg), Sodium 78mg (86mg with LS canned broth)

TOTAL SODIUM AND FAT PER INGREDIENT
Sodium:
  1½ lb veal - 435mg
  1 garlic clove - 1mg
  8 oz mushrooms - 6mg
  ½ cup Marsala wine - 11mg
  ½ cup BEEF STOCK - 10mg
    or LS canned broth - 60mg
  1 t LS beef bouillon - 5mg
Fat (Sat Fat):
  1½ lb veal - 12mg (4mg)
  1 T olive oil - 14mg (2mg)
  2 T NSA margarine -16mg (3mg)
    or NSA butter - 24mg (16mg)
  8 oz mushrooms - 1mg (0mg)
  ½ c BEEF STOCK - 1mg (0mg)
    or LS canned broth - 0mg

ROAST LEG OF LAMB WITH MUSTARD-ROSEMARY CRUST

Sodium Per Serving – 154mg
Serves 8

This lamb is covered with a garlic, rosemary, and mustard crust that helps keep the juices inside. I use a food processor, or pestle and mortar, to make the paste that is rubbed on the lamb. (Using a blender is not recommended, as the paste is too thick for a blender to be effective.)

1 (3-pound) boneless leg of lamb, excess fat trimmed, and lamb tied

4 garlic cloves, finely minced

2 tablespoons chopped fresh rosemary, or 2 teaspoons dried

1 tablespoon no-salt-added coarse-grain mustard[1]

¼ teaspoon garlic powder

¼ teaspoon ground black pepper

½ cup red wine, such as Merlot

½ cup BEEF STOCK (page 233) or canned low-salt beef broth

1 teaspoon (or 1 envelope) low-salt beef bouillon granules

1–2 teaspoons cornstarch, mixed with 1–2 tablespoons water to make a paste

1–2 tablespoons unsalted margarine or butter[2]

▷ Preheat oven to 350ºF (180ºC). Adjust shelf to middle of the oven.

▷ Place lamb in a shallow roasting pan. Mix garlic with rosemary, mustard, garlic powder, and pepper; rub all over lamb.

▷ Roast lamb, uncovered, in a preheated oven until thermometer reaches 140ºF (60ºC), about 1½ hours. Transfer lamb to a cutting board and let stand for 15 to 20 minutes. NOTE: Roast will continue cooking as it sits; internal temperature will rise to about 150ºF (65ºC) for medium doneness. For medium-rare, remove roast when the thermometer reaches 130ºF (55ºC).

▷ Slice lamb and serve with gravy.

▷ *For the gravy:* Pour off all but 1 tablespoon fat from roasting pan and place pan over medium-high heat. Add wine; stirring constantly, deglaze pan by scraping up any brown bits of lamb. Add beef stock and bouillon; cook, stirring frequently, until sauce has thickened to a gravy consistency, 2 to 3 minutes (if necessary, slowly add cornstarch paste, stirring constantly, until thickened to desired consistency). Just before serving, remove from heat and stir in margarine.

NUTRITIONAL INFO PER SERVING: Calories 345mg, Fat 13mg (Saturated Fat 4mg), Cholesterol 151mg, Carbohydrates 2mg (Fiber 0mg, Sugar 1mg), Sodium 154mg (162mg with LS canned broth)

COMMENTS:

1 Most coarse-grained mustard has 65mg sodium per teaspoon, look for no-salt-added brands with 10mg or less (see RESOURCES, page 272).

2 To reduce saturated fat, use trans-free margarine. Since it contains sodium (90mg per tablespoon), it will increase the sodium per serving to 169mg.

TOTAL SODIUM AND FAT PER INGREDIENT

Sodium:
3 lb leg of lamb - 871mg
4 garlic cloves - 2mg
2 T rosemary - 1mg
1 T mustard - 30mg
½ c red wine - 6mg
½ c BEEF STOCK - 10mg
  or LS canned broth - 162mg
1 t LS beef bouillon - 5mg
Fat (Sat Fat):
3 lb leg of lamb - 69mg (25mg)
½ c BEEF STOCK - 1mg (0mg)
  or LS canned broth - 0mg
1 T NSA margarine - 8mg (2mg)
  or NSA butter - 12mg (8mg)

1 *I think this sauce tastes best using a fruit-sweetened jam rather than a sugar-sweetened one. If you want a smooth sauce, use seedless jam.*

2 *To reduce saturated fat, use trans-free margarine. Since it contains sodium (90mg per tablespoon), it will increase the sodium per serving to 76mg.*

PORK CHOPS WITH RASPBERRY SAUCE

Sodium Per Serving – 53mg   Serves 4

This is so simple to prepare and absolutely devine! The sweet-tart taste of the raspberry sauce is the perfect compliment to the pork chops.

4 (4-ounce) boneless pork loin chops

½ teaspoon dried sage

½ teaspoon dried thyme

¼ teaspoon garlic or onion powder

⅛ teaspoon ground black pepper

1 tablespoon olive oil

Raspberry Sauce:

⅓ cup fruit sweetened raspberry jam[1]

2 tablespoons orange juice

1 tablespoon raspberry or balsamic vinegar

2 tablespoons dry sherry

2–3 drops hot pepper sauce, such as *Tabasco* (optional)

1 tablespoon unsalted margarine or butter[2]

▶ Combine sage, thyme, garlic powder, and pepper; rub over pork chops.

▶ Heat oil in a large skillet over medium-high heat; add chops. Lightly brown on both sides, 4 to 5 minutes per side. Transfer chops to a platter and keep warm while preparing sauce.

▶ *For the Raspberry Sauce:* In same skillet, stir in jam, orange juice, vinegar, sherry, and hot pepper sauce; bring to a boil. Cook, stirring constantly, until sauce has thickened to a gravy consistency, 2 to 3 minutes; stir in margarine. Serve over pork chops.

NUTRITIONAL INFO PER SERVING: Calories 234mg, Fat 10mg (Saturated Fat 2mg), Cholesterol 64mg, Carbohydrates 12mg (Fiber 0mg, Sugar 11mg), Sodium 53mg

TOTAL SODIUM AND FAT PER INGREDIENT

Sodium:
  1 lb pork chops - 206mg
  2 T sherry - 3mg
  2 drops hot pepper sauce - 4mg
Fat (Sat Fat):
  1 lb pork chops - 17mg (6mg)
  1 T olive oil - 14mg (2mg)
  1 T NSA margarine - 8mg (2mg)
   or NSA butter - 12mg (8mg)

FRUIT STUFFED PORK TENDERLOIN

Sodium Per Serving – 70mg   Serves 6

This is a family favorite at Easter and other special occasions. The colorful stuffing makes a beautiful presentation and the apple-brandy flavored gravy is a delicious accompaniment.

1½ pound boned pork loin roast[1]

1 tablespoon fresh rosemary, crumbled, or 1 teaspoon dried

¼ teaspoon garlic powder

⅛ teaspoon ground black pepper

2 teaspoons minced roasted garlic[2]

5–6 dried apricots, chopped

¼ cup dried cranberries[3]

2 tablespoons chopped fresh flat-leaf (Italian) parsley

1–2 tablespoons prepared horse-radish[4]

Gravy:

¼ cup brandy[5]

1 cup CHICKEN STOCK *(page 232)* or canned low-salt chicken broth

⅓ cup apple juice or cider

1 teaspoon (or 1 envelope) low-salt chicken bouillon granules

1–2 teaspoons cornstarch, mixed with 1–2 tablespoons water to make a paste

▷ Preheat oven to 350°F (180°C).

▷ Slit pork lengthwise, but not quite all the way through, to form a deep pocket. Sprinkle the inside with rosemary, garlic powder, pepper, and garlic. Stuff with apricots, cranberries, and parsley. Roll up and tie with heavy string, securing at 1 inch intervals. Rub horseradish over the outside of the roast.

▷ Heat oil in a large skillet over medium-high heat; brown roast on all sides. Remove roast and insert a thermometer; place in a shallow roasting pan. Bake in a preheated oven until the internal temperature registers 160°F (71°C), about 1½ hours. Transfer roast to a cutting board and let stand 10 minutes while preparing gravy.

▷ *For the gravy:* Place roasting pan (with juices) over medium-high heat; stir in brandy and deglaze pan by scraping up any browned bits of pork. Add chicken stock, apple juice, and bouillon; bring to a boil. Cook, stirring frequently, until sauce begins to thicken. If needed, gradually add cornstarch paste, stirring contantly, until it thickens to a gravy consistency.

▷ Slice the pork and serve with gravy on the side.

NUTRITIONAL INFO PER SERVING: Calories 206mg, Fat 5mg (Saturated Fat 1mg), Cholesterol 76mg, Carbohydrates 9mg (Fiber 1mg, Sugar 7mg), Sodium 73mg (91mg with LS canned broth)

COMMENTS:

[1] *Most pork loins come pre-packaged in brine and have up to 400mg sodium per 4-ounce serving. Fresh packaged roasts without the brine have 60mg or less sodium per serving.*

[2] *I like to make extra roasted garlic (see COOKING TIP, Roasting Garlic, page 185) and keep it on hand to use in different dishes.*

Bottled roasted garlic may be used, although I think the flavor of fresh roasted garlic is far superior to the bottled variety.

[3] *Currants may also be substituted for the cranberries.*

[4] *Rubbing horseradish onto the roast helps lock in the juices and keeps moisture from escaping during the cooking process.*

[5] *Madeira, Marsala, or a dry red wine may also be used.*

TOTAL SODIUM AND FAT PER INGREDIENT

Sodium:
1½ lb pork tenderloin - 340mg
2 garlic cloves - 2mg
5 dried apricots - 2mg
¼ c dried cranberries - 1mg
2 T parsley - 4mg
1 T horseradish - 60mg
1 t LS chicken bouillon - 5mg
⅓ c apple juice - 3mg
1 c CHICKEN STOCK - 20mg
  or LS canned broth - 130mg
Fat (Sat Fat):
1½ lb pork loin - 23mg (8mg)
1 T horseradish - 3mg (0mg)
1 c CHICKEN STOCK - 1mg (0mg)
  or LS canned broth - 2mg (1mg)

COMMENTS:

COMMENTS:

1 *Sea bass, cod, or monkfish may be substituted for the red snapper.*

2 *To reduce saturated fat, use trans-free margarine (or a combination of trans-free and unsalted). Since it contains sodium (90mg per tablespoon), it will increase the sodium per serving to 179mg.*

3 *A dry white wine, such as Chardonnay, may also be used instead of the sake or vermouth.*

RED SNAPPER BEURRE MEUNIERE

Sodium Per Serving – 111mg   Serves 4

Beurre Meunière simply means the fish is coated in flour, then sautéed, and served in a lemony butter sauce with a hint of tarragon. This elegant dish takes less than 10 minutes from start to finish and will win rave reviews from any fish lover.

4 red snapper filets (about 1½ pounds)[1]

2 tablespoons all-purpose flour

¼ teaspoon garlic or onion powder

⅛ teaspoon ground black pepper

1 tablespoon olive oil

3 tablespoons unsalted margarine or butter, divided[2]

1 shallot, finely minced

1 garlic clove, finely minced

¼ cup sake or vermouth[3]

1 tablespoon fresh lemon juice

1 tablepoon chopped fresh tarragon, or 1½ teaspoons dried

2–3 drops hot pepper sauce, such as *Tabasco*

▷ Combine flour, garlic powder, and pepper; dredge snapper in flour, shaking off any excess.

▷ Heat oil in a large skillet over medium heat; add snapper. Cook fish until golden brown, 2 to 3 minutes; turn and cook until fish flakes easily with a fork, 2 to 3 minutes. Transfer to a platter and keep warm while preparing sauce.

▷ *For the sauce:* In another skillet, melt 1 tablespoon margarine over medium heat; add shallots and garlic. Cook, stirring constantly, until shallots are soft, about 2 minutes; add sake, lemon juice, and tarragon. Cook, stirring constantly, until reduced slightly.

▷ Remove skillet from heat and stir in remaining 2 tablespoons margarine; mix in hot pepper sauce. Spoon sauce over fish and garnish with lemon slices and fresh parsley, if desired.

NUTRITIONAL INFO PER SERVING: Calories 293mg, Fat 12mg (Saturated Fat 2mg), Cholesterol 63mg, Carbohydrates 6mg (Fiber 0mg, Sugar 0mg), Sodium 111mg

TOTAL SODIUM AND FAT PER INGREDIENT

Sodium:
  1 lb red snapper - 435mg
  1 shallot - 1mg
  1 garlic clove - 1mg
  ¼ c sake - 1mg
  2 drops hot pepper sauce - 4mg
Fat (Sat Fat):
  1 lb red snapper - 9mg (1mg)
  2 T olive oil - 28mg (4mg)
  3 T NSA margarine - 24mg (5mg)
   or NSA butter - 36mg (24mg)

ORANGE ROUGHY IN CREAMY LEEK SAUCE

Sodium Per Serving – 93mg   Serves 4

Orange Roughy is a mild-tasting fish that comes from New Zealand and is low in both fat and sodium (18mg per ounce). I'm not sure where this recipe came from, but I've added sake (vermouth or white wine may be substituted), which, with the leeks, compliments the fish very well. Use the sauce on other mild-tasting fish, like sole, cod, flounder, and haddock.

2 tablespoons unsalted or trans-free margarine[1]

2 leeks (white and lite green parts), sliced[2]

½ teaspoon dried thyme

4 orange roughy fillets (about 1 pound)[3]

¼ teaspoon onion powder

⅛ teaspoon ground black pepper

½ cup half-and-half or light cream

¼ cup sake[4]

2 tablespoons chopped fresh chives or green onions (green part only)

▸ Melt margarine in a large skillet over medium heat; add leeks and thyme. Cook, stirring frequently, until leeks start to soften, about 5 minutes. Decrease heat to low; cover and cook, stirring occasionally, until leeks are soft, 10 minutes.

▸ Season fish with onion powder and pepper; arrange fish on top of leeks. Add half-and-half and sake; cover and cook until fish is opaque, about 8 minutes. Transfer fish to a platter and keep warm while preparing sauce.

▸ Raise heat to medium-high and bring to boil; continue cooking, stirring frequently, until slightly thickened, about 3 minutes. Pour over fish and garnish with chives.

NUTRITIONAL INFO PER SERVING: Calories 201mg, Fat 8mg (Saturated Fat 4mg), Cholesterol 34mg, Carbohydrates 9mg (Fiber 1mg, Sugar 2mg), Sodium 93mg

COMMENTS:

1 *To reduce saturated fat, use trans-free margarine. Since it contains sodium (90mg per tablespoon), it will increase the sodium per serving to 138mg.*

2 *For additional info on cleaning and storing leeks, see* FOOD NOTE, *page 176.*

3 *May also substitute cod, flounder, sole, or haddock.*

4 *Vermouth or a dry white wine, such as Chardonnay, may be used instead of sake.*

TOTAL SODIUM AND FAT PER INGREDIENT

Sodium:
  2 leeks - 36mg
  1 lb orange roughy - 286mg
  ½ c half-and-half - 50mg
    or light cream - 41mg
  ¼ c sake - 1mg

Fat (Sat Fat):
  2 T NSA margarine - 16mg (3mg)
    or NSA butter - 24mg (16mg)
  1 lb orange roughy - 3mg (2mg)
  ½ c half-and-half - 14mg (9mg)
    or light cream - 37mg (23mg)

COMMENTS:

1 *Cooked or canned no-salt-added salmon may be used (see RESOURCES, page 272).*

2 *See FOOD NOTE, page 171, for shallot information.*

3 *See COMMENTS #2, page 133, for low-salt horseradish brands.*

4 *For info on making bread crumbs, see COOKING TIP, page 46.*

5 *See Eggs and Egg Substitutes, page 38, for a comparison of fat and sodium in eggs and egg substitutes.*

6 *To reduce saturated fat, use trans-free margarine. Since it contains sodium (90mg per tablespoon), it will increase the sodium per serving to 136mg.*

To keep fat and sodium to a minimum, use a combination of trans-free and unsalted.

TOTAL SODIUM AND FAT PER INGREDIENT

Salmon Cakes:
Sodium:
1 lb salmon - 267mg
2 green onions - 8mg
2 shallots - 4mg
2 T lite mayonnaise - 120mg
1 T horseradish - 60mg
2½ c LS bread crumbs - 120mg
2 eggs - 124mg
   or ½ c egg substitute - 200mg
Fat (Sat Fat):
1 lb salmon- 49mg (10mg)
2 T lite mayonnaise - 6mg (0mg)
2½ c LS crumbs - 3mg (3mg)
2 eggs - 8mg (2mg)
   or ½ c egg substitute - 0mg

Orange Butter Sauce:
Sodium:
¼ c OJ concentrate - 2mg
1 shallot - 2mg
Fat (Sat Fat):
⅓ c NSA margarine - 43mg (8mg)
   or NSA butter - 64mg (43mg)

SALMON CAKES

Sodium Per Serving – 161mg   Makes 8 cakes

Although crab cakes are a favorite for many people, they usually have too much sodium for a low-salt diet. Depending on the variety, each fish cake can range anywhere from 249mg to 711mg. If you're a fan of crab cakes, you'll love this version made with salmon. Serve it plain or with a light butter sauce.

1 pound salmon filet, cubed[1]	**¼ teaspoon garlic or onion powder**
2 green onions, chopped (white and lite green parts)	**⅛ teaspoon ground black pepper**
2 shallots, chopped[2]	**½ teaspoon sugar substitute or sugar**
3 tablespoons lemon juice	**2½ cups low-salt unseasoned bread crumbs[4]**
2 tablespoons lite mayonnaise or mayonnaise-like dressing	**2 eggs, lightly beaten, or ½ cup egg substitute[5]**
1 tablespoon prepared horse-radish[3]	ORANGE OR LEMON BUTTER SAUCE *(recipes follow)*
1 teaspoon grated lemon peel	

▸ Combine salmon, green onions, shallots, lemon juice, mayonnaise, horseradish, lemon peel, garlic powder, pepper, and sweetener in a food processor; pulse until coarsely chopped. Transfer to a bowl; mix in bread crumbs and eggs. Form into 8 patties.

▸ *To oven bake:* Place cakes on a baking sheet and bake in a preheated oven at 475°F (240°C) for 15 to 18 minutes, or until golden brown.

▸ *To pan fry:* Heat 1 tablespoon oil in a large skillet over medium-high heat; cook cakes until lightly browned on each side, about 4 minutes per side. Remove and drain on paper towels. *NOTE: Salmon cakes are also good when grilled until lightly brown on each side.*

▸ Serve with ORANGE OR LEMON BUTTER SAUCE.

NUTRITIONAL INFO PER SERVING: Calories 323mg, Fat 17mg (Saturated Fat 4mg), Cholesterol 160mg, Carbohydrates 13mg (Fiber 1mg, Sugar 2mg), Sodium 161mg

ORANGE BUTTER SAUCE

Sodium Per Serving – 1mg   **Makes about ¾ cup**

This butter sauce is also good on most mild-tasting or grilled fish.

⅓ cup unsalted margarine or butter, divided[6]	**1 shallot, finely minced**
¼ cup orange juice concentrate	**1 teaspoon white wine vinegar or white balsamic vinegar**

▶ Melt 1 tablespoon margarine in a pan over medium heat; stir in orange juice, shallots, and vinegar. Add remaining 5 tablespoons margarine, 1 tablespoon at a time, stirring until melted before adding next piece. Serve over fish or salmon cakes.

NUTRITIONAL INFO PER SERVING: Calories 125mg, Fat 11mg (Saturated Fat 2mg), Cholesterol 0mg, Carbohydrates 8mg (Fiber 0mg, Sugar 7mg), Sodium 1mg

---

VARIATION
LEMON BUTTER SAUCE
Instead of orange juice and vinegar, substitute 1½ tablespoons lemon juice and 2 tablespoons white wine; proceed as directed.

NUTRITIONAL INFO PER SERVING: Calories 99mg, Fat 11mg (Saturated Fat 2mg), Cholesterol 0mg, Carbohydrates 1mg (Fiber 0mg, Sugar 0mg), Sodium 1mg

TUNA IN MARSALA SAUCE

Sodium Per Serving – 46mg   Serves 4

My friend, Margaret Napora, prepared this dish for a spur-of-the-moment dinner. It is so simple and absolutely divine — fresh fish is a must!

4 yellowfin or albacore tuna steaks (about 1 pound)[1]

¼ teaspoon garlic powder

⅛ teaspoon ground black pepper

1 tablespoon olive oil

4 tablespoons unsalted margarine or butter[2]

1 shallot, minced

1 garlic clove, finely minced

½ cup Marsala wine[3]

Juice of 1 lemon (about 2 tablespoons)

1 tablespoon minced fresh herbs, such as chives, tarragon, or flat-leaf (Italian) parsley

▶ Season tuna with garlic powder and pepper.

▶ Heat oil in skillet over medium-high heat; cook steaks for 3 to 4 minutes per side (medium-rare). Transfer tuna to a platter and keep warm while preparing sauce.

▶ *For the sauce:* In same skillet, decrease heat to medium and melt margarine; add shallots and garlic. Cook, stirring constantly, for 2 minutes; add wine, scraping up any browned bits. Bring to boil; cook, stirring frequently, until sauce is reduced by about half, 2 to 3 minutes. Stir in lemon juice and fresh herbs. Spoon over the tuna and serve.

NUTRITIONAL INFO PER SERVING: Calories 275mg, Fat 13mg (Saturated Fat 2mg), Cholesterol 51mg, Carbohydrates 5mg (Fiber 0mg, Sugar 1mg), Sodium 46mg

COMMENTS:

1 *Halibut or swordfish may be substituted for the tuna.*

2 *To reduce saturated fat, use trans-free margarine. Since it contains sodium (90mg per tablespoon), it will increase the sodium per serving to 136mg.*
To keep fat and sodium to a minimum, use a combination of trans-free and unsalted.

3 *Madeira or red wine may be substituted for the Marsala wine.*

TOTAL SODIUM AND FAT PER INGREDIENT

Sodium:
1 lb yellowfin tuna - 168mg
1 shallot - 2mg
1 garlic clove - 1mg
½ c Marsala wine - 11mg
Fat (Sat Fat):
1 lb yellowfin tuna - 4mg (1mg)
1 T olive oil - 14mg (2mg)
¼ c NSA margarine - 32mg (6mg)
or NSA butter - 48mg (32mg)

1 *Swordfish may be substituted for mahi mahi. Other alternatives are monkfish and tuna, but they won't be as sweet as the mahi mahi.*

2 *To reduce saturated fat, use trans-free margarine. Since it contains sodium (90mg per tablespoon), it will increase the sodium per serving to 168mg.*

To keep fat and sodium to a minimum, use a combination of trans-free and unsalted.

GRILLED MAHI MAHI ALMONDINE

Sodium Per Serving – 100mg   Serves 4

This grilled dish brings back memories of my days in Hawaii. It's simple enough for everyday faire, but also is an elegant dinner party entrée.

4 mahi mahi filets (about 1 pound)[1]

¼ teaspoon garlic powder

⅛ teaspoon ground black pepper

1 garlic clove, finely minced

2½ teaspoons lemon juice, divided

¼ cup olive oil

3 tablespoons unsalted margarine or butter[2]

⅓ cup sliced almonds

1 tablespoon chopped fresh flat-leaf (Italian) parsley

▸ Season mahi mahi with garlic powder and pepper and place in a shallow pan.

▸ Mix together garlic, 2 teaspoons lemon juice, and oil; pour over fish and marinate 30 minutes or more, turning fish several times. Remove fish from marinade and place skin-side down on a preheated grill that has been coated with nonstick cooking spray; grill mahi mahi, brushing frequently with marinade, until it flakes easily, 4 or 5 minutes on each side; transfer fish to a platter.

▸ Meanwhile, melt margarine in a skillet over medium-high heat; add almonds. Cook, stirring frequently, until almonds are a light, golden brown, 2 to 3 minutes; add reserved ½ teaspoon lemon juice and pour over fish. Garnish with parsley and serve.

NUTRITIONAL INFO PER SERVING: Calories 338mg, Fat 25mg (Saturated Fat 4mg), Cholesterol 83mg, Carbohydrates 5mg (Fiber 3mg, Sugar 1mg), Sodium 100mg

TOTAL SODIUM AND FAT PER INGREDIENT

Sodium:
  1 lb mahi mahi - 399mg
  1 garlic clove - 1mg
Fat (Sat Fat):
  1 lb mahi mahi - 3mg (1mg)
  ¼ c olive oil - 56mg (12mg)
  ⅓ c sliced almonds - 45mg (3mg)
  3 T NSA margarine - 24mg (5mg)
   or NSA butter - 36mg (24mg)

FOOD NOTE

COMPARISON OF FRESH FISH AND SEAFOOD

There is a wide difference in the amount of sodium in fish and seafood species. Listed from least amount of sodium to the most, the following figures are based on a 3-ounce serving of fresh fish:

Fish	Sodium	Fish	Sodium	Fish	Sodium
Monkfish	15mg	Crayfish	53mg	Swordfish	76mg
Rainbow Trout	28mg	Perch	53mg	Pollack	78mg
Tuna	31mg	Atlantic	64mg	Oysters, Pacific	90mg
Pike, Northern	33mg	Snapper	54mg	Eastern	151mg
Walleye	43mg	Orange Roughy	54mg	Shrimp	126mg
Catfish, Wild	37mg	Pompano	55mg	Scallops	137mg
Farmed	45mg	Haddock	58mg	Lobster, Spiny	150mg
Salmon, Chinook	40mg	Bass, Sea	58mg	Northern	252mg
Atlantic	50mg	Freshwater	60mg	Mussels	243mg
Pink	57mg	Sole (fFounder)	69mg	Crab	
Cod	46mg	Mackerel		Blue or Dungeness	250mg
Halibut	46mg	Pacific or Atlantic	75mg	Alaskan King	711mg
Sturgeon	46mg	King	134mg	Abalone	256mg
Clams	48mg	Mahi Mahi	75mg	Cuttlefish	316mg

HORSERADISH GRILLED SALMON

Sodium Per Serving – 94mg   Serves 6

Salmon is a part of every Northwesterner's diet and during the summer months it is not uncommon to have salmon several nights a week. This is our favorite way of grilling it and it comes out moist and succulent every time.

1½–2 pounds salmon filet, cut into 3 or 4 large pieces[1]

¼ teaspoon garlic powder

⅛ teaspoon ground white pepper

¼ cup lowfat sour cream

1 heaping tablespoon prepared horseradish[2]

1 tablespoon lite mayonnaise or mayonnaise-type dressing

Lemon wedges

▸ Preheat barbecue or gas grill. Remove the small pin bones

▸ Sprinkle salmon with garlic powder and pepper. Mix together sour cream, horseradish, and mayonnaise; coat all sides of the salmon.

▸ Place fish, skin-side down, on a preheated grill coated with vegetable cooking spray. Grill 5 to 6 minutes; turn fish over and continue cooking until fish flakes easily with a fork, about 3 minutes. Transfer fish to a platter and serve with lemon wedges.

NOTE: If barbecuing over coals, you can also push the coals to the outside of the grill and "bake" the salmon for 9 to 14 minutes (depending on the heat of the fire). If you do this, it is not necessary to turn the salmon.

NUTRITIONAL INFO PER SERVING: Calories 232mg, Fat 14mg (Saturated Fat 3mg), Cholesterol 71mg, Carbohydrates 1mg (Fiber 0mg, Sugar 0mg), Sodium 94mg

COMMENTS:

1 The variety of salmon determines the amount of sodium per serving. See FOOD NOTE *below for a comparison.* CAUTION: *Salmon has small pin bones that run the length of the filet. Before grilling, remove with tweezers or needle-nose pliers.*

2 Prepared horseradish averages 50mg sodium per teaspoon. There are several brands with 20mg or less, such as **Beaver, Heluva Good,** *and* **Inglehoffer.**

FOOD NOTE

SALMON COMPARISON

The variety of salmon determines the amount of sodium, fat, and cholesterol. The following compares a 3-ounce serving of uncooked salmon.

Variety	Cal	Fat	Sat Fat	Chol	Sod
Atlantic, wild	121	5	1	47	37
Coho, wild	124	5	1	38	39
Coho, farmed	136	7	2	43	40
Sockeye	143	7	1	53	40
Chinook	152	9	3	43	40
Chum	102	3	1	63	43
Atlantic, farmed	156	9	2	50	50
Pink	99	3	0	44	57
Smoked	100	16	1	20	667
Lox	99	4	1	20	1,700

TOTAL SODIUM AND FAT PER INGREDIENT

Sodium:
1½ lb salmon - 401mg
¼ c LF sour cream - 40mg
1 T horseradish - 60mg
1 T lite mayonnaise - 60mg
Fat (Sat Fat):
1½ lb salmon - 74mg (15mg)
¼ c LF sour cream - 6mg (2mg)
1 T horseradish - 3mg (0mg)
1 T lite mayonnaise - 3mg (0mg)

COMMENTS:

1 *To reduce saturated fat, use trans-free margarine. Since it contains sodium (90mg per tablespoon), it will increase the sodium per serving to 134mg in the broiled salmon recipe and 172mg in the shrimp dish.*

To keep both fat and sodium to a minimum, use a combination of trans-free and unsalted.

2 *Ready-to-eat pesto averages 730mg sodium per ¼ cup. Several lower salt varieties have 230mg or less (see RESOURCES, page 272).*

BROILED SALMON WITH PESTO

Sodium Per Serving – 89mg   Serves 4

Another simple and delicious way to prepare salmon.

1–1½ pounds salmon filet

¼ teaspoon garlic powder

⅛ teaspoon ground black pepper

2 tablespoons unsalted margarine or butter, melted[1]

Juice of ½ lemon (about 1 tablespoon)

¼–½ cup QUICK PESTO (*page 154*) **or ready-to-eat basil pesto**[2]

> Season salmon with garlic powder and pepper. Place skin-side down in a baking pan. Mix together margarine and lemon juice; pour over the salmon.

> Broil about 5 inches from the heat source until fish flakes easily with a fork, 8 to 10 minutes. Transfer salmon to a platter; spread 1–2 tablespoons pesto on top of fish and serve.

NUTRITIONAL INFO PER SERVING: Calories 294mg, Fat 21mg (Saturated Fat 4mg), Cholesterol 67mg, Carbohydrates 2mg (Fiber 0mg, Sugar 0mg), Sodium 89mg

---

TOTAL SODIUM AND FAT PER INGREDIENT

Salmon with Tarragon Butter:
Sodium:
  1 lb salmon - 267mg
  ¼ c QUICK PESTO - 88mg
    or ready-to-eat - 230mg
Fat (Sat Fat):
  1 lb salmon - 49mg (10mg)
  2 T NSA margarine - 16mg (3mg)
    or NSA butter - 24mg (16mg)
  ¼ c QUICK PESTO - 20mg (2mg)
    or ready-to-eat - 34mg (6mg)

Shrimp in Garlic Butter:
Sodium:
  1 lb shrimp - 503mg
  1 garlic clove - 1mg
  3 T vermouth - 3mg
  1 T parsley - 2mg
Fat (Sat Fat):
  1 lb shrimp - 6mg (1mg)
  1 T olive oil - 14mg (2mg)
  2 T NSA margarine - 16mg (3mg)
    or NSA butter - 24mg (16mg)

SHRIMP IN GARLIC BUTTER

Sodium Per Serving – 127mg   Serves 4

This is for all you garlic lovers!

1 pound large shrimp, peeled and deveined

1 tablespoon olive oil

2 tablespoons unsalted margarine or butter[1]

2–3 garlic cloves, crushed

¼ teaspoon garlic powder

⅛ teaspoon ground white pepper

3 tablespoons dry vermouth or white wine

3 tablespoons lemon juice (about 1 large lemon)

1 tablespoon chopped fresh flat-leaf (Italian) parsley (optional)

> Heat oil in a large skillet over medium-high heat; add shrimp. Cook, stirring frequently, until shrimp begins to turn pink; decrease heat to medium-low.

> Stir in margarine, garlic, garlic powder, and pepper; add vermouth and lemon juice. Cook, stirring constantly, for 1 minute; serve immediately with parsley sprinkled on top.

NUTRITIONAL INFO PER SERVING: Calories 169mg, Fat 9mg (Saturated Fat 2mg), Cholesterol 129mg, Carbohydrates 2mg (Fiber 0mg, Sugar 1mg), Sodium 127mg

SHRIMP CURRY

Sodium Per Serving – 120mg   Serves 4

*This recipe was developed while living in Hawaii. The original called for **Lipton's** Onion Soup Mix, which has too much sodium for a low-salt lifestyle. I've come up with an alternative that tates very much like the original. Serve with a variety of condiments, so that each person can add whatever they like.*

⅓ cup unsalted margarine or butter[1]

¼ cup dried minced onion

2–3 tablespoons curry powder[2]

1 tablespoon (or 3 envelopes) low-salt beef bouillon granules

1 teaspoon onion or garlic powder

1 teaspoon dried parsley flakes

½ teaspoon sugar substitute or sugar

½ teaspoon celery seed

¼ teaspoon ground ginger

⅛ teaspoon ground black pepper

1 pound small shrimp, cooked[3]

1 (15-ounce) can no-salt-added applesauce

¾ cup lowfat sour cream

½ cup lowfat milk

6 cups cooked rice

Condiments:

Raisins

Chopped green onions (white and lite green parts)

Diced pineapple

Chopped hard boiled egg

Shredded coconut

Unsalted peanuts

Low-salt chutney[1]

▶ In a saucepan over medium heat, combine all ingredients, except rice and condiments; cook, stirring occasionally, until heated through, 5 to 10 minutes.

▶ Serve over rice and top with condiments of your choice.

NUTRITIONAL INFO PER SERVING (WITHOUT CONDIMENTS): Calories 412mg, Fat 13mg (Saturated Fat 4mg), Cholesterol 96mg, Carbohydrates 69mg (Fiber 2mg, Sugar 17mg), Sodium 120mg

COMMENTS:

1 *To reduce saturated fat, use trans-free margarine. Since it contains sodium (90mg per tablespoon), it will increase the sodium per serving to 200mg.*

To keep fat and sodium to a minimum, use a combination of trans-free and unsalted.

2 *I like a lot of heat and use hot curry powder, however, any variety of curry may be used. For additional info on curry, see FOOD NOTE, page 198.*

3 *Canned shrimp may be used, however it has more sodium (196mg per 4 ounces) than fresh (168mg)*

4 *Mango chutney goes well with shrimp, unfortunately many brands have 170mg sodium or more per tablespoon. There are several low-salt chutneys, including **Steel's**, which offers a no-salt-added mango with 2mg. See RESOURCES, page 272, for more information.*

TOTAL SODIUM AND FAT PER INGREDIENT

Sodium:
- ¼ c dried onion - 3mg
- 2 T curry - 7mg
- 1 T LS beef bouillon - 15mg
- 1 t onion powder - 2mg
- 1 t parsley flakes - 1mg
- ½ t celery seed - 2mg
- 1 lb shrimp - 503mg
- 15 oz NSA applesauce - 16mg
- ¾ c LF sour cream - 102mg
- ½ c LF milk - 58mg
- 6 c cooked rice - 9mg

Fat (Sat Fat):
- ⅓ c NSA margarine - 43mg (8mg) or NSA butter - 64mg (43mg)
- 2 T curry - 2mg (0mg)
- 1 lb shrimp - 6mg (1mg)
- 15 oz NSA applesauce - 1mg (0mg)
- ¾ c LF sour cream - 20mg (12mg)
- ½ c LF milk - 3mg (1mg)
- 6 c cooked rice - 3mg (0mg)

TOTAL SODIUM AND FAT PER INGREDIENT

Sodium:
1 shallot - 2mg
1 lb crab - 664mg
3 eggs - 210mg
  or ¾ c egg substitute - 300mg
¾ c LF milk - 86mg
¼ c LF sour cream - 34mg
2 T white wine - 2mg
2 drops hot pepper sauce - 4mg
4 oz NSA Swiss cheese - 40mg
1 Basic Pie Crust - 159mg
  or store-bought - 400mg

Fat (Sat Fat):
2 T NSA margarine - 16mg (3mg)
  or NSA butter - 24mg (16mg)
1 lb crab - 2mg (1mg)
3 eggs - 15mg (5mg)
  ot ¾ c egg substitute - 0mg
¾ c LF milk - 3mg (1mg)
¼ c LF sour cream - 7mg (4mg)
4 oz NSA Swiss - 32mg (20mg)
1 Basic Pie Crust - 66mg (12mg)
  or store-bought - 56mg (16mg)

CRAB QUICHE

Sodium Per Serving – 195mg   Serves 4

Crab lovers, beware! Alaskan king crab is very high in sodium (237mg per ounce), but other crab varieties, like blue or Dungeness are much less (83mg per ounce). By using the latter in this dish, you'll have lots of crab flavor, but very little sodium.

2 tablespoons unsalted margarine or butter[1]

1 shallot, minced

1 tablespoon flour

8 ounces cooked crab meat, such as blue or Dungeness[2]

3 eggs, or ¾ cup egg substitute[3]

¾ cup lowfat milk

¼ cup lowfat sour cream

2 tablespoons dry white wine or sherry

¼ teaspoon garlic powder

⅛ teaspoon ground white pepper

2–3 drops hot pepper sauce, such as *Tabasco*

4 ounces no-salt-added Swiss cheese, shredded (about 1 cup)

1 Basic Pie Crust (page 229) or unbaked pie shell[4]

⅛ teaspoon hot paprika or cayenne pepper[5]

▸ Preheat oven to 350°F (180°C).

▸ Melt margarine in a skillet over medium heat; add shallots. Cook, stirring frequently, until shallots soften, about 2 minutes; stir in flour and crab meat. Set aside.

▸ In a large bowl, beat together eggs, milk, sour cream, wine, garlic powder, white pepper, and hot pepper sauce; stir in crab mixture.

▸ Sprinkle half the cheese in the pie shell, pour in crab mixture; top with remaining cheese. Sprinkle with paprika and bake in a preheated oven for 40 to 45 minutes, or until eggs are set and knife inserted in center comes out clean. Allow quiche to cool slightly at room temperature, 5 to 10 minutes, before serving.

NUTRITIONAL INFO PER SERVING: Calories 393mg, Fat 23mg (Saturated Fat 7mg), Cholesterol 155mg, Carbohydrates 28mg (Fiber 1mg, Sugar 2mg), Sodium 195mg (235mg with store-bought shell)

FOOD NOTE

CRAB COMPARISON

The variety of crab determines the amount of sodium, fat, and cholesterol. The following compares a 3-ounce serving of uncooked crab.

Variety	Cal	Fat	Sat Fat	Chol	Sod
Blue	74	1	0	66	249
Dungeness	73	1	1	50	251
Queen	77	1	0	47	458
Alaskan King	71	1	0	36	711
Imitation	87	1	0	17	715

SCALLOPS WITH BEURRE BLANC SAUCE

Sodium Per Serving – 190mg

Serves 6

This is an outstanding way to serve scallops. Once you try this butter sauce, you'll never eat scallops any other way!

1½–2 pounds large scallops (about 4–6 per person)

¼ teaspoon garlic powder

⅛ teaspoon ground white pepper

2 tablespoons all-purpose flour

2 tablespoons olive oil

BEURRE BLANC SAUCE *(recipe follows)*

1 tablespoon chopped fresh flat-leaf (Italian) parsley

▶ Prepare BEURRE BLANC SAUCE and keep warm while cooking scallops.

▶ Pat scallops dry and sprinkle with garlic powder and pepper; dredge in flour, shaking off any excess.

▶ Heat oil in a large skillet over medium-high heat; add scallops. Cook, turning once, until golden brown and opaque in center, about 3 minutes per side. Do not overcook. Remove from skillet and serve with sauce on top. Garnish with parsley.

NUTRITIONAL INFO PER SERVING (WITH SAUCE): Calories 328mg, Fat 24mg (Saturated Fat 9mg), Cholesterol 63mg, Carbohydrates 0mg (Fiber 0mg, Sugar 0mg), Sodium 190mg

BEURRE BLANC SAUCE

Sodium Per Serving – 7mg

Makes about ¾ cup

This classic French sauce is usually made with butter. To cut the saturated fat and cholesterol, I use half butter and half margarine. This sauce is also delicious on vegetables and other seafood.

¾ cup water

3 tablespoons white balsamic vinegar[1]

3 tablespoons tarragon vinegar[1]

2 shallots, finely minced

2 tablespoons half-and-half or light cream

10 tablespoons unsalted butter or margarine, or a combination of both[2]

▶ In a saucepan over medium-high heat; boil the water, balsamic and tarragon vinegars, and shallots until 2 tablespoons liquid remains, about 10 minutes. Stir in half-and-half; decrease heat to low. Add margarine and butter, 1 tablespoon at a time, stirring constantly until melted.

▶ Strain sauce through a fine-mesh sieve, pressing with the back of a spoon to remove as much liquid as possible; return strained sauce to pan and keep warm until ready to serve.

NUTRITIONAL INFO PER SERVING: Calories 178mg, Fat 19mg (Saturated Fat 8mg), Cholesterol 26mg, Carbohydrates 2mg (Fiber 0mg, Sugar 0mg), Sodium 7mg

---

COMMENTS:

1 *I like to use two kinds of vinegar, one of which is usually an herbal variety. Instead of white balsamic, use white wine vinegar.*

2 *To reduce saturated fat, use trans-free margarine. Since it contains sodium (90mg per tablespoon), it will increase the sodium per serving to 265mg (and 82mg for the sauce).*

To keep both fat and sodium to a minimum, use a combination of trans-free and unsalted.

TOTAL SODIUM AND FAT PER INGREDIENT

Scallops:
Sodium:
1½ lb scallops - 1095mg
1 T parsley - 2mg
Fat (Sat Fat):
1½ lbs scallops - 5mg (1mg)
2 T olive oil - 28mg (4mg)

Beurre Blanc Sauce:
Sodium:
2 shallots - 4mg
2 T half-and-half - 12mg
   or light cream - 12mg
Fat (Sat Fat):
2 T half-and-half - 3mg (2mg)
   or light cream - 6mg (2mg)
10 T NSA butter - 240mg (160mg)
   or margarine - 160mg (30mg)

COMMENTS:

1 *This recipe is very versatile and any variety of vegetables may be used. I particularly like the combination of herbes de Provence with mushrooms, snow peas, and broccoli.*

2 *Any variety or combination of mushrooms may be used. For additional info on mushroom varieties, see FOOD NOTE, page 44.*

3 *Herbes de Provence is a blend of herbs commonly used in French cooking and is available in supermarkets. See COMMENTS #1, page 107, for additional information.*

4 *Spreadable cheeses range anywhere from 60mg to 450mg per 2 tablespoons. Alouette (available in many supermarkets) has several varieties that range from 60mg to 110mg.*

VEGGIES IN CREAM CHEESE SAUCE

Sodium Per Serving – 101mg   Serves 4

This creamy and delicious stroganoff is ready in less than 15 minutes. For variety, add whatever veggies you like and serve it over rice or pasta.

1 tablespoon olive oil
½ sweet onion, sliced
2 cups broccoli florets[1]
2 cups snow peas, pinch off tips
5 ounces mushrooms, sliced (about 2 cups)[2]
1 garlic clove, minced
1 teaspoon lemon juice
½ teaspoon (or ½ envelope) chicken bouillon granules

¼ cup water
¼ teaspoon herbes de Provence[3]
⅛ teaspoon ground black pepper
½ cup lowfat sour cream
4 ounces (½ cup) whipped cream cheese or spreadable cheese, such as *Alouette*[4]
4 cups cooked rice or pasta

▸ Heat oil in a large skillet over medium-high heat; add onions, broccoli, peas, and mushrooms. Cook, stirring frequently, until onions are translucent, about 4 minutes.

▸ Add garlic, lemon juice, bouillon, water, herbes de Provence, and pepper; cook, stirring occasionally, until veggies are tender, about 5 minutes.

▸ Stir in sour cream and cream cheese; heat through and pour over rice or pasta.

NUTRITIONAL INFO PER SERVING: Calories 435mg, Fat 15mg (Saturated Fat 7mg), Cholesterol 28mg, Carbohydrates 63mg (Fiber 6mg, Sugar 8mg), Sodium 101mg

TOTAL SODIUM AND FAT PER INGREDIENT

Sodium:
½ sweet onion - 6mg
2 c broccoli - 38mg
2 c snow peas - 15mg
8 oz mushrooms - 4mg
1 garlic clove - 1mg
½ t LS chicken bouillon - 3mg
¼ t herbes de Provence - 3mg
½ c LF sour cream - 68mg
4 oz whipped cheese - 260mg
  or spreadable cheese - 298mg
4 c cooked rice - 6mg
  or pasta - 6mg
Fat (Sat Fat):
1 T olive oil - 14mg (2mg)
2 c snow peas - 1mg (0mg)
½ c LF sour cream - 14mg (8mg)
4 oz whip cheese - 28mg (18mg)
  or spreadable cheese - 20mg (12mg)
4 c cooked rice - 2mg (0mg)
  or pasta - 4mg (1mg)

ONION, MUSHROOM AND CHEVRE TART

Sodium Per Serving – 102mg   Serves 6–8

The filling for this yummy tart is also great in strudel or baked in small tart cups and served as an appetizer.

1 **BASIC PIE CRUST** *(page 229),* **or unbaked pie shell**[1]

1 **tablespoon olive oil**

1 **tablespoon unsalted margarine or butter**[2]

½ **sweet onion, thinly sliced**

1 **shallot, finely minced**

1 **pound mushrooms, sliced (about 6½ cups, use a combination, such as shiitake, button, or crimini)**[3]

1 **tablespoon roasted minced garlic**[4]

¼ **teaspoon garlic powder**

⅛ **teaspoon ground black pepper**

4 **ounces Chèvre cheese, softened**[5]

½ **cup lowfat sour cream**

2 **tablespoons lowfat milk or half-and-half**

2 **eggs, or ½ cup egg substitute**[6]

1 **teaspoon chopped fresh thyme, or ¼ teaspoon dried**

▸ Preheat oven to 350°F (180°C).

▸ Prick crust with a fork; line bottom of shell with aluminum foil. Pour pie weights into the pie shell to hold its shape while baking (for info on pie weights, *see* COOKING TIP, *page 247*). Bake for 10 minutes in a preheated oven; remove weights and bake 5 minutes more. Remove from oven and let cool slightly. *NOTE: If using a refrigerated or frozen pie shell, this step is not necessary.*

▸ Meanwhile, heat oil and margarine in a skillet over medium heat; add onions and shallots. Cook, stirring frequently, until the onions are translucent, 3 to 4 minutes. Add mushrooms, garlic, garlic powder, and pepper; cook, stirring frequently, until mushrooms are soft and most of the liquid is absorbed, about 10 minutes. Let cool slightly.

▸ In a bowl, mix together the Chèvre, sour cream, and half-and-half; beat in eggs, one at a time. Set aside.

▸ Spread mushroom mixture on the bottom of the precooked crust; pour egg mixture over the onions. Sprinkle with thyme and bake in a preheated oven for 20 minutes, or until golden brown.

NUTRITIONAL INFO PER SERVING: Calories 367mg, Fat 23mg (Saturated Fat 4mg), Cholesterol 85mg, Carbohydrates 31mg (Fiber 2mg, Sugar 3mg), Sodium 102mg (142mg with store-bought shell)

COMMENTS:

1 *If purchasing a prepared shell, look for those with 55mg or less sodium per serving.*

2 *To reduce saturated fat, use trans-free margarine. Since it contains sodium (90mg per tablespoon), it will increase the sodium per serving to 117mg (158mg with a store-bought shell).*

3 *See* FOOD NOTE, *page 44, for info on mushroom varieties.*

4 *To roast garlic, see* ROASTING GARLIC, *page 185.*

5 *Chèvre usually has the least sodium of the goat cheeses. Choose brands with 50mg or less per ounce.*

6 *See* Eggs and Egg Substitutes, *page 38, for a comparison of fat and sodium in eggs and egg substitutes.*

TOTAL SODIUM AND FAT PER INGREDIENT

Sodium:
1 BASIC PIE CRUST   150mg
  or store-bought - 400mg
½ sweet onion - 6mg
1 shallot - 2mg
12 oz mushrooms - 18mg
1 T garlic - 3mg
4 oz Chèvre - 200mg
½ c LF sour cream - 68mg
2 T LF milk - 14mg
  or half-and-half - 14mg
2 eggs - 140mg
  or ½ c egg substitute - 200mg

Fat (Sat Fat):
1 BASIC PIE CRUST - 66mg (12mg)
  or store-bought - 56mg (16mg)
1 T olive oil - 14mg (2mg)
1 T NSA margarine - 8mg (2mg)
  or NSA butter - 12mg (8mg)
12 oz mushrooms - 2mg (0mg)
4 oz Chèvre - 24mg (0mg)
½ c LF sour cream - 14mg (8mg)
2 T LF milk - 1mg (0mg)
  or half-and-half - 2mg (1mg)
2 eggs - 10mg (3mg)
  or ½ c egg substitute - 0mg

TOTAL SODIUM AND FAT PER INGREDIENT

Sodium:
1 leek - 18mg
1 shallot -2mg
1 garlic clove - 1mg
1 portobello mushroom - 3mg
1 c mushrooms - 2mg
½ t thyme -1mg
1 zucchini - 20mg
½ c broccoli - 15mg
½ c sun-dried tomatoes - 90mg
¼ c water chestnuts - 5mg
½ c LF sour cream - 68mg
2 t dijon mustard - 240mg
4 oz NSA Swiss cheese - 40mg
8 phyllo sheets - 368mg

Fat (Sat Fat):
1 T olive oil - 14mg (2mg)
1 T NSA margarine - 8mg (2mg)
  or NSA butter - 12mg (8mg)
½ c dried tomatoes - 8mg (1mg)
½ c LF sour cream - 14mg (8mg)
4 oz NSA Swiss - 32mg (20mg)
6 phyllo sheets - 2mg (0mg)

VEGETABLE STRUDEL WITH RED PEPPER COULIS

Sodium Per Serving – 153mg   Serves 6

Not only is this colorful strudel full of flavor, but it also is surprisingly easy to make. To shorten preparation time, make the filling and RED PEPPER COULIS *in advance and refrigerate until ready to use.*

1 tablespoon olive oil	⅛ teaspoon ground black pepper
1 tablespoon unsalted or trans-free margarine[1]	1 zucchini, shredded
1 leek, chopped (white and some green parts), or ½ cup chopped sweet onion[2]	½ cup broccoli, chopped
	½ cup oil-packed sun-dried tomatoes, drained and chopped
1 shallot, chopped	¼ cup water chestnuts, chopped
1 garlic clove, minced	½ cup lowfat sour cream
1 portobello mushroom, chopped	2 teaspoons Dijon-style mustard
1 cup chopped mushrooms (such as shiitake, oyster, or crimini)[3]	4 ounces shredded no-salt-added Swiss cheese (about 1 cup)
¾ teaspoon dried tarragon	8 (13 x 9-inch) sheets phyllo (fillo) dough[4]
½ teaspoon dried thyme	Butter-flavored spray[5]
¼ teaspoon garlic powder	RED PEPPER COULIS (page 141)

▶ Preheat oven to 350ºF (180ºC).

▶ Heat oil and margarine in a skillet over medium heat; add leeks. Cook, stirring constantly, until leeks are translucent, about 3 to 4 minutes. Add shallots and garlic, cook stirring constantly, until you smell the garlic, 1 to 2 minutes.

▶ Add mushrooms, tarragon, thyme, garlic powder, and pepper; cook until mushrooms soften, about 5 minutes. Stir in zucchini, broccoli, tomatoes, and water chestnuts; cover and simmer, stirring occasionally, until veggies are tender, about 5 minutes.

▶ Mix together sour cream and mustard; stir into mushroom mixture. Add cheese and mix thoroughly; remove from heat and let cool slightly.

▶ *To prepare strudel:* Place 1 sheet of phyllo dough on a flat surface; spray with butter-flavored spray. Place another sheet on top of the dough and spray with butter spray; repeat twice more, until there is a total of 4 sheets. Place half the mushroom mixture in the center of the dough; roll into a log, folding in both ends about an inch. Repeat with remaining sheets of phyllo and mushroom mixture.

▶ Place strudels on a baking sheet and spray tops with butter-flavored spray; cut several diagonal slits in top about 1-inch apart. Bake in a preheated oven for 30 minutes or until golden brown. Remove and let stand 5 minutes before slicing into serving pieces. Top with RED PEPPER COULIS and serve.

NUTRITIONAL INFO PER SERVING (WITH SAUCE): Calories 287mg, Fat 16mg (Saturated Fat 6mg), Cholesterol 22mg, Carbohydrates 27mg (Fiber 4mg, Sugar 8mg), Sodium 153mg

RED PEPPER COULIS

Sodium Per Serving – 9mg   Serves 4

Coulis (koo-LEE) is a puréed sauce, usually made from fruits or vegetables. The fresh flavor of the roasted red peppers in this coulis is delicious. Serve over burgers, pastas, on pizzas, or add a dollop to a creamy vegetable soup.

2 red bell peppers, roasted[1]	**1 tablespoon white balsamic vinegar**[3]
¼ cup oil-packed sun-dried tomatoes, drained and chopped[2]	**1 teaspoon (or 1 envelope) low-salt chicken bouillon granules**
¾ cup water	**¼ teaspoon garlic powder**
1 tablespoon dry sherry	**⅛ teaspoon ground black pepper**

▸ Place all ingredients in a blender or food processor and pulse until the consistency of a thick spaghetti sauce. (NOTE: If too thick, stir in additional water.) Pour purée into a saucepan and place over medium heat; cook, stirring frequently, until heated through, about 3 to 4 minutes. Pour over entrée and serve.

NUTRITIONAL INFO PER SERVING: Calories 63mg, Fat 3mg (Saturated Fat 0mg), Cholesterol 0mg, Carbohydrates 7mg (Fiber 2mg, Sugar 4mg), Sodium 9mg

VARIATION

CHIPOTLE PEPPER SAUCE

For a smoky, spicy sauce, add 1–2 teaspoons minced chipotle chilies in adobo sauce. (NOTE: Adobo is a spicy tomato sauce with a smoked flavor. You can find chipotle chiles in the Hispanic section of many large supermarkets.)

NUTRITIONAL INFO PER SERVING: Calories 64mg, Fat 3mg (Saturated Fat 0mg), Cholesterol 0mg, Carbohydrates 7mg (Fiber 2mg, Sugar 4mg), Sodium 20mg

---

COOKING TIP

ROASTING PEPPERS

Roasting intensifies the flavor of peppers and is far more flavorful than canned or bottled varieties.

In the broiler – Broil about 5 inches from the heat, turning frequently, until peppers are blackened on all sides, 10 to 15 minutes. Remove and cool *(see note below)*.

Over a gas flame – Hold the pepper with tongs over a medium flame, turning as it blackens, about 10 to 15 minutes. Let cool *(see note below)*.

Stove-top – In a cast-iron skillet over medium-high heat, cook pepper, turning frequently, until blacked on all sides, 10 to 15 minutes. Let cool *(see note below)*.

NOTE: Once blackened, place peppers in a paper bag and let cool 15 minutes. Remove and peel, the skin should easily pull away from the peppers.

COMMENTS:

1 *Roasting peppers brings out their sweetness. There are several ways to roast peppers, see COOKING TIP below.*

To save time, bottled peppers may be used, but the flavor of fresh roasted peppers is far superior to the bottled variety.

2 *Sun-dried tomatoes come bottled in olive oil or dried in bags. Generally, bottled tomatoes have less sodium than packaged, but read labels carefully, some brands have added sodium. Either are okay to use, but the latter must be reconstituted in warm water for 30 minutes before using. Drain tomatoes before chopping.*

3 *White balsamic vinegar is made from white grapes and is combined with white wine vinegar. Although milder and sweeter, it also is not as overpowering in salads as the darker balsamic vinegar.*

TOTAL SODIUM AND FAT PER INGREDIENT

Sodium:
2 red bell peppers - 4mg
¼ c sun-dried tomatoes - 40mg
1 T dry sherry - 2mg
1 t LS chicken bouillon - 5mg
Fat (Sat Fat):
¼ c dried tomatoes - 20mg (2mg)

COMMENTS:

1 To reduce saturated fat, use trans-free margarine. Since it contains sodium (90mg per tablespoon), it will increase the sodium per serving to 122mg (64mg for the MUSHROOM SAUCE).

2 See COMMENTS #6, page 155, for a comparison of fresh Romano and Parmesan, versus the canned variety.

3 Shallots look like small onions and have a mild garlic flavor. For additional info on choosing and storing shallots, see FOOD NOTE, page 171.

4 Any variety or combination of mushrooms may be used. For additional info on mushroom varieties, see FOOD NOTE, page 44.

TOTAL SODIUM AND FAT PER INGREDIENT
Creamy Polenta:
Sodium:
1 t LS chicken bouillon - 5mg
1 c cornmeal - 4mg
¼ c Parmesan - 300mg
Fat (Sat Fat):
1 c cornmeal - 2mg (0mg)
2 T NSA margarine - 16mg (3mg)
   or NSA butter - 24mg (16mg)
¼ c Parmesan - 4mg (2mg)

Mushroom Sauce:
Sodium:
½ sweet onion - 6mg
1 shallot - 2mg
2 garlic cloves - 2mg
½ c Madeira - 10mg
½ c white wine - 6mg
8 oz mushrooms - 9mg
2 c CHICKEN STOCK - 40mg
   or canned LS broth - 260mg
1 T cornstarch - 1mg
Fat (Sat Fat):
1 T olive oil - 14mg (2mg)
8 oz mushrooms - 1mg (0mg)
2 c CHICKEN STOCK - 2mg (0mg)
   or canned LS broth - 4mg (2mg)
2 T NSA margarine - 16mg (3mg)
   or NSA butter - 24mg (16mg)

CREAMY POLENTA WITH MUSHROOM SAUCE

Sodium Per Serving – 96mg   Serves 4

Polenta is a mainstay of Italy and is prepared in a variety of ways, using cheese and/or vegetables. Serve it as a main entrée or side dish.

4 cups water

1 teaspoon (or 1 envelope) low-salt chicken bouillon granules

1 cup yellow cornmeal

2 tablespoons unsalted margarine or butter[1]

2 ounces reduced fat grated Parmesan cheese (about ¼ cup)[2]

MUSHROOM SAUCE (recipe follows)

▸ In a large saucepan over medium-high heat, bring water and bouillon to a boil; add cornmeal, stirring constantly, a little at a time. Decrease heat to low; cook, stirring occasionally, until cornmeal has thickened to an oatmeal consistency, about 30 minutes. Stir in margarine and Parmesan; serve in bowls topeed with mushroom sauce

NUTRITIONAL INFO PER SERVING: Calories 369mg, Fat 14mg (Saturated Fat 2mg), Cholesterol 9mg, Carbohydrates 39mg (Fiber 4mg, Sugar 3mg), Sodium 96mg

---

MUSHROOM SAUCE

Sodium Per Serving – 19mg   Serves 4

This delicious sauce is also good served over steaks, chicken, pasta, or rice.

2 tablespoons olive oil

½ sweet onion, chopped

1 shallot, minced[3]

2 garlic cloves, minced

½ cup Madeira or Marsala wine

½ cup dry white wine

8 ounces sliced mushrooms (about 3½ cups), such as crimini, portobello, oyster, or dried porcinis[4]

¼ teaspoon dried rosemary or thyme

¼ teaspoon garlic powder

⅛ teaspoon ground black pepper

2 cups CHICKEN STOCK (page 232) or canned low-salt chicken broth

1 tablespoon unsalted margarine or butter, melted[1]

1 tablespoon cornstarch

▸ Heat oil in a large saucepan over medium-high heat; add onions and shallots. Cook, stirring frequently, until onions are translucent, 3 to 4 minutes. Add garlic and cook, stirring constantly, until you smell the garlic, 1 to 2 minutes.

▸ Add Madeira and white wine; bring to a boil and continue cooking until liquid nearly evaporates, about 10 minutes.

▷ Add mushrooms, garlic powder, rosemary, pepper, and chicken stock; bring to a boil. Decrease heat to medium-low and simmer, uncovered, for 10 minutes.

▷ Mix together margarine and cornstarch; add to mushroom mixture. Cook, stirring frequently, until sauce thickens slightly, about 2 to 3 minutes.

NUTRITIONAL INFO PER SERVING: Calories 185mg, Fat 8mg (Saturated Fat 1mg), Cholesterol 8mg, Carbohydrates 10mg (Fiber 1mg, Sugar 3mg), Sodium 19mg

VEGGIE BURGERS

Sodium Per Serving – 85mg   Serves 4

These burgers go together quickly using a food processor. Even guests who love their meat, enjoy this tasty delights.

Burgers:

1 cup uncooked bulgur[1]

1 carrot, shredded

1 celery stalk, minced

½ cup sweet onion, minced

½ green bell pepper, minced

1 garlic clove, finely minced

1 cup no-salt-added kidney or black beans, rinsed and drained

1 (8-ounce) can low-salt vegetable juice cocktail, such as *V-8*

1 egg, lightly beaten, or ¼ cup egg substitute[2]

4–5 drops hot pepper sauce, such as *Tabasco*

2 tablespoons chopped fresh flat-leaf (Italian) parsley

½ teaspoon dried basil

¼ teaspoon garlic powder

⅛ teaspoon ground black pepper

1 cup unsalted or low-salt bread crumbs, plain or seasoned[3]

4 HAMBURGER BUNS (page 220), or low-salt bread

4 slices low-salt Swiss cheese (optional)

Sliced onion

Sliced tomato

Lettuce leaves

▷ Preheat broiler.

▷ In a food processor, add bulgur, carrot, celery, onion, bell pepper, garlic, beans, vegetable juice, egg, hot pepper sauce, parsley, basil, garlic powder, and pepper; pulse until a paste-like consistency. Transfer to a large bowl, mix in bread crumbs and shape into patties.

▷ Broil, turning once, until lightly browned and crisp on both sides, about 4 minutes per side. Serve on buns; top with cheese, onion, tomato, lettuce, and other condiments of your choice.

NUTRITIONAL INFO PER BURGER (WITHOUT BUN & CONDIMENTS): Calories 318mg, Fat 4mg (Saturated Fat 0mg), Cholesterol 47mg, Carbohydrates 61mg (Fiber 12mg, Sugar 5mg), Sodium 85mg

COMMENTS:

1 *Instead of bulgur, substitute couscous.*

2 *See* Eggs and Egg Substitutes, *page 38, for a comparison of fat and sodium in eggs and egg substitutes.*

3 *You can also make fresh bread crumbs by tearing 1–2 slices of dried low-salt bread into pieces. Place in blender or food processor and pulse until desired coarseness. For additional info on making bread crumbs, see* COOKING TIP, *page 48.*

TOTAL SODIUM AND FAT PER INGREDIENT

Sodium:
1 c bulger - 24mg
1 carrot - 42mg
1 celery stalk - 32mg
½ c onion - 2mg
½ bell pepper - 2mg
1 garlic clove - 1mg
1 c NSA kidney beans - 22mg
8 oz NSA V-8 juice - 140mg
1 egg - 62mg
  or ¼ c egg substitute - 0mg
4 drops hot pepper sauce - 8mg
2 T parsley - 4mg
Fat (Sat Fat):
1 c bulgur - 2mg (0mg)
1 egg - 4mg (1mg)
  or ¼ c egg substitute - 0mg
1 c NSA bread crumbs - 8mg (0mg)

VEGETABLE CREPES WITH CHEESE SAUCE

Sodium Per Serving – 156mg   Serves 4

This is a great recipe for using leftover vegetables from the refrigerator. This goes together quickly using tortillas, and the mild cheese sauce is a perfect topping.

1 tablespoon olive oil

½ sweet onion, thinly sliced (or 1 leek, white and lite green parts)

1 garlic clove, minced

4 cups mixed veggies, sliced, shredded, or cubed (such as red bell pepper, mushrooms, broccoli, snow peas, zuccini, and carrots)

¼ cup water chestnuts, chopped[1]

¼ cup dry sherry

¼ teaspoon garlic powder

⅛ teaspoon ground black pepper

1 teaspoon spice combination[2]

4 large low-salt burrito-sized flour tortillas[3]

1½ cups CHEESE SAUCE (*page 145*)

2 tablespoons chopped fresh flat-leaf (Italian) parsley or cilantro (optional)

▷ Preheat oven to 150°F (75°C). If using microwave to heat tortillas (*see "To warm tortillas" below*), *it is not necessary to preheat oven.*

▷ Heat oil in a skillet over medium heat; add onion. Cook, stirring frequently, until onions are translucent, 2 to 3 minutes; add garlic and cook, stirring constantly, until you smell the garlic, 1 to 2 minutes. Add mixed veggies, water chestnuts, sherry, garlic powder, pepper, and spice combination; cook 10 minutes until veggies are tender and liquid is absorbed.

▷ To warm tortillas:

In the microwave – Warm tortillas for 30 seconds on high. NOTE: Warm just before preparing, as they harden when they cool.

In the oven – Preheat oven to 150°F (75°C), wrap tortillas in aluminum foil and place in oven until heated through, about 5 minutes.

In oil – Heat 1 tablespoon vegetable or canola oil in a skillet over medium-high heat; quickly warm each tortilla, turning once, 15 to 20 seconds per side.

▷ Place one-fourth the filling on each warm tortilla and roll up; continue with remaining filling and tortillas. *NOTE: For a crisper crepe, cook in 2 tablespoons oil until golden brown and crisp on both sides, 3 to 4 minutes.*

▷ Pour cheese sauce on top of crepes and sprinkle with chopped parsley (or cilantro if using the spicy spice combo.)

NUTRITIONAL INFO PER SERVING: Calories 420mg, Fat 21mg (Saturated Fat 7mg), Cholesterol 29mg, Carbohydrates 30mg (Fiber 5mg, Sugar 7mg), Sodium 156mg

CHEESE SAUCE

Sodium Per Serving – 50mg   Makes about 1½ cups

This easy-to-prepare cheese sauce has a mild flavor. It also goes well with vegetables, burgers, and biscuits.

2 tablespoons unsalted margarine or butter[1]

2 tablespoons all-purpose flour

1 teaspoon (or 1 envelope) low-salt chicken bouillon granules

⅔ cup water[2]

⅔ cup lowfat milk

½ cup dry sherry or white wine

½ teaspoon Dijon-style mustard

½ teaspoon mustard powder

2–3 drops hot pepper sauce, such as *Tabasco*

4 ounces no-salt-added Swiss cheese, shredded (about 1 cup)

⅛ teaspoon ground black pepper

Freshly grated nutmeg or paprika

1–2 tablespoons chopped fresh flat-leaf (Italian) parsley (optional)

▸ Melt margarine in a saucepan over medium-high heat; add flour. Cook, stirring constantly, until flour paste begins to brown, 1 to 2 minutes; decrease heat to medium.

▸ Mix in bouillon, water, and milk; bring to a boil. Decrease heat to medium-low; cook, stirring frequently, until thickened to a gravy consistency, 4 to 5 minutes.

▸ Add Dijon-style mustard, mustard powder, hot pepper sauce, and cheese; cook, stirring constantly, until cheese has melted, about 2 minutes. Season with pepper and nutmeg; serve.

NUTRITIONAL INFO PER SERVING: Calories 221mg, Fat 13mg (Saturated Fat 6mg), Cholesterol 29mg, Carbohydrates 10mg (Fiber 0mg, Sugar 3mg), Sodium 50mg

COMMENTS:

1 *To reduce saturated fat, use trans-free margarine. Since it contains sodium (90mg per tablespoon), it will increase the sodium per serving to 95mg.*

2 *For a richer-tasting sauce, use* CHICKEN STOCK *(page 232) or canned low-salt chicken broth instead of water.*

TOTAL SODIUM AND FAT PER INGREDIENT

Sodium:
   1 t LS chicken bouillon - 5mg
   ⅔ c LF milk - 76mg
   ⅓ c sherry - 10mg
   ½ t Dijon mustard - 60mg
   2 drops hot pepper sauce - 4mg
   4 oz NSA Swiss cheese - 40mg
   1 T parsley - 2mg
Fat (Sat Fat):
   2 T NSA margarine - 16mg (3mg)
      or NSA butter - 24mg (16mg)
   ⅔ c LF milk - 3mg (1mg)
   4 oz NSA Swiss - 32mg (20mg)

COMMENTS:

1 *To reduce saturated fat, use trans-free margarine. Since it contains sodium (90mg per tablespoon), it will increase the sodium per serving to 127mg.*

2 *For information on preparing and storing shallots, see FOOD NOTE, page 171.*

3 *Any type or combination of mushrooms may be used. See FOOD NOTE, page 44, for different varieties of mushrooms.*

4 *See Eggs and Egg Substitutes, page 38, for a comparison of fat and sodium in eggs and egg substitutes.*

5 *May also use ¼ teaspoon ground nutmeg, but the taste of fresh nutmeg is far superior to ground.*

TOTAL SODIUM AND FAT PER INGREDIENT

Sodium:
½ sweet onion - 6mg
2 shallots - 4mg
4 oz mushrooms - 4mg
1 garlic clove - 1mg
3 eggs - 210mg
  or ¾ c egg substitute - 300mg
8 oz tofu - 9mg
½ c LF ricotta - 180mg
2 oz NSA Swiss cheese - 20mg
¼ c LF milk - 26mg
10 oz spinach - 210mg
Fat (Sat Fat):
1 T olive oil - 14mg (2mg)
1 T NSA margarine - 8mg (2mg)
  or NSA butter - 12mg (8mg)
3 eggs - 15mg (5mg)
  or ¾ c egg substitute - 0mg
8 oz tofu - 5mg (1mg)
½ c LF ricotta - 12mg (8mg)
2 oz NSA Swiss - 16mg (10mg)
¼ c LF milk - 1mg (0mg)
10 oz spinach - 2mg (1mg)

CRUSTLESS SPINACH–MUSHROOM QUICHE

Sodium Per Serving – 112mg	Serves 6 as an entrée, 8 as a side dish

This recipe was given to me by a vegetarian friend. It is so good and no one will ever know it contains tofu . . . unless you tell them! This also makes a nice side dish to serve with poultry or beef.

1 tablespoon olive oil
1 tablespoon unsalted margarine or butter[1]
½ sweet onion, diced
2 shallots, chopped[2]
4 ounces mushrooms, chopped (about 1½ cups)[3]
1 garlic clove, minced
¼ teaspoon dried basil
¼ teaspoon garlic or onion powder
¼ teaspoon dried tarragon
¼ teaspoon dried thyme
⅛ teaspoon ground black pepper

3 eggs, beaten, or ¾ cup egg substitute[4]
8 ounces firm tofu
½ cup lowfat ricotta cheese
2 ounces no-salt-added Swiss cheese, shredded (about ½ cup)
¼ cup lowfat milk
1 (10-ounce) package frozen chopped spinach, thawed and moisture squeezed out
⅛ teaspoon freshly grated nutmeg[5]

▸ Preheat oven to 350°F (180°C). Coat a 9-inch quiche or pie dish with nonstick cooking spray.

▸ Heat oil and margarine in a skillet over medium heat; add onions, shallots and mushrooms. Cook, stirring frequently, until onions are translucent, 3 to 4 minutes; add garlic, basil garlic powder, tarragon, thyme, and pepper. Cook, stirring constantly, until you smell the garlic, 1 to 2 minutes; remove from heat and let cool slightly.

▸ Mix together the eggs, tofu, ricotta, Swiss cheese, milk, and spinach; add to onion mixture. Pour into prepared quiche dish and sprinkle with nutmeg.

▸ Bake in a preheated oven for 30 minutes, or until custard has set and top is lightly browned. Cool for 10 minutes, then cut into wedges and serve.

NUTRITIONAL INFO PER 6 SERVINGS: Calories 200mg, Fat 12mg (Saturated Fat 5mg), Cholesterol 125mg, Carbohydrates 9mg (Fiber 2mg, Sugar 5mg), Sodium 112mg

STUFFED BAKED POTATOES

Serves 4

Potatoes are very low in sodium (18mg for a large russet) and are great as a main course meal. The toppings you can use are endless. Here are a few of our favorites.

4 large russet potatoes, scrubbed and rubbed with vegetable oil

2–3 cups filling/topping of your choice *(see Variations below)*

▷ Preheat oven to 425°F (220°C). Arrange oven rack in middle of the oven.

▷ Pierce the potatoes several times with a fork. Place potatoes on rack and bake for 60 minutes, or until tender and cooked through. Split lengthwise and top with filling of your choice.

NUTRITIONAL INFO PER SERVING: Varies depending on filling or topping (see below).

FILLINGS / TOPPINGS

STROGANOFF STUFFED POTATOES

Evenly divide 2–3 cups VEGGIES IN CREAM SAUCE *(page 138)* and pour over potatoes.

NUTRITIONAL INFO PER POTATO: Calories 427mg, Fat 18mg (Saturated Fat 8mg), Cholesterol 28mg, Carbohydrates 57mg (Fiber 8mg, Sugar 9mg), Sodium 111mg

NOTE: The following variations contain some chicken or turkey:

CHILI STUFFED POTATOES

Evenly divide 2–3 cups TEXAS-STYLE TURKEY CHILI *(page 70)* and pour over potatoes. Top with sour cream, shredded no-salt-added Swiss cheese, and chopped green onions.

NUTRITIONAL INFO PER POTATO: Calories 502mg, Fat 16mg (Saturated Fat 6mg), Cholesterol 58mg, Carbohydrates 62mg (Fiber 12mg, Sugar 7mg), Sodium 171mg

CREAMY CHEESY CHICKEN STUFFED POTATOES

Evenly divide 2–3 cups CREAMY CHEESY CHICKEN *(page 101)* and pour over potatoes. *NOTE: Cut large chunks of chicken into bite-size pieces,*

NUTRITIONAL INFO PER POTATO: Calories 358mg, Fat 8mg (Saturated Fat 3mg), Cholesterol 44mg, Carbohydrates 42mg (Fiber 3mg, Sugar 3mg), Sodium 91mg

CHICKEN-MUSHROOM ALFREDO STUFFED POTATOES

Evenly divide 2–3 cups CHICKEN-MUSHROOM ALFREDO *(page 152)* and pour over potatoes.

NUTRITIONAL INFO PER POTATO: Calories 537mg, Fat 11mg (Saturated Fat 2mg), Cholesterol 16mg, Carbohydrates 88mg (Fiber 8mg, Sugar 4mg), Sodium 73mg

COMMENTS:

1 *Most supermarkets carry lower salt pasta sauces, such as* **Colavita** *Marinara or* **Classico** *Roasted Garlic, averaging about 220mg sodium per ½ cup. Other sauces with less than 100mg sodium are also available from online grocers (see RESOURCES, page 272, for more info).*

2 *When cooking pasta, it is not necessary to add salt to the water. If you want additional flavor, stir in 1–2 teaspoons low-salt chicken bouillon granules to the water, before cooking the pasta.*

15-MINUTE SPAGHETTI

Sodium Per Serving – 114mg   Serves 6

This spur-of-the-moment dish uses ingredients you usually have on hand and is a great way to jazz up that store-bought pasta sauce.

- **1 tablespoon olive oil**
- **½ cup chopped sweet onion, or 1 leek, sliced (white and lite green parts)**
- **1 shallot, minced**
- **1 garlic clove, minced**
- **2 cups mixed vegetables, sliced or chopped (such as zucchini, mushrooms, and broccoli)**
- **¼ teaspoon dried basil**
- **¼ teaspoon dried oregano**
- **¼ teaspoon dried thyme**
- **1 (26-ounce) jar low-salt pasta sauce or lower salt pasta sauce[1]**
- **12 ounces spaghetti noodles, cooked[2]**

▷ Heat oil in a skillet over medium-high heat; add onions and shallots. Cook, stirring frequently, until onions are translucent, 2 to 3 minutes; add garlic and cook, stirring constantly, until you smell the garlic, 1 to 2 minutes.

▷ Stir in vegetables, basil, oregano, and thyme; cook, stirring frequently, until vegetables are nearly tender, 4 to 5 minutes. Add pasta sauce and cook until heated through, about 5 minutes.

▷ Combine sauce and cooked spaghetti; mixing well. Serve with Parmesan, if desired.

NUTRITIONAL INFO PER SERVING: Calories 344mg, Fat 4mg (Saturated Fat 1mg), Cholesterol 11mg, Carbohydrates 67mg (Fiber 5mg, Sugar 16mg), Sodium 114mg (247mg with lower salt pasta sauce)

TOTAL SODIUM AND FAT PER INGREDIENT

Sodium:
- ½ c sweet onion - 5mg
- 1 shallot - 2mg
- 1 garlic clove - 1mg
- 2 c mixed vegetables - 128mg
- 26 oz LS pasta sauce - 522mg
  or lower salt sauce - 1,320mg
- 12 oz spaghetti - 24mg

Fat (Sat Fat):
- 1 T olive oil - 14mg (2mg)
- 26 oz LS pasta sauce - 6mg (0mg)
  or lower salt sauce - 6mg (0mg)
- 12 oz spaghetti - 5mg (1mg)

FOOD NOTE

PASTA SHAPES

Pasta comes in a variety of shapes and sizes and each shape serves a different purpose. Pasta falls into the following general categories:

Long/straight (such as spaghetti, linguine, and vermicelli) – generally the thinner varieties are for light sauces and the broader strips for thicker sauces.

Lasagna – use in baked dishes or spread with filling and roll up.

Curly (such as fusilli and rotini spirals) – very versatile, use with most any sauce, soups, and salads.

Small tubular (such as elbow macaroni, penne, and ziti) – very versatile, use in soups, salads, and a variety of sauces.

Large tubular (such as manicotti and cannelloni) – these are generally stuffed with cheese, meat, and/or vegetables.

Specialty (such as farfalle, shells, and orzo) – use in soups, salads, and with most sauces.

PASTA WITH SUN-DRIED TOMATO CREAM SAUCE

Sodium Per Serving – 93mg   Serves 4

This yummy pasta goes together quickly with a prepared alfredo sauce and using leftover cooked chicken has this dish ready in less than 15 minutes.

- 1 tablespoon olive oil
- 1 tablespoon unsalted or trans-free margarine[1]
- 1 garlic clove, minced
- 1 shallot, minced
- 4 ounces sliced mushrooms (about 1½ cups)
- 2 (4-ounce) boneless, skinless chicken breasts, cubed[2]
- ½ cup oil-packed sun-dried tomatoes, drained and chopped[3]
- ¼ teaspoon garlic powder

- ⅛ teaspoon ground black pepper
- 1 (15-ounce) jar *Walden Farms* Alfredo Sauce[4]
- 2 tablespoons dry white wine or sherry
- 8 ounces fettucine or spaghetti noodles, cooked per package directions[5]
- Parmesan cheese (optional)
- Chopped fresh flat-leaf (Italian) parsley (optional)

▷ Heat oil and margarine in a skillet over medium heat; add garlic and shallots. Cook, stirring constantly, until you smell the garlic, 1 to 2 minutes.

▷ Add mushrooms, chicken, sun-dried tomatoes, garlic powder, and pepper; cook, stirring frequently, until mushrooms soften and chicken is not longer pick, about 5 minutes.

▷ Stir in alfredo sauce and wine; cook, stirring occasionally, until heated through, 2 to 3 minutes.

▷ Mix together fettucine and alfredo sauce; serve with parsley and Parmesan sprinkled on top.

NUTRITIONAL INFO PER SERVING: Calories 367mg, Fat 9mg (Saturated Fat 2mg), Cholesterol 33mg, Carbohydrates 48mg (Fiber 2mg, Sugar 3mg), Sodium 93mg

---

COMMENTS:

1 *To reduce saturated fat, use trans-free margarine. Since it contains sodium (90mg per tablespoon), it will increase the sodium per serving to 115mg.*

2 *Leftover cooked chicken may also be used.*

3 *See* COMMENTS #3, *page 141, for information on sun-dried tomatoes.*

4 *Most prepared alfredo sauce averages 540mg sodium per ¼ cup.* **Walden Farms** *offers a low-carb, calorie-free alfredo sauce with only 20mg sodium per serving (see* RESOURCES, *page 272, for online sources).*

5 *When cooking pasta, it is not necessary to add salt to the water. If you want additional flavor, stir in 1–2 teaspoons low-salt chicken bouillon granules to the cooking water.*

TOTAL SODIUM AND FAT PER INGREDIENT

Sodium:
- 1 garlic clove - 1mg
- 1 shallot - 2mg
- 4 oz mushrooms - 4mg
- 8 oz chicken breast - 146mg
- ½ c sun-dried tomatoes - 80mg
- 1½ c alfredo sauce - 120mg
- 2 T white wine - 2mg
- 8 oz fettucine noodles - 16mg

Fat (Sat Fat):
- 1 T olive oil - 14mg (2mg)
- 1 T NSA margarine - 8mg (2mg)
  or NSA butter - 12mg (8mg)
- 8 oz chicken breast - 3mg (1mg)
- ½ c dried tomatoes - 8mg (1mg)
- 8 oz fettucine noodles - 3mg (1mg)

1 *A combination of turkey or chicken may be used instead of beef and pork (although lower in fat, the meatballs won't be as moist). Depending on the ground meat used, the amount of sodium will vary (per 4 ounces): pork - 64mg, lean beef - 76mg, veal - 93mg, turkey breast - 107.*

2 *To make fresh bread crumbs, see* COOKING TIP, *page 46. If using unseasoned crumbs, double the Italian spice blend to 2 teaspoons.*

3 *See* Eggs and Egg Substitutes, *page 38, for a comparison of fat and sodium in eggs and egg substitutes.*

4 *See* COMMENTS #1, *page 154, for a comparison of sodium in grated cheeses.*

5 *Instead of Italian seasoning, use ¼ teaspoon dried basil, ¼ teaspoon dried oregano, ¼ teaspoon dried rosemary, and ¼ teaspoon dried thyme.*

TOTAL SODIUM AND FAT PER INGREDIENT

Sodium:
8 oz beef - 148mg
8 oz pork - 125mg
½ c onion - 2mg
¼ c parsley - 6mg
¼ c LF milk - 26mg
1 egg - 70mg
 or ¼ c egg substitute - 115mg
2 T reduced fat Parmesan - 150mg
½ t red pepper flakes - 2mg
3 c MARINARA SAUCE - 548mg
Fat (Sat Fat):
8 oz beef - 34mg (13mg)
8 oz pork - 47mg (18mg)
½ c LS crumbs - 4mg (0mg)
¼ c LF milk - 1mg (0mg)
1 egg - 5mg (2mg)
 or ¼ c egg substitute - 0mg
3 c MARINARA SAUCE - 21mg (3mg)

MEATBALLS WITH MARINARA SAUCE

Sodium Per Serving – 176mg   Serves 6

This is a great family meal that my northern Italian grandmother taught me as a child. Either bake the moist and flavorful meatballs in the oven or cook them on the stove-top. Serve these meatballs with just the MARINARA SAUCE *or on top of spaghetti noodles.*

½ pound ground sirloin[1]

½ pound ground pork[1]

½ cup low-salt seasoned bread crumbs[2]

½ cup minced onion

3 tablespoons chopped fresh flat-leaf (Italian) parsley

1 garlic clove, finely minced

¼ cup lowfat milk

1 egg, beaten, or ¼ cup egg substitute[3]

2 tablespoons reduced fat grated Parmesan cheese[4]

1 teaspoon Italian seasoning[5]

½ teaspoon crushed red pepper flakes (optional)

¼ teaspoon onion or garlic powder

¼ teaspoon ground black pepper

3 cups MARINARA SAUCE (page 151)

Parmesan cheese (optional)

▸ In a large bowl, mix the sirloin and pork with the bread crumbs, onion, parsley, garlic, milk, egg, Parmesan, Italian seasoning, red pepper flakes, onion powder, and pepper. Shape into 1¼-inch balls. Cook in one of the following ways:

In the marinara sauce: Heat 1 tablespoon oil in a skillet over medium-high heat; add meatballs. Cook, turning frequently, until brown on all sides, about 5 minutes. Decrease heat to medium-low and add MARINARA SAUCE; simmer, covered, until cooked through, 30 to 45 minutes.

In the oven: Preheat oven to 375°F (190°C). Coat a large baking dish with nonstick vegetable spray. Place meatballs in prepared dish and bake until light brown and cooked through, 20 to 25 minutes; add to MARINARA SAUCE.

By frying: Heat 2 tablespoons olive oil in a nonstick skillet over medium heat; add meatballs. Cook, turning several times, until browned on both sides and cooked through, 10 to 15 minutes; add to MARINARA SAUCE.

▸ Serve with Parmesan or place on top of a bed of cooked spaghetti noodles.

NUTRITIONAL INFO PER SERVING: Calories 352mg, Fat 18mg (Saturated Fat 6mg), Cholesterol 82mg, Carbohydrates 23mg (Fiber 4mg, Sugar 8mg), Sodium 176mg

VARIATION

SICILIAN MEATBALLS

   Add ½ cup dried currants, raisins, or dried cranberries to the meatball mixture; proceed as directed.

NUTRITIONAL INFO PER APPETIZER: Calories 281mg, Fat 15mg (Saturated Fat 5mg), Cholesterol 82mg, Carbohydrates 19mg (Fiber 1mg, Sugar 8mg), Sodium 85mg

MARINARA SAUCE

Sodium Per Serving – 92mg   About 3 cups

This fresh sauce is rich and spicy and doesn't take long to cook. For a more concentrated flavor, simmer over low heat at least 3 hours or all day.

1½ tablespoons olive oil

1 onion, chopped

2 garlic cloves, finely minced

2 (16-ounce) cans no-salt-added diced tomatoes, undrained[1]

1 (6-ounce) can no-salt-added tomato paste[1]

¼ cup red wine

1 teaspoon dried oregano

½ teaspoon dried basil

¼ teaspoon garlic powder

⅛ teaspoon ground black pepper

⅛ teaspoon salt (optional)

2 bay leaves

▷ Heat oil in a skillet over medium-high heat; cook onions, stirring frequently, until they are translucent, about 3 to 4 minutes. Add garlic and cook, stirring constantly, until you smell the garlic, 1 to 2 minutes.

▷ Stir in diced tomatoes, tomato paste, wine, oregano, bay leaves, and pepper. Decrease heat to medium-low and simmer 15 to 30 minutes (the less the sauce cooks, the fresher it tastes).

NUTRITIONAL INFO PER SERVING: Calories 107mg, Fat 4mg (Saturated Fat 1mg), Cholesterol 0mg, Carbohydrates 13mg (Fiber 4mg, Sugar 7mg), Sodium 92mg

COMMENTS:

1 *Several manufacturers make no-salt-added tomato products with 50mg or less sodium per ½ cup serving. See* RESOURCES, *page 272, for additional information.*

FOOD NOTE

TOMATO PASTE, PUREE AND SAUCE

When your recipe calls for tomato puree and all you have is tomato sauce or tomato paste, what do you do? Here are the differences between these three tomato products and how to use them interchangeably.

Tomato paste – Thick concentrated, strained tomatoes, average amount of sodium is 522mg per ¼ cup (no-salt-added brands have about 40mg). Substitute with tomato puree or sauce, using twice as much as the recipe calls for and reducing another liquid in the recipe to compensate for the added liquid.

Tomato puree – Thinner than paste and has not been cooked down as long, average sodium is 249mg per ¼ cup (no-salt-added brands have about 20mg). Substitute 3 parts tomato paste, plus 5 parts water. *NOTE: In Britain, tomato puree is the same as tomato paste in the U.S.*

Tomato sauce – Thinner than puree and is usually seasoned, average sodium is 371mg per ¼ cup (no-salt-added brands have about 20mg). Substitute tomato puree or use 3 parts tomato paste, plus 4 parts water.

TOTAL SODIUM AND FAT PER INGREDIENT

Sodium:
  1 onion - 3mg
  2 garlic cloves - 2mg
  32 oz NSA diced tomatoes - 210mg
  6 oz NSA tomato paste - 42mg
  ¼ c red wine - 2mg
Fat (Sat Fat):
  1½ T olive oil - 21mg (3mg)

COMMENTS:

1 To reduce saturated fat, use trans-free margarine. Since it contains sodium (90mg per tablespoon), increase the sodium per serving to 79mg.

2 Any type or combination of mushrooms may be used. For additional info on mushroom varieties, see FOOD NOTE, page 44.

3 When cooking pasta, it is not necessary to add salt to the water. If you want additional flavor, stir in 1–2 teaspoons low-salt chicken bouillon granules to the cooking water.

CREAMY MUSHROOM PASTA

Sodium Per Serving – 33mg   Serves 4

This delcious pasta goes together quickly and uses ingredients you usually have on hand.

- **1 tablespoon olive oil**
- **2 tablespooons unsalted margarine or butter[1]**
- **1 pound mushrooms, sliced (about 6 cups)[2]**
- **2 shallots, chopped**
- **2 garlic cloves, minced**
- **¼ teaspoon garlic powder**
- **⅛ teaspoon ground black pepper**
- **¾ cup CHICKEN STOCK *(page 232)* or canned low-salt chicken broth**

- **1 teaspoon (or 1 envelope) low-salt chicken bouillon granules**
- **1 cup fresh or frozen peas**
- **1 tablespoon fresh chopped thyme, or 1 teaspoon dried**
- **½ cup lowfat sour cream**
- **8 ounces linguine noodles, cooked[3]**

▸ Heat oil and margarine in a large skillet over medium heat; add mushrooms and shallots. Cook, stirring frequently, until onions are translucent, 3 to 5 minutes; add garlic, garlic powder, and pepper. Cook, stirring constantly, until you smell the garlic, 1 to 2 minutes.

▸ Stir in chicken stock, bouillon, peas, and thyme; bring to a boil. Decrease heat to medium-low and simmer, covered, until peas are tender, about 4 minutes.

▸ Remove from heat and stir in sour cream; mix with linguine.

NUTRITIONAL INFO PER SERVING: Calories 371mg, Fat 12mg (Saturated Fat 4mg), Cholesterol 11mg, Carbohydrates 52mg (Fiber 3mg, Sugar 3mg), Sodium 33mg

TOTAL SODIUM AND FAT PER INGREDIENT

Sodium:
- 1 lb mushrooms - 18mg
- 2 shallots - 4mg
- 2 garlic cloves - 2mg
- ¾ c CHICKEN STOCK - 15mg or LS canned broth - 98mg
- 1 t LS chicken bouillon - 5mg
- 1 c peas - 2mg
- ½ c LF sour cream - 68mg
- 8 oz linguine - 16mg

Fat (Sat Fat):
- 1 T olive oil - 14mg (2mg)
- 2 T NSA margarine - 16mg (3mg) or NSA butter - 24mg (16mg)
- 1 lb mushrooms - 2mg (0mg)
- ¾ c CHICKEN STOCK - 1mg (0mg) or LS canned broth - 2mg (1mg)
- ½ c LF sour cream - 14mg (8mg)
- 8 oz linguine - 3mg (1mg)

VARIATION

CHICKEN-MUSHROOM ALFREDO

Reduce the fresh thyme to 1½ teaspoons (or ½ teaspoon dried) and eliminate the chicken stock, bouillon, and sour cream; instead stir in 8 ounces cooked cubed chicken, 1 (15-ounce) jar *Walden Farms* Alfredo Sauce *(see COMMENTS #3, page 149),* and 2 tablespoons dry white wine; proceed as directed.

NUTRITIONAL INFO PER SERVING: Calories 385mg, Fat 10mg (Saturated Fat 2mg), Cholesterol 33mg, Carbohydrates 50mg (Fiber 3mg, Sugar 3mg), Sodium 78mg

TURKEY SAUSAGE AND EDAMAME PASTA

Sodium Per Serving – 301mg   Serves 4

This recipe came about when trying to find more uses for edamame beans. The results were pleasantly surprising . . . hope you enjoy!

- 1 tablespoon olive oil
- 2 mild Italian sausages (about 6 ounces)[1]
- 1 tablespoon unsalted margarine or butter[2]
- 1 small sweet onion, chopped
- 8 ounces sliced mushrooms (about 3 cups)
- 1 tablespoon minced roasted garlic[3]
- 2 cups CHICKEN STOCK (page 232) or canned low-salt chicken broth
- 1 tablespoons (or 3 envelopes) low-salt chicken bouillon granules
- ¼ cup dry sherry

- 1 cup broccoli florets
- 1 cup edamame beans[4]
- 1 (16-ounce) can no-salt-added diced tomatoes, drained[5]
- ¼ teaspoon dried basil
- ¼ teaspoon garlic or onion powder
- ⅛ teaspoon ground black pepper
- ¼ teaspoon crushed red pepper flakes
- 1 teaspoon sugar substitute or sugar
- 1 tablespoon lemon juice
- 8 ounces linguine or spaghetti noodles, broken up

▷ Heat oil in a skillet over medium heat; brown sausage on all sides. Remove and slice into small, bite-sized pieces; return to skillet and add margarine. Once melted, add onions and mushrooms; cook, stirring frequently, until onions are translucent, 4 to 5 minutes. Add garlic; cook, stirring frequently, until you smell the garlic, 1 to 2 minutes.

▷ Stir in water, bouillon, sherry, broccoli, edamame beans, tomatoes, basil, garlic powder, black pepper, red pepper flakes, sweetener, lemon juice, and linguine; bring to a boil. Decrease heat to medium-low; cover and simmer, stirring occasionally, until pasta is nearly cooked, about 15 minutes. Uncover and cook another 5 minutes to reduce liquid. Serve with Parmesan on top, if desired.

NUTRITIONAL INFO PER SERVING: Calories 504mg, Fat 16mg (Saturated Fat 3mg), Cholesterol 20mg, Carbohydrates 61mg (Fiber 6mg, Sugar 6mg), Sodium 301mg (357mg with canned LS broth)

COMMENTS:

1 *Although Italian sausage is high in sodium (160mg per ounce), a small amount will give you plenty of spicy flavor.*

2 *To reduce saturated fat, use trans-free margarine. Since it contains sodium (90mg per tablespoon), it will increase the sodium per serving to 324mg.*

3 *To roast garlic, see COOKING TIP, page 185. Bottled roasted garlic (found in the produce section of most supermarkets) may also be used.*

4 *Edamame (pronounced e duh MA-may) are soy beans that are low in sodium and high in vitamins. They have a sweet, nutty flavor and are found in the frozen food section of most supermarkets.*

5 *Several manufacturers make no-salt-added tomato products with 50mg or less sodium per ½ cup serving. See RESOURCES, page 272, for additional information*

TOTAL SODIUM AND FAT PER INGREDIENT

Sodium:
- 6 oz Italian sausage - 958mg
- 1 sm sweet onion - 9mg
- 8 oz mushrooms - 8mg
- 1 T roasted garlic - 3mg
- 2 c CHICKEN STOCK - 40mg
  or LS canned broth - 260mg
- 1 T LS chicken bouillon - 15mg
- ¼ c sherry - 5mg
- 1 c broccoli - 19mg
- 2 c CHICKEN STOCK - 2mg (0mg)
  or LS canned broth - 4mg (2mg)
- 1 c edamame - 25mg
- 16 oz NSA tomatoes - 105mg
- 8 oz spaghetti - 16mg

Fat (Sat Fat):
- 1 T olive oil - 14mg (2mg)
- 6 oz Italian sausage - 14mg (5mg)
- 2 T NSA margarine - 16mg (3mg)
  or NSA butter - 24mg (16mg)
- 1 c edamame - 12mg (1mg)
- 8 oz spaghetti - 3mg (1mg)

QUICK PESTO

Sodium Per Serving – 52mg   Serves 4

This delicious pesto, with less oil than most, is very versatile—toss with pasta, use on pizzas, sandwiches, grilled salmon, and steaks, or mix with cream cheese for a delicious dip or spread. This makes about 1 cup pesto and can be made two weeks ahead of time (keep in a covered container in the refrigerator).

¼ cup chopped fresh basil

¼ cup chopped fresh flat-leaf (Italian) parsley

¼ cup pine nuts, walnuts, or almonds

¼ cup reduced fat grated Parmesan cheese[1]

2 garlic cloves, smashed and coarsley chopped

¼ teaspoon garlic powder

¼ teaspoon ground black pepper

¼ cup olive oil

▷ Place basil, parsley, pine nuts, Parmesan, garlic, garlic powder, and pepper in a blender or food processor. With machine running, gradually add oil; process until a smooth paste. Mix with warm pasta noodles and serve.

NUTRITIONAL INFO PER 2 TABLESPOONS: Calories 134mg, Fat 14mg (Saturated Fat 2mg), Cholesterol 1mg, Carbohydrates 3mg (Fiber 0mg, Sugar 0mg), Sodium 52mg

---

VARIATION

Sun-Dried Tomato Pesto

Add 1½ cups oil-packed sun-dried tomatoes, increase the Parmesan cheese to ½ cup and the garlic to 3 cloves. Add to the ingredients in the blender or food processor; proceed as directed. Makes about 2 cups.

NUTRITIONAL INFO PER 2 TABLESPOONS: Calories 104mg, Fat 9mg (Saturated Fat 1mg), Cholesterol 1mg, Carbohydrates 5mg (Fiber 1mg, Sugar 2mg), Sodium 71mg

TOTAL SODIUM AND FAT
PER INGREDIENT

Sodium:
  ¼ c parsley - 8mg
  ¼ c pine nuts - 1mg
  ¼ c Parmesan - 300mg
  2 garlic cloves - 2mg
Fat (Sat Fat):
  ¼ c pinenuts - 23mg (2mg)
  ¼ c Parmesan - 4mg (0mg)
  ¼ c olive oil - 56mg (8mg)

LINGUINE WITH CLAM SAUCE

Sodium Per Serving – 172mg   Serves 6

Many clam sauce recipes use bottled clam juice, which is high in sodium (280mg per ¼ cup). This tasty dish lowers the sodium by using the juice from canned clams. Adding a few fresh clams on top takes this from everyday faire to an elegant dinner entrée.

1 tablespoon olive oil	½ cup half-and-half or light cream[3]
1 tablespoon unsalted margarine or butter[1]	¼ cup white wine
2 shallots, chopped	½ teaspoon garlic powder
4 garlic cloves, finely minced	¼ teaspoon ground black pepper
1 (10-ounce) can baby clams, drained and liquid reserved	¼ teaspoon crushed red pepper flakes[3]
1 (10-ounce) can baby clams, drained	12 ounces linguine, freshly cooked[4]
½ cup chopped flat-leaf (Italian) parsley[2]	¼ cup reduced fat grated Parmesan cheese[5]

▸ Heat oil and margarine in a large skillet over medium heat; add shallots. Cook, stirring frequently, until shallots soften, 2 to 3 minutes, add garlic and continue stirring until you smell the garlic, 1 to 2 minutes.

▸ Stir in reserved clam juice, parsley, half-and-half, wine, garlic powder, black pepper, and red pepper flakes. Decrease heat to medium-low and simmer until liquid has thickened to a thin sauce consistency, 10 to 12 minutes. (NOTE: This is the final consistency of the sauce, if it is still too thin, continue to cook until the desired consistency.)

▸ Stir in clams and heat through; pour over cooked linguine and toss well. *NOTE: Do not hurry this process, as you want the linguine to absorb as much of the clam sauce as possible.* Add more ground black pepper, if desired, and serve with Parmesan cheese.

NUTRITIONAL INFO PER SERVING: Calories 399mg, Fat 9mg (Saturated Fat 2mg), Cholesterol 53mg, Carbohydrates 51mg (Fiber 1mg, Sugar 0mg), Sodium 172mg

COMMENTS:

1 *To reduce saturated fat, use trans-free margarine. Since it contains sodium (90mg per tablespoon), it will increase the sodium per serving to 187mg.*

2 *For variety, substitute fresh basil instead of the parsley.*

3 *Add more pepper flakes for a spicier flavor.*

4 *If linguine is slightly under-cooked it will absorb more of the clam sauce.*

5 *Although freshly grated cheese is superior in flavor to the canned variety, it often contains more sodium. Romano generally is lower in sodium than Parmesan (340mg per ounce versus 454mg, and canned Parmesan has 150mg or less).*

TOTAL SODIUM AND FAT PER INGREDIENT
Sodium:
 2 shallots - 4mg
 4 garlic cloves - 4mg
 20 oz clams - 631mg
 ½ c parsley - 16mg
 ½ c half-and-half - 50mg
   or light cream - 48mg
 ¼ c white wine - 3mg
 ¼ t crushed red pepper - 1mg
 12 oz linguine - 24mg
 ¼ c Parmesan - 300mg
Fat (Sat Fat):
 1 T olive oil - 14mg (2mg)
 1 T NSA margarine - 8mg (2mg)
   or NSA butter - 12mg (8mg)
 20 oz clams - 8mg (0mg)
 ½ c half-and-half - 14mg (9mg)
   or light cream - 24mg (16mg)
 12 oz linguine - 4mg (1mg)
 ¼ c Parmesan - 4mg (0mg)

COMMENTS:

1 *There are many low-sodium pasta sauces available, choose varieties with less than 250mg per ½ cup serving. See RESOURCES, page 272.*

2 *See Eggs and Egg Substitutes, page 38, for a comparison of fat and sodium in eggs and egg substitutes.*

3 *Omitting the olives reduces the sodium per serving to 231mg.*

4 *Fresh mozzarella usually comes packaged in water and low in sodium (15mg per ounce). Read labels carefully, as some brands are packaged in brine, which increases the sodium substantially.*

5 *Although freshly grated cheese is superior in flavor to the canned variety, it often contains more sodium. Romano generally is lower in sodium than Parmesan (340mg per ounce versus 454mg, and canned Parmesan has 150mg or less).*

TOTAL SODIUM AND FAT PER INGREDIENT

Sodium:
4½ c Marinara Sauce - 548mg
1 lb LF ricotta - 720mg
8 oz NSA Swiss - 80mg
2 eggs - 140mg
 or ½ c egg substitute - 200mg
2 oz ripe olives - 298mg
1 T cinnamon - 3mg
4 oz fresh mozzarella - 60mg
2 oz Parmesan - 300mg

Fat (Sat Fat):
4½ c Marinara - 21mg (3mg)
9 lasagna noodles - 4mg (0mg)
1 lb LF ricotta - 48mg (32mg)
8 oz NSA Swiss - 64mg (40mg)
2 eggs - 10mg (3mg)
 or ½ c egg substitute - 0mg
¼ c walnuts - 19mg (2mg)
2 oz ripe olives - 4mg (0mg)
4 oz mozzarella - 28mg (6mg)
2 oz Parmesan - 4mg (0mg)

LASAGNA WITH A CINNAMON TWIST

Sodium Per Serving – 269mg   Serves 6

This lasagna is different than most with its unique cinnamon flavor, and it goes together quickly with premade spaghetti sauce. By the way, most frozen and restaurant lasagna is relatively high in sodium, averaging about 600mg per serving.

4½–5 cups Marinara Sauce (page 151), **or 1½ (28-ounce) jars low-salt pasta sauce, divided**[1]

9 lasagna noodles, cooked per package directions

1 pound lowfat ricotta cheese

8 ounces shredded no-salt-added Swiss cheese (about 3 cups)

2 eggs, beaten, or ½ cup egg substitute[2]

¼ cup chopped walnuts

½ (4-ounce) can sliced ripe olives, drained (optional)[3]

1 tablespoon cinnamon powder

1 tablespoon sugar substitute or sugar

4 ounces fresh mozzarella, sliced, chopped, or grated[4]

2 ounces reduced fat grated Parmesan cheese (about ¼ cup)[5]

▷ Preheat oven to 350ºF (180ºC).

▷ Spread ½ cup spaghetti sauce in bottom of a large rectangular baking dish. Place 3 lasagna noodles on top of the sauce, covering the bottom of the dish.

▷ In a large bowl, mix together ricotta, Swiss cheese, eggs, walnuts, olives, cinnamon, sweetener, and ½ cup spaghetti sauce; spread half the cheese mixture over the lasagne noodles and top with 1½ cups pasta sauce. Layer with 3 more lasagna noodles, spread remaining cheese mixture and pasta sauce on top; cover with the last 3 noodles.

▷ Top with mozzarella and Parmesan cheeses. Cover with aluminum foil and bake in a preheated oven for 1 hour. Remove and let sit for 10 minutes before serving.

NUTRITIONAL INFO PER SERVING: Calories 505mg, Fat 25mg (Saturated Fat 12mg), Cholesterol 119mg, Carbohydrates 38mg (Fiber 5mg, Sugar 13mg), Sodium 269mg

VARIATION
Vegetable Lasagna

Set aside 1 cup sauce for the bottom of the dish and to mix with the cheese. Add 2–3 cups sliced or chopped vegetables, such as mushrooms, broccoli, and zucchini, to the remaining 3½ cups sauce; proceed as directed.

NUTRITIONAL INFO PER SERVING: Calories 426mg, Fat 19mg (Saturated Fat 8mg), Cholesterol 94mg, Carbohydrates 39mg (Fiber 5mg, Sugar 11mg), Sodium 202mg

PESTO, TOMATO AND FRESH MOZZARELLA PIZZA

Sodium Per Serving – 159mg   Makes 4 individual pizzas

Two slices of a 12-inch cheese pizza averages 500mg sodium or more. This lower-salt favorite is especially good in the summer when there is an abundance of fresh basil and tomatoes.

4 (8-inch) flatbreads *(see* QUICK HERBAL FLATBREAD AND PIZZA DOUGH *(page 219)*[1]

1 cup QUICK PESTO *(page 154)* **or prepared pesto**[2]

2 garlic cloves, finely minced

6 basil leaves, thinly sliced

2 tomatoes, sliced

½ cup pine nuts

4 ounces fresh herbal mozzarella, chopped or thinly sliced[4]

▷ Preheat oven to 350°F (180°C). Arrange oven rack to lowest level.

▷ Place 2 flatbreads on a pizza stone or baking sheet; spread with pesto. Sprinkle with garlic and basil; place tomato slices on top and sprinkle with pine nuts and mozzarella. Repeat with remaining 2 flatbreads. *NOTE: For a fresher tomato taste, prepare the pizza without the tomatoes and add them after the pizza has baked.*

▷ Bake pizza in a preheated oven on the lowest rack for 20 minutes, or until crust is lightly browned and cheese has melted.

NUTRITIONAL INFO PER PIZZA: Calories 674mg, Fat 41mg (Saturated Fat 11mg), Cholesterol 74mg, Carbohydrates 58mg (Fiber 4mg, Sugar 4mg), Sodium 159mg

---

CHICKEN, SPINACH AND SUN-DRIED TOMATO PIZZA

Sodium Per Serving – 258mg   Makes 4 individual pizzas

Another easy, yummy pizza that uses leftover chicken.

4 (8-inch) flatbreads *(see* QUICK HERBAL FLATBREAD AND PIZZA DOUGH, *page 219)*[1]

¾ cup SUN-DRIED TOMATO PESTO *(page 154)*[2]

12–16 spinach leaves[3]

2 cups cooked chicken breast, sliced

½ small sweet onion, thinly sliced, such as Vidalia[5]

4 ounces fresh herbal mozzarella, chopped or thinly sliced[4]

▷ Preheat oven to 350°F (180°C). Arrange oven rack to lowest level.

▷ Place 2 flatbreads on a pizza stone or baking sheet; spread with pesto. Layer with spinach, chicken, onion, and mozzarella. Repeat with remaining 2 flatbreads.

▷ Bake pizza in a preheated oven on the lowest rack for 20 minutes, or until crust is lightly browned and cheese has melted.

NUTRITIONAL INFO PER SERVING: Calories 638mg, Fat 30mg (Saturated Fat 11mg), Cholesterol 107mg, Carbohydrates 55mg (Fiber 5mg, Sugar 5mg), Sodium 258mg

---

COMMENTS:

1 Low-salt pita bread or flour tortillas may also be used.

2 Prepared pesto averages over 700mg sodium per ¼ cup, but there are a few lower salt varieties with less than 250mg.

3 Fresh basil leaves may be substituted, except place them on the pizza during the last 4 or 5 minutes of cooking.

4 See COMMENTS #4, page 156, for info on fresh mozzarella.

5 Caramelized onions are also delicious on this pizza (see COOKING TIP, Caramelizing Onions, page 41).

TOTAL SODIUM AND FAT PER INGREDIENT

Pesto, Tomato Pizza:
Sodium:
  4 flatbreads - 144mg
  1 c QUICK PESTO - 156mg
  2 garlic cloves - 2mg
  2 tomatoes - 12mg
  ½ c pine nuts - 1mg
  4 oz fresh mozzarella - 320mg
Fat (Sat Fat):
  4 flatbreads - 27mg (5mg)
  1 c QUICK PESTO - 42mg (5mg)
  2 tomatoes - 1mg (0mg)
  ½ c pine nuts - 46mg (3mg)
  4 oz mozzarella - 48mg (32mg)

Chicken, Spinach Pizza:
Sodium:
  4 flatbreads - 144mg
  ¾ c TOMATO PESTO - 320mg
  12 spinach leaves - 95mg
  2 c chicken breast - 146mg
  ½ sm sweet onion - 5mg
  4 oz fresh mozzarella - 320mg
Fat (Sat Fat):
  4 flatbreads - 27mg (5mg)
  1 c TOMATO PESTO - 42mg (5mg)
  2 c chicken breast - 3mg (1mg)
  4 oz mozzarella - 48mg (32mg)

COMMENTS:

1 *Soy sauce has 914mg sodium per tablespoon, lite soy averages 660mg, however, there are several brands with less than 400mg:* **House of Tsang** *Less Salt (280mg),* **Rice Road** *(300mg), and* **Angostura** *(390mg).*

2 *If using rice wine vinegar, be aware that some brands have added sodium.*

MOO GOO GAI PAN

Sodium Per Serving – 257mg   Serves 4

While living in Hawaii, I picked up several delicious recipes, this is one of my favorites. Moo Goo Gai Pan is nothing more than chicken and sliced mushrooms. This version also includes carrots, snow peas, and water chestnuts. While many Asian dishes are high in sodium, because of MSG (monosodium glutamate) and soy sauce, this lower-salt dish uses lite soy sauce and no MSG.

2 (4-ounce) boneless, skinless chicken breasts, sliced in thin strips

1½ tablespoons lite soy sauce[1]

2 tablespoons dry sherry or rice wine vinegar[2]

1 tablespoon cornstarch

1 tablespoon olive oil

8 ounces sliced mushrooms (about 3 cups)

2 carrots, sliced on the diagonal

2–3 green onions, chopped

3 garlic cloves, minced

2 cups snow peas

½ cup CHICKEN STOCK (page 232) or canned low-salt chicken broth

½ teaspoon low-salt chicken bouillon granules

2 tablespoons sugar substitute or sugar

1 (8-ounce) can sliced water chestnuts, drained

½ cup no-salt-added bamboo shoots

4 cups cooked rice

▸ Mix together soy sauce, sherry, cornstarch, and oil; add chicken strips and marinate for 20 minutes.

▸ In a skillet over medium-high heat; add chicken and marinade. Cook, stirring frequently, until chicken begins to brown, 2 to 3 minutes. Stir in mushrooms, and carrots; cook stirring frequently, until mushrooms soften, about 3 minutes. Add green onions and garlic; cook, stirring constantly, until you smell the garlic, about 1 minute.

▸ Stir in peas, chicken stock, bouillon, sweetener, water chestnuts, and bamboo shoots; decrease heat to medium-low. Cook, stirring occasionally, until carrots are done, about 5 minutes; serve over rice.

NUTRITIONAL INFO PER SERVING: Calories 393mg, Fat 5mg (Saturated Fat 1mg), Cholesterol 35mg, Carbohydrates 60mg (Fiber 4mg, Sugar 6mg), Sodium 257mg

TOTAL SODIUM AND FAT PER INGREDIENT

Sodium:
8 oz chicken breast - 146mg
1½ T lite soy sauce - 734mg
2 T sherry - 3mg
1 T cornstarch - 1mg
8 oz mushrooms - 4mg
2 carrots - 84mg
2 green onions - 8mg
3 garlic cloves - 3mg
2 c snow peas - 10mg
½ c CHICKEN STOCK - 10mg or
  LS canned broth - 65mg
½ t LS chicken bouillon - 3mg
8 oz water chestnuts - 20mg
½ c NSA bamboo shoots - 2mg
4 c cooked rice - 6mg
Fat (Sat Fat):
8 oz chicken breast - 3mg (1mg)
1 T olive oil - 14mg (2mg)
8 oz mushrooms - 1mg (0mg)
½ c CHICKEN STOCK - 1mg (0mg)
  or LS canned broth - 1mg (1mg)
4 c cooked rice - 2mg (0mg)

SWEET AND SOUR PORK

Sodium Per Serving – 95mg   Serves 4

This is a simple, yet delicious preparation of this traditional Chinese dish. Serve with steamed rice.

- 1 pound boneless pork loin, cut into 1-inch cubes[1]
- 2 tablespoons all-purpose flour
- 1 tablespoon cornstarch
- ¼ teaspoon onion powder
- 2 tablespoons olive oil
- 2 celery stalks, sliced horizontally into ½-inch pieces
- 1 bell pepper, cut into thin strips

- ½ sweet onion, thinly sliced
- 1 (8-ounce) can pineapple tidbits in its own juice[2]
- ⅓ cup no-salt-added ketchup
- 1 tablespoon low-salt prepared mustard
- 1 teaspoon cider vinegar
- ½ teaspoon low-salt Worcestershire sauce

▷ Place pork, flour, cornstarch, and onion powder in a paper bag and shake until all pieces are coated.

▷ Heat oil in a large skillet over medium-high heat; add pork. Fry, turning frequently, until brown and crispy on all sides, 8 to 10 minutes. Remove pork and keep warm.

▷ In same skillet, add celery, bell pepper, onion, and pineapple (including juice); decrease heat to medium and cook, stirring frequently, until vegetables begin to soften, about 5 minutes.

▷ Stir in ketchup, mustard, vinegar, and Worcestershire; cook, stirring frequently, for 2 minutes. Mix in pork and heat through; serve with rice.

NUTRITIONAL INFO PER SERVING: Calories 314mg, Fat 12mg (Saturated Fat 3mg), Cholesterol 72mg, Carbohydrates 24mg (Fiber 2mg, Sugar 16mg), Sodium 95mg

COMMENTS:

1 *Most pork loins come pre-packaged in brine and have up to 400mg sodium per 4-ounce serving. Fresh packaged roasts without the brine have 60mg or less sodium per serving.*

2 *Tidbits are a good size for this dish, larger chunks may also be used, but cut them in half.*

TOTAL SODIUM AND FAT PER INGREDIENT

Sodium:
- 1 lb pork loin - 231mg
- 1 T cornstarch - 1mg
- 2 celery stalks - 64mg
- 1 bell pepper - 4mg
- ½ sweet onion - 6mg
- 8 oz pineapple in juice - 2mg
- ⅓ c NSA ketchup - 32mg
- 1 T LS mustard - 30mg
- ½ t Worcestershire - 10mg

Fat (Sat Fat):
- 1 lb pork loin - 19mg (7mg)
- 2 T olive oil - 27mg (4mg)

COMMENTS:

1 See FOOD NOTE, page 73, for info on no-salt-added beans.

2 See COMMENTS #2, page 42, for low-salt salsa info.

3 Surprisingly, chili powder contains sodium (26mg per teaspoon). Look for no-salt-added brands (see RESOURCES, page 272, for more info).

4 There are several unsalted spicy seasonings that are used for cajun or barbecue rubs that may be used. Also, if your market has a Hispanic section, check the dried spices in bags for a no-salt taco seasoning.

5 Look for Mexican oregano in the Hispanic section of the supermarket. It's flavor is more pungent than regular oregano.

6 Omitting the olives reduces the sodium to 153mg per serving.

EASY FIESTA CASSEROLE

Sodium Per Serving – 171mg   Serves 6

This yummy casserole is made with ingredients I always have on hand.

½ pound ground lean turkey or beef

½ sweet onion, chopped

1 (15-ounce) no-salt-added black or kidney beans, rinsed and drained[1]

1 cup low-salt tomato-based salsa[2]

¼ teaspoon no-salt-added chili powder[3]

¼ teaspoon garlic powder

¼ teaspoon no-salt-added taco or spicy seasoning[4]

⅛ teaspoon ground cumin

⅛ teaspoon dried oregano[5]

⅛ teaspoon ground black pepper

2 cups crushed low-salt tortilla chips (about 3 ounces)

1 cup lowfat sour cream

2 tablespoons (about 9 small) chopped ripe olives (optional)[6]

1 (4-ounce) can diced green chiles

1 (15-ounce) can no-salt-added whole corn, drained

1–2 tomatoes, chopped

4 ounces no-salt-added Swiss cheese, shredded (about 1 cup)

2 ounces lowfat Cheddar cheese, shredded (about ½ cup)

▶ Preheat oven to 350°F (180°C). Coat a large rectangular baking dish with nonstick cooking spray.

▶ In a skillet over medium heat; cook meat 4 to 5 minutes, stirring frequently and breaking up into small chunks. Add onion, beans, salsa, chili powder, garlic powder, taco seasoning, cumin, oregano, and black pepper; reduce heat to medium-low and cover. Cook, stirring occasionally, until meat is no longer pink, 5 to 10 minutes.

▶ Spread crushed tortilla chips over bottom of prepared baking dish, layer turkey mixture on top, followed by sour cream, green chiles, corn, olives, tomatoes, and shredded cheeses. Cover with foil and bake for 20 to 30 minutes, until cheese is bubbly and lightly browned. Serve with additional salsa.

NUTRITIONAL INFO PER SERVING: Calories 280mg, Fat 12mg (Saturated Fat 6mg), Cholesterol 37mg, Carbohydrates 25mg (Fiber 6mg, Sugar 5mg), Sodium 171mg

TOTAL SODIUM AND FAT PER INGREDIENT

Sodium:
- ½ lb ground turkey - 130mg
- ½ sweet onion - 6mg
- 15 oz NSA black beans - 45mg
- 1 c LS salsa - 320mg
- ¼ t NSA chili powder - 6mg
- 3 oz LS tortilla chips - 126mg
- 1 c LF sour cream - 136mg
- 2 T ripe olives - 146mg
- 4 oz green chiles - 100mg
- 15 oz NSA corn - 30mg
- 1 tomato - 6mg
- 4 oz NSA Swiss cheese - 40mg
- 2 oz LF Cheddar cheese - 280mg

Fat (Sat Fat):
- 1 lb ground turkey - 2mg (0mg)
- 3 oz LS tortilla chips - 18mg (3mg)
- 1 c LF sour cream - 27mg (16mg)
- 2 T ripe olives - 2mg (0mg)
- 15 oz NSA corn - 3mg (0mg)
- 4 oz NSA Swiss - 32mg (20mg)
- 2 oz LF Cheddar - 12mg (8mg)

QUICK FAJITAS

Sodium Per Serving – 123mg   Serves 4

This is another recipe that has been passed on to me from sources unknown. We particularly like the combination of the peppers and cumin with the lime and orange juices.

8 ounces flank steak or skinless, boneless chicken breasts, sliced into thin strips[1]

1 tablespoon olive oil

½ red bell pepper, sliced

½ green bell pepper, sliced

½ sweet onion, sliced

1 teaspoon no-salt-added chili powder[2]

1 teaspoon ground cumin

½ teaspoon dried oregano

¼ teaspoon garlic powder

¼ teaspoon ground black pepper

3 tablespoons lime juice

2 tablespoons orange juice

4 (10 or 12-Inch) low-salt whole wheat tortillas or 8 (6 or 7-inch) corn tortillas[3]

Optional Condiments:

Shredded no-salt-added Swiss and lowfat Cheddar cheese (optional)

Chopped fresh cilantro

Chopped tomatoes

Shredded lettuce

Low-salt salsa

COMMENTS:

1 *These are best made with beef, but chicken is a close second.*

2 *Surprisingly, chili powder contains sodium (26mg per teaspoon). Look for no-salt-added brands, like* **The Spice Hunter** *(see RESOURCES, page 272, for more info).*

3 *Most 10-inch flour tortillas average 335mg sodium, but a few manufacturers, such as* **Adios Carbs** *and* **Tumaro's,** *offer low-sodium ones (see RESOURCES, page 272, for additional information).*

Corn tortillas average 3mg sodium per tortilla (shelf-stable shells have 150mg)

▷ Heat oil in a skillet over medium heat; add beef. Cook, stirring frequently, until no longer pink, about 2 minutes, add red and green peppers and onions. Cook, stirring frequently, until onions and peppers begin to soften, 3 to 4 minutes. Stir in chili powder, cumin, oregano, garlic powder, pepper, lime juice, and orange juice; cook, stirring frequently, for 2 minutes.

▷ Fill warmed tortillas with chicken mixture; add optional condiments as desired.

NUTRITIONAL INFO PER BEEF FAJITA (WITHOUT CONDIMENTS): Calories 306mg, Fat 19mg (Saturated Fat 7mg), Cholesterol 40mg, Carbohydrates 15mg (Fiber 4mg, Sugar 3mg), Sodium 123mg (46mg with corn tortillas)

NUTRITIONAL INFO PER CHICKEN FAJITA (WITHOUT CONDIMENTS): Calories 223mg, Fat 8mg (Saturated Fat 1mg), Cholesterol 33mg, Carbohydrates 15mg (Fiber 4mg, Sugar 3mg), Sodium 121mg (44mg with corn tortillas)

TOTAL SODIUM AND FAT PER INGREDIENT

Sodium:
8 oz lean beef - 152mg
  or chicken breast - 146mg
½ red bell pepper - 1mg
½ green bell pepper - 2mg
½ sweet onion - 6mg
1 t ground cumin - 4mg
4 LS flour tortillas - 328mg
  or 8 corn tortillas - 21mg
Fat (Sat Fat):
8 oz lean beef - 45mg (26mg)
  or chicken breast - 3mg (1mg)
1 T olive oil - 14mg (2mg)
4 LS flour tortillas - 16mg (0mg)
  or 8 corn tortillas - 7mg (0mg)

CHICKEN BURRITOS WITH TOMATILLO SAUCE

Sodium Per Serving – 202mg   Serves 6

These delicious burritos, covered in a yummy tomatillo sauce, are ready in less than 30 minutes.

¼ cup dry sherry

2 boneless, skinless chicken breasts (about 8 ounces), cooked and cut into thin strips[1]

1 cup mixed vegetables, chopped (such as zucchini, broccoli, mushrooms, corn, and carrots)

1 cup no-salt-added black or kidney beans

6 (10 to 12-inch) low-salt flour tortillas[2]

TOMATILLO SAUCE *(page 163)*

3 ounces shredded no-salt-added Swiss cheese (about ¾ cup)[3]

1 ounce shredded lowfat Cheddar cheese (about ¼ cup)[3]

▸ Combine sherry, chicken, veggies, and beans in a saucepan over medium heat; cover and cook, stirring occasionally, until veggies are tender, about 5 minutes.

▸ Equally divide mixture and place in tortillas; roll up and pour TOMATILLO SAUCE over burritos. Top with cheese and serve.

NUTRITIONAL INFO PER SERVING: Calories 349mg, Fat 12mg (Saturated Fat 4mg), Cholesterol 40mg, Carbohydrates 31mg (Fiber 11mg, Sugar 5mg), Sodium 202mg

COMMENTS:

1 *Use leftover chicken or cook by any preferred method, such as poached (see COOKING TIP, page 115), roasted, or mixed with ¼ cup low-salt salsa and cooked in 1 tablespoon olive oil.*

2 *Most 10-inch flour tortillas average 335mg sodium, but a few manufacturers, such as **Adios Carbs** and **Tumaro's**, offer low-sodium ones (see RESOURCES, page 272, for additional information).*

3 *Cheddar has about 140mg sodium per ounce versus 10mg for NSA Swiss. A little Cheddar adds flavor, while keeping salt to a minimum.*

TOTAL SODIUM AND FAT PER INGREDIENT

Sodium:
¼ c sherry - 5mg
8 oz chicken breast - 146mg
1 c mixed veggies - 64mg
1 c NSA black beans - 22mg
6 LS flour tortillas - 492mg
3 oz NSA Swiss cheese - 30mg
1 oz LF Cheddar cheese - 140mg
Fat (Sat Fat):
8 oz chicken breast - 3mg (1mg)
6 LS flour tortillas - 24mg (0mg)
3 oz NSA Swiss - 24mg (15mg)
1 oz LF Cheddar - 6mg (4mg)

FOOD NOTE

TOMATILLOS

A relative of the tomato, tomatillos look like green tomatoes, but have a thin papery husk. Their flavor is tart with a hint of lemon, and they are most often used to make green salsa (salsa verde).

Selection: Tomatillos are used most often in an unripened state. Choose firm tomatillos that are bright green with tight-fitting, unblemished husks; avoid those that are beginning to turn a light yellow, as they will be too ripe.

Preparation: Before using, remove husk and wash to remove stickiness. There are several ways to cook tomatillos:

Boiling: Bring a pot of water to a boil over high heat; add peeled tomatillos and cook until soft but still whole, 3 to 4 minutes. NOTE: Tomatillos will burst and get mushy if cooked too long.

Grilling: Heat a skillet (preferably cast iron) over high heat; add whole tomatillos and grill, turning occasionally, until browned on all sides, about 5 minutes.

Roasting: Either place tomatillos in a pan and broil 2 inches from heat, turning until all sides are blistered and charred, 6 to 7 minutes; or place in a pan and roast in a preheated oven at 350ºF (180ºC) for 15 to 20 minutes.

Storage: Place in a paper bag and store in the refrigerator up to 4 weeks.

TOMATILLO SAUCE

Sodium Per Serving – 52mg   Serves 4

This is a mild sauce if you omit the hot peppers, but if you like it hot, you can add degrees of heat by the number and type of peppers used and whether or not you include the seeds. Ready in less than 30 minutes, it is also good with grilled halibut or other firm fish. Canned tomatillos are found in the Hispanic section (fresh ones in the produce section) of many supermarkets.

1 tablespoon olive oil

1 small onion, chopped (about ½ cup)

2 garlic cloves

1 (4-ounce) can diced green chiles

2 (13-ounce) cans tomatillos, drained[1]

1 cup CHICKEN STOCK (page 232) or canned low-salt chicken broth

2 tablespoons fresh lime juice

1 teaspoon (or 1 envelope) low-salt chicken bouillon granules

1 teaspoon ground cumin

1 teaspoon dried oregano[2]

1 teaspoon sugar substitute or sugar

2 jalapeño or serrano peppers, (optional)[3]

¼ cup chopped fresh cilantro

▷ Heat oil in a skillet over medium-high heat; add onions. Cook, stirring frequently, until onions are soft, 3 to 4 minutes; add garlic. Cook, stirring constantly, until you smell the garlic, 1 to 2 minutes; stir in green chiles, tomatillos, chicken stock, lime juice, bouillon, cumin, oregano, sweetener, and jalapeños. Decrease heat to low and simmer, uncovered, until the tomatillos are mushy, about 25 minutes.

▷ Remove sauce from heat and stir in cilantro; let cool slightly. Pour into a blender or food processor and pulse until smooth; return to saucepan and reheat. Serve over burritos, enchiladas, or grilled fish. Top with more cilantro, if desired

---

NUTRITIONAL INFO PER SERVING: Calories 77mg, Fat 3mg (Saturated Fat 0mg), Cholesterol 3mg, Carbohydrates 11mg (Fiber 5mg, Sugar 4mg), Sodium 52mg

COMMENTS:

1 Fresh tomatillos may be used (24 tomatillos or about 4 cups is equivalent to 26 ounces of canned), see FOOD NOTE, page 162, for selecting and cooking information.

2 Mexican oregano is stronger and more pungent than other dried oregano and is available in the Hispanic foods section of many supermarkets.

3 On a scale of 1 to 5, jalapeños are a 3, with most of the heat contained in the seeds and veins. See FOOD NOTE, page 235, for a listing of peppers and the amount of heat in each.

CAUTION: When handling hot chiles, wear rubber gloves, as the oils of the pepper can be very potent. A piece of plastic wrap or a sandwich bag also works to hold the pepper. If you should touch the pepper with your bare fingers, wash your hands thoroughly and be sure to keep your fingers away from your eyes or you'll be in sheer agony!

TOTAL SODIUM AND FAT PER INGREDIENT

Sodium:
  1 sm onion - 2mg
  2 garlic cloves - 2mg
  4 oz green chiles - 100mg
  26 oz tomatillos - 180mg
  1 c CHICKEN STOCK - 20mg
    or canned LS broth - 130mg
  1 t LS chicken bouillon - 5mg
  1 t cumin - 4mg
  ¼ c cilantro - 2mg
Fat (Sat Fat):
  1 T olive oil - 14mg (2mg)
  1 c CHICKEN STOCK - 1mg (0mg)
    or canned LS broth - 2mg (1mg)

1 Cooked chicken instead of the beef is also good in this dish.

2 Corn tortillas average 3mg sodium per tortilla (shelf-stable shells have 150mg). Most 7-inch flour tortillas average 234mg sodium, but a few manufacturers offer low-sodium ones (see RESOURCES, page 272).

BEEF QUESADILLAS

Sodium Per Serving – 191mg   Serves 4

Quesadillas are like Mexican pizzas—put just about anything you want between two corn or flour tortillas and fry. Serve with lettuce, tomato, GUACAMOLE (page 42), sour cream, and salsa, if desired.

2 cups cooked beef, sliced, shredded, or cubed[1]

½ small sweet onion, thinly sliced

1–2 tomatoes, diced

1 (4-ounce) can diced green chiles

2 tablespoons chopped ripe olives (optional)

2 tablespoons chopped fresh cilantro

4 ounces shredded no-salt-added Swiss cheese (about 1 cup)

2 ounces shredded lowfat Cheddar cheese (about ½ cup)

8 (6-inch) corn or low-salt flour tortillas[2]

Vegetable or canola oil for frying (about ¼ cup)

Toppings, such as lettuce, tomato, avocado (or guacamole), sour cream, jalapeños, and low-salt salsa

▷ Evenly divide beef and place on 4 tortillas; layer with onions, tomato, green chiles, olives, cilantro, and cheeses. Top with a tortilla, making a sandwich.

▷ Heat oil in a skillet over medium-high heat; fry tortilla sandwich, carefully turning, until golden brown and crisp on both sides, about 2 minutes per side. Cut each quesadilla into quarters and serve with desired condiments.

NUTRITIONAL INFO PER SERVING (WITHOUT TOPPINGS AND OIL FOR FRYING): Calories 514mg, Fat 24mg (Saturated Fat 10mg), Cholesterol 135mg, Carbohydrates 30mg (Fiber 4mg, Sugar 2mg), Sodium 191mg

---

TOTAL SODIUM AND FAT PER INGREDIENT

Sodium:
2 c lean beef - 164mg
½ sweet onion - 5mg
1 tomato - 6mg
4 oz green chiles - 100mg
2 T ripe olives - 146mg
2 T cilantro - 1mg
8 corn tortillas - 21mg
  or LS flour tortillas - 656mg
4 oz NSA Swiss cheese - 40mg
2 oz LF cheddar cheese - 280mg

Fat (Sat Fat):
2 c lean beef - 30mg (10mg)
2 T ripe olives - 2mg (0mg)
8 corn tortillas - 7mg (0mg) or
  LS flour tortillas - 32mg (0mg)
4 oz NSA Swiss - 32mg (20mg)
2 oz LF Cheddar - 12mg (8mg)
1 T olive oil - 14mg (2mg)

STUFFED QUESADILLAS

Sodium Per Serving – 109mg   Serves 6

This is one our most favorite put-together-quickly meals. It takes about 15 minutes and is very yummy. Set out the condiments in bowls and let each person select the toppings of their choice.

¼ cup dry sherry[1]

1 medium red potato, cubed

1 cup fresh or frozen broccoli, chopped

1 cup fresh or frozen cauliflower, chopped

1 cup fresh or frozen mixed vegetables (such as carrots, mushrooms, and corn)

1 cup no-salt-added black or kidney beans[2]

6 low-salt large (burrito-size) flour tortillas[3]

2 tablespoons unsalted margarine or butter[4]

Optional Toppings:

Chopped onion

Chopped tomato

Shredded lettuce

Sliced avocado (optional)

Shredded no-salt-added Swiss cheese and/or lowfat Cheddar cheese

Nonfat or lowfat sour cream or plain yogurt

Low-salt salsa[5]

Chopped cilantro (optional)

▷ In a saucepan over medium heat, add sherry, potatoes, broccoli, cauliflower, mixed vegetables, and beans. Cook, covered, until potatoes are done, about 6 to 8 minutes. *NOTE: Do not let liquid boil dry, if necessary, add more sherry or water to keep vegetables from burning.*

▷ Evenly divide vegetable mixture and place in the center of each tortilla, fold in half.

▷ Melt margarine in a skillet over medium heat; fry filled tortillas until golden brown on both sides, 2 to 3 minutes per side. Repeat with remaining tortillas; add desired toppings and serve.

NUTRITIONAL INFO PER QUESADDILA (WITHOUT TOPPINGS): Calories 239mg, Fat 7mg (Saturated Fat 1mg), Cholesterol 0mg, Carbohydrates 30mg (Fiber 8mg, Sugar 2mg), Sodium 109mg

COMMENTS:

1 *You may substitute white wine or water for the sherry, but the flavor of the sherried vegetables is what makes this dish special.*

2 *Instead of beans, increase the amount of other vegetables by 1 cup.*

3 *Most flour tortillas are high in sodium (335mg per 10-inch tortilla), however, several low-carb varieties have less than 125mg per tortilla (see RE-SOURCES, page 272).*

4 *To reduce saturated fat, use trans-free margarine. Since it contains sodium (90mg per tablespoon), it will increase the sodium per serving to 121mg.*

5 *Look for salsa with 40mg so-dium or less per 2 tablespoons. See RESOURCES, page 272, for low-salt brands.*

TOTAL SODIUM AND FAT PER INGREDIENT

Sodium:
 ¼ c sherry - 5mg
 1 red potato - 20mg
 1c broccoli - 19mg
 1 c cauliflower - 30mg
 1 c mixed vegetables - 64mg
 1 c NSA black beans - 23mg
 6 LS flour tortillas - 492mg
 Optional Toppings (per serving):
  Tomatoes - 2mg
  Avocado - 2mg
  Lettuce - 1mg
  NSA Swiss cheese - 5mg
  LF cheddar cheese - 23mg
Fat (Sat Fat):
 6 LS flour tortillas - 24mg (0mg)
 2 T NSA margarine - 16mg (3mg)
  or NSA butter - 24mg (16mg)
 Optional Toppings (per serving):
  Avocado - 5mg (1mg)
  NSA Swiss - 6mg (3mg)
  LF Cheddar - 1mg (1mg)

TOTAL SODIUM AND FAT PER INGREDIENT

Sodium:
8 ounces ground turkey - 160mg
¼ c LS salsa - 80mg
8 corn tortillas - 21mg
  or 6 LS flour tortillas - 492mg
Optional Toppings (per serving):
  Tomatoes - 2mg
  Avocado - 2mg
  Lettuce - 1mg
  NSA Swiss cheese - 5mg
  LF cheddar cheese - 23mg
Fat (Sat Fat):
1 T olive oil - 14mg (2mg)
8 oz ground turkey - 14mg (4mg)
6 corn tortillas - 5mg (0mg)
  or 6 LS flour - 24mg (0mg)
Optional Toppings (per serving):
  Avocado - 5mg (1mg)
  NSA Swiss - 6mg (3mg)
  LF Cheddar - 1mg (1mg)

YUMMY TURKEY TACOS

Sodium Per Serving – 79mg   Makes 6–8 tacos

We have these turkey tacos as often as possible and the best part . . . they're ready in about 15 minutes.

1 tablespoon olive oil

6–8 ounces ground lean turkey breast

¼ teaspoon no-salt-added chili powder[1]

¼ teaspoon hot chili or taco spices)[2]

¼ teaspoon garlic powder

⅛ teaspoon cumin

⅛ teaspoon ground black pepper

¼–½ cup low-salt tomato-based salsa[3]

8 (6-inch) corn tortillas or 6 (10-inch) low-salt whole wheat tortillas[4]

Vegetable or canola oil for frying (about ¼ cup)

Optional Toppings:

Chopped tomatoes

Sliced avocado, sliced

Chopped sweet onion

Shredded lettuce

Shredded no-salt-added Swiss cheese[5]

Shredded lowfat Cheddar cheese[5]

Chopped fresh cilantro

Low-salt salsa[3]

▷ Heat oil in a skillet over medium heat; add turkey, chili powder, hot chili spices, garlic powder, cumin, and pepper. Brown meat, stirring frequently and breaking up any chunks, until no longer pink, about 5 minutes. Stir in ¼–½ cup salsa; decrease heat to low and keep warm while frying tortillas.

▷ Heat vegetable oil in another skillet over medium-high heat; place one tortilla in hot oil and fry until golden and slightly crisp, turn, fold in half, and continue to fry each side until slightly crisp. Remove and drain on paper towels; repeat with remaining tortillas. Fill with meat mixture and desired condiments.

NUTRITIONAL INFO PER TACO (WITHOUT OPTIONAL TOPPINGS AND OIL FOR FRYING): Calories 217mg, Fat 12mg (Saturated Fat 4mg), Cholesterol 28mg, Carbohydrates 18mg (Fiber 4mg, Sugar 1mg), Sodium 79mg (138mg with LS flour tortillas)

GRILLED FISH TACOS

Sodium Per Serving – 127mg   Makes 6 tacos

If you've never had fish tacos, you're in for a treat. Grill marinated fish, add fresh corn salsa, and you've got a delicious, but simple meal. Serve with a side of REFRIED BEANS *(page 192) and a tossed salad.*

1 pound halibut, cut into bite-size pieces[1]

2 tablespoons lime juice

¼ cup dry white wine

2 tablespoons olive oil, divided

1½ cups FRESH CORN RELISH (page 235)

6 (6-inch) corn or low-salt flour tortillas, grilled[2]

4 ounces no-salt-added Swiss cheese, shredded (about 1 cup)[3]

2 ounces lowfat Cheddar cheese, shredded (about ½ cup)[3]

¼ cup chopped fresh cilantro

▶ Combine lime juice, wine, and 2 tablespoons olive oil; pour over halibut and marinate for 30 minutes.

▶ Grill fish until done (meat will be opaque and still moist inside), about 5 minutes.

▶ Mix grilled fish with FRESH CORN RELISH; evenly divide and fill tortillas. Mix Swiss and Cheddar cheeses together and add to tacos; top with cilantro and salsa, if desired.

NUTRITIONAL INFO PER TACO: Calories 339mg, Fat 16mg (Saturated Fat 6mg), Cholesterol 49mg, Carbohydrates 23mg (Fiber 4mg, Sugar 3mg), Sodium 127mg (206mg with LS flour tortillas)

COMMENTS:

1 *Any firm fish, such as tuna or salmon may be used.*

2 *Grill tortillas for 1 minute on each side until they start to brown.*

Corn tortillas average 3mg sodium per tortilla (shelf-stable shells have 150mg). Most 7-inch flour tortillas average 234mg sodium, but a few manufacturers offer low-sodium ones (see RESOURCES*, page 272).*

3 *Cheddar has about 140mg sodium per ounce versus 10mg for NSA Swiss. Mixing in a little Cheddar adds flavor, while keeping salt to a minimum.*

TOTAL SODIUM AND FAT PER INGREDIENT

Sodium:
  1 lb halibut - 245mg
  ¼ c white wine - 3mg
  1½ c CORN RELISH - 18mg
  6 corn tortillas - 16mg
    or LS flour tortillas - 492mg
  4 oz NSA Swiss cheese - 40mg
  2 oz LF cheddar cheese - 280mg
  ¼ c cilantro - 2mg
Fat (Sat Fat):
  1 lb halibut - 10mg (1mg)
  2 T olive oil - 27mg (4mg)
  1½ c CORN RELISH - 1mg (0mg)
  6 corn tortillas - 5mg (0mg)
    or LS flour tortillas - 24mg (0mg)
  4 oz NSA Swiss - 32mg (20mg)
  2 oz LF Cheddar - 12mg (8mg)

1 *Canned black beans average 480mg sodium per ½ cup, 50% less salt varieties have 260mg, and no-salt-added brands (NSA) 15mg. NSA beans, such as* **Eden**, **Nature's Choice**, *and* **American Prairie**, *and low-salt brands, like* **Westbrae Natural**, *are found in many supermarkets or health food stores.*

2 *Most bottled salsas average 139mg sodium per 2 table-spoons, but there are many delicious low-salt varieties with less than 80mg. See RE-SOURCES, page 272, for low-salt brands.*

3 *Corn tortillas average 3mg sodium per tortilla (shelf-stable shells have 150mg). Most 7-inch flour tortillas average 234mg sodium, but a few manufacturers offer low-sodium ones (see RESOURCES, page 272).*

TOSTADAS WITH CHICKEN AND GUACAMOLE

Sodium Per Serving – 146mg   Makes 4–6 tostadas

A tostada is nothing more than a salad on a tortilla shell. You won't believe how easy this is to put together, the only thing you have to cook is the tortilla shell. Oh, and did I mention that these are absolutely delicious!

GUACAMOLE *(page 42)*

1 tablespoon lime juice, divided

1 cup no-salt-added black or kidney beans, drained[1]

2 green onions (white and light green parts), chopped

1 tablespoon low-salt tomato-based salsa[2]

2 (4-ounce) boneless, skinless chicken breast halves, cooked and shredded (about 2 cups)

1–2 tomatoes, chopped

2 tablespoons chopped fresh cilantro

1 teaspoon ground cumin

¼ teaspoon garlic powder

⅛ teaspoon ground black pepper

4–6 (6-inch) corn tortillas[3]

Vegetable oil for frying (about ¼ cup)

2 cups shredded lettuce

3 ounces no-salt-added Swiss cheese, shredded (about ¾ cup)

1 ounce lowfat Cheddar cheese, shredded (about ¼ cup)

½ cup low-salt salsa[2]

▷ Mix together GUACAMOLE, 1 teaspoon lime juice, beans, and green onions; set aside.

▷ In another bowl, combine chicken, tomato, remaining 2 teaspoons lime juice, cilantro, cumin, garlic powder, and pepper; set aside.

▷ Heat oil in a skillet over medium-high heat; fry tortillas, one at a time, until crisp and golden on both sides.

▷ Evenly divide chicken and spread on each tortilla; top with guacamole and lettuce. Sprinkle with cheese and top with salsa.

NUTRITIONAL INFO PER SERVING (WITHOUT OIL FOR FRYING): Calories 364mg, Fat 17mg (Saturated Fat 6mg), Cholesterol 59mg, Carbohydrates 31mg (Fiber 10mg, Sugar 2mg), Sodium 146mg

TOTAL SODIUM AND FAT PER INGREDIENT

Sodium:
1 c GUACAMOLE - 27mg
1 c NSA black beans - 22mg
2 green onions - 8mg
½ c + 1 T LS salsa - 180mg
8 oz chicken breast - 146mg
1 tomato - 6mg
2 T cilantro - 1mg
1 t cumin - 4mg
4 corn tortillas - 11mg
2 c lettuce - 9mg
3 oz NSA Swiss cheese - 30mg
1 oz LF cheddar cheese - 140mg
Fat (Sat Fat):
1 c GUACAMOLE - 30mg (4mg)
8 oz chicken breast - 3mg (1mg)
4 corn tortillas - 3mg (0mg)
3 oz NSA Swiss - 24mg (15mg)
1 oz LF Cheddar - 6mg (4mg)

SIDE DISHES

COMMENTS:

1 Either thick or thin asparagus may be used, see FOOD NOTE below for preparation and storage information.

ASPARAGUS WITH TARRAGON VINAIGRETTE

Sodium Per Serving – 9mg

Serves 4

The combination of tarragon and vinegar with asparagus is a perennial favorite and goes nicely with grilled entrées.

20–24 asparagus spears, trimmed[1]

1 tablespoon tarragon or white wine vinegar

1 tablespoon olive oil

¼ teaspoon Dijon-style mustard

½ teaspoon dried tarragon

¼ teaspoon garlic powder

⅛ teaspoon ground black pepper

▸ Cook asparagus by any method desired *(see below)*.

▸ Mix together vinegar, oil, mustard, tarragon, garlic powder, and pepper; pour over asparagus, gently stirring to coat. Serve immediately.

NUTRITIONAL INFO PER SERVING: Calories 48mg, Fat 4mg (Saturated Fat 1mg), Cholesterol 0mg, Carbohydrates 3mg (Fiber 2mg, Sugar 2mg), Sodium 9mg

---

FOOD NOTE

ABOUT ASPARAGUS

Asparagus is high in folic acid, a good source of potassium, and low in sodium (3mg per cup). There is little taste difference between thick or thin stalks, but if you want the most tender, choose thicker stalks. Thinner spears are picked early in the season and tend to be more chewy. NOTE: Prepare asparagus as soon as possible; the longer it sits, the tougher it becomes, regardless of size.

Preparation: Select bright green firm stalks with compact tips. Snap off the tough ends with your hands; they will break naturally at the point that is tough and chewy. Or you can peel the tough outer skin with a vegetable peeler (this is not necessary if using thin stalks, only the ends need trimming). To cook:

Boil – Place in boiling water; cook 5 to 8 minutes. NOTE: Do not overcook. Perfectly cooked asparagus is bright green and crisp-tender; it is not mushy.

Steam – Place asparagus in the upper half of a steamer over boiling water; cook 7 to 12 minutes.

Microwave – Place asparagus and 1–2 tablespoons water in a covered dish and microwave on high 3 to 4 minutes.

Roast – Drizzle a little olive oil on the asparagus and place in an oven-proof dish; roast in a preheated oven at 400°F (200°C) until tender, 10 to 15 minutes (depending on thickness of spears).

Grill – Coat asparagus with 1–2 tablespoons olive oil (place asparagus and oil in a plastic bag, seal and roll asparagus in oil until well coated); place on a hot grill and cook for several minutes, turning once, until asparagus has softened enough to wiggle slightly when picked up with tongs.

Storage: Wrap fresh asparagus in a damp cloth and place in a plastic bag with holes; store in the refrigerator 3 to 4 days. If wilted, refresh by removing ¼ inch from the cut end and standing in water for 5 minutes. *To freeze:* Blanch by boiling or microwaving 1 to 2 minutes, cool in ice water, and drain. Place in plastic bags and freeze for up to 9 months. *NOTE: Do not defrost before cooking and do not refreeze.*

TOTAL SODIUM AND FAT PER INGREDIENT

Sodium:
 20 asparagus - 6mg
 ¼ t dijon mustard - 30mg
Fat (Sat Fat):
 1 T olive oil - 14mg (2mg)

CARAMELIZED SHALLOTS AND ASPARAGUS

Sodium Per Serving – 3mg   Serves 4

This is by far our most favorite asparagus preparation and one of the most requested of my recipes. Incredibly simple and absolutely scrumptous!

1 tablespoon olive oil

1 tablespoon unsalted margarine or butter[1]

2 shallots, minced

1 teaspoon sugar substitute or sugar[2]

20–24 asparagus spears, trimmed

▸ Heat oil and margarine in a large skillet over medium-low heat, add shallots. Cook, stirring occasionally, until shallots are lightly browned and caramelized, 15 to 20 minutes; mix in sweetener.

▸ Meanwhile, cook asparagus by any method desired *(see* FOOD NOTE, *page 170)* until crisp tender. Add asparagus to shallots, tossing to coat; transfer asparagus to a bowl and top with excess shallots. Serve immediately.

NUTRITIONAL INFO PER SERVING: Calories 71mg, Fat 6mg (Saturated Fat 1mg), Cholesterol 0mg, Carbohydrates 5mg (Fiber 2mg, Sugar 2mg), Sodium 3mg

COMMENTS:

1 *To reduce saturated fat, use trans-free margarine. Since it contains sodium (90mg per tablespoon), it will increase the sodium per serving to 25mg.*

2 *For a discussion of the differences between sugar and sugar substitutes, see Sweeteners, page 37.*

FOOD NOTE

ABOUT SHALLOTS

Shallots look like small onions, but are similar to garlic, as they separate into multiple cloves. They are mild in flavor, somewhere between an onion and garlic. Shallots may be used in place of onions in many recipes and add more flavor to most any dish.

Preparation: Remove the outer skin and cook the same as onions and garlic. *NOTE: Do not let them go beyond light brown in color or they may taste bitter.*

Selection: Choose shallots with well-formed heads; avoid those that have started to sprout.

Storage: Will keep for several months in a cool dry area.

TOTAL SODIUM AND FAT PER INGREDIENT

Sodium:
2 shallots - 4mg
20 asparagus - 6mg
Fat (Sat Fat):
1 T olive oil - 14mg (2mg)
1 T NSA margarine - 8mg (2mg)
or NSA butter - 12mg (8mg)

COMMENTS:

1 *To reduce saturated fat, use trans-free margarine. Since it contains sodium (90mg per tablespoon), it will increase the sodium per serving to 74mg.*

2 *For information on shallots, see* FOOD NOTE, *page 171.*

3 *Sliced almonds are also a nice addition instead of Parmesan. This will decrease the sodium to 10mg per serving.*

BROCCOLI IN LEMON-SHALLOT BUTTER

Sodium Per Serving – 29mg   Serves 4

I love shallots; they add an extra depth to dishes, and any chance I have to use them, I do. I think you'll like this simple yet delicious way of preparing broccoli.

1 broccoli head (about 1½ pounds), cut into florets	**2 teaspoons lemon juice**
2 tablespoons unsalted margarine or butter[1]	**¼ teaspoon garlic or onion powder**
1 shallot, chopped (about 2 tablespoons)[2]	**⅛ teaspoon ground black pepper**
	1 tablespoon reduced fat grated Parmesan cheese[3]

▶ Cook broccoli by any method desired *(see* FOOD NOTE *below)* until bright green and crisp tender.

▶ Meanwhile, melt margarine in a skillet over medium heat; add shallots. Cook, stirring frequently, until shallots are translucent, about 3 minutes. Stir in lemon juice, garlic powder, and pepper; tossing with broccoli until well coated. Sprinkle with Parmesan and serve.

NUTRITIONAL INFO PER SERVING: Calories 56mg, Fat 5mg (Saturated Fat 1mg), Cholesterol 0mg, Carbohydrates 4mg (Fiber 1mg, Sugar 0mg), Sodium 29mg

TOTAL SODIUM AND FAT PER INGREDIENT

Sodium:
1½ lb broccoli - 38mg
1 shallot - 2mg
1 T Parmesan - 75mg
Fat (Sat Fat):
1½ lb broccoli - 1mg (0mg)
2 T NSA margarine - 16mg (3mg)
  or NSA butter - 24mg (16mg)
1 T Parmesan - 1mg (0mg)

FOOD NOTE

ABOUT BROCCOLI

Broccoli is a member of the cabbage family and is an excellent source for vitamins C and A, potassium, and a multitude of other vitamins and minerals. High in fiber and low in sodium (29mg per cup), this nutritional powerhouse helps reduce the risk of cancer, heart disease, and other ailments.

Selection: Choose broccoli with compact floret clusters that are dark green, sage, or purple-green in color, depending on the variety. There should be no yellowing (which indicates it is past its prime) and the stalks should be firm. A bunch, weighing 1½ to 2 pounds, when cleaned and trimmed, will yield 1 pound of broccoli, enough for 4 people. Both the stalk and floret can be eaten raw or cooked.

Preparation: Since the stalks take longer to cook than the florets, split stalks larger than 1 inch halfway up or cut into smaller uniform pieces. You can also cook the stalks for 2 to 3 minutes before adding the florets. To cook:

Microwave – Place florets in a covered dish with 1–2 tablespoons water and microwave on high 3 to 4 minutes. If cooking the whole stalk; place in a spoke pattern (with florets in the center), add 1–2 tablespoons water, and microwave on high 6 to 10 minutes.

Steam – Place broccoli in upper half of steamer over boiling water; cook, covered, 2 to 3 minutes. Remove lid to allow the strong odors to escape; replace lid and continue cooking 3 to 4 minutes.

Boil – Bring water to a boil; add broccoli, and cook 5 to 7 minutes.

Stir-fry – Cook over medium-high heat, stirring frequently, for 2 minutes; add a little water or broth, cover, and continue cooking 2 to 3 minutes.

Storage: Place in an open bag in the refrigerator for up 4 to 5 days. *To freeze:* Blanch by boiling or microwaving 1 to 2 minutes, cool in ice water, and drain. Place in plastic bags and freeze for up to a year.

CARROTS AND SUGAR SNAP PEAS IN THYME SAUCE

Sodium Per Serving – 29mg   Serves 4

Snow peas may also be substituted for the sugar snap peas in this delicious and colorful dish.

- 1 tablespoon unsalted margarine or butter[1]
- 2 medium carrots, peeled and cut on the diagonal, or 12-16 baby carrots (about 8 ounces)
- 2 tablespoons chopped onion[2]
- 1 garlic clove, minced
- ¼ teaspoon garlic or onion powder
- ¼ teaspoon dried thyme
- ⅛ teaspoon ground black pepper
- ⅓ cup CHICKEN STOCK (page 232) or canned low-salt chicken broth
- ½ teaspoon (or 1 envelope) low-salt chicken bouillon granules
- 1 cup sugar snap peas
- 1 teaspoon cornstarch

▶ Melt margarine in a large skillet over medium heat; add carrots, onions, and garlic. Cook, stirring frequently, until onions are translucent, 2 to 3 minutes; add garlic powder, thyme, and pepper.

▶ Stir in half the chicken stock and cook 2 to 3 minutes; add the bouillon and peas. Cook until peas are tender, about 2 minutes longer.

▶ Mix remaining broth and cornstarch together; gradually add to peas, stirring constantly, until sauce thickens to a gravy consistency, 1 to 2 minutes.

NUTRITIONAL INFO PER SERVING: Calories 68mg, Fat 2mg (Saturated Fat 0mg), Cholesterol 1mg, Carbohydrates 10mg (Fiber 3mg, Sugar 4mg), Sodium 29mg

---

VARIATION

GINGERED PEAS AND CARROTS

This variation adds a hint of sweetness. Instead of thyme, add 2 thin slices of fresh ginger (or ¼ teaspoon ground) and ½ teaspoon sugar substitute (or sugar); proceed as directed. *NOTE: Before serving, remove the ginger.*

NUTRITIONAL INFO PER SERVING: Calories 68mg, Fat 2mg (Saturated Fat 0mg), Cholesterol 1mg, Carbohydrates 10mg (Fiber 3mg, Sugar 4mg), Sodium 29mg

---

COMMENTS:

1 *To reduce saturated fat, use trans-free margarine. Since it contains sodium (90mg per tablespoon), it will increase the sodium per serving to 48mg.*

2 *A chopped shallot may be substituted for the onion.*

TOTAL SODIUM AND FAT PER INGREDIENT
Sodium:
- 2 carrots - 84mg
- 2 T onion - 1mg
- 1 garlic clove - 1mg
- ⅓ c CHICKEN STOCK - 7mg
  or LS canned broth - 43mg
- ½ t LS chicken bouillon - 3mg
- 1 c snap peas - 7mg

Fat (Sat Fat):
- 1 T NSA margarine - 8mg (2mg)
  or NSA butter - 12mg (8mg)
- ⅓ c CHICKEN STOCK - 0mg
  or LS canned broth - 1mg (0mg)
- 1 c snap peas - 1mg (0mg)

SPICY CARROTS WITH CURRANTS

Sodium Per Serving – 67mg   Serves 6

This sweet and spicy combination is a perfect accompaniment to blander dishes.

1 tablespoon olive oil

6 medium carrots, sliced on the diagonal, or baby carrots (about 1 pound)

¼ teaspoon garlic powder

⅛ teaspoon cayenne pepper, or to taste[1]

⅛ teaspoon ground cumin

⅛ teaspoon ground black pepper

½ cup CHICKEN STOCK (page 232) or canned low-salt chicken broth[2]

½ teaspoon (or ½ envelope) low-salt chicken bouillon granules

1 tablespoon unsalted margarine or butter[3]

1 tablespoon sugar substitute or sugar[4]

½ teaspoon molasses

¼ teaspoon ground cinnamon

¼ cup currants or raisins

▷ Heat oil in a skillet over medium heat; add carrots, garlic powder, cayenne pepper, cumin, and black pepper. Cook, stirring frequently, until carrots begin to soften, 3 to 4 minutes; add chicken stock and bouillon. Bring to a boil; decrease heat to low, cover, and simmer until carrots are crisp-tender and nearly done, about 5 minutes.

▷ Add margarine, sugar, molasses, and cinnamon; cook, stirring frequently, until liquid has evaporated and carrots are glazed, 2 to 3 minutes. Stir in currants and serve.

NUTRITIONAL INFO PER SERVING: Calories 99mg, Fat 6mg (Saturated Fat 1mg), Cholesterol 0mg, Carbohydrates 11mg (Fiber 3mg, Sugar 6mg), Sodium 67mg

FOOD NOTE

ABOUT CARROTS

Carrots are extremely versatile—they may be eaten raw or cooked in various way. Their sweet flavor also makes them a favorite in muffins, breads, and other desserts. Although carrots are low in calories and high in fiber, they also contain a lot of sodium (an average carrot has 50mg). Parsnips are a good substitute for carrots in cooked dishes and have substantially less sodium (about 7mg). *CAUTION: Do not eat raw parsnips, they contain toxins that are destroyed once they are cooked.*

Selection: Select carrots that are firm and uniform in color, avoid any that are cracked, have large green areas at the crown (a little green is okay), or are limp. If stems are attached, choose ones that are fresh-looking.

Storage: Wrap in a paper towel, place in a plastic bag, and store in the refrigerator up to a month. Do not place near fruits, like apples or pears, as they produce a gas that speeds up the ripening process.

ROASTED VEGETABLES

Sodium Per Serving – 30mg   Serves 8

Roasting brings out the sweetness of vegetables, giving them a wonderful rich flavor. Cut vegetables into uniform sizes so they will all be done at the same time.

3 large carrots, sliced in 1½-inch chunks[1]

2 cups Brussels sprouts (about ½ pound), halved lengthwise

8 small red potatoes, quartered

1 medium yam or sweet potato, cut into 1½-inch cubes

2–3 tablespoons olive oil[2]

2 teaspoons dried basil

2 teaspoons dried rosemary, crumbled

1 teaspoon dried oregano

1 teaspoon dried thyme

½ teaspoon garlic powder

½ teaspoon ground black pepper

▷ Preheat oven to 350°F (180°C).

▷ Mix all the ingredients together until well coated (either mix in a large bowl or on the baking sheet), place on a rimmed baking sheet. Roast in a preheated oven until vegetables are tender and golden brown, about 40 minutes.

NUTRITIONAL INFO PER SERVING: Calories 158mg, Fat 4mg (Saturated Fat 1mg), Cholesterol 0mg, Carbohydrates 29mg (Fiber 5mg, Sugar 3mg), Sodium 30mg

---

COMMENTS:

1 *Instead of carrots, use parsnips, which are similar in taste, but have less sodium (1 carrot has 42mg, 1 parsnip 7mg).*

2 *Use just enough oil to thoroughly coat all the vegetables.*

TOTAL SODIUM AND FAT PER INGREDIENT

Sodium:
3 carrots - 126mg
2 c Brussels sprouts - 44mg
8 sm red potatoes - 41mg
1 yam - 27mg

Fat (Sat Fat):
2 T olive oil - 28mg (4mg)
2 c Brussels sprouts - 1mg (0mg)
8 sm red potatoes - 1mg (0mg)
1 yam - 1mg (0mg)

CORN, LEEK AND SNAP PEA SAUTE

Sodium Per Serving – 11mg   Serves 8

Colorful, simple and very tasty . . . what more can you ask?

2 tablespoons unsalted margarine or butter[1]

3 leeks, chopped (white and light green parts)

1 red bell pepper, thinly sliced

1 garlic clove, finely minced

1 teaspoon dried thyme

¼ teaspoon garlic powder

⅛ teaspoon ground black pepper

1 (10-ounce) package frozen corn, thawed (about 2 cups)

½ cup CHICKEN STOCK (page 232) or canned low-salt chicken broth[2]

½ teaspoon (or ½ envelope) low-salt chicken bouillon granules

2 cups fresh sugar snap or snow peas, or 1 (10-ounce) package, frozen

▷ Melt margarine in a large skillet over medium heat; add leeks, bell pepper, garlic, thyme, garlic powder, and pepper. Cook, stirring frequently, until leeks are soft, 8 to 10 minutes.

▷ Add corn, chicken stock, and bouillon; cook, uncovered, until liquid is reduced by half, about 5 minutes.

▷ Stir in peas; cook, uncovered, until heated through, 1 to 2 minutes.

NUTRITIONAL INFO PER SERVING: Calories 84mg, Fat 2mg (Saturated Fat 0mg), Cholesterol 1mg, Carbohydrates 15mg (Fiber 2mg, Sugar 4mg), Sodium 11mg

TOTAL SODIUM AND FAT PER INGREDIENT

Sodium:
  3 leeks - 54mg
  1 red bell pepper - 2mg
  1 t thyme - 1mg
  1 garlic clove - 1mg
  10 oz corn - 9mg
  ½ c CHICKEN STOCK - 10mg
    or LS canned broth - 65mg
  1 t LS chicken bouillon - 5mg
  2 c snap peas - 5mg
Fat (Sat Fat):
  2 T NSA margarine - 16mg (3mg)
    or NSA butter - 24mg (16mg)
  10 oz corn - 2mg (0mg)
  ½ c CHICKEN STOCK - 1mg (0mg)
    or LS canned broth - 1mg (1mg)

FOOD NOTE

ABOUT LEEKS

Leeks are available year round, but are at their peak in the spring and fall. Choose small to medium leeks with crisp, bright green leaves and a white bulb. Smaller leeks are the most tender.

Cleaning: Leeks contain a lot of hidden dirt and it's important to clean them thoroughly. Cut off the root end and the top leaves (which can be used in a stock or soup), leaving a little of the green. Slit the leeks in half lengthwise and wash the trapped dirt away by gently spreading the leaves apart and rinsing.

Storage: Wrap in a damp paper towel and place in a plastic bag; store in the refrigerator up to a week.

GREEN BEANS SUPREME

Sodium Per Serving – 49mg   Serves 6

This creamy casserole is a take-off on an old family favorite.

2 tablespoons unsalted or trans-free margarine[1]

1 medium onion, chopped

2 tablespoons all-purpose flour, mixed with 2 tablespoons water to make a paste

½ teaspoon finely grated lemon peel

¼ teaspoon garlic powder

¼ teaspoon ground black pepper

2 (10-ounce) packages frozen French-cut green beans, thawed

3 tablespoons chopped fresh flat-leaf (Italian) parsley

1 (15-ounce) can low-salt cream of mushroom soup, or 1 cup lowfat sour cream[2]

2 ounces low-fat Cheddar cheese, shredded (about ½ cup)

Topping:

2 ounces no-salt-added Swiss cheese, shredded (about ½ cup)

¼ cup unsalted or low-salt bread crumbs[3]

▷ Preheat oven to 350°F (180°C). Coat a 2-quart baking dish with vegetable cooking spray.

▷ Melt margarine in a skillet over medium heat; cook onion, stirring frequently, until onions are translucent, 3 to 4 minutes. Gradually stir in flour paste, lemon peel, garlic powder, and pepper; cook, stirring constantly, until flour begins to brown, about 3 minutes. Add beans, parsley, soup, and Cheddar cheese; mix well.

▷ Place mixture in prepared baking dish; sprinkle with Swiss cheese and bread crumbs. Bake, uncovered, in a preheated oven until topping is golden brown, about 30 minutes.

NUTRITIONAL INFO PER SERVING: Calories 175mg, Fat 8mg (Saturated Fat 3mg), Cholesterol 14mg, Carbohydrates 21mg (Fiber 3mg, Sugar 2mg), Sodium 49mg

---

VARIATION

HERB SEASONED GREEN BEAN CASSEROLE

For an herbal flavor, mix together the bread crumbs with ½ teaspoon dried basil, ½ teaspoon dried parsley, ¼ teaspoon dried oregano, ⅛ teaspoon garlic powder, ⅛ teaspoon ground black pepper, and ⅛ teaspoon dried thyme; proceed as directed.

NUTRITIONAL INFO PER SERVING: Calories 175mg, Fat 8mg (Saturated Fat 3mg), Cholesterol 14mg, Carbohydrates 21mg (Fiber 3mg, Sugar 2mg), Sodium 49mg

---

COMMENTS:

1 *To reduce saturated fat, use trans-free margarine. Since it contains sodium (90mg per tablespoon), it will increase the sodium per serving to 71mg.*

2 *The mushroom soup adds a richness that you don't get with sour cream.*

3 *Make fresh bread crumbs by pulsing 1–2 slices of low-salt bread in a food processor. For additional tips, see COOKING TIP, page 46.*

TOTAL SODIUM AND FAT PER INGREDIENT

Sodium:
 1 onion - 3mg
 20 oz green beans - 17mg
 3 T parsley - 6mg
 15 oz NSA soup - 65mg
   or 1 c LF sour cream - 136mg
 2 oz LF Cheddar cheese - 280mg
 2 oz NSA Swiss cheese - 20mg

Fat (Sat Fat):
 2 T NSA margarine - 16mg (3mg)
   or NSA butter - 24mg (16mg)
 20 oz green beans - 1mg (0mg)
 15 oz NSA soup - 14mg (4mg)
   or 1 c LF sour cream -
     27mg (16mg)
 2 oz LF Cheddar - 12mg (8mg)
 2 oz NSA Swiss - 16mg (10mg)
 ½ c NSA crumbs - 8mg (0mg)

COMMENTS:

1 *To reduce saturated fat, use trans-free margarine. Since it contains sodium (90mg per tablespoon), it will increase the sodium per serving to 24mg.*

2 *For additional information on cleaning and storing leeks, see FOOD NOTE, page 176.*

GREEN BEANS AND LEEKS IN TARRAGON SAUCE

Sodium Per Serving – 9mg   Serves 6

This is a simple, yet elegant way to prepare green beans. I love the combination of the tarragon, leeks, and green beans.

¾ pound green beans, trimmed (about 3 cups)

1 teaspoon olive oil

1 tablespoon unsalted or trans-free margarine[1]

1 leek, sliced (white and light green parts)[2]

¼ teaspoon dried tarragon

¼ teaspoon garlic powder

⅛ teaspoon ground black pepper

1 teaspoon (or 1 envelope) low-salt chicken bouillon granules

½ cup Madeira wine

▸ Bring a large pan of water to a boil over high heat; add green beans. Cook, covered, until crisp tender, 4 to 5 minutes; drain.

▸ Meanwhile, heat oil and margarine in a skillet over medium heat; add leeks, tarragon, garlic powder, and pepper. Cook, stirring frequently, for 8 to 10 minutes, until leeks are soft. Stir in bouillon and Madeira; add beans and toss until well-coated.

NUTRITIONAL INFO PER SERVING: Calories 76mg, Fat 2mg (Saturated Fat 0mg), Cholesterol 0mg, Carbohydrates 9mg (Fiber 2mg, Sugar 2mg), Sodium 9mg

VARIATION

CREAMY TARRAGON GREEN BEANS

For a creamy sauce, stir into the beans, 1 tablespoon lowfat milk and 1 tablespoon nonfat (or lowfat) sour cream before serving.

NUTRITIONAL INFO PER SERVING: Calories 122mg, Fat 4mg (Saturated Fat 1mg), Cholesterol 1mg, Carbohydrates 14mg (Fiber 3mg, Sugar 3mg), Sodium 18mg

GREEN BEANS IN SHALLOT SAUCE

Use 1 large chopped shallot instead of the leek and substitute sake for the Madeira; proceed as directed.

NUTRITIONAL INFO PER SERVING: Calories 105mg, Fat 3mg (Saturated Fat 1mg), Cholesterol 0mg, Carbohydrates 11mg (Fiber 3mg, Sugar 2mg), Sodium 10mg

TOTAL SODIUM AND FAT PER INGREDIENT

Sodium:
¾ lb green beans - 20mg
1 leek - 18mg
1 t LS chicken bouillon - 5mg
½ c Madeira - 11mg

Fat (Sat Fat):
1 t olive oil - 5mg (1mg)
1 T NSA margarine - 8mg (2mg)
  or NSA butter - 12mg (8mg)

WILD MUSHROOMS IN MADEIRA SAUCE

Sodium Per Serving – 6mg　　　　　　　　　　　　　　Serves 4

Wild mushrooms are much more flavorful than button mushrooms. Any combination of cultivated and wild mushrooms works well in this dish.

1 tablespoon olive oil

1 tablespoon unsalted margarine or butter[1]

2 green onions, chopped (white and green parts)

1 garlic clove, minced

5 ounces sliced wild or cultivated mushrooms, such as shiitake, portobello, oyster, or crimini (about 2 cups)[2]

1 teaspoon (or 1 envelope) low-salt chicken bouillon granules

¼ cup Madeira[3]

½ teaspoon dried thyme

¼ teaspoon garlic powder

⅛ teaspoon ground black pepper

▷ Heat oil and margarine in a skillet over medium heat; add onions and garlic, cook, stirring frequently, until onions soften, 1 to 2 minutes. Add mushrooms; cook, stirring frequently, until mushrooms soften, 4 to 5 minutes.

▷ Stir in bouillon, Madeira, thyme, garlic powder and pepper; simmer, uncovered, until liquid is nearly gone, about 5 minutes.

NUTRITIONAL INFO PER SERVING: Calories 86mg, Fat 6mg (Saturated Fat 1mg), Cholesterol 0mg, Carbohydrates 5mg (Fiber 1mg, Sugar 2mg), Sodium 6mg

---

VARIATION

WILD MUSHROOM AND WALNUT SAUTE

Add ½ teaspoon dried sage or rosemary (or 1 tablespoon fresh) to the mushrooms; proceed as directed. Top with chopped walnuts before serving.

NUTRITIONAL INFO PER SERVING: Calories 135mg, Fat 10mg (Saturated Fat 1mg), Cholesterol 0mg, Carbohydrates 6mg (Fiber 1mg, Sugar 2mg), Sodium 6mg

COMMENTS:

1 *To reduce saturated fat, use trans-free margarine. Since it contains sodium (90mg per tablespoon), it will increase the sodium per serving to 28mg.*

2 *For additional information on choosing and preparing mushrooms, see FOOD NOTE, page 44.*

3 *Red wine may be used instead, but I think the creamy flavor of Madeira is far superior in this dish.*

TOTAL SODIUM AND FAT PER INGREDIENT

Sodium:
2 green onions - 8mg
1 garlic clove - 1mg
2 c mushrooms - 6mg
1 t LS chicken bouillon - 5mg
¼ c Madeira - 5mg
Fat (Sat Fat):
1 T olive oil - 14mg (2mg)
1 T NSA margarine - 8mg (2mg)
　or NSA butter - 12mg (8mg)

CARAMELIZED ONION TART

Sodium Per Serving – 58mg   Serves 8

This deliciously mild onion tart is so versatile—serve it as a first course, side dish, or even a main entrée.

1 BASIC PIE CRUST *(page 229)* **or unbaked pie shell**[1]

2 tablespoons olive oil

2 tablespoons unsalted or trans-free margarine[2]

3 large yellow onions, sliced[3]

¼ teaspoon garlic powder

⅛ teaspoon white pepper[4]

2 eggs, beaten, or ½ cup egg substitute[5]

¼ cup lowfat sour cream

¼ teaspoon freshly grated or ground nutmeg

▸ Preheat oven to 425°F (220°C). Arrange oven rack on lowest position.

▸ Prick crust with a fork; line bottom of shell with aluminum foil. Pour pie weights into the pie shell to hold its shape while baking *(for info on pie weights, see* COOKING TIP, *page 247)*. Bake in preheated oven for 5 minutes; remove weights. Return to oven and bake for 5 minutes more; remove shell from oven and let cool slightly. *NOTE: If using a refrigerated or frozen pie shell, this step is not necessary.*

▸ Heat oil and margarine in a large skillet over medium heat; cook onions, stirring frequently, until they begin to brown, about 5 minutes. Decrease heat to medium-low; stir in garlic powder and pepper. Cook, stirring occasionally, until onions are dark brown and carmelized, 20 to 30 minutes; remove from heat and let cool slightly.

▸ Add eggs and sour cream to onions, mixing well; pour into prepared pie crust. and sprinkle nutmeg over the top. Bake in a preheated oven until filling is set, 35 to 40 minutes; let stand for 5 minutes before removing from oven. Cut into wedges and serve.

NUTRITIONAL INFO PER SERVING: Calories 346mg, Fat 21mg (Saturated Fat 4mg), Cholesterol 73mg, Carbohydrates 32mg (Fiber 2mg, Sugar 4mg), Sodium 58mg (98mg with store-bought shell)

VARIATION

CARAMELIZED ONION TART WITH PARMESAN

This tart is great tasting with or without the Parmesan, but the addition of the cheese kicks this up a notch. Sprinkle 2 tablespoons grated Parmesan cheese on top of the tart before baking.

NUTRITIONAL INFO PER SERVING: Calories 352mg, Fat 21mg (Saturated Fat 4mg), Cholesterol 74mg, Carbohydrates 33mg (Fiber 2mg, Sugar 4mg), Sodium 83mg (123mg with store-bought shell)

ONION CASSEROLE

Sodium Per Serving – 71mg   Serves 8

My mother-in-law asked me to reduce the fat and salt in this rich favorite of hers. Although I haven't tasted the original, this version tasted so good, I had to share it with you.

2 tablespoons olive oil

5 tablespoons unsalted margarine or butter, divided[1]

2 large onions, sliced

¼ teaspoon garlic powder

⅛ teaspoon ground cumin

⅛ teaspoon paprika

⅛ teaspoon ground black pepper

25 low-salt saltine crackers, crumbled[2]

3 ounces no-salt-added Swiss cheese, shredded (about ¾ cup)

1 ounce lowfat Cheddar cheese, shredded (about ¼ cup)

2 large eggs, or ½ cup egg substitute[3]

⅔ cup lowfat milk

▸ Preheat oven to 350°F (180°C). Coat a 2-quart casserole dish with nonstick cooking spray.

▸ Heat oil and 1 tablespoon margarine in a skillet over medium heat; add onions, garlic powder, cumin, paprika, and pepper. Cook, stirring frequently, until onions are translucent and start to brown, about 5 minutes.

▸ Melt remaining 4 tablespoons margarine and mix with crackers; cover the bottom of a prepared baking dish with three-fourths of the crumbs, reserving one-fourth to use on top. Arrange onions over the crumbs and cover with the Swiss and Cheddar cheeses.

▸ In a small bowl, mix eggs and milk together; pour over onions. Top with remaining crumbs. Bake, uncovered, in a preheated oven for 40 to 45 minutes, until top is lightly browned.

NUTRITIONAL INFO PER SERVING: Calories 204mg, Fat 15mg (Saturated Fat 4mg), Cholesterol 66mg, Carbohydrates 12mg (Fiber 1mg, Sugar 3mg), Sodium 71mg

COMMENTS:

1 *To reduce saturated fat, use trans-free margarine. Since it contains sodium (90mg per tablespoon), it will increase the sodium per serving to 127mg.*

2 *Be aware of the differences in sodium between saltines with unsalted tops and those labeled low sodium. Unsalted tops average 110mg per 0.5 ounce, reduced sodium have 75mg, and low sodium saltines, 35mg.*

Other low-salt crackers may be used, but saltines is our preference.

3 *Even though egg substitutes have more sodium than eggs (115mg versus 70mg per large egg), most brands have very little or no fat. To keep fat and sodium to a minimum, use a combination of eggs and egg substitute.*
See Eggs and Egg Substitutes, page 38, for a comparison of fat and sodium in eggs and egg substitutes.

TOTAL SODIUM AND FAT PER INGREDIENT

Sodium:
2 onions - 9mg
25 LS saltines - 175mg
3 oz NSA Swiss cheese - 30mg
1 oz LF Cheddar cheese - 140mg
2 eggs - 140mg
  or ½ c egg substitute - 200mg
⅔ c LF milk - 77mg
Fat (Sat Fat):
2 T olive oil - 28mg (4mg)
5 T NSA margarine - 40mg (8mg)
  or NSA butter - 60mg (40mg)
25 LS saltines - 10mg (0mg)
3 oz NSA Swiss - 24mg (15mg)
1 oz LF Cheddar - 6mg (4mg)
2 eggs - 10mg (3mg)
  or ½ c egg substitute - 0mg
⅔ c LF milk - 3mg (1mg)

COMMENTS:

1 *For a comparison of sodium and fat within cream cheese varieties, see* FOOD NOTE, *page 43.*

2 *There are several low-salt croutons available, look for those with 35mg sodium or less per 0.5-ounce serving.*

PEAS AND ONIONS AU GRATIN

Sodium Per Serving – 84mg   Serves 4

This is an old stand-by and goes together quickly when you use the microwave.

½ (10-ounce) package frozen no-salt-added peas, thawed

½ (10-ounce) package frozen pearl onions, thawed

2 tablespoons water

2 ounces (¼ cup) Neufchâtel or lowfat cream cheese[1]

2 tablespoons nonfat or lowfat milk

1 garlic clove, minced

¼ teaspoon ground black pepper

½ cup HERBED GARLIC CROUTONS *(page 228),* or low-salt seasoned croutons[2]

▸ *Microwave:* Place peas, onions, and water in a microwave-proof dish and microwave on high until tender, 3 to 4 minutes; drain. Stir in cream cheese, milk, garlic, and pepper; microwave 2 minutes until heated through.

▸ *Stove-top:* Place peas, onions, and water in a saucepan over medium-high heat; cover and cook until tender, 4 to 5 minutes. Stir in cream cheese, milk, garlic, and pepper; cook until heated through and cheese has melted, about 4 minutes.

▸ Sprinkle with croutons and serve.

NUTRITIONAL INFO PER SERVING: Calories 128mg, Fat 6mg (Saturated Fat 2mg), Cholesterol 11mg, Carbohydrates 18mg (Fiber 3mg, Sugar 3mg), Sodium 84mg

TOTAL SODIUM AND FAT PER INGREDIENT

Sodium:
  5 oz NSA peas - 14mg
  5 oz pearl onions - 20mg
  ¼ c Neufchatel - 220mg
    or LF cream cheese - 300mg
  2 T LF milk - 16mg
  1 garlic clove - 1mg
  ½ c HERBED CROUTONS - 46mg
    or LS packaged - 100mg
Fat (Sat Fat):
  ¼ c Neufchatel - 12mg (8mg)
    or LF cream cheese - 9mg (6mg)
  2 T LF milk - 1mg (0mg)
  ½ c HERB CROUTONS -10mg (1mg)
    or LS packaged - 2mg (0mg)

FOOD NOTE

ABOUT PEAS

Peas are typically classified as fresh, field, or pod:

Fresh peas – small, round, and green; grown in a pod and generally harvested in the early summer. Also known by other names such as sweet pea, green pea, garden pea, or English pea. The fresh pea is eaten raw or used as an ingredient in salads, soups, stews, casseroles, and other dishes. Fresh peas are available as a raw podded pea, canned as a shelled pea, and frozen.

Field peas – grown, dried, and then split or used whole for use in purées, soups, and dishes requiring thickening. Varieties of the field pea include the green and yellow pea (either split or whole), the chickpea, and the black-eyed pea.

Pod peas – grown so that both the pod and the pea can be eaten either raw or cooked; examples are snow and sugar snap peas.

BAKED IDAHOES WITH CARAMELIZED SHALLOTS

Sodium Per Serving – 31mg   Serves 8

Caramelized shallots add elegance to these cheesy potatoes. Prepare the potatoes several hours ahead of time and reheat before serving.

4 large russet potatoes (about 3 pounds)

1 teaspoon olive oil

2 tablespoons unsalted margarine or butter[1]

½ cup lowfat sour cream

⅓ cup lowfat milk

¼ teaspoon garlic or onion powder

⅛ teaspoon white pepper

4 ounces no-salt-added Swiss cheese, shredded (about 1 cup)

Pinch hot paprika or cayenne pepper

Shallot Topping:

1 tablespoon olive oil

1 tablespoon unsalted margarine or butter[1]

8 shallots, thinly sliced[2]

½ teaspoon sugar substitute or sugar

2 tablespoons chopped flat-leaf (Italian) parsley (optional)

▷ Preheat oven to 400°F (200°C).

▷ Rub potatoes with olive oil and pierce in several places with a fork. Bake until tender, about 1 hour; transfer to a wire rack and cool slightly.

▷ Slice potatoes lengthwise; using a spoon, scoop out the flesh, leaving a ¼-inch thick shell, and place potato flesh in a bowl. Mash with 2 tablespoons margarine, sour cream, and milk; add garlic powder and pepper. (If needed, add 1–2 tablespoons more milk until potatoes are a creamy consistency.) Stir in the Swiss cheese; divide evenly and spoon into potato shells. Sprinkle tops with paprika.

▷ *For the Shallot Topping:* Meanwhile, heat 1 tablespoon oil and 1 tablespoon margarine in a skillet over medium heat; add shallots. Cook, stirring frequently, until shallots are translucent, 3 to 4 minutes; decrease heat to low and continue cooking for 15 to 20 minutes, until shallots are dark brown and have caramelized. Stir in sweetener; divide evenly and spoon on top of potatoes.

▷ Bake potatoes in a preheated oven at 350°F (180°C) until heated through, 15 to 20 minutes; sprinkle with parsley and serve.

NUTRITIONAL INFO PER SERVING: Calories 286mg, Fat 12mg (Saturated Fat 5mg), Cholesterol 18mg, Carbohydrates 38mg (Fiber 2mg, Sugar 2mg), Sodium 31mg

COMMENTS:

1 *To reduce saturated fat, use trans-free margarine. Since it contains sodium (90mg per tablespoon), it will increase the sodium per serving to 65mg.*

2 *Shallots look like small onions and have a mild garlic flavor. For additional information on preparation and storage of shallots, see COMMENTS, page 171.*

TOTAL SODIUM AND FAT PER INGREDIENT

Sodium:
- 4 russet potatoes - 74mg
- ½ c LF sour cream - 80mg
- ⅓ c LF milk - 38mg
- 4 oz NSA Swiss cheese - 40mg
- 8 shallots - 16mg
- 2 T parsley - 4mg

Fat (Sat Fat):
- 4 russet potatoes - 1mg (0mg)
- 1 T + 1 t olive oil - 19mg (3mg)
- 3 T NSA margarine - 24mg (5mg)
- or NSA butter - 36mg (24mg)
- ½ c LF sour cream - 16mg (10mg)
- ⅓ c LF milk - 2mg (0mg)
- 4 oz NSA Swiss - 32mg (20mg)

PAN-ROASTED POTATOES

Sodium Per Serving – 15mg   Serves 4–6

This easy-to-prepare family favorite is great with eggs or as a side dish with grilled poultry or meat.

1 tablespoon olive oil

5–6 small red or Yukon Gold potatoes, cubed (about 2 pounds)

¼ teaspoon dried basil

¼ teaspoon garlic or onion powder

⅛ teaspoon ground black pepper

½ cup chopped sweet onion

½ cup chopped red bell pepper

1 cup sliced mushrooms

▸ Heat oil in a large skillet over medium heat; add potatoes, basil, garlic powder, and pepper. Cook, stirring frequently, until potatoes begin to brown, 4 to 5 minutes.

▸ Stir in the onion, bell pepper, and mushrooms; decrease heat to medium-low. Cover, and continue cooking until potatoes are done, about 10 minutes.

NUTRITIONAL INFO PERSERVING: Calories 197mg, Fat 4mg (Saturated Fat 1mg), Cholesterol 0mg, Carbohydrates 36mg (Fiber 4mg, Sugar 4mg), Sodium 15mg

PERFECT MASHED POTATOES

Sodium Per Serving – 26mg   Serves 5–6

The secret to delicious mashed potatoes is leaving the skins on and cooking them whole. Potatoes are very porous and absorb liquids easily, by leaving the potatoes whole and unpeeled, the flavor is not "diluted" by the water. The same principle applies when mashing the potatoes, the first ingredient added will be absorbed by the potatoes. To get a rich, creamy flavor, margarine or butter is added first, followed by the milk and other additions.

6 small russet potatoes (about 2 pounds)[1]

2 teaspoons (or 2 envelopes) low-salt chicken bouillon granules

¼ cup unsalted margarine or butter, melted[2]

½ cup lowfat milk

2 tablespoons lowfat sour cream[3]

¼ teaspoon garlic or onion powder

⅛ teaspoon ground white pepper

¼ cup chopped chives or green onions (green part only)

⅛ teaspoon paprika

▸ Place whole, unpeeled potatoes and bouillon in a pot and cover with water; bring to boil over high heat. Decrease heat to medium and cook until potatoes are tender, about 20 minutes; drain.

▷ Peel potatoes, if desired, and mash. *NOTE: A potato ricer makes the smoothest and fluffiest potatoes, but a food mill, potato masher, or electric mixer may be used. Avoid overmixing, particularly with a mixer, which can produce gluey, gummy potatoes.* Add margarine and mix; gradually stir in milk and sour cream. Mix in garlic powder, pepper, and green onions; sprinkle with paprika and serve.

NOTE: For the best consistency, serve as soon as possible. However, you can prepare the dish the day before, cover, and refrigerate. Bring to room temperature before reheating. *In the microwave:* Cover and microwave, stirring every 2 minutes, until heated through, about 5 minutes. *In the oven:* Cover and bake in a preheated 350°F (180°C) oven about 20 minutes, or until heated through.

NUTRITIONAL INFO PER SERVING: Calories 217mg, Fat 8mg (Saturated Fat 2mg), Cholesterol 4mg, Carbohydrates 33mg (Fiber 2mg, Sugar 3mg), Sodium 26mg

---

VARIATIONS

ROASTED GARLIC MASHED POTATOES

Roast 1–2 heads of garlic *(see* COOKING TIP *below)*; once cooled, squeeze out cooked cloves. Add to potatoes before mashing; proceed as directed.

NUTRITIONAL INFO PER SERVING: Calories 226mg, Fat 8mg (Saturated Fat 2mg), Cholesterol 4mg, Carbohydrates 35mg (Fiber 2mg, Sugar 3mg), Sodium 27mg

FRIED POTATO PATTIES

Use up leftover potatoes by shaping into 3-inch patties and frying in 1 tablespoon unsalted margarine (or butter) over medium heat until brown on both sides.

NUTRITIONAL INFO PER SERVING: Calories 231mg, Fat 9mg (Saturated Fat 2mg), Cholesterol 4mg, Carbohydrates 33mg (Fiber 2mg, Sugar 3mg), Sodium 26mg

---

COOKING TIP

ROASTING GARLIC

Roasting garlic mellows its flavor, giving a slightly sweet, creamy, non-bitter taste. Roast several heads at a time and use on pizzas, in sauces and vegetable dishes; as a spread on bread when mixed with unsalted butter (or margarine) and Parmesan; or in recipes that call for garlic. Save any unused heads for later use.

To roast: Preheat the oven to 375°F (190°C). Cut the top third off each head of garlic; do not remove outer skins. Place the heads, cut sides up, in a small baking dish and drizzle a teaspoon of olive oil over the top of each head. Cover tightly or wrap in aluminum foil; roast in a preheated oven for 1 hour, or until cloves are soft and golden. Remove and let sit for 15 minutes, until cool enough to handle; squeeze out cloves (they should pop out easily).

Storage: Place unused cloves in a jar, add oil from the baking dish, cover and store in the refrigerator up to a week.

SCALLOPED POTATOES WITH SUN-DRIED TOMATO PESTO

Sodium Per Serving – 92mg   Serves 8

My neighbor, Gigi Wooldridge, gave me this recipe. I've eliminated most of the salt and made a few other changes, but I think you'll enjoy these flavorful scalloped potatoes. Although you can purée the pesto in a blender, a food processor works best. SUN-DRIED TOMATO PESTO *(page 154) may be substituted for the pesto ingredients below.*

Pesto:

1 cup oil-packed sun-dried tomatoes, undrained

½ cup fresh basil

3 tablespoons reduced fat grated Parmesan cheese[1]

2 garlic cloves, smashed and coarsely chopped

¼ teaspoon garlic powder

⅛ teaspoon ground black pepper

8 small red or Yukon Gold potatoes, thinly sliced (about 3 pounds)

4 ounces no-salt-added Swiss cheese, shredded (about 1 cup)

2 ounces lowfat Cheddar cheese, shredded (about ½ cup)

1 cup CHICKEN STOCK *(page 232)* **or canned low-salt chicken broth**

1 teaspoon (or 1 envelope) low-salt chicken bouillon granules

▷ Preheat oven to 350°F (180°C). Coat a 2-quart casserole or baking dish with nonstick cooking spray.

▷ *To make the pesto:* Place the tomatoes, basil, Parmesan, garlic, garlic powder, and pepper in a food processor or blender; pulse until a smooth paste. (If too dry, add a little olive oil while the machine is running.)

▷ Mix the pesto with the potatoes and arrange half the potatoes in the bottom of a prepared casserole dish. Mix the two cheeses together; spreading half on the potatoes and reserving the remaining cheese. Top with the rest of the potatoes.

▷ Mix the chicken stock and bouillon together; pour over potatoes. Cover with foil and bake in a preheated oven for 30 minutes; remove foil and spread remaining cheese on top. Bake for 20 to 25 minutes more, until potatoes are tender.

NUTRITIONAL INFO PER SERVING: Calories 222mg, Fat 7mg (Saturated Fat 4mg), Cholesterol 20mg, Carbohydrates 31mg (Fiber 3mg, Sugar 3mg), Sodium 92mg (106mg with canned low-salt broth)

BAKED FRENCH FRIES

Sodium Per Serving – 11mg   Serves 4

These spicy, lowfat French fries are baked in the oven; double the spices if you want even more flavor.

2 tablespoons olive oil

½ teaspoon chili powder

½ teaspoon garlic powder

½ teaspoon hot paprika[1]

¼ teaspoon onion powder

⅛ teaspoon ground black pepper

4 russet potatoes (about 2 pounds), unpeeled and cut into wedges

▷ Preheat oven to 400°F (200°C).

▷ Mix olive oil, garlic powder, chili powder, paprika, onion powder, and pepper together. Mix with potatoes, coating all sides.

▷ Place potatoes in a single layer on a baking sheet. Bake in a preheated oven, turning every 10 minutes until tender and evenly browned, about 40 minutes.

NUTRITIONAL INFO PER SERVING: Calories 232mg, Fat 7mg (Saturated Fat 1mg), Cholesterol 0mg, Carbohydrates 39mg (Fiber 3mg, Sugar 1mg), Sodium 11mg

SUCCOTASH

Sodium Per Serving – 9mg   Serves 8

This has been a family staple for years. For non-lima bean fans, substitute edamame (soy beans).

2 cups fresh or frozen lima beans[2]

¼ cup unsalted margarine or butter[3]

½ sweet onion, chopped

2 cups fresh or frozen corn kernels

⅛ teaspoon onion powder

⅛ teaspoon ground black pepper

2 tomatoes, chopped

2 teaspoons chopped fresh basil, or ½ teaspoon dried

1 teaspoon sugar substitute or sugar

2 tablespoons chopped chives or green onions (green part only) (optional)

▷ If using frozen lima beans, cook according to package directions; drain.

▷ Melt margarine in a large skillet over medium heat; cook onion, stirring frequently, until translucent, about 4 minutes. Add lima beans, corn, onion powder, and pepper; decrease heat to low, cover, and simmer until vegetables are tender, 15 to 20 minutes.

▷ Stir in tomatoes, basil, and sweetener; heat through. Sprinkle with chives and serve.

NUTRITIONAL INFO PER SERVING: Calories 130mg, Fat 4mg (Saturated Fat 1mg), Cholesterol 0mg, Carbohydrates 20mg (Fiber 4mg, Sugar 4mg), Sodium 9mg

COMMENTS:

1 *Paprika comes in sweet or hot varieties. Most American paprika is sweet, while the Hungarian variety is more pungent. Hungarian is available in ethnic or gourmet shops and some large supermarkets. If unable to find, use cayenne pepper.*

2 *Edamame (pronounced eh-duh-mah-may) are soybeans which may be used as a substitute for lima beans. They are very low in sodium, have a sweet, nutty flavor, and are available in the frozen food section of most supermarkets (fresh beans are found in some larger grocery stores).*

3 *To reduce saturated fat, use trans-free margarine. Since it contains sodium (90mg per tablespoon), it will increase the sodium per serving to 54mg.*

TOTAL SODIUM AND FAT PER INGREDIENT

Baked French Fries:
Sodium:
 2 lb russet potatoes - 43mg
Fat (Sat Fat):
 2 lb russet potatoes - 1mg (0mg)
 2 T olive oil - 28mg (4mg)

Succotash:
Sodium:
 2 c lima beans - 40mg
 2 c corn - 10mg
 ½ sweet onion - 6mg
 2 tomatoes - 12mg
Fat (Sat Fat):
 ¼ c NSA margarine - 32mg (6mg)
  or NSA butter - 48mg (32mg)
 2 c corn - 3mg (0mg)
 2 tomatoes - 1mg (0mg)

SOUFFLED SWEETS

Sodium Per Serving – 35mg | Serves 8

This is a holiday favorite with our family, even the finicky eaters who love the slightly sweet, orange flavor.

4 red-skinned sweet potatoes or yams (about 2 pounds)[1]

3 tablespoons unsalted margarine or butter[2]

¼ cup orange juice

¼–⅓ cup sugar substitute or sugar[3]

2 teaspoons (or 2 envelopes) low-salt chicken bouillon granules

1 teaspoon vanilla extract

¼ teaspoon garlic or onion powder

⅛ teaspoon ground white pepper

3 egg whites, beaten until stiff peaks form

▸ Preheat oven to 400ºF (200ºC). Coat a 2-quart casserole or baking dish with nonstick cooking spray.

▸ Pierce potatoes in several places with a fork; place on baking sheet and bake for 45 to 50 minutes, or until soft. Remove and let cool slightly.

▸ Reduce oven temperature to 350ºF (180ºC).

▸ Once potatoes are cool enough to handle, peel and mash; mix in margarine. Stir in orange juice, sweetener, bouillon, vanilla, garlic powder, and white pepper. Potatoes should have the consistency of mashed potatoes; if too dry, add more orange juice.

▸ Gently fold in egg whites; pour into the prepared baking dish. Bake, uncovered, for 30 to 35 minutes, until top begins to turn golden brown.

NUTRITIONAL INFO PER SERVING: Calories 207mg, Fat 3mg (Saturated Fat 1mg), Cholesterol 0mg, Carbohydrates 41mg (Fiber 6mg, Sugar 2mg), Sodium 35mg

CREAMED SPINACH

Sodium Per Serving – 76mg   Serves 8

People on low-sodium diets should normally avoid creamed spinach. A half-cup serving is both high in sodium and fat (about 335mg sodium, 13mg fat, and 4mg saturated fat). This lightened up version is not only rich and creamy, but also low in sodium and fat.

3 tablespoons unsalted margarine or butter[1]

¼ cup all-purpose flour

1 cup nonfat or lowfat milk

1 teaspoon olive oil

¼ cup finely chopped onion

2 (10-ounce) packages frozen chopped spinach, thawed and water squeezed out[2]

½ cup lowfat sour cream

¼ teaspoon garlic or onion powder

⅛ teaspoon ground white pepper

¼ teaspoon freshly ground nutmeg[3]

▸ *To make white sauce:* Melt margarine in a saucepan over medium heat; add flour. Cook, stirring constantly, until flour begins to change to a golden color, about 2 minutes. Slowly add milk, stirring constantly, until mixture becomes thick and smooth; set aside.

▸ Heat oil in a skillet over medium heat; add onions. Cook, stirring frequently, until onions are translucent, 2 to 3 minutes; set aside.

▸ Cook spinach according to package directions until almost done; decrease heat to medium-low. Stir in white sauce, sour cream, garlic powder, and pepper; cook until well blended and heated through, 4 to 5 minutes. Top with nutmeg and serve.

NUTRITIONAL INFO PER SERVING: Calories 107mg, Fat 6mg (Saturated Fat 2mg), Cholesterol 7mg, Carbohydrates 9mg (Fiber 2mg, Sugar 3mg), Sodium 76mg

COMMENTS:

1 *To reduce saturated fat, use trans-free margarine. Since it contains sodium (90mg per tablespoon), it will increase the sodium per serving to 109mg.*

2 *When using frozen spinach, be aware that some brands (oftentimes less expensive brands) have a chemical taste that may adversely affect this dish.*

May also substitute 1½ pounds fresh spinach, cooked by any desired method.

3 *Pre-ground nutmeg may be used, but the taste of freshly ground nutmeg is far superior.*

FOOD NOTE

ABOUT SPINACH

Spinach is rich in cancer-fighting antioxidants and is a vitamin and mineral powerhouse. It is relatively fat free, but contains a significant amount of sodium (1 cup raw spinach has 24mg).

Selection: Choose spinach with deep green leaves that are unwilted and free of any yellowing.

Preparation: Wash spinach before using, as there may be dirt trapped between the leaves. Here are several ways to cook spinach:

Sauté: Place the spinach and a few drops of water in a pot; place over medium heat. Cover and cook, stirring frequently, until spinach wilts, about 4 to 5 minutes.

Steam: Place spinach in a steamer over boiling water and cook until wilted, 5 to 8 minutes.

Microwave: Cover and place in microwave; cook on high until tender, 4 to 6 minutes.

Storage: Loosely pack unwashed spinach in a plastic bag and keep in the refrigerator for 3 or 4 days. (Washed spinach will rot and decay quicker than unwashed.)

TOTAL SODIUM AND FAT PER INGREDIENT

Sodium:
1 cup LF milk - 115mg
¼ c onion - 2mg
20 oz spinach - 420mg
½ c LF sour cream - 68mg
Fat (Sat Fat):
1 t olive oil - 5mg (1mg)
3 T NSA margarine - 24mg (5mg)
  or NSA butter - 36mg (24mg)
1 cup LF milk - 5mg (2mg)
20 oz spinach - 4mg (1mg)
½ c LF sour cream - 14mg (8mg)

SQUASH AND APPLE GRATIN

Sodium Per Serving – 63mg   Serves 8

This is my low-salt version of a recipe that a neighbor brought to a potluck dinner. The combination of apples and squash with the cheesy bread crumbs is a perfect accompaniment to most any fish, meat, or poultry dish.

Topping:

3 slices low-salt bread, processed to coarse crumbs, or 1½ cups unsalted or low-salt bread crumbs[1]

2 tablespoons unsalted margarine or butter, melted[2]

1 teaspoon fresh thyme, chopped, or ¼ teaspoon dried

4 ounces no-salt-added Swiss cheese, shredded (about 1 cup)

2 ounces lowfat Cheddar cheese, shredded (about ½ cup)

Gratin:

1 tablespoon olive oil

3 tablespoons unsalted margarine or butter, divided

3 leeks, sliced (white and light green parts)[3]

½ cup apple juice or cider

½ cup lowfat milk

3 tablespoons lowfat sour cream

2 teaspoons fresh thyme, chopped, or ½ teaspoon dried

1 teaspoon ground cinnamon

½ teaspoon ground allspice

¼ teaspoon garlic powder

¼ teaspoon ground black pepper

2 apples (such as Braeburn or Fuji), peeled, cored, and thinly sliced

1 pound butternut squash, peeled, quartered and thinly sliced (about 3¼ cups)[4]

▷ Preheat oven to 350°F (180°C). Coat a 2-quart gratin or baking dish with nonstick cooking spray.

▷ *For the topping:* Combine bread crumbs and margarine in a bowl; mix in 1 teaspoon fresh thyme, Swiss, and Cheddar cheeses. Set aside.

▷ *For the gratin:* Heat oil and 1 tablespoon margarine in a large skillet over medium heat; add leeks. Cook, stirring frequently, until lightly browned, about 10 minutes; add apple juice and cook 2 minutes. Add milk, sour cream, remaining teaspoon fresh thyme, cinnamon, allspice, garlic powder, and pepper; stir well and set aside.

▷ In another skillet, melt remaining 2 tablespoons margarine over medium heat; add apples. Cook, gently turning, until most slices are brown and limp, about 10 minutes; add to leek mixture.

▷ Combine squash with the leek and apple mixtures; place in a prepared gratin dish and sprinkle with bread crumb topping. Bake, uncovered, in a preheated oven for 1 hour, or until the crust is golden brown. Remove and let sit 15 minutes before serving.

NUTRITIONAL INFO PER SERVING: Calories 242mg, Fat 14mg (Saturated Fat 6mg), Cholesterol 20mg, Carbohydrates 25mg (Fiber 3mg, Sugar 9mg), Sodium 63mg

TOMATO, ONION AND GOAT CHEESE TART

Sodium Per Serving – 64mg   Serves 6–8

This tart is a great summertrime treat when made with fresh, juicy tomatoes from the garden. It also may be served as a main course or the same ingredients can be used as toppings for a great-tasting pizza.

1 **BASIC PIE CRUST** *(page 229),* **or** unbaked pie shell[1]

1 tablespoon olive oil

½ large sweet onion, thinly sliced

¼ teaspoon garlic powder

⅛ teaspoon ground black pepper

3–4 tomatoes (such as Roma or beefsteak), cored and sliced crosswise ¼-inch thick

2 garlic cloves, finely minced

4 ounces goat cheese[2]

2–3 tablespoons chopped fresh basil leaves

▸ Preheat oven to 350°F (180°C).

▸ Prick crust with a fork, line bottom of shell with aluminum foil and pour pie weights into crust to hold its shape while baking *(see* COOKING TIP, *page 247, for info on pie weights)*; bake in a preheated oven for 20 minutes. Remove weights and foil; return to oven and bake 10 minutes more, or until crust is golden brown. Remove and let cool.

▸ Meanwhile, heat oil in a skillet over medium heat; add onions, garlic powder, and pepper. Cook, stirring frequently, until onions are translucent, about 5 minutes. Let cool slightly.

▸ Spread onions on the bottom of the precooked crust; arrange tomatoes, slightly overlapping, on top of the onions. Sprinkle with garlic and cheese; top with basil. Broil tart about 6 inches from heat for 3 minutes, or until cheese starts to melt.

NUTRITIONAL INFO PER SERVING: Calories 291mg, Fat 17mg (Saturated Fat 5mg), Cholesterol 9mg, Carbohydrates 28mg (Fiber 2mg, Sugar 2mg), Sodium 64mg (104mg with store-bought shell)

VARIATION

TOMATO, LEEK AND CHEESE TART

In place of onions, substitute 2 thinly sliced leeks (white and some green parts) and add 1 tablespoon unsalted margarine or butter to the skillet. Cook leeks, stirring frequently, until softened, about 10 minutes; proceed as directed.

NUTRITIONAL INFO PER SERVING: Calories 317mg, Fat 19mg (Saturated Fat 5mg), Cholesterol 9mg, Carbohydrates 32mg (Fiber 2mg, Sugar 3mg), Sodium 69mg (109mg with store-bought shell)

COMMENTS:

1 *If purchasing a prepared pie crust, look for shells with 55mg or less sodium per serving.*

2 *Goat (or chèvre) cheese can range from sweet and mild to tangy and sharp. Semi-soft varieties average 146mg sodium per ounce, soft brands, 104mg, and some imports are as low as 50mg.*

Fresh mozzarella may also be used, but check label, as some brands are packaged in brine.

TOTAL SODIUM AND FAT PER INGREDIENT

Sodium:
1 BASIC PIE CRUST - 159mg
  or store bought - 400mg
½ sweet onion - 6mg
3 tomatoes - 18mg
2 garlic cloves - 2mg
4 oz goat cheese - 200mg

Fat (Sat Fat):
1 BASIC PIE CRUST - 66mg (12mg)
  or store bought - 56mg (16mg)
1 T olive oil - 14mg (2mg)
4 oz goat cheese - 24mg (17mg)

QUICK REFRIED BEANS

Sodium Per Serving – 17mg   Makes 2 cups

Canned refried beans average 530mg sodium per half a cup. The following is a good low-salt substitute to use in tacos, burritos, or bean dips.

1 (15-ounce) can no-salt-added kidney beans, drained[1]

½ cup CHICKEN STOCK (page 232), or canned low-salt chicken broth

1 teaspoon (or 1 envelope) low-salt chicken bouillon granules

1 tablespoon olive oil

1 tablespoon unsalted margarine or butter[2]

½ cup finely minced sweet onion

1 garlic clove, finely minced

1 teaspoon ground cumin

½ teaspoon garlic or onion powder

½ teaspoon ground black pepper

Pinch cayenne pepper

Shredded no-salt-added Swiss cheese (optional)

▷ In a small bowl, mash beans and 2 tablespoons chicken stock using a potato masher, ricer, or wooden spoon, adding more stock as needed until smooth and creamy. Set aside.

▷ Heat oil and margarine in a skillet over medium heat; add onions. Cook, stirring frequently, until onions are golden brown and caramelized, about 5 minutes.

▷ Add garlic; cook, stirring constantly, until you smell the garlic, 1 to 2 minutes. Decrease heat to medium; stir in beans, cumin, garlic powder, black pepper, and cayenne. Cook, stirring occasionally, until heated through, about 5 minutes. Sprinkle cheese on top and serve.

NUTRITIONAL INFO PER SERVING: Calories 138mg, Fat 6mg (Saturated Fat 1mg), Cholesterol 2mg, Carbohydrates 16mg (Fiber 8mg, Sugar 1mg), Sodium 17mg

VARIATION

REFRIED BLACK BEANS

Substitute 1 (15-ounce) can no-salt-added black beans for the kidney beans and increase the cumin to 1½ teaspoons; proceed as directed.

NUTRITIONAL INFO PER SERVING: Calories 139mg, Fat 6mg (Saturated Fat 1mg), Cholesterol 2mg, Carbohydrates 16mg (Fiber 8mg, Sugar 1mg), Sodium 17mg

KILLER COWBOY BEANS

Sodium Per Serving – 137mg   Serves 16

While visiting friends in Placerville, California, I tasted the most delicious beans at a cowboy poetry reading, unfortunately they were loaded with sodium and fat. When I got home, I tried to duplicate the taste, and this is the result, but without the salt and fat. The beans are extremely hot and spicy, if you want less heat, cut back on the jalapeños.

1 tablespoon olive oil

1 pound lean ground turkey or beef

¼ teaspoon garlic powder

⅛ teaspoon ground black pepper

1 sweet onion, chopped

1 green bell pepper, chopped

4 garlic cloves, finely minced

3 (15-ounce) cans no-salt-added black beans[1]

3–4 jalapeños, chopped[2]

1 (7-ounce) can diced green chiles

1 (28-ounce) can crushed tomatoes in puree

1 (15-ounce) can no-salt-added diced tomatoes

1 (8-ounce) can no-salt-added tomato sauce or puree (about 1 cup)

1 cup no-salt-added ketchup

2 cups CHICKEN STOCK *(page 232)*, or canned low-salt chicken broth

2 teaspoons (or 2 envelopes) low-salt chicken bouillon granules

3 tablespoons no-salt-added chili powder

2 teaspoons ground cumin

2 teaspoons dried oregano

1 teaspoon no-salt-added spicy seasoning mix, such as taco, cajun, or barbecue[4]

▷ Heat oil in a large pot over medium heat; add meat. Cook, stirring frequently and crumbling with a fork (you want little bits of meat, not chunks), until no longer pink, about 10 minutes; add onion and bell pepper. Cook, stirring frequently, until onion has softened, about 4 minutes; decrease heat to medium-low. Add remaining ingredients and simmer, covered, for 1 hour.

NUTRITIONAL INFO PER SERVING: Calories 163mg, Fat 3mg (Saturated Fat 1mg), Cholesterol 18mg, Carbohydrates 21mg (Fiber 8mg, Sugar 8mg), Sodium 137mg (164mg with LS canned broth)

COMMENTS:

1 *Instead of canned beans, use dried beans (to cook, see COOKING TIP, page 40). A 16-ounce package yields about 5–6 cups cooked beans.*

2 *See COMMENTS #3, page 163, for information on handling hot peppers.*

3 *Most chili powders contain sodium (26mg per teaspoon). Look for no-salt-added brands, like The Spice Hunter (see RESOURCES, page 272).*

4 *There are several unsalted spicy seasonings that are often used in cajun or barbecue rubs that may be used. Also, if your market has a Hispanic section, check the dried spices for packages of no-salt taco seasoning (see RESOURCES, page 272).*

TOTAL SODIUM AND FAT PER INGREDIENT

Sodium:

1 lb ground turkey - 320mg
  or ground beef - 299mg
1 sweet onion - 12mg
1 bell pepper - 4mg
4 garlic cloves - 4mg
45 oz NSA black beans - 135mg
7 oz green chiles - 160mg
28 oz tomatoes in puree - 1,235mg
15 oz NSA diced tomatoes - 105mg
8 oz NSA tomato sauce - 60mg
  or tomato puree - 150mg
1 c NSA ketchup - 96mg
2 c CHICKEN STOCK - 40mg
  or canned LS broth - 260mg
2 t LS chicken bouillon - 10mg
2 t cumin - 8mg

Fat (Sat Fat):

1 T olive oil - 14mg (2mg)
1 lb ground turkey - 28mg (8mg)
  or ground beef - 68mg (27mg)
2 c CHICKEN STOCK - 2mg (0mg)
  or LS canned broth - 4mg (2mg)
2 T NSA chili powder - 2mg (0mg)

COMMENTS:

1 *Lemon peel adds flavor to the broth. Using a zester or knife, remove as large a portion of lemon peel as possible (avoiding the bitter white membrane); proceed as directed.*

2 *This dish uses the more familiar Moroccan or quick-cooking couscous, which looks like tiny golden pellets. Israeli or pearl couscous, found in health food stores and in the kosher section of many supermarkets, has larger pearl-sized granules and is usually boiled instead of steamed. If using the latter, boil for 8 minutes and drain; proceed as directed.*

3 *To reduce saturated fat, use trans-free margarine. Since it contains sodium (90mg per tablespoon), it will increase the sodium per serving to 32mg.*

4 *Shallots look like small onions and have a mild garlic flavor. For additional preparation and storage info, see* FOOD NOTE, *page 171.*

HERBED COUSCOUS

Sodium Per Serving – 17mg   Serves 6

Couscous, originating in North Africa, is made of semolina, the same durham wheat from which many pasta noodles are made. It takes little time to prepare and is a delicious alternative to rice or potatoes. Fresh herbs make the difference in this colorful dish.

2 cups CHICKEN STOCK (page 232) or canned low-salt chicken broth

1 teaspoon (or 1 envelope) low-salt chicken bouillon granules

1 ribbon lemon peel[1]

1 (10-ounce) package couscous (about 1½ cups)[2]

1–2 tablespoons lemon juice

1 tablespoon unsalted margarine or butter[3]

2 shallots, finely minced[4]

1 red bell pepper, chopped

4 green onions, thinly sliced

¼ cup chopped fresh basil

¼ cup chopped fresh parsley

¼ teaspoon freshly ground black pepper

▸ Place chicken stock, bouillon, and lemon peel in a saucepan over medium-high heat; bring to a boil. Remove lemon peel; stir in couscous and lemon juice. Cover and remove from heat; let stand until all liquid is absorbed, about 5 minutes.

▸ Meanwhile, melt margarine in a skillet over medium heat; add shallots. Cook, stirring frequently, until golden brown, about 5 minutes.

▸ Fluff couscous with a fork, breaking up any lumps; stir in shallots, bell pepper, green onions, basil, and parsley. Season with pepper and serve.

NUTRITIONAL INFO PER SERVING: Calories 205mg, Fat 2mg (Saturated Fat 0mg), Cholesterol 5mg, Carbohydrates 38mg (Fiber 3mg, Sugar 1mg), Sodium 17mg (60mg with canned LS broth)

TOTAL SODIUM AND FAT PER INGREDIENT

Sodium:
2 c CHICKEN STOCK - 40mg
  or LS canned broth - 260mg
1 t LS chicken bouillon - 5mg
1½ c couscous - 26mg
2 shallots - 4mg
1 red bell pepper - 2mg
4 green onions - 16mg
½ c parsley - 8mg
Fat (Sat Fat):
2 c CHICKEN STOCK - 2mg (0mg)
  or LS canned broth - 4mg (2mg)
1½ c couscous - 2mg (0mg)
1 T NSA margarine - 8mg (2mg)
  or NSA butter - 12mg (8mg)

VARIATIONS

SUN-DRIED TOMATO-BASIL COUSCOUS

Add ½ cup drained and chopped oil-packed sun-dried tomatoes before serving.

NUTRITIONAL INFO PER SERVING: Calories 225mg, Fat 3mg (Saturated Fat 0mg), Cholesterol 5mg, Carbohydrates 40mg (Fiber 4mg, Sugar 3mg), Sodium 30mg (74mg with canned LS broth)

COUSCOUS WITH DRIED APRICOTS AND PINE NUTS

Add ½ cup chopped dried apricots and ½ cup toasted pine nuts before serving.

NUTRITIONAL INFO PER SERVING: Calories 307mg, Fat 10mg (Saturated Fat 1mg), Cholesterol 5mg, Carbohydrates 46mg (Fiber 4mg, Sugar 8mg), Sodium 18mg (62mg with canned LS broth)

BASIC STEAMED RICE

Sodium Per Serving – 6mg   Serves 6

This is a basic, never fail steamed rice recipe. Adding chicken bouillon to the water gives the rice more flavor.

2 cups rice[1]

4 cups water

1 tablespoon (or 3 envelopes) low-salt chicken bouillon granules

▶ Combine all ingredients in a saucepan and bring to a boil over high heat. Decrease heat to low; cover, and simmer until rice is tender and all liquid is absorbed, about 45 minutes. (If rice is done, but some liquid remains, adjust lid so that steam can escape from the pan; continue to cook until all liquid is absorbed.) Fluff with a fork and serve.

NUTRITIONAL INFO PER SERVING: Calories 230mg, Fat 0mg (Saturated Fat 0mg), Cholesterol 0mg, Carbohydrates 50mg (Fiber 1mg, Sugar 1mg), Sodium 0mg

COMMENTS:

1 *Any kind of rice may be used, but the type determines the cooking time and amount of water that is used. See* FOOD NOTE *below for more information.*

FOOD NOTE

ABOUT RICE

Varieties: Rice comes in brown and white varieties:

Brown — contains the entire grain but without the husk; has a chewy, nutty taste with slightly more nutrients than white; takes twice as long to cook as white.

White — without the husk, bran, and germ; is lighter and more tender in taste.

Rice is then classified by size:

Long-grain — long, thin grains that cook up fluffy and don't stick together; best for side dishes.

Medium-grain — shorter and fatter than long-grain; starchier than long-grain, but more fluffy than short-grain; good all-purpose rice.

Short-grain — nearly round grains; high starch content, causing the grains to stick together; use in Asian cooking and risottos (arborio rice)

Brown and white rice also come in converted (has less nutrients than brown, but more than white) and instant varieties (is precooked and dehydrated, so it takes less time to cook, but lacks taste and texture). *NOTE: If you are watching carbohydrates, instant has half the carbs as other kinds of rice.*

Preparation: Generally, to cook rice, use 2 parts water to 1 part rice; white takes 20 to 30 minutes, brown about 45 minutes.

Storage: White rice keeps indefinitely in an airtight container in a cool, dark place, while brown rice will keep up to 6 months (store in refrigerator for a longer shelf life).

TOTAL SODIUM AND FAT PER INGREDIENT

Sodium:
  2 c white rice - 18mg
    or brown rice - 26mg
  1 T LS chicken bouillon - 15mg
Fat (Sat Fat):
  2 c white rice - 2mg (0mg)
    or brown rice - 10mg (2mg)

1 *To reduce saturated fat, use trans-free margarine. Since it contains sodium (90mg per tablespoon), it will increase the sodium per serving to 48mg.*

2 *Shallots look like small onions and have a mild flavor, somewhere between an onion and garlic (see FOOD NOTE, About Shallots, page 171, for additional info).*

3 *Any kind of rice may be used, but the type determines the cooking time and amount of water that is used. See FOOD NOTE, page 195, for more information.*

4 *Almonds may be used instead of the pecans.*

RICE PILAF WITH PECANS AND CURRANTS

Sodium Per Serving – 18mg   Serves 6

This delicious pilaf is quick and easy to prepare.

2 tablespoons unsalted margarine or butter[1]

2 shallots, chopped[2]

1 cup uncooked rice[3]

1 carrot, shredded

⅓ cup currants or raisins

1 teaspoon finely shredded orange peel

¼ teaspoon ground cinnamon

¼ teaspoon onion powder

¼ teaspoon ground black pepper

⅛ teaspoon cayenne pepper

2 cups CHICKEN STOCK *(page 232)* or canned low-salt chicken broth

2 teaspoons (or 2 envelopes) low-salt chicken bouillon granules

¼ cup pecans, toasted and coarsely chopped[4]

▸ Melt margarine in a saucepan over medium heat; add shallots. Cook, stirring frequently, until shallots soften, 2 to 3 minutes; add rice. Cook, stirring frequently, until rice begins to turn golden, 3 to 4 minutes. Stir in carrot, currants, orange peel, cinnamon, onion powder, black pepper, and cayenne; mix thoroughly.

▸ Stir in chicken stock and bouillon; bring to a boil. Decrease heat to low and simmer, covered, until liquid is absorbed and rice is tender, about 45 minutes. Fluff with a fork and stir in pecans; serve.

NUTRITIONAL INFO PER SERVING: Calories 196mg, Fat 6mg (Saturated Fat 1mg), Cholesterol 5mg, Carbohydrates 29mg (Fiber 1mg, Sugar 1mg), Sodium 18mg

---

VARIATION

WILD RICE AND CRANBERRY PILAF

Replace ½ cup of the uncooked rice with ½ cup wild rice; decrease currants to ¼ cup and add ¼ cup dried cranberries. Proceed as directed.

NUTRITIONAL INFO PER SERVING: Calories 199mg, Fat 7mg (Saturated Fat 1mg), Cholesterol 5mg, Carbohydrates 30mg (Fiber 2mg, Sugar 5mg), Sodium 18mg

TOTAL SODIUM AND FAT PER INGREDIENT

Sodium:
2 shallots - 4mg
1 c rice - 9mg
1 carrot - 42mg
2 c CHICKEN STOCK - 40mg
  or LS chicken broth - 260mg
2 t LS chicken bouillon - 10mg
Fat (Sat Fat):
2 T NSA margarine - 16mg (3mg)
  or NSA butter - 24mg (16mg)
1 c rice - 1mg (0mg)
¼ c pecans - 20mg (2mg)
2 c CHICKEN STOCK - 2mg (0mg)
  or LS chicken broth - 4mg (2mg)

RISOTTO

Sodium Per Serving – 102mg

Serves 4

This is a basic risotto that takes about 30 minutes to prepare. Unlike steamed rice, which can be left unattended, risotto requires you to be nearby, so you can stir it every few minutes.

1 tablespoon olive oil

1 tablespoon unsalted margarine or butter[1]

½ sweet onion, finely chopped

1 cup arborio rice[2]

½ cup dry white wine or vermouth

4–5 cups CHICKEN STOCK *(page 232)* or canned low-salt chicken broth

1 tablespoon (or 3 envelopes) low-salt chicken boulllon granules

¼ cup reduced fat grated Parmesan cheese[3]

▶ Heat oil in a saucepan over medium heat; add onion. Cook, stirring frequently, until onion softens; add rice, stirring until the rice is coated with the oil. Add wine and cook, stirring frequently, until most of the wine is absorbed.

▶ Add chicken stock in ½ cup increments, stirring frequently, after each addition until liquid is absorbed. Continue adding the stock and allowing liquid to absorb, until rice is creamy and tender, about 20 minutes. Stir in Parmesan and serve.

NUTRITIONAL INFO PER SERVING: Calories 314mg, Fat 8mg (Saturated Fat 1mg), Cholesterol 16mg, Carbohydrates 44mg (Fiber 0mg, Sugar 2mg), Sodium 102mg

VARIATION

LEMON RISOTTO

Before serving, stir in 1 tablespoon fresh lemon juice, 2 teaspoons grated lemon peel, and 1 tablespoon chopped fresh flat-leaf (Italian) parsley.

NUTRITIONAL INFO PER SERVING: Calories 315mg, Fat 8mg (Saturated Fat 1mg), Cholesterol 16mg, Carbohydrates 45mg (Fiber 0mg, Sugar 2mg), Sodium 102mg

COMMENTS:

1 *To reduce saturated fat, use trans-free margarine. Since it contains sodium (90mg per tablespoon), it will increase the sodium per serving to 124mg.*

2 *Arborio rice is a fat, short-grain rice from Italy that absorbs lots of liquid without getting mushy. It is used most often for risotto and paella dishes. A short-grain white rice may be used, but the risotto will not be as creamy.*

3 *Although freshly grated cheese is superior in flavor to the canned variety, it often contains more sodium. Romano generally is lower in sodium than Parmesan (340mg per ounce versus 454mg, and canned Parmesan has 150mg or less)*

TOTAL SODIUM AND FAT PER INGREDIENT

Sodium:
½ sm sweet onion - 4mg
1 c arborio rice - 2mg
½ c white wine - 6mg
4 c CHICKEN STOCK - 80mg
  or LS chicken broth - 520mg
1 T LS chicken bouillon - 15mg
¼ c Parmesan - 300mg

Fat (Sat Fat):
1 T olive oil - 14mg (2mg)
1 T NSA margarine - 8mg (2mg)
  or NSA butter - 12mg (8mg)
1 c arborio rice - 1mg (0mg)
4 c CHICKEN STOCK - 4mg (0m)
  or LS canned broth - 8mg (4mg)
¼ c Parmesan - 4mg (0mg)

COMMENTS:

1 To reduce saturated fat, use trans-free margarine. Since it contains sodium (90mg per tablespoon), it will increase the sodium per serving to 38mg.

2 I like a little heat in this dressing and use a hot curry powder, but a mild type may be used. See FOOD NOTE below for additional info.

3 For variety, substitute dried cranberries or cherries for the raisins.

4 Toasting nuts intensifies their flavor, see COOKING TIP, page 90 for toasting methods.

DRIED FRUIT AND CURRY RICE DRESSING

Sodium Per Serving – 10mg

Serves 10–12

This dressing is great as a stuffing or side dish. It's full of flavor and goes very well with poultry or fish dishes.

1½ cups long-grain white and brown rice

2 cups CHICKEN STOCK *(page 232)* or canned low-salt chicken broth

2 teaspoons (or 2 envelopes) low-salt chicken bouillon granules

1 cup water

2 tablespoons unsalted margarine or butter, melted[1]

½ sweet onion, chopped

1 celery stalk, chopped

1 garlic clove, minced

½ teaspoon garlic powder

½ teaspoon ground black pepper

½ teaspoon dried thyme

1 apple, cored and diced

1 tablespoon curry powder[2]

½ cup dried prunes, chopped

½ cup dried apricots, chopped

¼ cup raisins or currants[3]

¼ cup almonds or pecans, chopped and toasted[4]

▸ In a large saucepan, combine rice, chicken stock, bouillon, and water; bring to a boil over high heat. Decrease heat to medium-low; cover and cook until rice is done, 35 to 40 minutes. If not using right away, cover and refrigerate until ready to use; reheat in the microwave.

▸ Meanwhile, melt margarine in a large skillet over medium heat; add onion, celery, garlic, garlic powder, pepper, and thyme. Cook, stirring frequently, until onion is translucent, about 4 minutes; add apples and curry. Cook, stirring frequently, until apples begin to soften, 2 to 3 minutes; mix into rice.

▸ Stir in prunes, apricots, raisins, and almonds, mixing well. Cool slightly and use as a stuffing or serve immediately as a side dish.

NUTRITIONAL INFO PER SERVING: Calories 245mg, Fat 5mg (Saturated Fat 1mg), Cholesterol 4mg, Carbohydrates 48mg (Fiber 4mg, Sugar 14mg), Sodium 15mg

TOTAL SODIUM AND FAT PER INGREDIENT

Sodium:
¾ c white rice - 7mg
¾ c brown rice - 10mg
2 c CHICKEN STOCK - 40mg
  or LS canned broth - 260mg
2 t LS chicken bouillon - 10mg
½ sweet onion - 6mg
1 celery stalk - 32mg
1 garlic clove - .1mg
1 apple - 1mg
1 T curry - 4mg
½ c prunes - 2mg
½ c dried apricots - 7mg
¼ c raisins - 4mg

Fat (Sat Fat):
¾ c white rice - 1mg (0mg)
¾ c brown rice - 4mg (1mg)
2 c CHICKEN STOCK - 2mg (0mg)
  or LS canned broth - 4mg (2mg)
2 T NSA margarine - 16mg (3mg)
  or NSA butter - 24mg (16mg)
1 T curry - 1mg (0mg)
¼ cup almonds - 13mg (1mg)

▌ FOOD NOTE ▐

CURRY POWDER

Curry powder is a blend of herbs and spices, varying by region. There are thousands of curries, ranging from complex (up to 20 or more ingredients) to simple (4 or 5 components). Depending on the spices and herbs used, curry can vary greatly in flavor and heat—from hot and spicy to mild and sweet. Its distinctive yellow color comes from turmeric, the primary ingredient; other commonly used ingredients are cayenne pepper, ginger, coriander, fennel, chili powder, cumin, cloves, and cardamom.

Varieties: Commercial curry powder comes in two basic varieties—standard and Madras (the hottest). Garam masala, used in Indian cooking, is another variety of curry.

Storage: Curry powder quickly loses its pungency and should be stored in an airtight container for up to 2 months.

RICE STUFFING WITH ALMONDS AND OLIVES

Sodium Per Serving – 61mg   Serves 4

The yummy side dish is great with poultry dishes, especially HERB ROASTED GAME HENS *(page 118), and cooks up in less than 30 minutes.*

2 tablespoons unsalted margarine or butter[1]

½ cup uncooked rice[2]

1¼ cups CHICKEN STOCK *(page 232)* **or canned low-salt chicken broth**

1 teaspoon (or 1 envelope) low-salt chicken bouillon granules

1 egg, beaten, or ¼ cup egg substitute[3]

2 tablespoons minced ripe olives

¼ cup slivered almonds

2 tablespoons unsalted or low-salt bread crumbs[4]

▶ Melt margarine in a skillet over medium-high heat; add rice. Cook, stirring frequently, until golden brown, about 4 to 5 minutes; stir in chicken stock and bouillon. Decrease heat to low; cover and simmer until rice is cooked, about 20 minutes.

▶ Stir in egg, olives, almonds, and bread crumbs; cook, stirring frequently, until egg sets up and is no longer runny. Use as a stuffing or side dish.

NUTRITIONAL INFO PER SERVING: Calories 254mg, Fat 14mg (Saturated Fat 2mg), Cholesterol 54mg, Carbohydrates 24mg (Fiber 3mg, Sugar 1mg), Sodium 61mg

NOTES:

1 *To reduce saturated fat, use trans-free margarine. Since it contains sodium (90mg per tablespoon), it will increase the sodium per serving to 106mg.*

2 *I like to use a medium-grain brown rice, but any type will work.*

3 *See* Eggs and Egg Substitutes, *page 38, for a comparison of fat and sodium in eggs and egg substitutes.*

4 *To make bread crumbs, dry 1 slice of low-salt bread in the oven. Tear into pieces and place in food processor and pulse until desired coarseness. For additional info on making bread crumbs, see* COOKING TIP, *page 46.*

TOTAL SODIUM AND FAT PER INGREDIENT

Sodium:
½ c rice - 4mg
1¼ c CHICKEN STOCK - 25mg
  or LS canned broth - 150mg
1 t LS chicken bouillon - 5mg
1 egg - 70mg
  or ¼ c egg substitute - 100mg
2 T ripe olives - 146mg

Fat (Sat Fat):
2 T NSA margarine - 16mg (3mg)
  or NSA butter - 24mg (16mg)
½ c rice - 3mg (1mg)
1¼ c CHICKEN STOCK - 1mg (0mg)
  or LS canned broth - 2mg (0mg)
1 egg - 5mg (2mg)
  or ¼ c egg substitute - 0mg
2 T ripe olives - 2mg (0mg)
¼ c almonds - 30mg (2mg)
2 T LS crumbs - 1mg (0mg)

HERBED BREAD STUFFING WITH DRIED CRANBERRIES

Sodium Per Serving – 29mg   Makes 12 cups

This flavorful stuffing is perfect for the holidays or anytime you have chicken, turkey, or pork. For variety, substitute other dried fruits for the cranberries.

1 loaf EVERYDAY MULTIGRAIN BREAD (page 218) **or 1 (16-ounce) loaf low-salt bread, cubed and toasted (about 10 cups)**[1]

2 tablespoons unsalted margarine or butter[2]

1 large sweet onion, chopped

3 celery stalks, finely chopped

¼ teaspoon garlic powder

¼ teaspoon ground black pepper

1 garlic clove, finely minced

1 teaspoon dried sage

½ teaspoon dried rosemary, crumbled

½ teaspoon dried thyme

1 cup chopped dried cranberries[3]

1–1½ cups CHICKEN STOCK (page 232) **or canned low-salt chicken broth**

1 egg, beaten, or ¼ cup egg substitute[4]

▸ Preheat oven to 325°F (160°C). Adjust oven shelf to middle level. Coat a 3-quart casserole dish with nonstick cooking spray.

▸ Spread the bread cubes in a shallow baking pan; bake until dry and a light golden color, about 25 minutes. Remove and cool; then transfer to a large bowl.

▸ Meanwhile, melt margarine in a large skillet over medium heat; add onion, celery, garlic powder, and pepper. Cook, stirring frequently, until onions are translucent, 3 to 4 minutes; add garlic and cook, stirring frequently, until you smell the garlic, 1 to 2 minutes. Remove from heat; stir in sage, rosemary, and thyme.

▸ Add onion mixture to the bread cubes and toss lightly; stir in cranberries, chicken stock, and egg, mixing well. *NOTE: Use 1 cup stock if you like it dry or all of the stock if you want it moist.*

▸ Transfer to prepared casserole dish, cover with foil; bake in the middle of a preheated oven for 30 minutes. Remove foil and bake until stuffing is heated through and bread is golden brown, about 30 minutes longer.

NOTE: Stuffing can be assembled the day before, covered, and refrigerated. Bring to room temperature before baking.

NUTRITIONAL INFO PER SERVING: Calories 229mg, Fat 6mg (Saturated Fat 1mg), Cholesterol 35mg, Carbohydrates 42mg (Fiber 3mg, Sugar 10mg), Sodium 29mg

BREAKFAST AND LUNCH

COMMENTS:

1 *Even though egg substitutes have more sodium than eggs (115mg versus 70mg per large egg), most brands have very little or no fat. To keep fat and sodium to a minimum, use a combination of eggs and egg substitute. See* Eggs and Egg Substitutes, *page 38, for a comparison of fat and sodium in eggs and egg substitutes.*

2 *Any low-salt tomato-based salsa works. Also, mango or peach salsa is a nice accompaniment to the eggs. Look for brands with 40mg or less sodium per 2 tablespoons. See* RESOURCES, *page 272, for more information.*

THE MIXUP

Sodium Per Serving – 82mg   Serves 4

We have this breakfast almost every weekend. Just about any vegetables work—green onions, asparagus, zucchini, roasted red peppers, tomatoes, and spinach—but the following is our favorite combination.

1 tablespoon olive oil

2 small red potatoes, diced (about 1½ cups)

½ teaspoon dried basil

¼ teaspoon garlic powder

⅛ teaspoon black pepper

Pinch cayenne (optional)

½ cup chopped sweet onion

1 cup sliced mushrooms

½ cup broccoli florets, cut into pieces (optional)

¼ cup diced red bell pepper

4 eggs, beaten with 1–2 tablespoons water or milk, or 1 cup egg substitute[1]

2 ounces no-salt-added Swiss cheese, shredded (about ½ cup)

Low-salt salsa (optional)[2]

▷ Heat oil in a skillet over medium heat; add potatoes, basil, garlic powder, pepper, and cayenne. Cook, stirring occasionally, until potatoes begin to brown, about 5 minutes.

▷ Stir in onions, mushrooms, broccoli, and red pepper; cover and cook, stirring occasionally, until potatoes are tender, about 5 minutes.

▷ Pour eggs over the potato mixture; once eggs begin to set, add cheese. Decrease heat to medium-low; cover and cook until cheese is melted, 2 to 3 minutes. Serve with salsa.

NUTRITIONAL INFO PER SERVING: Calories 207mg, Fat 13mg (Saturated Fat 5mg), Cholesterol 225mg, Carbohydrates 12mg (Fiber 2mg, Sugar 2mg), Sodium 82mg

TOTAL SODIUM AND FAT PER INGREDIENT
Sodium:
1 med red potato - 13mg
½ c sweet onion - 4mg
¼ c red bell pwpper - 1mg
1 c mushrooms - 2mg
½ c broccoli - 10mg
½ c red bell pepper - 1mg
4 eggs - 280mg or
  1 c egg substitute - 400mg
2 oz NSA Swiss cheese - 20mg
Fat (Sat Fat):
1 T olive oil - 14mg (2mg)
4 eggs - 20mg (6mg)
  or 1 c egg substitute - 0mg
2 oz NSA Swiss - 16mg (10mg)

VARIATION

SAUSAGE MIXUP

Add 2 ounces low-sodium meatless breakfast sausage patties (break into small chunks) with the onions and mushrooms; proceed as directed.

NUTRITIONAL INFO PER SERVING: Calories 226mg, Fat 14mg (Saturated Fat 5mg), Cholesterol 225mg, Carbohydrates 13mg (Fiber 3mg, Sugar 2mg), Sodium 127mg

NIGHT BEFORE WESTERN SOUFFLE

Sodium Per Serving – 154mg   Serves 10–12

This delicious make-ahead breakfast soufflé is one of my most requested recipes. Salsa, particularly a sweet salsa like peach or mango, goes well with this dish. Make it the night before and bring it to room temperature before putting it in the oven.

8 slices EVERYDAY MULTIGRAIN BREAD *(page 218)*, **torn into pieces**[1]

8 ounces sliced mushrooms (about 6½ cups)

½ sweet onion, chopped

1 (4-ounce) can diced green chiles

1 red bell pepper, chopped

1 (15-ounce) no-salt-added whole corn, drained

3 low sodium meatless breakfast sausage patties, broken into small chunks (about 4½ ounces)[2]

4 eggs, or 1 cup egg substitute[3]

2 cups lowfat milk

½ teaspoon garlic powder

½ teaspoon paprika

½ teaspoon ground black pepper

¼ teaspoon dried sage

¼ teaspoon dried thyme

4 ounces no-salt-added Swiss cheese, shredded (about 1 cup)

2 ounces lowfat Cheddar cheese, shredded (about ½ cup)

1 tomato, chopped

▷ Coat a rectangular baking dish with nonstick cooking spray. Cover bottom with bread pieces; spread mushrooms on top. Continue layering with onions, green chiles, bell pepper, and corn; finish with crumbled sausage on top of veggies.

▷ Combine eggs, milk, garlic powder, paprika, pepper, sage, and thyme; pour over veggies. Top with cheeses and tomato; cover and refrigerate overnight.

▷ Preheat oven to 350°F (180°C).

▷ Bring soufflé to room temperature; then bake, covered, for 1 hour. Let stand 5 minutes before cutting into squares. Serve with salsa, if desired.

NUTRITIONAL INFO PER SERVING: Calories 302mg, Fat 11mg (Saturated Fat 4mg), Cholesterol 115mg, Carbohydrates 40mg (Fiber 4mg, Sugar 9mg), Sodium 154mg

COMMENTS:

1 *Any low-salt bread with 40mg or less sodium per slice will work.*

2 *Although most breakfast sausage has too much sodium for a low-salt diet, there are several good-tasting, lower sodium sweet turkey sausages and vegetarian patties, such as* **Gardenburger** *Breakfast Sausage (120mg per 1.5-ounce patty). See RESOURCES, page 272, for more info.*

3 *See Eggs and Egg Substitutes, page 38, for a comparison of fat and sodium in eggs and egg substitutes.*

TOTAL SODIUM AND FAT PER INGREDIENT

Sodium:
8 sl MULTIGRAIN BREAD - 200mg
8 oz mushrooms - 7mg
½ sweet onion - 4mg
4 oz green chiles - 100mg
1 red bell pepper -2mg
15 oz NSA corn - 30mg
3 LS sausage - 360mg
4 eggs - 280mg
  or 1 c egg substitute - 400mg
2 c LF milk - 230mg
4 oz NSA Swiss cheese - 40mg
2 oz LF Cheddar cheese - 280mg
1 tomato - 6mg
Fat (Sat Fat):
8 sl MULTIGRAIN - 21mg (4mg)
8 oz mushrooms - 1mg (0mg)
15 oz NSA corn - 3mg (1mg)
4 eggs - 20mg (6mg)
  or 1 c egg substitute - 0mg
2 c LF milk - 10mg (4mg)
4 oz NSA Swiss - 32mg (20mg)
2 oz LF Cheddar - 12mg (8mg)

BACON AND VEGETABLE FRITTATA

Sodium Per Serving – 153mg   Serves 4

I liken a frittata to an omelet pizza, all the ingredients are slowly baked in the skillet and then served as a large round omelet. This is a basic frittata, the ingredients may be varied to your liking by adding meat, different vegetables, and cheeses.

1 teaspoon olive oil

2 slices lower sodium bacon, cut into small pieces[1]

½ cup chopped sweet onion

½ red bell pepper, chopped

½ zucchini, chopped

¼ teaspoon garlic powder

⅛ teaspoon ground black pepper

1½ cups spinach leaves, coarsely chopped

6 eggs or 1½ cups egg substitute[2]

¼ teaspoon hot pepper sauce, such as *Tabasco*

2 ounces no-salt-added Swiss cheese, shredded (about ½ cup)

1–2 tomatoes chopped

1–2 tablespoons chopped fresh basil

▷ Heat oil in a large 12-inch nonstick skillet over medium heat; add bacon and cook, turning frequently, until lightly browned, 3 to 4 minutes. Add onion, bell pepper, zucchini, garlic powder, and pepper; cook, stirring frequently, until vegetables have softened, about 5 minutes. Add spinach and cook, stirring constantly, until wilted, about 1 minute.

▷ In a bowl, whisk eggs with hot pepper sauce and pour over vegetable mixture; decrease heat to medium-low. Cover and cook, without stirring, until eggs are set, about 5 to 6 minutes; sprinkle eggs with cheese, tomatoes, and basil. Cover and cook until cheese has melted, 2 to 3 minutes. Cut into wedges and serve.

NUTRITIONAL INFO PER SERVING: Calories 209mg, Fat 14mg (Saturated Fat 6mg), Cholesterol 333mg, Carbohydrates 6mg (Fiber 1mg, Sugar 3mg), Sodium 153mg

BREAKFAST TACOS

Sodium Per Serving – 49mg   Serves 8

This yummy alternative to scrambled eggs is baked instead of fried. Use either corn or low-sodium flour tortillas.

1 tablespoon olive oil

2 small red potatoes, diced (about 1 cup)

¼ teaspoon no-salt-added chili powder[1]

¼ teaspoon garlic or onion powder

⅛ teaspoon dried cumin

⅛ teaspoon dried oregano

⅛ teaspoon ground black pepper

¼ red or green bell pepper, chopped

2 green onions, chopped (white and green parts)

4 eggs, beaten, or 1 cup egg substitute[2]

2 tablespoons lowfat milk

4 ounces no-salt-added Swiss cheese, shredded (about ½ cup)

8 (7–8-inch) corn or low-salt flour tortillas[3]

Optional garnishes:

Chopped tomato

Chopped onion

Guacamole (page 12)

Low-salt salsa[4]

Chopped cilantro

▷ Preheat oven to 350°F (180°C).

▷ Heat oil in a skillet over medium heat; add potatoes, chili powder, garlic powder, cumin, oregano, and black pepper. Cook, stirring frequently, until potatoes begin to brown, about 5 minutes.

▷ Stir in red pepper and onions; cover and cook, stirring occasionally, until potatoes are tender, 5 to 8 minutes.

▷ Pour eggs over the potato mixture; once eggs begin to set, stir gently and continue cooking until eggs are done.

▷ Equally divide egg mixture and fill each tortilla; top with cheese, fold in half, and place in a baking dish. Bake in a preheated oven for 10 to 15 minutes, until lightly browned and crisp. Serve with chopped tomato, onion, guacamole, salsa, and cilantro.

NUTRITIONAL INFO PER TACO: Calories 180mg, Fat 9mg (Saturated Fat 4mg), Cholesterol 119mg, Carbohydrates 17mg (Fiber 2mg, Sugar 1mg), Sodium 49mg (126mg with LS flour tortillas)

COMMENTS:

1 *Surprisingly, chili powder contains sodium (26mg per teaspoon). Look for no-salt-added brands, like* **The Spice Hunter** *(see RESOURCES, page 272, for more info).*

2 *See* Eggs and Egg Substitutes, *page 38, for a comparison of fat and sodium in eggs and egg substitutes.*

3 *When it comes to tortillas, fresh corn have the least sodium (3mg per 6-inch tortilla versus 234mg for a 7-inch flour). (NOTE: Shelf-stable shells average 150mg each.) A few manufacturers offer low-sodium flour tortillas (see RESOURCES, page 272).*

4 *Most bottled salsas average 139mg sodium per 2 tablespoons, a few low-salt varieties have 40mg or less. See* RESOURCES, *page 272, for more information.*

TOTAL SODIUM AND FAT PER INGREDIENT

Sodium:
2 red potatoes - 9mg
½ red bell pepper - 1mg
2 green onions - 8mg
⅛ t cumin - 1mg
4 eggs - 280mg
  or 1 c egg substitute - 400mg
2 T LF milk - 14mg
4 oz NSA Swiss cheese - 40mg
8 corn tortillas - 40mg
  or LS flour tortillas - 656mg
Fat (Sat Fat):
1 T olive oil - 14mg (2mg)
4 eggs - 20mg (6mg)
  or 1 c egg substitute - 0mg
2 T LF milk - 1mg (0mg)
4 oz NSA Swiss - 32mg (20mg)
8 corn tortillas - 8mg (0mg)
  or LS flour - 32mg (0mg)

TOTAL SODIUM AND FAT PER INGREDIENT

Sodium:
1 BASIC PIE CRUST - 159mg
  or store-bought - 400mg
1½ lb red potatoes - 38mg
½ c sweet onion - 4mg
4 sl LS bacon - 240mg
4 oz NSA Swiss cheese - 40mg
4 eggs - 280mg
  or 1 c egg substitute - 400mg
1 c LF milk - 115mg
¼ t LS Worcestershire - 5mg
Fat (Sat Fat):
1 BASIC PIE CRUST - 66mg (12mg)
  or store-bought - 56mg (16mg)
1 T olive oil - 14mg (2mg)
1 T NSA margarine - 8mg (2mg)
  or NSA butter - 12mg (8mg)
1½ lb red potatoes - 1mg (0mg)
4 sl LS bacon - 12mg (4mg)
4 oz NSA Swiss - 32mg (20mg)
4 eggs - 20mg (6mg)
  or 1 c egg substitute - 0mg
1 c LF milk - 5mg (2mg)

QUICHE LORRAINE

Sodium Per Serving – 147mg   Serves 6

Quiche Lorraine is a French classic that can be served for breakfast, lunch, or dinner. Traditionally high in salt, by using low-sodium bacon and Swiss cheese, the amount of salt is significantly reduced.

1 BASIC PIE CRUST *(page 229)* or unbaked pie shell[1]

1 tablespoon olive oil

1 tablespoon unsalted margarine or butter[2]

1½ pounds red potatoes, shredded

½ cup chopped sweet onions

¼ teaspoon garlic or onion powder

⅛ teaspoon ground black pepper

4 slices lower sodium bacon, crisply cooked and crumbled[3]

4 ounces no-salt-added Swiss cheese, shredded (about 1 cup)

4 eggs, or 1 cup egg substitute[4]

1 cup lowfat milk

¼ teaspoon low-salt Worcestershire sauce

2 tablespoons all-purpose flour

½ teaspoon dry mustard

¼ teaspoon dried basil

⅛ teaspoon cayenne pepper

Tomato slices (optional)

▷ Preheat oven to 350ºF (180ºC).

▷ Prick crust with a fork, line bottom of shell with aluminum foil and pour pie weights into crust to hold its shape while baking *(see* COOKING TIP, *page 247, for info on pie weights)*; bake in a preheated oven for 10 minutes. Remove weights and foil; return to oven and bake 10 minutes more, or until crust is golden brown. Remove and let cool.

▷ Heat oil and margarine in a large skillet over medium-high heat; add potatoes, onions, garlic powder, and black pepper. Cook, stirring frequently, until potatoes are lightly browned, about 4 minutes; stir in bacon and remove from heat.

▷ Spoon potato mixture into partially-baked pie crust; sprinkle with cheese.

▷ Beat eggs slightly; mix with milk, Worcestershire sauce, flour, mustard, basil, and cayenne. Pour over potatoes.

▷ Bake in a preheated oven for 45 minutes or until a knife inserted in the center

NUTRITIONAL INFO PER SERVING: Calories 490mg, Fat 26mg (Saturated Fat 8mg), Cholesterol 165mg, Carbohydrates 47mg (Fiber 3mg, Sugar 4mg), Sodium 147mg (187mg with store-bought shell)

POTATO CRUSTED BREAKFAST PIZZA

Sodium Per Serving – 65mg   Serves 6

The potatoes, arranged in concentric circles, act as the crust for this morning dish and creates a beautiful presentation for a brunch or buffet. And the best part . . . it's ready in 30 minutes.

2 tablespoons olive oil, divided

2 medium red potatoes, thinly sliced (about ¾ pound)

½ teaspoon Tuscan spice mix, divided[1]

¼ teaspoon garlic powder, divided

⅛ teaspoon ground black pepper, divided

½ medium sweet onion, sliced

2–3 garlic cloves, finely minced

1 cup mixed veggies, sliced or cut into bite-size pieces[2]

4 eggs, or 1 cup egg substitute[3]

2 tablespoons lowfat milk

1 green onion, chopped (white and green parts)

1 tomato, chopped

4 ounces no-salt-added Swiss cheese, shredded (about 1 cup)

1 roasted red pepper[4]

▸ Preheat oven to 350°F (180°C).

▸ Rub a large oven proof skillet with 1 tablespoon oil. Arrange potatoes on the bottom of the skillet in a circular design beginning on the outside and working toward the center (each slice overlapping the last). Sprinkle half the Tuscan spice mix, half the garlic powder, and half the pepper over the potatoes. Place potatoes over medium heat and fry until potatoes are golden brown on the bottom (do not turn), about 5 minutes.

▸ Meanwhile, heat remaining 1 tablespoon oil in another skillet over medium heat; add onion, garlic, mixed veggies, and remaining Tuscan spice mix, garlic powder, and pepper. Cook, stirring frequently, until veggies are tender. Remove from heat; mix in eggs and milk. Pour over potatoes and top with cheese, green onions, and tomatoes; arrange red pepper slices on top in a spoke-like pattern.

▸ Bake in a preheated oven for 10 to 15 minutes, until eggs are set. Remove and place on a platter; sprinkle with parsley, if desired, and serve.

NUTRITIONAL INFO PER SERVING: Calories 217mg, Fat 13mg (Saturated Fat 5mg), Cholesterol 158mg, Carbohydrates 14mg (Fiber 2mg, Sugar 3mg), Sodium 65mg

VARIATION

SAUSAGE, CHEESE AND POTATO MORNING PIZZA

Crumble 2 low-salt meatless breakfast patties (about 3 ounces) and cook with the mixed vegetables; proceed as directed. (See COMMENTS #2, page 203, for information on meatless sausage.)

NUTRITIONAL INFO PER SERVING: Calories 234mg, Fat 15mg (Saturated Fat 5mg), Cholesterol 158mg, Carbohydrates 15mg (Fiber 3mg, Sugar 3mg), Sodium 105mg

COMMENTS:

1 *Tuscan spice blends are found in most supermarkets. To make your own, mix together equal amounts of dried rosemary, sage, thyme, and basil.*

2 *Use a combination of vegetables, such as broccoli, corn, mushrooms, and zucchini.*

3 *Even though egg substitutes have more sodium than eggs (115mg versus 70mg per large egg), most brands have very little or no fat. To keep fat and sodium to a minimum, use a combination of eggs and egg substitute. See Eggs and Egg Substitutes, page 38, for a comparison of fat and sodium in eggs and egg substitutes.*

4 *Substitute bottled roasted red sweet peppers for the roasted pepper, cut into strips; proceed as directed. (For info on roasting peppers, see COOKING TIP, page 141.)*

TOTAL SODIUM AND FAT PER INGREDIENT

Sodium:
2 red potatoes - 20mg
½ c sweet onion - 4mg
2 garlic clove - 2mg
4 eggs - 280mg
  or 1 c egg substitute - 320mg
2 T LF milk - 15mg
1 green onion - 4mg
1 tomato - 8mg
1 red pepper - 2mg
4 oz NSA Swiss cheese - 40mg
Fat (Sat Fat):
2 T olive oil - 28mg (4mg)
4 eggs - 20mg (6mg)
  or 1 c egg substitute - 0mg
4 oz NSA Swiss - 32mg (20mg)

1 *Mascarpone, similar to cream cheese, is low in sodium, but high in fat. See* FOOD NOTE, *page 43, for a comparison of fat and sodium in cream cheese varieties.*

2 *See* COOKING TIP, Toasting Nuts, *page 90, for toasting options.*

3 *See* Eggs and Egg Substitutes, *page 38, for a comparison of fat and sodium in eggs and egg substitutes.*

4 *Because sugar substitutes differ from sugar in sweetness, the amount needed depends on the sweetener used:*
Splenda or sugar - ¼ *cup*
Fructose - 3 tablespoons
For additional information, see Sweeteners, *page 37.*

5 *To reduce saturated fat, use trans-free margarine. Since it contains sodium (90mg per tablespoon), it will increase the sodium per serving to 169mg.*

APRICOT STUFFED FRENCH TOAST

Sodium Per Serving – 146mg   **Serves 8**

This recipe was given to me some time ago and is perfect for a special occasion breakfast or brunch. Filled with a cream cheese-apricot mixture and topped with an apricot sauce, it is both delicious and easy to make. I like to use mascarpone and a low fat cream cheese to keep both fat and sodium to a minimum.

½ cup chopped dried apricots

¾ cup orange juice, divided

⅔ cup apricot preserves (preferably fruit sweetened)

4 ounces (½ cup) mascarpone[1]

4 ounces (½ cup) lowfat cream cheese[1]

¼ cup chopped pecans or almonds, toasted[2]

16 slices No Knead French Bread

4 eggs, or 1 cup egg substitute[3]

¼ cup nonfat or lowfat milk

3–4 tablespoons sugar substitute or sugar[4]

1 tablespoon grated orange zest

1 teaspoon vanilla extract

2 tablespoons unsalted margarine or butter[5]

▸ In a small saucepan, mix together apricots and ¼ cup orange juice; place on medium-high and bring to a boil. Reduce heat to low and simmer 10 minutes; remove and cool to room temperature.

▸ *For the syrup:* In another small saucepan, combine preserves and remaining ½ cup orange juice; place on medium-high and bring to a boil. Cook, stirring occasionally, until thickened to a syrup consistency, about 3 minutes; remove from heat and let cool slightly.

▸ In a small bowl, combine mascarpone, cream cheese, pecans, and dried apricot mixture. Equally divide filling and spread on 8 slices of bread; top with remaining bread, making 8 sandwiches.

▸ Combine eggs, milk, sweetener, orange zest, and vanilla. Dip each sandwich into the egg mixture; turn, until both sides are coated.

▸ Melt margarine in a skillet or griddle over medium-high heat; fry sandwiches until brown on both sides. Serve with apricot preserve syrup.

NUTRITIONAL INFO PER SERVING: Calories 530mg, Fat 21mg (Saturated Fat 7mg), Cholesterol 135mg, Carbohydrates 73mg (Fiber 4mg, Sugar 18mg), Sodium 146mg

TOTAL SODIUM AND FAT PER INGREDIENT

Sodium:
½ c apricots - 7mg
¾ c orange juice - 2mg
8 oz whipped cheese - 520mg
1 loaf French Bread - 307mg
  or LS bread - 420mg
¼ c NF milk - 54mg
4 eggs - 280mg
  or 1 c egg substitute - 400mg
Fat (Sat Fat):
8 oz whipped cheese - 56mg (36mg)
¼ c pecans - 41mg (3mg)
1 loaf French Bread - 14mg (2mg)
  or LS bread - 16mg (4mg)
4 eggs - 20mg (6mg)
  or 1 c egg substitute - 0mg
2 T NSA margarine - 16mg (3mg)
  or NSA butter - 24mg (16mg)

BLUEBERRY PANCAKES

Sodium Per Serving – 80mg   Serves 4–6

Packaged pancake mixes average 484mg sodium per 6-inch pancake. By using, no-salt-added baking powder, you can make these thick, dense pancakes that are low in sodium.

1½ cups all-purpose flour[1]	1½ cups lowfat milk
3–4 tablespoons sugar substitute or sugar[2]	½ teaspoon vanilla extract
	¼ teaspoon ground cinnamon
2 tablespoons no-salt-added baking powder[3]	1 tablespoon unsalted margarine or butter, melted[5]
2 eggs, lightly beaten, or ½ cup egg substitute[4]	1 cup fresh or frozen blueberries

▷ In a large bowl, mix together flour, sweetener, and baking powder.

▷ In another bowl, beat eggs, milk, vanilla, cinnamon, and margarine; gradually add to flour.

▷ Heat a lightly oiled griddle or skillet over medium heat; working in batches, pour batter onto griddle, using ¼ cup batter per pancake. Top each pancake with 6–8 blueberries; cook until browned on both sides, about 2 minutes per side. Serve with syrup or jam.

NUTRITIONAL INFO PER SERVING: Calories 294mg, Fat 7mg (Saturated Fat 2mg), Cholesterol 114mg, Carbohydrates 46mg (Fiber 2mg, Sugar 9mg), Sodium 80mg

POTATO PANCAKES

Sodium Per Serving – 31mg   Serves 4–6

Potato pancakes can be served anytime; these are easy to fix and taste great.

1 pound Yukon gold or russet potatoes, grated and moisture squeezed out	¼ teaspoon onion powder
	⅛ teaspoon ground black pepper
1 egg, lightly beaten, or ¼ cup egg substitute[4]	1 tablespoon olive oil
½ sweet onion, chopped	1 tablespoon unsalted margarine or butter[5]
1 teaspoon all-purpose flour	1 (15-ounce) can no-salt-added applesauce

▷ Mix together potatoes, egg, onion, flour, onion powder, and pepper.

▷ Heat oil and margarine in a skillet over medium heat; cook potatoes until browned on both sides, about 5 minutes per side. Serve with applesauce.

NUTRITIONAL INFO PER SERVING: Calories 282mg, Fat 7mg (Saturated Fat 1mg), Cholesterol 53mg, Carbohydrates 56mg (Fiber 4mg, Sugar 23mg), Sodium 31mg

COMMENTS:

1 *For additional nutrition, replace ½ cup flour with whole-wheat flour.*

2 *See* COMMENTS #4, *page 208, for sugar and sugar substitute information.*

3 *For info on no-salt-added baking powder, see* COMMENTS #1, *page 222.*

4 *See* Eggs and Egg Substitutes, *page 38, for a comparison of fat and sodium in eggs and egg substitutes.*

5 *To reduce saturated fat, use trans free margarine. Since it contains sodium (90mg per tablespoon), it will increase the sodium per serving to 100mg (33mg in the Potato Pancakes).*

TOTAL SODIUM AND FAT PER INGREDIENT

Blueberry Pancakes:
Sodium:
  1½ c flour - 5mg
  2 eggs - 140mg
    or ½ c egg substitute - 200mg
  1½ c LF milk - 173mg
  1 c blueberries - 1mg
Fat (Sat Fat):
  1½ c flour - 2mg (0mg)
  2 eggs - 10mg (3mg)
    or ½ c egg substitute - 0mg
  1½ c LF milk - 8mg (3mg)
  1 T NSA margarine - 8mg (2mg)
    or NSA butter - 12mg (8mg)

Potato Pancakes:
Sodium:
  1 lb potatoes - 32mg
  1 egg - 70mg
    or ¼ c egg substitute - 100mg
  ½ sm sweet onion - 4mg
  15 oz applesauce - 16mg
Fat (Sat Fat):
  1 lb potatoes - 1mg (0mg)
  1 egg - 5mg (2mg)
    or ¼ c egg substitute - 0mg
  1 T NSA margarine - 8mg (2mg)
    or NSA butter - 12mg (8mg)
  15 oz applesauce - 1mg (0mg)
  1 T olive oil - 14mg (2mg)

COMMENTS:

1 *Canned tuna averages any-where from 35mg to 221mg sodium per 2 ounces (very low sodium has 35mg, low sodium averages 120mg, and regular tuna, 221mg).*

2 *If the tuna is too dry for your taste, add 1–2 tablespoons more yogurt.*

3 *If using store-bought bread, look for varieties with 60mg or less per slice.*

TUNA SANDWICHES

Sodium Per Serving – 161mg   Makes 3 sandwiches

This is one of our favorite sandwiches. It's light and flavorful and not loaded with mayonnaise.

1 (6.5-ounce) can very low sodium tuna (or albacore)[1]

2 tablespoons minced onion

1 tablespoon sweet pickle relish

2 tablespoons lite mayonnaise or mayonnaise-type dressing[2]

2 tablespoons plain lowfat yogurt

6 slices EVERYDAY MULTIGRAIN BREAD *(page 218)* **or other low-salt bread**

Lettuce leaves

Tomato slices

▸ Mix together tuna, onion, pickle relish, and mayonnaise. Spread one-third mixture on 3 slices of bread; top with lettuce, tomato, and remaining bread.

NUTRITIONAL INFO PER SANDWICH: Calories 455mg, Fat 9mg (Saturated Fat 1mg), Cholesterol 57mg, Carbohydrates 78mg (Fiber 5mg, Sugar 9mg), Sodium 161mg (231mg with store-bought LS bread)

VARIATION

OPEN-FACED AVOCADO-TUNA GRILL

Divide tuna and spread equally on 3 slices of bread. Top with sliced avocado and 1 slice Swiss cheese. Broil about 5 inches from heat until cheese melts, 2 to 3 minutes. NOTE: The bread will be soft; if you want it toasted, do so before adding the tuna and placing it under the broiler.

NUTRITIONAL INFO PER SANDWICH: Calories 413mg, Fat 17mg (Saturated Fat 5mg), Cholesterol 61mg, Carbohydrates 44mg (Fiber 4mg, Sugar 5mg), Sodium 184mg (219mg with store-bought LS bread)

TOTAL SODIUM AND FAT PER INGREDIENT

Sodium:
6.5 oz NSA tuna - 105mg
2 T onion - 1mg
1 T pickle relish - 80mg
2 T lite mayonnaise - 120mg
2 T LF yogurt - 22mg
6 sl EVERYDAY MULTIGRAIN - 150mg
  or LS bread - 360mg
3 lettuce leaves - 2mg
3 sl tomato - 3mg
Fat (Sat Fat):
6.5 oz NSA tuna - 3mg (0mg)
2 T lite mayonnaise - 6mg (0mg)
2 T LF yogurt - 1mg (0mg)
6 sl MULTIGRAIN - 16mg (3mg)
  or LS bread - 6mg (1mg)

CURRIED CHICKEN SALAD SANDWICH

Sodium Per Serving – 184mg   Serves 4

This goes together quickly with leftover chicken. Serve on low-salt bread, in a pita pocket, or roll up in a low-sodium flour tortilla. This also makes a yummy salad when served on romaine leaves.

2 cups cooked chicken, diced

1 apple, diced

½ cup cashews, chopped

1 celery stalk, diced

¼ cup currants or raisins

2 tablespoons lowfat mayonnaise or mayonnaise-type dressing

2 tablespoons lowfat plain yogurt

2 tablespoons low-salt mango chutney[1]

⅛ teaspoon black pepper

½–1 teaspoon curry powder[2]

8 slices EVERYDAY MULTIGRAIN BREAD *(page 218)*, **or other low-salt bread, or 4 pita pockets, cut in half**

▸ Mix all ingredients together. Evenly divide and spread on bread or place in pita pocket halves.

NUTRITIONAL INFO PER SERVING: Calories 661mg, Fat 18mg (Saturated Fat 4mg), Cholesterol 92mg, Carbohydrates 99mg (Fiber 6mg, Sugar 22mg), Sodium 184mg

ROAST BEEF, HORSERADISH AND BLUE CHEESE WRAPS

Sodium Per Serving – 207mg   Serves 8

This wrap is perfect for leftover beef; the horseradish and blue cheese add a zesty flavor to this delicious wrap. For a milder taste, use Swiss cheese. This filling also is good on sandwiches or in pitas.

1 ounce Stilton blue cheese, crumbled (about ¼ cup)[3]

1–1½ tablespoons prepared horseradish

1 tablespoon lowfat mayonnaise or mayonnaise-type dressing

2 tablespoons lowfat sour cream

½ teaspoon Dijon-style mustard

½ teaspoon garlic powder

½ teaspoon ground black pepper

½ small sweet onion, thinly sliced (such as Vidalia)

4 (1-ounce) slices roast beef[4]

1 roasted red pepper, sliced, or 1 (4-ounce) jar roasted red peppers, drained

4 (10-inch) low-salt flour tortillas[5]

▸ Mix together sour cream, horseradish, mayonnaise, blue cheese, mustard, garlic powder, and pepper. Divide equally and spread on each tortilla; layer onions, roast beef, and red peppers. Roll up and cut in half diagonally.

NUTRITIONAL INFO PER SERVING: Calories 234mg, Fat 11mg (Saturated Fat 3mg), Cholesterol 34mg, Carbohydrates 15mg (Fiber 4mg, Sugar 2mg), Sodium 207mg

---

COMMENTS:

1 *Mango chutney averages 170mg sodium or more per tablespoon. Some brands have 70mg or less (see RE-SOURCES, page 272).*

2 *A sweet, rather than hot, curry goes well with this. For additional info on curry, see* FOOD NOTE, *page 198.*

3 *Stilton is milder and firmer than other blue cheeses, plus it has much less sodium.*

4 *Use leftover beef you've pre-pared; most packaged beef has over 400mg sodium per ounce.*

5 *See COMMENTS #2, page 162, for low-salt tortilla info.*

TOTAL SODIUM AND FAT PER INGREDIENT

Curried Chicken Sandwiches:
Sodium:
2 c chicken - 207mg
½ c NSA cashews - 11mg
1 celery stalk - 32mg
¼ c currants - 4mg
2 T lite mayonnaise - 120mg
2 T LF yogurt - 15mg
2 T mango chutney - 140mg
8 sl MULTIGRAIN BREAD - 200mg
Fat (Sat Fat):
2 c chicken - 10mg (3mg)
½ c NSA cashews - 32mg (7mg)
2 T lite mayonnaise - 6mg (0mg)
2 T LF yogurt - 1mg (0mg)
8 sl MULTIGRAIN BREAD - 21mg (4mg)

Roast Beef / Horseradish Wraps:
Sodium:
1 oz Stilton cheese - 220mg
1 T horseradish - 60mg
1 T lite mayonnaise - 60mg
2 T LF sour cream - 15mg
½ t Dijon mustard - 60mg
½ sweet onion - 5mg
4 oz beef - 75mg
1 red bell pepper - 2mg
4 LS flour tortillas - 328mg
Fat (Sat Fat):
1 oz Stilton cheese - 9mg (5mg)
1 T horseradish - 3mg (0mg)
1 T lite mayonnaise - 3mg (0mg)
2 T LF yogurt - 3mg (2mg)
4 oz beef - 9mg (4mg)
4 LS flour tortillas - 16mg (0mg)

COMMENTS:

1 *Most prepared hummus contains 53mg sodium per tablespoon.*

2 *If using store-bought bread, look for varieties with 60mg or less per slice.*

VEGGIE SANDWICHES WITH HUMMUS

Sodium Per Serving – 109mg   Serves 4

This healthy vegetarian sandwich is great with leftover hummus and raw vegetables.

1 cup SPICY ROASTED RED PEPPER HUMMUS *(page 40)*, **or low-salt prepared hummus[1]**

8 slices OLIVE-SAGE BREAD *(page 218)*, **or other low-salt bread[2]**

½ cucumber, sliced

6–8 mushrooms, sliced

½ red bell pepper, sliced

4 thick slices sweet onion

1–2 tomatoes, sliced

4 (1-ounce) slices low-salt Swiss cheese

2 cups alfalfa sprouts or shredded lettuce

▸ Equally divide hummus and spread on each slice of bread; layer 4 slices with cucumber, mushrooms, bell pepper, onions, tomato, cheese, and alfalfa sprouts. Top with remaining bread slices and serve. *NOTE: This is also good with melted cheese; place open-faced sandwich without sprouts in a broiler for 2 to 3 minutes until cheese melts. Top with sprouts and remaining bread; serve.*

NUTRITIONAL INFO PER SERVING: Calories 513mg, Fat 17mg (Saturated Fat 6mg), Cholesterol 27mg, Carbohydrates 69mg (Fiber 7mg, Sugar 6mg), Sodium 109mg (142mg with store-bought LS bread)

VARIATION

CREAM CHEESE, AVOCADO AND VEGGIE SANDWICH

Omit the hummus and use ½ cup whipped cream cheese; spread 2 tablespoons on 4 slices of bread. Proceed as directed, omitting the Swiss cheese and adding sliced avocado instead.

NUTRITIONAL INFO PER SANDWICH: Calories 445mg, Fat 16mg (Saturated Fat 6mg), Cholesterol 21mg, Carbohydrates 62mg (Fiber 8mg, Sugar 5mg), Sodium 121mg (154mg with store-bought LS bread)

TOTAL SODIUM AND FAT PER INGREDIENT

Sodium:
8 sl OLIVE-SAGE BREAD - 189mg
   or LS bread - 320mg
½ c RED PEPPER HUMMUS - 6mg
½ cucumber - 2mg
6 mushrooms - 4mg
½ red bell pepper - 1mg
½ sweet onion - 5mg
1 tomato - 6mg
4 oz Swiss cheese - 40mg
2 c alfalfa sprouts - 4mg

Fat (Sat Fat):
8 sl OLIVE BREAD - 8mg (1mg)
   or LS bread - 6mg (1mg)
½ c HUMMUS - 1mg (0mg)
4 oz Swiss cheese - 32mg (20mg)

SLOPPY JOES

Sodium Per Serving – 122mg   Serves 4

This childhood favorite is not only fast and easy, but it also tastes delicious.

1 pound ground beef or turkey[1]

½ small sweet onion, thinly sliced (such as Vidalia)

1 green bell pepper, chopped

1 celery stalk, finely chopped

¾ cup CHILI SAUCE *(page 238)*

¼ cup no-salt-add ketchup

1 tablespoon low-salt Worcestershire sauce

1 teaspoon prepared low-salt mustard

¼ teaspoon garlic powder

⅛ teaspoon ground black pepper

4 HAMBURGER BUNS *(see page 220)*[2]

▶ In a large pot or Dutch oven over medium heat, add beef, onion, bell pepper, and celery; cook, stirring frequently and crumbling the beef, until meat is not longer pink, about 5 minutes. Drain any liquid or fat from the meat.

▶ Add CHILI SAUCE, ketchup, Worcestershire, mustard, garlic, and pepper; decrease heat to medium-low and simmer, uncovered, until mixture has thickened to a chili-like consistency, 35 to 45 minutes.

▶ Equally divide meat mixture and pour over buns.

NUTRITIONAL INFO PER SERVING (WITH GROUND BEEF): Calories 377mg, Fat 24mg (Saturated Fat 9mg), Cholesterol 84mg, Carbohydrates 17mg (Fiber 2mg, Sugar 10mg), Sodium 122mg

NUTRITIONAL INFO PER SERVING (WITH GROUND TURKEY): Calories 239mg, Fat 8mg (Saturated Fat 2mg), Cholesterol 68mg, Carbohydrates 17mg (Fiber 2mg, Sugar 10mg), Sodium 126mg

COMMENTS:

1 *To lower fat, use lean ground turkey breast, instead of beef (see recipe Nutritional Info for a comparison).*

2 *Store-bought buns average 206mg per roll; a few brands have 150mg or less, such as* **Arnold**, **Food for Life**, **Giant**, *and* **Wenner** *(see RESOURCES, page 272, for more info).*

TOTAL SODIUM AND FAT PER INGREDIENT

Sodium:
1 lb lean beef - 304mg
   or turkey breast - 320mg
½ sweet onion - 5mg
1 green bell pepper - 4mg
1 celery stalk - 32mg
¾ c CHILI SAUCE - 19mg
¼ c ketchup - 24mg
1 T Worcestershire - 60mg
1 t LS mustard - 10mg
4 HAMBURGER BUNS - 30mg
   or store-bought - 600mg
Fat (Sat Fat):
1 lb lean beef - 91mg (35mg)
   or turkey breast - 28mg (8mg)
4 HAMBURGER BUNS - 3mg (0mg)
   or store-bought - 24mg (4mg)

YOGURT GRUEL WITH GRANOLA AND NUTS

Sodium Per Serving – 90mg   Serves 2

My husband and father-in-law eat this nearly every day for either breakfast or lunch. Vary it by using different flavors of yogurt or fruit, or omitting the fruit.

12 ounces lowfat fruit-flavored yogurt[1]

1 cup fresh fruit, cut into bite-size chunks (such as an apple, peach, berries, or banana)

½ cup Go Lean Crunch or other lowfat granola cereal[2]

⅓ cup unsalted dry roasted mixed nuts, chopped[3]

▷ Mix yogurt with fruit; sprinkle with cereal and nuts.

NUTRITIONAL INFO PER SERVING: Calories 278mg, Fat 12mg (Saturated Fat 7mg), Cholesterol 3mg, Carbohydrates 36mg (Fiber 6mg, Sugar 19mg), Sodium 90mg

FRESH FRUIT SMOOTHIE

Sodium Per Serving – 2mg   Serves 2

These are the best smoothies, they're thick and delicious, a meal in itself. Just about any fruit works, but this is our favorite combination.

¾–1 cup orange juice[4]

1 peach, quartered

1 banana, cut in half

½ cup fresh or frozen berries

▷ Place all ingredients in a blender and pulse until smooth; pour into glasses and serve.

NUTRITIONAL INFO PER SERVING: Calories 134mg, Fat 0mg (Saturated Fat 0mg), Cholesterol 0mg, Carbohydrates 32mg (Fiber 5mg, Sugar 23mg), Sodium 2mg

BREADS AND BAKED GOODS

BREADS, BUNS AND DOUGH

OTHER BAKED GOODS

TOPPINGS

COMMENTS:

1 Be sure the yeast is not past its expiration date. Fresh yeast will produce a higher, lighter loaf.

2 I think a little salt is needed for flavor, but the bread tastes good without it. Without salt, each slice has 1mg sodium.

WHY IS SALT USED IN BREAD?

In addition to flavor, salt controls the fermentation of the yeast, preventing the bread from overrising during the initial risings. This is necessary so that there will be enough oomph for the final rise and during baking.

Although breads may be made without salt, to compensate for the loss of energy, a sweetener (which enhances yeast growth) is needed. Also, herbs and/or spices are often added for the loss of flavor the salt provides.

Depending on the bread, I like to use a tablespoon of sweetener and anywhere from a pinch to ⅛ teaspoon salt (a pinch adds about 155mg sodium to the whole loaf or about 13mg per slice, ⅛ teaspoon adds 291mg or about 18mg per slice).

Also, bread that is made without salt will have a coarser texture.

TOTAL SODIUM AND FAT PER INGREDIENT

Sodium:
  1 pkg yeast - 4mg
  4 c flour - 10mg
  ⅛ t salt - 291mg
Fat (Sat Fat):
  1 pkg yeast - 1mg (0mg)
  4 c flour - 5mg (1mg)
  1 T NSA margarine - 8mg (2mg)
   or NSA butter - 12mg (8mg)

NO KNEAD FRENCH BREAD

Sodium Per Serving – 19mg   Makes two 6-inch loaves (16 slices)

This is tasty French bread that requires no kneading. Allow about 5 hours until the bread comes out of the oven. Makes one large loaf or two 6" round loaves.

1 tablespoon active dry yeast[1]
1¾ cups lukewarm water, divided
4 cups all-purpose or bread flour
1 tablespoon sugar substitute or sugar

⅛ teaspoon salt (optional)[2]
1 tablespoon unsalted margarine or butter, melted

▸ Dissolve yeast in 1 cup lukewarm water.

▸ While yeast softens, sift flour, sweetener, and salt together; stir in dissolved yeast. Gradually add remaining ¾ cup water, adding just enough until dough holds together; mix with a spoon or a mixer *(see* FOOD NOTE, *page 217),* until dough is soft and sticky. Cover with a clean cloth, place in a warm spot, and let rise until double its size, 2 to 3 hours.

▸ Punch down and hit a few times with your fist to remove air bubbles. Divide into two portions and place in two well-greased 6-inch round baking dishes (or make one large loaf and place in a well-greased loaf pan).

▸ Cover with a clean cloth and let rise to the top of the baking dish; brush with melted margarine. Bake in a preheated oven at 400°F (200°C) for 1 hour, or until golden brown. Let cool before slicing.

Bread Machine Method:

▸ *For one large loaf:* Place ingredients in the bread machine according to manufacturer's directions; start on *normal* or *basic* cycle. *See IMPORTANT below.*

NOTE: To eliminate the hole in the bottom of the bread caused by the paddle, gently lift out the dough at beginning of bake cycle. Remove paddle and return dough to the machine; continue on the *bake* cycle.

▸ *For two small loaves:* Follow directions for one loaf, except start on *dough* instead of *normal* cycle. *See IMPORTANT below.* When cycle is finished, remove dough and divide into two portions and place in two well-greased 6-inch round baking dishes. Cover and let rise to the top of the baking dish; bake as directed.

IMPORTANT: Because the amount of humidity affects the wetness or dryness of the dough, after a few minutes into the first cycle, check the consistency of the dough. If necessary, add more flour or water until dough holds together, but is still sticky.

NUTRITIONAL INFO PER SLICE: Calories 120mg, Fat 1mg (Saturated Fat 0mg), Cholesterol 0mg, Carbohydrates 24mg (Fiber 1mg, Sugar 0mg), Sodium 19mg

ROSEMARY HERB BREAD

Sodium Per Serving – 18mg | Makes a 1½ pound loaf (12 servings)

Here is another great bread machine recipe that I often serve at family holiday feasts. Plus, it makes the best sandwiches with leftover turkey or meatloaf.

1 tablespoon unsalted margarine or butter[1]

⅓ cup chopped sweet onion

3 cups bread flour[2]

1½ tablespoons powdered buttermilk[3]

1 cup water[3]

1 tablespoon dried basil

1 tablespoon dried rosemary, crumbled

1½ tablespoons sugar substitute or sugar

Pinch salt (optional)[4]

1 tablespoon active dry yeast

▸ Melt margarine in a small skillet over medium heat; add onion and cook, stirring frequently, until onions are translucent, 4 to 5 minutes. Let cool slightly.

▸ Place flour, buttermilk powder, water, basil, rosemary, sweetener, salt, and yeast in bread machine according to manufacturer's directions. Start on *normal* or *basic* cycle.

▸ After 5 minutes into the first cycle, check the consistency of the dough. If necessary, add more flour or water until dough holds together, but is still sticky.

NOTE: To eliminate hole in the bottom of the bread from the paddle, gently lift out the dough at beginning of bake cycle. Remove paddle and return dough to the machine; continue on the *bake* cycle.

▸ Let bread cool before slicing.

NUTRITIONAL INFO PER SLICE: Calories 138mg, Fat 1mg (Saturated Fat 0mg), Cholesterol 1mg, Carbohydrates 26mg (Fiber 1mg, Sugar 1mg), Sodium 18mg

COMMENTS:

1 *To reduce saturated fat, use trans-free margarine. Since it contains sodium (90mg per tablespoon), it will increase the sodium per serving to 26mg.*

2 *Bread flour is made specifically for bread making and has more gluten in it, which produces a larger, more-structured loaf than with all-purpose flour.*

3 *Substitute 1 cup nonfat or lowfat milk for the powdered buttermilk and water.*

4 *Although I usually add a pinch of salt, this bread tastes fine without it (each slice without salt is 6mg). See COMMENTS, Why Is Salt Used in Bread?, page 216, for additional information.*

COOKING TIP

BREAD MAKING WITHOUT A BREAD MACHINE

Electric Mixer: Using the flat beater, mix all the dough ingredients together at medium speed until the dough begins to get some shape, about 5 to 8 minutes. (NOTE: You may want to change to the dough hook, once the dough is well mixed.) Transfer to a lightly oiled bowl, cover and let rise; proceed as directed.

Food processor: Using dough hook, place all ingredients in processor; pulse until dough is smooth and sticky, about 1 to 2 minutes. Transfer to a lightly oiled bowl, cover and let rise; proceed as directed.

By hand: Place half the dry ingredients in a large bowl, forming a well in the center; pour in the wet ingredients. Mix with a wooden spoon, or your hands, until smooth; gradually add remaining flour until dough is stiff and workable; proceed as directed. *NOTE: You may not use all the flour.*

TOTAL SODIUM AND FAT PER INGREDIENT

Sodium:
⅓ c sweet onion - 2mg
1½ T dried buttermilk - 50mg
3 c bread flour - 8mg
Pinch salt - 155mg
1 T yeast - 6mg

Fat (Sat Fat):
1 T NSA margarine - 8mg (2mg)
  or NSA butter - 12mg (8mg)
1½ T dried buttermilk - 1mg (0mg)
3 c bread flour - 7mg (1mg)
1 T yeast - 1mg (0mg)

TOTAL SODIUM AND FAT PER INGREDIENT

Olive-Sage Bread:
Sodium:
1½ T dried buttermilk - 50mg
3 c bread flour - 8mg
3 T c ripe olives - 219mg
1 T yeast - 6mg
Fat (Sat Fat):
1½ T dried buttermilk - 1mg (0mg)
3 c bread flour - 7mg (1mg)
3 T c ripe olives - 3mg (0mg)
1 T yeast - 1mg (0mg)

Everyday Multigrain Bread:
Sodium:
⅓ c 8-grain cereal - 7mg
½ c NF milk - 54mg
  or LF milk - 58mg
1 egg - 70mg
  or ¼ c egg substitute - 100mg
2½ c bread flour - 7mg
¾ c whole wheat flour - 5mg
Dash salt - 155mg
4 t yeast - 8mg
Fat (Sat Fat):
⅓ c 8-grain cereal - 3mg (1mg)
½ c NF milk - 0mg
  or LF milk - 3mg (1mg)
1 egg - 5mg (2mg)
  or ¼ c egg substitute - 0mg
2½ c bread flour - 6mg (1mg)
¾ c whole wheat flour - 2mg (0mg)
2 T NSA margarine - 16mg (3mg)
  or NSA butter - 24mg (16mg)
⅓ c sunflower seeds - 21mg (2mg)
4 t yeast - 1mg (0mg)

OLIVE-SAGE BREAD

Sodium Per Serving – 24mg   Makes a 1½ pound loaf (12 servings)

One of our favorite Italian restaurants, Cafe Juanita in Kirkland, Washington, serves a delicious olive-sage bread. My version tastes almost as good and is made either in a bread machine or by hand.

3 cups bread flour[1]
1 cup water[2]
1½ tablespoons powdered buttermilk[2]
3 tablespoons chopped ripe olives

2 tablespoons dried sage
1–1½ tablespoons sugar substitute or sugar
1 tablespoon active dry yeast

▸ Place all ingredients in bread machine per manufacturer's instructions; start on *light crust* setting. Let cool before slicing. NOTE: To make by hand, see COOKING TIP, page 217, for directions.

NOTE: To eliminate hole in the bottom of the bread from the paddle, gently lift out the dough at beginning of bake cycle. Remove paddle and return dough to the machine; continue on the *bake* cycle.

NUTRITIONAL INFO PER SLICE: Calories 133mg, Fat 1mg (Saturated Fat 0mg), Cholesterol 1mg, Carbohydrates 26mg (Fiber 1mg, Sugar 1mg), Sodium 24mg

EVERYDAY MULTIGRAIN BREAD

Sodium Per Serving – 25mg   Makes a 1½ pound loaf (12 servings)

This healthy multigrain bread is ideal for sandwiches. Although the directions are for a bread machine, you can also make this without one (see COOKING TIP, page 217, for instructions).

⅓ cup 8-grain cereal
½ cup nonfat or lowfat milk
½ cup water
1 egg, lightly beaten, or ¼ cup egg substitute
2½ cups bread flour
¾ cup whole wheat flour

2 tablespoons unsalted margarine or butter[3]
2–4 tablespoons honey[4]
Pinch salt (optional)
⅓ cup raw, unsalted sunflower seeds
4 teaspoons active dry yeast

▸ Place all ingredients in bread machine according to machine directions. Start on *light crust* setting. (See NOTE above to eliminate hole in bottom of bread.) Let cool before slicing.

NUTRITIONAL INFO PER SLICE: Calories 197mg, Fat 4mg (Saturated Fat 1mg), Cholesterol 16mg, Carbohydrates 38mg (Fiber 3mg, Sugar 4mg), Sodium 25mg

QUICK HERBAL FLATBREAD AND PIZZA CRUST

Sodium Per Serving – 37mg   Makes 8 flatbreads

Flatbreads are popular in middle eastern culture. This version uses herbs and spices to make a delicious bread that can also be used as a pizza crust.

3½ cups all-purpose or bread flour[1]

⅓ cup cornmeal

2 teaspoons sugar substitute or sugar

2 teaspoons active dry yeast

½ teaspoon garlic powder

½ teaspoon dried oregano

½ teaspoon dried rosemary, crumbled

½ teaspoon dried thyme

¼ teaspoon ground black pepper

Pinch salt (optional)[2]

½ cup lowfat milk

2 tablespoons olive oil

1 egg, lightly beaten, or ¼ cup egg substitute[3]

½ cup warm water

2 tablespoons unsalted margarine or butter, melted[4]

> In a large bowl, mix together flour, cornmeal, sweetener, yeast, garlic powder, oregano, rosemary, thyme, black pepper, and salt. Add milk, oil, egg, and warm water; stir until a soft dough forms.

> Turn out onto floured work surface and knead 5 to 10 minutes; cover and let rest one hour. Divide into 8 portions and roll out each into 8-inch round pieces.

> *Baking method:* Place on a baking sheet and brush with margarine. Bake in a preheated oven at 400° F (200° C) for 10 to 12 minutes, or until golden brown.

> *Frying method:* Heat a cast-iron skillet over high heat until very hot. Place one flatbread in skillet; cook 1 to 2 minutes per side until just browned. Keep warm; repeat with remaining flatbreads.

> *Broiling method:* Brush with margarine or water and broil 3 inches from the heat until browned, about 3 minutes; turn and brown on other side.

NUTRITIONAL INFO PER FLATBREAD: Calories 289mg, Fat 7mg (Saturated Fat 1mg), Cholesterol 28mg, Carbohydrates 51mg (Fiber 2mg, Sugar 2mg), Sodium 37mg

COMMENTS:

1 *Replace some white flour with ½ to 1 cup whole wheat. Although healthier, it will make a denser dough.*

2 *I think a little salt is needed for taste, but is equally good without it (each flatbread without salt is 18mg).*

3 *Even though egg substitutes have more sodium than eggs (115mg versus 70mg per large egg), most brands have very little or no fat. To keep fat and sodium to a minimum, use a combination of eggs and egg substitute. See Eggs and Egg Substitutes, page 38, for a comparison of fat and sodium in eggs and egg substitutes.*

4 *To reduce saturated fat, use trans-free margarine. Since it contains sodium (90mg per tablespoon), it will increase the sodium per serving to 59mg.*

TOTAL SODIUM AND FAT PER INGREDIENT

Sodium:
3½ c flour - 11mg
⅓ c cornmeal - 1mg
2 t yeast - 4mg
Pinch salt - 155mg
½ c LF milk - 68mg
1 egg - 70mg
  or ¼ c egg substitute - 100mg
Fat (Sat Fat):
3½ c flour - 4mg (1mg)
⅓ c cornmeal - 1mg (0mg)
2 t yeast - 1mg (0mg)
½ c LF milk - 3mg (1mg)
2 T olive oil - 28mg (4mg)
1 egg - 5mg (2mg)
  or ¼ c egg substitute - 0mg
2 T NSA margarine - 16mg (3mg)
  or NSA butter - 24mg (16mg)

HAMBURGER BUNS

Sodium Per Serving – 62mg   Makes 8 large buns

These are the best-tasting light and fluffy buns. You won't believe how easy they are to make. Use your bread machine to do the kneading, then simply divide into balls, flatten and bake. You will never eat store-bought again!

2 cups bread flour	**1 cup lowfat milk**
1 cup whole wheat flour[1]	**2 teaspoons active dry yeast[5]**
⅛ teaspoon salt (optional)[2]	**1 tablespoon unsalted margarine or butter, melted (optional)[6]**
2 tablespoons honey[3]	**Dried onion or sesame seeds (optional)**
3 tablespoons canola oil	
1 egg, lightly beaten, or ¼ cup egg substitute[4]	

▸ Place bread flour, whole wheat flour, salt, sweetener, oil, egg, milk, and yeast in bread machine per manufacturer's instructions; select *dough* setting.

▸ When cycle is finished, remove dough and place on floured work surface; punch down dough and divide into 8 equal pieces. Form into balls, then flatten into a smooth, even 3½-inch circle. Place on a lightly greased baking sheet; cover with a damp towel and let rise 30 minutes until double in size.

▸ Brush tops with melted margarine and sprinkle with dried onions or sesame seeds. Bake in a preheated 350°F (180°C) oven for 10 to 15 minutes, or until lightly brown. *NOTE: If adding dried onion or sesame seeds, brush top with melted butter or margarine and sprinkle on desired topping.*

NUTRITIONAL INFO PER SERVING: Calories 246mg, Fat 7mg (Saturated Fat 1mg), Cholesterol 29mg, Carbohydrates 42mg (Fiber 3mg, Sugar 3mg), Sodium 62mg

VARIATION

CINNAMON BUNS

Increase the sweetener by 2 tablespoons and mix with ¼ teaspoon ground cinnamon. Also, increase the margarine to 2 tablespoons. Instead of dividing the dough into 8 buns, roll out on a floured surface until it is about 10 x 12 inches.

Brush the dough with margarine; sprinkle with the sweetener/cinnamon mixture. Roll up tightly and cut into 10 buns. Place on greased baking sheet; bake in a preheated 350°F (180°C) oven, about 15 minutes, or until lightly brown. Ice with **CREAM CHEESE FROSTING** *(page 267)*, if desired.

NUTRITIONAL INFO PER APPETIZER: Calories 205mg, Fat 7mg (Saturated Fat 1mg), Cholesterol 23mg, Carbohydrates 32mg (Fiber 2mg, Sugar 1mg), Sodium 49mg

MANGO BREAD

Sodium Per Serving – 20mg   Approximately 12 slices

This family recipe was given to me years ago by an old Hawaiian woman, whose grandmother made this bread for the early missionaries. It is absolutely delicious, especially with fresh coconut. If you have the time to use fresh coconut, you're in for a treat.

2 cups all-purpose flour

1½ tablespoons no-salt-added baking powder[1]

⅓–½ cup sugar substitute or sugar[2]

2 teaspoons ground cinnamon

2 cups diced mango

¾ cup canola or vegetable oil

1 tablespoon lemon or lime juice

1 teaspoon vanilla extract

½ cup raisins

½ cup chopped walnuts

½ cup freshly grated or packaged coconut

3 eggs, slightly beaten, or ¾ cup egg substitute[3]

▸ Preheat oven to 350°F (180°C). Lightly oil and flour a 9 x 5-inch loaf pan.

▸ In a large bowl, sift together flour and baking powder; add sugar and cinnamon. Make a well in the center and add remaining ingredients, stirring just enough to mix. Pour into prepared pan and bake for 15 minutes, lower heat to 325° (180°C) and bake for 45 to 55 minutes, or until a toothpick inserted in center comes out clean.

NUTRITIONAL INFO PER SLICE: Calories 297mg, Fat 19mg (Saturated Fat 3mg), Cholesterol 53mg, Carbohydrates 27mg (Fiber 2mg, Sugar 8mg), Sodium 20mg

COMMENTS:

1 *See* COMMENTS #1, *page 222, for no-salt-added baking powder info.*

2 *Because sugar substitutes differ from sugar in sweetness, the amount needed depends on the sweetener used:*
   Splenda or sugar - ½ cup
   Fructose - ⅓ cup
   For additional information, see Sweeteners, page 37.

3 *Even though egg substitutes have more sodium than eggs (115mg versus 70mg per large egg), most brands have very little or no fat. To keep fat and sodium to a minimum, use a combination of eggs and egg substitute. See Eggs and Egg Substitutes, page 38, for a comparison of fat and sodium in eggs and egg substitutes.*

FOOD NOTE

ABOUT COCONUTS

Selection: Fresh coconuts purchased at the market are often rancid; consequently, choosing the right coconut can help reduce your odds of getting a bad one.

Feel the weight and gently shake it — a fresh coconut is very heavy and has lots of liquid inside that you can hear sloshing when shaken.

Look for cracks and mold — the shell should be intact and free of cracks; any mold, mildew, or black spots, particularly around the 3 "eyes", indicates it's rancid.

Preparation: Most people drain the coconut prior to opening it, as it can get quite messy. To drain, pierce the eyes at the top of the shell with a knife or ice pick. The liquid should be fairly clear and smell fresh. If it is cloudy or smells bad, throw the coconut away. Once drained, there are several ways to open it:

Place in plastic bag and drop on pavement — it may take several drops, but will break in several pieces.

Gently tap the shell — use a rock or hammer, tapping around the middle (or diameter) of the coconut until a crack forms; continue tapping until the shell breaks in half.

Bake drained coconut — place in a preheated oven at 350°F (180°C) for about 25 minutes, remove and lightly tap the shell with a hammer until it breaks.

Freeze for an hour — remove and lightly tap with a hammer until it breaks.

Storage: Once the coconut is opened, separate the meat from the shell, peel the thin brown layer, and grate. One coconut yields about 3–3 1/2 cups grated coconut. Store in the refrigerator 2 to 3 days in a sealed bag or jar.

TOTAL SODIUM AND FAT PER INGREDIENT

Sodium:
   2 c flour - 6mg
   2 t cinnamon - 2mg
   2 c mango - 7mg
   ½ c raisins - 8mg
   ½ c walnuts - 1mg
   ½ c coconut - 8mg
   3 eggs - 210mg
   or ¾ c egg substitute - 300mg

Fat (Sat Fat):
   2 c flour - 2mg (0mg)
   2 c mango - 1mg (0mg)
   ¾ c canola oil - 164mg (12mg)
   ½ c walnuts - 38mg (4mg)
   ½ c coconut - 13mg (12mg)
   3 eggs - 15mg (5mg)
   or ¾ c egg substitute - 0mg

COMMENTS:

1 *Baking powder has 488mg sodium per teaspoon. Featherweight makes a salt-free baking powder that can be used instead. I find that doubling the amount called for in a recipe gives the best results.*

2 *To reduce saturated fat, use trans-free margarine. Since it contains sodium (90mg per tablespoon), it will increase the sodium per serving to 78mg.*

To keep fat and sodium to a minimum, use a combination of trans-free and unsalted.

3 *Because sugar substitutes differ from sugar in sweetness, the amount needed depends on the sweetener used:*

Splenda or sugar - ½ cup
Fructose - ⅓ cup
For additional info, see Sweeteners, page 37.

4 *See Eggs and Egg Substitutes, page 38, for a comparison of fat and sodium in eggs and egg substitutes.*

CORNBREAD

Sodium Per Serving – 31mg   Makes 15 squares

My mother-in-law loves this cornbread. It is slightly sweet and is the perfect accompaniment to a bowl of bean soup or chili.

1 cup yellow cornmeal
1 cup all-purpose flour
2½ tablespoons no-salt-added baking powder[1]
½ cup unsalted margarine or butter, at room temperature[2]
⅓–½ cup sugar substitute or sugar[3]
3 eggs, or ¾ cup egg substitute[4]

⅓ cup lowfat milk
¼ cup lowfat sour cream
1 (15-ounce) can no-salt-added cream-style corn
1 (4-ounce) can diced green chiles
4 ounces no-salt-added Swiss cheese, shredded (about 1 cup)

▷ Preheat oven to 350°F (180°C). Lightly grease a rectangular baking dish.

▷ In a large bowl, combine cornmeal, flour, and baking powder.

▷ In another bowl, cream together the margarine and sweetener; beat in eggs, one at a time. Stir in milk, sour cream, corn, chiles, and Swiss cheese; add to cornmeal mixture, stirring until smooth.

▷ Pour batter into prepared baking dish; bake in preheated oven for 45 minutes, or until a toothpick inserted in the center comes out clean. Cut into 15 squares (3 rows by 5 rows).

NUTRITIONAL INFO PER SQUARE: Calories 173mg, Fat 8mg (Saturated Fat 3mg), Cholesterol 51mg, Carbohydrates 19mg (Fiber 1mg, Sugar 2mg), Sodium 31mg

TOTAL SODIUM AND FAT PER INGREDIENT

Sodium:
1 c cornmeal - 4mg
1 c flour - 3mg
3 eggs - 210mg
  or ¾ cup egg substitute - 300mg
15 oz NSA cream corn - 30mg
4 oz green chiles - 100mg
2 oz NSA Swiss cheese - 40mg
⅓ c LF milk - 38mg
¼ c LF sour cream - 34mg

Fat (Sat Fat):
1 c cornmeal - 2mg (0mg)
1 c flour - 1mg (0mg)
½ c NSA margarine - 64mg (12mg)
  or NSA butter - 96mg (64mg)
3 eggs - 15mg (5mg)
  or ¾ cup egg substitute - 0mg
15 oz NSA corn - 3mg (0mg)
2 oz NSA Swiss - 32mg (20mg)
⅓ c LF milk - 2mg (0mg)
¼ c LF sour cream - 7mg (4mg)

VARIATION
JALAPENO CORNBREAD

Substitute 1–2 seeded and chopped jalapeños for the chiles; proceed as directed.

NUTRITIONAL INFO PER SQUARE: Calories 169mg, Fat 8mg (Saturated Fat 3mg), Cholesterol 51mg, Carbohydrates 18mg (Fiber 1mg, Sugar 2mg), Sodium 24mg

HERBED BUTTERMILK BISCUITS

Sodium Per Serving – 31mg   Makes 12 biscuits

These light and fluffy biscuits are delicious with soups and stews or with COUNTRY GRAVY *(page 97) on top.*

2 cups all-purpose flour

2 tablespoons no-salt-added baking powder[1]

1 tablespoon sugar substitute or sugar

⅛ teaspoon salt (optional)[2]

½ cup unsalted margarine or butter[3]

½ cup lowfat milk, mixed with ¼ teaspoon lemon juice, let sit for 5 to 10 minutes[4]

2 tablespoons lowfat sour cream

1 cup chopped chives or green onions (green part only)

¼ teaspoon dried basil

¼ teaspoon garlic powder

¼ teaspoon dried tarragon

¼ teaspoon dried thyme

⅛ teaspoon ground black pepper

▸ Preheat oven to 425° F (220° C).

▸ In a large bowl, combine flour, baking powder, sweetener, and salt; cut in margarine until mixture resembles coarse granules. *NOTE: This step goes quickly using a food processor.*

▸ Stir in the milk and sour cream, mixing until just combined and dough sticks together (if too dry, add a little more milk).

▸ Form dough into a ball and place on a lightly floured surface; flatten into an 8-inch round, about ½-inch thick. Cut into rounds, using a 2-inch diameter cutter. Repeat, gathering and flattening dough scraps and cutting out biscuits, until all dough is used.

▸ Place biscuits on a baking baking sheet; bake in a preheated oven for 15 to 20 minutes, or until golden brown. *NOTE: If not serving immediately, wrap cooled biscuits in aluminum foil and store at room temperature. Rewarm in a preheated oven at 350° F (175° C) for 5 to 10 minutes, or until heated through.*

NUTRITIONAL INFO PER BISCUIT: Calories 133mg, Fat 6mg (Saturated Fat 1mg), Cholesterol 2mg, Carbohydrates 17mg (Fiber 1mg, Sugar 1mg), Sodium 31mg

COMMENTS:

1 *See* COMMENTS #1, *page 222, for salt-free baking powder info.*

2 *While I think these taste best with a little bit of salt, it can be omitted without too much loss of flavor (each biscuit without salt is 7mg).*

3 *To reduce saturated fat, use trans-free margarine. Since it contains sodium (90mg per tablespoon), it will increase the sodium per serving to 91mg.*

   To keep fat and sodium to a minimum, use a combination of trans-free and unsalted.

4 *Reduced fat buttermilk may be substituted, but it will increase the sodium to 40mg per biscuit.*

TOTAL SODIUM AND FAT PER INGREDIENT

Sodium:
 2 c flour - 6mg
 ⅛ t salt - 291mg
 ½ c LF milk - 58mg
 2 T LF sour cream - 17mg
Fat (Sat Fat):
 2 c flour - 2mg (0mg)
 ⅓ c NSA margarine - 43mg (8mg)
   or NSA butter - 64mg (21mg)
 ½ c LF milk - 3mg (1mg)
 2 T LF sour cream - 3mg (2mg)

COMMENTS:

1 See COMMENTS #1, *page 222, for salt-free baking powder info.*

2 *Because sugar substitutes differ from sugar in sweetness, the amount needed depends on the sweetener used:*

   Splenda or sugar - 4 table-spoons

   Fructose - 3 tablespoons
   For additional info, see Sweeteners, page 37.

3 *To reduce saturated fat, use trans-free margarine. Since it contains sodium (90mg per tablespoon), it will increase the sodium per serving to 51mg.*

   To keep fat and sodium to a minimum, use a combination of trans-free and unsalted.

4 See *Eggs and Egg Substitutes, page 38, for a comparison of fat and sodium in eggs and egg substitutes.*

TOTAL SODIUM AND FAT PER INGREDIENT

Sodium:
 2¼ c flour - 6mg
 1 egg - 70mg
   or ¼ c egg substitute - 100mg
 ½ c LF milk - 58mg
 2 T LF sour cream - 17mg
Fat (Sat Fat):
 2¼ c flour - 3mg (0mg)
 ¼ c NSA margarine - 32mg (6mg)
   or NSA butter - 48mg (32mg)
 1 egg - 5mg (2mg)
   or ¼ c egg substitute - 0mg
 ½ c LF milk - 3mg (1mg)
 2 T LF sour cream - 3mg (2mg)

LEMON CURRANT SCONES

Sodium Per Serving – 15mg   Makes 8 scones

Hot scones and coffee, what a way to relax on a Sunday morning. These light and moist scones are quick to fix with a food processor. Make several hours ahead of time, cool completely before storing in an air-tight container.

2¼ cups all-purpose flour

1½ tablespoons no-salt-added baking powder[1]

3–4 tablespoons sugar substitute or sugar[2]

¼ cup unsalted margarine or butter[3]

1 egg, or ¼ cup egg substitute[4]

½ cup lowfat milk

2 tablespoon lowfat sour cream

1 teaspoon vanilla extract

1 tablespoon grated lemon peel

½ cup dried currants

▸ Preheat oven to 400ºF (200ºC). Lightly grease a baking sheet or line with aluminum foil or parchment paper.

▸ In a large bowl, combine flour, baking powder, and sweetener. Cut the margarine into the flour using a pastry blender or two knives, until mixture resembles coarse granules.

▸ In a small bowl, combine egg, milk, sour cream, vanilla, lemon peel, and currants; add to dry ingredients. Mix until dough comes together in a moist, sticky clump.

▸ With floured hands, form dough into a ball. Place on a lightly floured surface and flatten into a 8-inch round, about ¾ inch thick. Using a floured knife, slice in 8 wedges. Place scones on a prepared baking sheet; bake in a preheated oven for 20 minutes, or until golden brown. Serve warm or at room temperature.

NUTRITIONAL INFO PER SCONE: Calories 153mg, Fat 5mg (Saturated Fat 1mg), Cholesterol 23mg, Carbohydrates 23mg (Fiber 1mg, Sugar 1mg), Sodium 15mg

VARIATIONS

ORANGE CURRANT SCONES

   Instead of lemon peel, substitute 1 tablespoon orange peel.

NUTRITIONAL INFO PER SCONE: Calories 153mg, Fat 5mg (Saturated Fat 1mg), Cholesterol 23mg, Carbohydrates 23mg (Fiber 1mg, Sugar 1mg), Sodium 15mg

CHOCOLATE CHIP SCONES

   Instead of currants, add ½ cup miniature semisweet chocolate morsels and replace the lemon peel with 1 tablespoon grated orange peel.

NUTRITIONAL INFO PER SCONE: Calories 194mg, Fat 9mg (Saturated Fat 4mg), Cholesterol 23mg, Carbohydrates 25mg (Fiber 2mg, Sugar 1mg), Sodium 17mg

BLUEBERRY MUFFINS

Sodium Per Serving – 17mg | Makes 12 muffins

Most muffins are very high in sodium (averaging 505mg per medium-size muffin). This is because of the baking powder and baking soda used in most recipes. This version uses no-salt-added baking powder; although they won't rise as high as you may be accustomed, they will taste yummy. If using fresh or thawed blueberries, mixing them with a little flour before adding to the batter will keep it from turning blue.

2 cups all-purpose flour

1 tablespoon plus 1 teaspoon no-salt-added baking powder[1]

1/4 teaspoon ground cinnamon

3/4–1 cup sugar substitute or sugar[2]

1/3 cup unsalted margarine or butter[3]

2 eggs, beaten, or 1/2 cup egg substitute[4]

1/2 teaspoon vanilla extract

1/2 cup lowfat milk[5]

1/2 teaspoon lemon juice[5]

2 cups fresh or frozen blueberries[6]

▸ Preheat oven to 400°F (200°C). Line muffin pan with paper liners. *NOTE: These muffins tend to stick to the muffin pan and the liners help alleviate this. For the liners to peel off cleanly from the muffins, spray the liners with nonstick cooking spray.*

▸ In a bowl, combine the flour, baking powder, and cinnamon. *NOTE: If using fresh or thawed frozen berries, set 1/4 cup flour mixture aside.*

▸ In another large bowl, cream the sweetener and margarine until light and fluffy; beat in the eggs, one at a time. Mix in vanilla; add flour mixture and buttermilk, mixing until combined. Fold in blueberries.

▸ Pour into muffin cups and bake in a preheated oven for 20 to 25 minutes, or until golden brown and tops spring back when lightly touched.

NUTRITIONAL INFO PER MUFFIN: Calories 139mg, Fat 5mg (Saturated Fat 1mg), Cholesterol 36mg, Carbohydrates 20mg (Fiber 1mg, Sugar 3mg), Sodium 17mg

COMMENTS:

1 *See COMMENTS #1, page 222, for salt-free baking powder info.*

2 *Because sugar substitutes differ from sugar in sweetness, the amount needed depends on the sweetener used:*

    Splenda or sugar - 1 cup
    Fructose - 3/4 cup
For additional information, see Sweeteners, page 37.

3 *To reduce saturated fat, use trans-free margarine. Since it contains sodium, it will increase the sodium per muffin to 62mg.*

    To keep fat and sodium to a minimum, use a combination of trans-free and unsalted

4 *See Eggs and Egg Substitutes, page 38, for a comparison of fat and sodium in eggs and egg substitutes.*

5 *Substitute 1/2 cup lowfat buttermilk instead of the milk and lemon juice. This will increase the sodium per muffin to 23mg.*

6 *If using fresh or thawed blueberries, mix berries with 1/4 cup of the flour mixture to keep them from bleeding into the batter and turning it blue.*

TOTAL SODIUM AND FAT PER INGREDIENT

Sodium:
  2 c flour - 6mg
  2 eggs - 140mg
    or 1/2 c egg substitute - 200mg
  1/2 c LF milk - 58mg
  2 c blueberries - 2mg
Fat (Sat Fat):
  2 c flour - 3mg (0mg)
  1/3 c NSA margarine - 48mg (9mg)
    or NSA butter - 64mg (43mg)
  2 eggs - 10mg (3mg)
    or 1/2 c egg substitute - 0mg
  1/2 c LF milk - 3mg (1mg)
  2 c blueberries - 1mg (0mg)

COMMENTS:

1 See COMMENTS #1, page 222, for salt-free baking powder info.

2 To reduce saturated fat, use trans-free margarine. Since it contains sodium (90mg per tablespoon), it will raise the sodium per serving to 82mg.

3 Because sugar substitues differ from sugar in sweetness, the amount needed depends on the sweetener used:

Splenda or sugar - ⅔ cup
Fructose - ½ cup

For additional information, see Sweeteners, page 37.

4 Even though egg substitutes have more sodium than eggs (115mg versus 70mg per large egg), most brands have very little or no fat. To keep fat and sodium to a minimum, use a combination of eggs and egg substitute. See Eggs and Egg Substitutes, page 38, for a comparison of fat and sodium in eggs and egg substitutes.

POPPY SEED MUFFINS WITH LEMON GLAZE

Sodium Per Serving – 22mg   Makes 12 muffins

These moist muffins have a sweet, lemony glaze that taste, just like what you'd buy at the bakery.

2 cups all-purpose flour
1½ tablespoons no-salt-added baking powder[1]
2 tablespoons poppy seeds
½ cup (1 stick) unsalted margarine or butter[2]
½–⅔ cup sugar substitute or sugar[3]

2 eggs, or ½ cup egg substitute[4]
¾ cup lowfat milk
¼ cup lowfat sour cream
1 teaspoon vanilla extract
1 teaspoon finely grated lemon peel
LEMON GLAZE *(recipe follows)*

▸ Preheat oven to 375°F (190°C). Place liners in a muffin tin or coat pan with nonstick cooking spray.

▸ In a bowl, combine flour, baking powder, and poppy seeds; set aside.

▸ In another bowl, cream the margarine and sweetener until light and fluffly; beat in eggs, one at a time. Stir in milk, sour cream, and vanilla.

▸ Fold half the flour into the wet ingredients, mixing until just combined; repeat with remaining flour, taking care not to overmix.

▸ Divide evenly into 12 muffin cups; bake in a preheated oven for 20 to 25 minutes, or until golden brown and a toothpick inserted in the center comes out clean. Remove from oven and let cool 5 minutes; dunk muffin tops into LEMON GLAZE or drizzle over the tops. Let cool before eating.

NUTRITIONAL INFO PER MUFFIN: Calories 155mg, Fat 7mg (Saturated Fat 2mg), Cholesterol 38mg, Carbohydrates 18mg (Fiber 1mg, Sugar 1mg), Sodium 22mg

LEMON GLAZE

Sodium Per Serving – 0mg   Makes ¾ cup

This sweet glaze is delicious over most bakery products, like sweet breads, scones, or muffins.

½–⅔ cup sugar substitute or sugar[3]

Juice of 1 lemon (about 3 tablespoons)

▸ In a saucepan over medium heat, combine sweetener and lemon juice; cook, stirring frequently, until sweetener is dissolved. Drizzle over baked items or dunk while still warm; allow to cool before eating.

NUTRITIONAL INFO PER TABLESPOON: Calories 1mg, Fat 0mg (Saturated Fat 0mg), Cholesterol 0mg, Carbohydrates 0mg (Fiber 0mg, Sugar 0mg), Sodium 0mg

TOTAL SODIUM AND FAT PER INGREDIENT

Poppy Seed Muffins:
Sodium:
 2 c flour - 6mg
 2 eggs - 140mg
  or ½ c egg substitute - 200mg
 ¾ LF milk - 86mg
 ¼ LF sour cream - 34mg
Fat (Sat Fat):
 2 c fllour - 3mg (0mg)
 ½ c NSA margarine - 64mg (12mg)
  or NSA butter - 96mg (64mg)
 2 eggs - 10mg (3mg)
  or ½ c egg substitute - 0mg
 ¾ LF milk - 4mg (2mg)
 ¼ LF sour cream - 7mg (4mg)

CONDIMENTS, SAUCES AND OTHER BASICS

COMMENTS:

COMMENTS:

1 *Although freshly grated cheese is superior in flavor to the canned variety, it often contains more sodium. Romano generally is lower in sodium than Parmesan (340mg per ounce versus 454mg, but canned Parmesan has 150mg or less).*

2 *Instead of Italian seasoning, use 1 teaspoon dried basil, 1 teaspoon dried oregano, and 1 teaspoon dried thyme.*

3 ROSEMARY HERB BREAD *(page 217) is also nice to use for croutons. If using, omit Italian seasoning.*

HERBED GARLIC CROUTONS

Sodium Per Serving – 39mg   Makes 2½ cups (6 servings)

Once you taste these croutons, you'll never use store-bought again. For a buttery taste, coat with butter-flavored spray. Store croutons in an airtight container for up to a week.

3 tablespoons olive oil

1 tablespoon reduced fat grated Parmesan cheese (optional)[1]

1 tablespoon garlic powder

1 tablespoon Italian seasoning[2]

⅛ teaspoon onion powder

⅛ teaspoon ground black powder

1 loaf No KNEAD FRENCH BREAD *(page 216),* **or 6–8 slices low-salt bread, cubed (about 3–4 cups)[3]**

Butter-flavored spray (optional)

▸ In a large bowl, mix olive oil with Parmesan, garlic powder, Italian seasoning, onion powder, and pepper; stir in bread cubes, mixing well until bread is well coated. (You can also add all ingredients to a large container with a lid and shake until well coated.)

▸ To toast croutons:

Oven method: Preheat oven to 350ºF (180ºC). Spread on a baking sheet and spray with butter-flavored spray; bake in a preheated oven until lightly brown and crisp, 15 to 20 minutes.

Stove-top method: Melt 1 tablespoon unsalted margarine or butter in a large skillet over medium heat; toast croutons, tossing and stirring frequently, until golden brown and crisp, about 4 to 5 minutes. *CAUTION: The croutons can easily burn using this method, so watch them carefully.*

NUTRITIONAL INFO PER SERVING: Calories 231mg, Fat 8mg (Saturated Fat 1mg), Cholesterol 0mg, Carbohydrates 34mg (Fiber 2mg, Sugar 1mg), Sodium 39mg

TOTAL SODIUM AND FAT PER INGREDIENT

Sodium:
  1 T Parmesan cheese - 75mg
  1 T garlic powder - 2mg
  1 loaf No KNEAD FRENCH - 154mg
    or ½ loaf LS bread - 240mg

Fat (Sat Fat):
  3 T ollive oil - 42mg (6mg)
  1 T Parmesan - 1mg (0mg)
  1 loaf FRENCH BREAD - 7mg (1mg)
    or ½ loaf LS bread - 6mg (6mg)

BASIC PIE CRUST

Sodium Per Serving – 20mg   Serves 8

If you cannot find a premade pie shell with 55mg or less sodium per serving, this is a good alternative.

1½ cups all-purpose flour

1 tablespoon sugar substitute or sugar (optional)[1]

Pinch salt (optional)[2]

½ cup unsalted margarine or butter[3]

3 tablespoons cold water

▸ *To prepare crust by hand:* In a large bowl, mix together flour, sweetener, and salt. Using a pastry blender or two knives, cut the margarine into the flour until mixture resembles coarse granules. Stir in water, 1 tablespoon at a time, mixing after each addition until a dough forms.

▸ *To prepare crust with a food processor:* Place all ingredients in a food processor and pulse until dough starts to pull away from the sides. *NOTE: Do not overwork or crust will be tough.*

▸ Place dough on a floured surface and roll out to an 11-inch circle. Place in a 9-inch pie plate and flute edges; cover and refrigerate until ready to use.

NUTRITIONAL INFO PER SERVING: Calories 155mg, Fat 8mg (Saturated Fat 2mg), Cholesterol 0mg, Carbohydrates 18mg (Fiber 1mg, Sugar 0mg), Sodium 20mg

EGG ROLL WRAPS

Sodium Per Serving – 11mg   Makes 6 wrappers

Egg roll wrappers are a great substitute for puff pastry or pie dough in turnover recipes. Just spread your favorite filling on the wrapper, either fold in half on the diagonal or roll up; then fry or bake until golden brown.

2 cups all-purpose flour

Pinch salt (optional)[2]

1 egg, mixed with ⅓ cup water

▸ In a large bowl, mix flour and salt; make a well in the center of the bowl. Add egg, mixing well; if dough is too dry, add a little water until dough holds together.

▸ Dust the working surface lightly with cornstarch or flour; knead the dough until it is smooth and pliable. Cover with a damp cloth and let rest for 1 hour. Cut dough into 6 pieces; roll each piece into an 8x8-inch paper-thin square, adding flour as needed. *NOTE: If using for wontons, cut each into 4 equal squares.*

▸ *To store:* Lightly dust each side with cornstarch to keep from sticking together; wrap in plastic and store in refrigerator or freezer.

NUTRITIONAL INFO PER WRAPPER: Calories 163mg, Fat 1mg (Saturated Fat 0mg), Cholesterol 31mg, Carbohydrates 32mg (Fiber 1mg, Sugar 0mg), Sodium 11mg (37mg with salt)

COMMENTS:

1 *Use the sweetener if the crust is for a dessert, otherwise it is not necessary.*

2 *While I think this tastes best with a little salt, it is equally good without (each serving without salt is 2mg).*

3 *To reduce saturated fat, use trans-free margarine. Since it contains sodium (90mg per tablespoon), it will increase the sodium per serving to 110mg.*

To keep fat and sodium to a minimum, use a combination of trans-free and unsalted

---

TOTAL SODIUM AND FAT PER INGREDIENT

Basic Pie Crust:
Sodium:
  1½ c flour - 4mg
  Pinch salt - 155mg
Fat (Sat Fat):
  1½ c flour - 2mg (0mg)
  ½ c NSA margarine - 64mg (12mg)
    or NSA butter - 96mg (64mg)

Egg Roll Wraps:
Sodium:
  1 egg - 62mg
  2 c flour - 6mg
  Pinch salt - 155mg
Fat (Sat Fat):
  1 egg - 4mg (1mg)
  2 c flour - 2mg (0mg)

COMMENTS:

1 *While I think these taste best with a little salt, they are equally good without (each crepe without salt is 49mg).*

2 *Even though egg substitutes have more sodium than eggs (115mg versus 70mg per large egg), most brands have very little or no fat. To keep fat and sodium to a minimum, use a combination of eggs and egg substitute. See* Eggs and Egg Substitutes, *page 38, for a comparison of fat and sodium in eggs and egg substitutes.*

3 *To reduce saturated fat, use trans-free margarine. Since it contains sodium (90mg per tablespoon), it will increase the sodium per serving to 88mg.*

BASIC CREPES

Sodium Per Serving – 75mg   Makes 8–10 crepes

Making crepes is like making pancakes . . . quick and easy! These may be used in place of egg roll wrappers or tortillas; fill with anything from chicken and vegetables to strawberries and cream cheese.

1 cup all-purpose flour
2 teaspoons sugar substitute or sugar
Pinch salt (optional)[1]
2 eggs, or ½ cup egg substitute[2]

1 tablespoon unsalted margarine or butter, melted[3]
1⅓ cups lowfat milk

▸ Mix together all ingredients, either with a whisk or electric mixer; if batter is too thick, add 1–2 tablespoons more milk or water. Cover and refrigerate for 30 minutes to 1 hour.

▸ Coat a 7 or 8-inch nonstick skillet with nonstick cooking spray and place over medium heat. *NOTE: The correct temperature is important to cooking crepes properly. Depending on your cooktop, you may have to adjust the heat up or down, until you get the correct temperature.*

▸ Pour 2–3 tablespoons batter into skillet and swirl to coat the bottom; cook until the edges start to turn golden, about 1 minute. Loosen sides with spatula and turn; cook until golden brown, about 30 to 45 seconds. Transfer to a plate and repeat with remaining batter, adding more nonstick cooking spray, as needed.

NUTRITIONAL INFO PER CREPE: Calories 139mg, Fat 4mg (Saturated Fat 1mg), Cholesterol 75mg, Carbohydrates 19mg (Fiber 1mg, Sugar 3mg), Sodium 75mg

---

VARIATION

DESSERT CREPES

Increase sweetener to 2 tablespoons and add ¼ teaspoon vanilla extract to the batter; proceed as directed.

NUTRITIONAL INFO PER CREPE: Calories 39mg, Fat 4mg (Saturated Fat 1mg), Cholesterol 75mg, Carbohydrates 19mg (Fiber 1mg, Sugar 3mg), Sodium 75mg

---

TOTAL SODIUM AND FAT PER INGREDIENT

Sodium:
 1 c flour - 3mg
 Pinch salt - 155mg
 2 eggs - 140
  or ½ c egg substitute - 200mg
 1⅓ c LF milk - 150mg
Fat (Sat Fat):
 1 c flour - 1mg (0mg)
 2 eggs - 10mg (3mg)
 1 T NSA margarine - 8mg (2mg)
  or NSA butter - 12mg (8mg)
 1⅓ c LF milk - 7mg (3mg)

BLENDER MAYONNAISE

Sodium Per Serving – 15mg   Makes about 1½ cups

Once you've tried homemade mayonnaise, you won't want to use the commercial brands again. I've had this recipe for ages, unfortunately I do not know where it came from, so I cannot give credit to the creator.

1 egg[1]

2 tablespoons lemon juice or vinegar

½ teaspoon sugar substitute or sugar

½ teaspoon dry mustard

¼ teaspoon garlic powder

⅛ teaspoon paprika (optional)

Pinch cayenne pepper

⅛ teaspoon salt (optional)

1 cup canola or vegetable oil

▶ In a blender or food processor, combine egg, lemon juice, sweetener, mustard, garlic powder, paprika, cayenne, and salt; pulse at low speed until blended. Increase speed to high; slowly add oil in a steady stream, blending until smooth and creamy. If necessary, stop blender or processor and scrape down the sides. Keep refrigerated in a tightly covered jar for up to a month.

NUTRITIONAL INFO PER 1 TABLESPOON: Calories 84mg, Fat 9mg (Saturated Fat 1mg), Cholesterol 0mg, Carbohydrates 0mg (Fiber 0mg, Sugar 0mg), Sodium 15mg

COMMENTS:

1 *For a richer taste, 2 medium egg yolks may be substituted; this will decrease the sodium to 13mg per tablespoon.*

VARIATIONS

CHIPOTLE MAYONNAISE

Add 1 tablespoon chipotle chiles in adobo sauce (these are canned smoked jalapeños in tomato sauce, found in the Hispanic section of many supermarkets) to the ingredients in the blender or food processor; pulse until smooth.

NUTRITIONAL INFO PER SERVING: Calories 84mg, Fat 9mg (Saturated Fat 1mg), Cholesterol 9mg, Carbohydrates 0mg (Fiber 0mg, Sugar 0mg), Sodium 18mg

BASIL MAYONNAISE

To ½ cup **BLENDER MAYONNAISE**, add ¼ cup basil; place in a blender or food processor and pulse until smooth.

NUTRITIONAL INFO PER SERVING: Calories 42mg, Fat 5mg (Saturated Fat 0mg), Cholesterol 4mg, Carbohydrates 0mg (Fiber 0mg, Sugar 0mg), Sodium 8mg

NOTE: Use flavored mayonnaise in sandwiches, on vegetables, and fish cakes.

TOTAL SODIUM AND FAT PER INGREDIENT

Sodium:
  1 egg - 70mg
  ⅛ t salt - 291mg
Fat (Sat Fat):
  1 egg - 5mg (2mg)
  1 c canola oil - 218mg (15mg)

CHICKEN STOCK

Sodium Per Serving – 20mg   Makes about 10 cups

A good stock is far superior to any bouillon or canned broth and is very useful in low-salt cooking. Not only does it add lots of flavor and nutrients, but it has very little salt. The secret to a good, flavorful stock is browning the bones and vegetables before making the broth. Once the stock is completely chilled, freeze in paper cups in varying amounts (¼ cup to 1 cup) for later use. The stock can also be made in a crock pot—place all ingredients in the pot, cover and cook on low heat for 8 hours or overnight. This recipe works for either beef or chicken.

1 tablespoon olive oil

3–4 pounds chicken parts, such as necks, backs, wings, bones, and carcasses[1]

¼ teaspoon garlic powder

⅛ teaspoon ground black pepper

2 onions, unpeeled and quartered

3 celery stalks, including tops, chopped in 1-inch chunks

3 carrots, chopped in 1-inch chunks

3½ quarts water

4 garlic cloves, 2 whole and 2 crushed

6 fresh parsley sprigs[2]

6 fresh thyme sprigs[2]

6–8 black peppercorns

4 whole cloves

3 bay leaves

▷ Brown the bones and vegetables either on the stove-top or in the oven:

Stove-top browning: Heat oil in a large pot (at least 6 quarts) over medium heat; add bones and sprinkle with garlic powder and pepper. Cook, turning occasionally, until browned on all sides, about 15 minutes. Remove bones and set aside. To the same pot, add onions, celery, and carrots; cook, stirring frequently, until vegetables are a golden brown, about 10 minutes. Return bones to pot; decrease heat to low and proceed as directed below.

Oven browning: Place chicken parts and vegetables in a roasting pan and bake, uncovered, in a preheated oven at 450°F (230°C) until chicken and vegetables are brown, about 30 minutes. Remove from oven and drain off fat; place browned bones and vegetables in a large stockpot or Dutch oven over low heat.

▷ Add water, garlic, parsley, thyme, cloves, bay leaves, and peppercorns; cover, and simmer for 3 hours, occasionally skimming the froth from the top of the stock. *CAUTION: The froth contains impurities that should be removed, not stirred back into the stock.*

▷ Strain the stock through a collander and discard solids; strain again through a fine-mesh sieve or cheesecloth-lined collander. If using right away, refrigerate, uncovered, until slightly cooled, then remove fat that has formed on top. If not using right away, refrigerate until thoroughly chilled, then remove fat. Cover and refrigerate for up to a week or pour into paper cups in varying amounts (such as ¼ cup, ½ cup, and 1 cup) and freeze up to 3 months.

NUTRITIONAL INFO PER 1 CUP (values are approximates): Calories 35mg, Fat 1mg (Saturated Fat 0mg), Cholesterol 15mg, Carbohydrates 0mg (Fiber 0mg, Sugar 0mg), Sodium 20mg

LOW-SODIUM PICKLES

Sodium Per Serving – 5mg   Makes about 2½ quarts

This is an old recipe from an unknown source that contains no salt. According to my friend, Sally, who is a master canner, salt can be left out of fresh-packed or quick-processed pickles. However, when salt is omitted, there must be either the same amount or more of vinegar as water, or it must contain only vinegar. However, fermented pickles must have salt to kill unwanted organisms. Allow two days to prepare, as the cucumbers must stand overnight in cold water.

20–25 small pickling cucumbers (3 to 4 inches in length)

1-2 garlic cloves per quart[1]

3 fresh dill heads (4-inch diameter), or 1–2 tablespoons dill seed per quart

6 peppercorns per quart

1 tablespoon whole mixed pickling spice per quart

2 teaspoons whole mustard seed per quart

1 slice fresh horseradish per quart (optional)[2]

7½ cups white vinegar

7½ cups water

¼ cup sugar[3]

▷ Scrub cucumbers with a brush until clean. Cover with cold water and let sit overnight; drain.

▷ Sterilize several quart and/or pint jars. Place garlic, dill, peppercorns, pickling spice, mustard seed, and horseradish into hot sterilized jars; pack cucumbers into the jars.

▷ In a saucepan over medium-high heat, combine the vinegar, water, and sugar; bring to boil, stirring constantly, until sugar is dissolved. Pour over cucumbers, leaving ½-inch head space.

▷ Wipe jar rims with a towel dipped in hot water; place lid on jar and seal tightly. Lower jars into a 180°F (82°C) water bath and process for 30 minutes. *NOTE: Use a thermometer to be sure water stays at 180°F (82°C).*

▷ Carefully remove jars and cool thoroughly. Check seals by pressing the center of each lid; if it stays down, the jar is sealed. Store in a cool dry place for up to 1 year. If lid is not sealed, refrigerate for up to 3 weeks.

NUTRITIONAL INFO PER SERVING: Calories 45mg, Fat 0mg (Saturated Fat 0mg), Cholesterol 0mg, Carbohydrates 13mg (Fiber 1mg, Sugar 10mg), Sodium 5mg

COMMENTS:

1 *For a stronger garlic flavor, use 2 cloves per quart.*

2 *Horseradish adds a little zip and helps overcome the lack of salt. If you like the taste of horseradish, add a second piece per quart.*

3 *Sugar substitutes are not recommended, as the pickles have an undesirable flavor and are mushy instead of crisp.*

TO STERILIZE JARS:

There are two basic ways to sterilize jars:

Place empty jars in water and bring to a boil; boil for 10 minutes. Remove and drain.

Place lids and jars in a preheated oven at 225°F (110°C) for 10 minutes. Turn off oven and leave jars inside until ready to use.

NOTE: Use tempered glass jars designed for canning, not jars from store-bought products, such as pickle or mayonnaise jars.

TOTAL SODIUM AND FAT PER INGREDIENT

Sodium:
 20 cucumbers - 60mg
 1 clove - 3mg
 1 sl horseradish - 16mg
 7½ c white vinegar - 18mg
Fat (Sat Fat):
 20 cucumbers - 3mg (1mg)

COMMENTS:

1 *Because sugar substitutes differ from sugar in sweetness, the amount needed depends on the sweetener used. The following amounts produce a slightly tart relish (for a sweeter dish, increase sweetener by 2–4 tablespoons):*

   Splenda or sugar - ¾ cup
   Fructose - ½ cup
   For additional info, see Sweeteners, page 37.

2 *For even more flavor, use roasted corn:*

ROASTING CORN
   Pull back husks, remove silks, and replace husks before roasting:
   On the grill: *Place on grill and roast, turning often, until husks are browned and corn is tender, 12 to 15 minutes.*
   In the oven: *Bake at 350°F (180°C) for 40 minutes.*
   Stove-top: *Remove kernels from cobs; heat a dry skillet over high heat. Add corn and cook, stirring and tossing constantly until corn begins to darken, about 4 minutes.*

3 *See COMMENTS #2, page 235, on handling jalapeños.*

TOTAL SODIUM AND FAT PER INGREDIENT
Cranberry-Orange Relish:
Sodium:
 12 oz cranberries - 7mg
 3 T Grand Marnier - 4mg
Fat (Sat Fat):
 ½ c hazelnuts - 71mg (5mg)

Fresh Corn Relish:
Sodium:
 2½ c corn - 54mg
 ½ sweet onion - 6mg
 1 tomato - 6mg
 1 red bell pepper - 2mg
 ½ c cilantro - 4mg
 ½ t cumin - 2mg
Fat (Sat Fat):
 2½ c corn - 4mg (1mg)
 2 t olive oil - 10mg (1mg)

CRANBERRY-ORANGE RELISH WITH GRAND MARNIER

Sodium Per Serving – 1mg   Makes 4 cups

This relish is a family favorite during the holidays. We like it on the tart side, but if you like it sweeter, add more sweetener. For best results, use a food processor.

- 1 (12-ounce) bag frozen cranberries
- 1 navel orange, cut into chunks, or 2 tangerines, quartered
- ½ cup unsalted dry roasted hazelnuts (optional)
- ½–¾ cup sugar substitute or sugar[1]
- 3–4 tablespoons Grand Marnier or orange liqueur

▸ In a food processor, pulse frozen cranberries, oranges, and nuts together until coarsely ground. (Depending on the size of your processor, you may have to do this in several batches.) Transfer to a bowl and stir in sweetener, mixing well. Refrigerate for at least an hour; stir before serving.

NUTRITIONAL INFO PER ¼ CUP: Calories 70mg, Fat 4mg (Saturated Fat 0mg), Cholesterol 0mg, Carbohydrates 6mg (Fiber 2mg, Sugar 3mg), Sodium 1mg

FRESH CORN RELISH

Sodium Per Serving – 5mg   Makes 4 cups

This light and refreshing relish is great on poultry, fish, and in tacos. It can be served right away, but allowing it to chill for an hour enhances the flavor.

- 2½ cups fresh or frozen corn kernels (about 4 ears)[2]
- ½ sweet onion, chopped
- 1 tomato, seeded and chopped
- 1 red bell pepper, chopped
- ½ cup chopped fresh cilantro
- 1 jalapeño, seeded and chopped[3]
- ¼ cup fresh lime or lemon juice
- 2 teaspoons extra-virgin olive oil
- ½ teaspoon ground cumin

▸ Combine all ingredients; cover and refrigerate for 1 hour; stir before serving.

NUTRITIONAL INFO PER ½ CUP: Calories 31mg, Fat 1mg (Saturated Fat 0mg), Cholesterol 0mg, Carbohydrates 6mg (Fiber 1mg, Sugar 2mg), Sodium 5mg

Mango Salsa

Sodium Per Serving – 2mg   Makes 3 cups

This salsa is a great accompaniment to grilled fish, poultry, and pork. It also is delicious as a dip for tortilla chips.

2 mangos, peeled and cubed[1]

½ sweet onion, chopped

½ red bell pepper, chopped

¼ cup chopped fresh cilantro

2 tablespoons fresh lime or lemon juice

1 jalapeño or serrano pepper, seeded and chopped[2]

▸ Combine all ingredients; cover and refrigerate for 1 hour. Stir before serving.

NUTRITIONAL INFO PER ¼ CUP: Calories 27mg, Fat 0mg (Saturated Fat 0mg), Cholesterol 0mg, Carbohydrates 7mg (Fiber 1mg, Sugar 6mg), Sodium 2mg

VARIATION

Pineapple-Mango Salsa

Add ½ cup crushed pineapple (drained); proceed as directed.

NUTRITIONAL INFO PER ¼ CUP: Calories 32mg, Fat 0mg (Saturated Fat 0mg), Cholesterol 0mg, Carbohydrates 8mg (Fiber 1mg, Sugar 7mg), Sodium 2mg

Black Bean-Mango Salsa

Add 1 (15-ounce) can no-salt-add black beans (drained and rinsed).

NUTRITIONAL INFO PER ¼ CUP: Calories 39mg, Fat 0mg (Saturated Fat 0mg), Cholesterol 0mg, Carbohydrates 9mg (Fiber 3mg, Sugar 4mg), Sodium 4mg

FOOD NOTE

About Chile Peppers

There are many kinds of chile peppers ranging from mild to extremely hot. Based on the Scoville heat unit (SHU), which measures the amount of heat in chile peppers, here are a few of the more popular varieties, listed from hottest to mildest:

Habanero – these are the hottest of all chile peppers, ranging from 200,000 to over 300,000 SHU

Cayenne – very hot, especially red varieties, often used in Cajun cooking, 8,000–100,000 SHU

Serrano – hot, ranges from 7,000–25,000 SHU

Chipotle (smoked jalapeño) – hot, 10,000 SHU

Jalapeño – moderately hot, fresh are usually hotter than canned, 3,500–25,000 SHU

New Mexican – similar in size to Anaheims, but hotter, 4,500–5,000 SHU

Poblanos – mild, great for stuffing, 2,500–3,000 SHU

Anaheim – large mild chile, used for chile rellenos, 1,000–1,400 SHU

Ancho/Poblano – mild, 1,000 SHU

COMMENTS:

1 *If the mango is not very ripe, mix in 1 teaspoon sugar substitute or sugar with the salsa.*

2 *On a scale of 1 to 5, jalapeños are a 3, with most of the heat contained in the seeds and veins.*

CAUTION: When handling hot chiles, wear rubber gloves, as the oils of the pepper can be very potent. A piece of plastic wrap or a sandwich bag also works to hold the pepper. If you should touch the pepper with your bare fingers, wash your hands thoroughly and be sure to keep your fingers away from your eyes or you'll be in sheer agony!

TOTAL SODIUM AND FAT PER INGREDIENT

Sodium:
 2 mangos - 8mg
 ½ sweet onion - 6mg
 ½ red bell pepper - 1mg
 ¼ c cilantro - 2mg
Fat (Sat Fat):
 2 mangos - 1mg (0mg)

COMMENTS:

1 Roma or plum tomatoes are preferred, as they are less watery. Other varieties may be used, but will produce a thinner, watery salsa.

2 The pungency of chile peppers vary by the type of pepper, growing conditions, and time of year. Start with 2 peppers and add more until desired heat. NOTE: The heat will intensify the longer the salsa sits. See COMMENTS #2, page 235, for info on handling peppers.

3 To peel tomatoes: Bring a pot of water to a boil; place tomatoes in water for 10 seconds to loosen skins. Remove skins and crush.

Low-salt canned crushed tomatoes may be substituted for the fresh tomatoes.

4 I think a little salt enhances the flavor of this salsa, but is equally good without it.

TOTAL SODIUM AND FAT PER INGREDIENT

Mucho Caliente Tomato Salsa:
Sodium:
2 tomatoes - 12mg
½ sweet onion - 6mg
½ c cilantro - 4mg
Fat (Sat Fat):
2 tomatoes - 1mg (0mg)

Tex-Mex Hot Salsa:
Sodium:
2 lb tomatoes - 43mg
2 t garlic powder - 2mg
1 t cumin - 2mg
1 sm sweet onion - 9mg
½ c cilantro - 4mg
⅛ t salt - 291mg
Fat (Sat Fat):
2 lb tomatoes - 2mg (0mg)

MUCHO CALIENTE FRESH TOMATO SALSA

Sodium Per Serving – 3mg   Makes 2 cups

Simple and delicious; tastes just like the fresh salsa you'll find in Mexico.

2 tomatoes, chopped[1]

2–5 jalapeño or serrano chile peppers, seeded and chopped[2]

½ sweet onion, chopped

½ cup chopped fresh cilantro

1½ teaspoons fresh lime juice

▶ Combine all ingredients; cover and refrigerate for 1 hour. Stir before serving.

NUTRITIONAL INFO PER ¼ CUP: Calories 11mg, Fat 0mg (Saturated Fat 0mg), Cholesterol 0mg, Carbohydrates 2mg (Fiber 1mg, Sugar 1mg), Sodium 3mg

TEX-MEX HOT SAUCE

Sodium Per Serving – 11mg   Makes 4 cups

This salsa is briefly cooked and then puréed

2 pounds roma or plum tomatoes, peeled and crushed[3]

2 teaspoons garlic powder

1 tablespoon fresh lime or lemon juice

1 teaspoon cayenne pepper

½ teaspoon ground cumin

1 small sweet onion, chopped

2–10 jalapeño or serrano chile peppers, seeded and chopped[2]

½ cup chopped fresh cilantro

⅛ teaspoon salt (optional)[4]

▶ In a saucepan over medium-high heat; add all ingredients, mixing well. Bring to a boil; continue cooking 10 minutes. Remove from heat and let cool slightly.

▶ Place half the tomato mixture in a blender or food processor; pulse until a smooth consistency. Mix with remaining tomato mixture and refrigerate until ready to use. Will keep for up to a week in a covered container in the refrigerator. Can also store in the freezer for later use.

NUTRITIONAL INFO PER 2 TABLESPOONS: Calories 8mg, Fat 0mg (Saturated Fat 0mg), Cholesterol 0mg, Carbohydrates 2mg (Fiber 0mg, Sugar 1mg), Sodium 11mg

TEXAS-STYLE BARBECUE SAUCE

Sodium Per Serving – 29mg   Makes 4 cups

There are many regional styles of barbecue sauce, from hot and tangy to sweet and spicy. This tangy sauce is smokey-hot and slightly sweet. It cooks up in 30 minutes and will keep up to 2 weeks in an airtight container in the refrigerator.

1 tablespoon olive oil	**1 tablespoon molasses**
½ cup chopped onion	**1 tablespoon instant coffee, preferably espresso**[3]
3–4 garlic cloves, minced	
2–4 tablespoons chipotle peppers in adobo sauce[1]	**1 tablespoon no-salt-added chili powder**[4]
2 cups no-salt-added ketchup	**1 teaspoon mustard powder**
2 tablespoons low-salt Worcestershire sauce	**1 teaspoon garlic powder**
½ cup apple cider vinegar	**1 teaspoon onion powder**
⅓–½ cup sugar substitute or sugar[2]	

▷ Place all ingredients in a large pot and bring to a boil over medium high heat; decrease heat to medium low. Cook, stirring often, until the sauce has thickened to the desired consistency, about 30 minutes.

▷ Let cool completely before placing in jars with tight-fitting lids. Will keep up to 2 weeks in the refrigerator.

NUTRITIONAL INFO PER ¼ CUP: Calories 52mg, Fat 1mg (Saturated Fat 0mg), Cholesterol 0mg, Carbohydrates 11mg (Fiber 0mg, Sugar 10mg), Sodium29mg

COMMENTS:

[1] *Chipotle peppers are nothing more than smoked jalapenos in a spicy tomato sauce. Available in many supermarkets with the Hispanic foods.*

[2] *Because sugar substitutes differ from sugar in sweetness, the amount needed depends on the sweetener used:*
Splenda or sugar - ½ cup
Fructose - ⅓ cup
For additional information, see Sweeteners, page 37.

[3] *The stronger the flavor of the instant coffee, the better the sauce.*

[4] *Most chili powders contain sodium (26mg per teaspoon). See RESOURCES, page 272, for no-salt-added chili powder brands.*

TOTAL SODIUM AND FAT PER INGREDIENT

Sodium:
½ sweet onion - 2mg
3 garlic cloves - 3mg
2 T chipotle in adobo - 140mg
2 c NSA ketchup - 192mg
2 T Worcestershire - 120mg
½ c apple cider vinegar - 1mg
1 T molasses - 7mg
1 T instant coffee - 1mg
1 t onion powder - 2mg
Fat (Sat Fat):
1 T olive oil - 14mg (2mg)
2 T chipotle in adobo - 1mg (0mg)
1 T NSA chili powder - 1mg (0mg)
1 t mustard powder - 1mg (0mg)

CHILI SAUCE

Sodium Per Serving – 7mg   Makes 2 cups

Most bottled chili sauce is loaded with sodium (457mg per 2 tablespoons). This low-salt version simmers for a couple of hours on the stove and can be used on meatloaf, chicken, or as a substitute for ketchup. This will keep for many months in the refrigerator in a container with a tight-fitting lid.

4 large ripe tomatoes, chopped, or 1 (28-ounce) can no-salt-added whole or diced tomatoes

1 small sweet onion, chopped (about 1 cup)

½ cup chopped red bell pepper

½ cup chopped green bell pepper

¼–⅓ cup sugar substitute or sugar[1]

¼ cup cider vinegar

½ teaspoon ground allspice

½ teaspoon ground cinnamon

½ teaspoon ground cloves

¼ teaspoon ground black pepper

¼ teaspoon mustard powder

¼ teaspoon crushed red chile flakes

▷ Place all ingredients in a large pot and bring to a boil over medium-high heat; decrease heat to medium low. Stirring often, cook, uncovered, until the sauce has thickened to the desired consistency, 2 to 3 hours (this will depend on the juiciness of the tomatoes used).

▷ After 2 hours, check for sweetness, and add more sweetener, if needed. Let cool completely before placing in jars with tight-fitting lids.

NUTRITIONAL INFO PER ¼ CUP: Calories 29mg, Fat 0mg (Saturated Fat 0mg), Cholesterol 0mg, Carbohydrates 6mg (Fiber 2mg, Sugar 4mg), Sodium 7mg

TOTAL SODIUM AND FAT PER INGREDIENT

Sodium:

  4 tomatoes - 36mg

  1 sm sweet onion - 9mg

  ½ c red bell pepper - 1mg

  ½ c green bell pepper - 2mg

  ½ t cloves - 3mg

  ¼ t dried chili flakes - 1mg

Fat (Sat Fat):

  4 tomatoes - 1mg (0mg)

SHERRIED RAISIN SAUCE

Sodium Per Serving – 2mg   Makes 1½ cups

This is a luscious sauce that is great served over pork and vegetables, like carrots.

¾ cup raisins

1½ cups water

⅓–½ cup sugar substitute or sugar[1]

1½ tablespoons cornstarch

¼ teaspoon ground cloves

1 tablespoon unsalted margarine or butter[2]

½ cup dry sherry

▷ Combine raisins and water in a saucepan; simmer over low heat for 10 minutes.

▷ Mix together sweetener, cornstarch, and cloves; stir into raisins; cook, stirring constantly, until clear and thickened, about 5 minutes. Stir in margarine and sherry; heat through and serve warm.

NUTRITIONAL INFO PER 2 TABLESPOONS: Calories 52mg, Fat 1mg (Saturated Fat 0mg), Cholesterol 0mg, Carbohydrates 9mg (Fiber 0mg, Sugar 6mg), Sodium 2mg

BLACKBERRY WINE SAUCE

Sodium Per Serving – 1mg   Makes 1½ cups

This tangy berry sauce is the perfect accompaniment to salmon, chicken, and pork.

2 cups blackberries[3]

¼ cup water

3–4 tablespoons sugar substitute or sugar[1]

¼ cup red wine vinegar

1 tablespoon unsalted margarine or butter[2]

¼ cup minced onions or shallots

¼ cup dry red wine

¼ teaspoon garlic powder

▷ Place blackberries in a blender or food processor and pulse until puréed. (NOTE: If you want this free of seeds, strain purée through a fine-mesh sieve.)

▷ Combine water and sweetener in a saucepan over medium-high heat; cook, stirring frequently, until reduced to a thick syrup, 6 to 8 minutes. Remove from heat; stir in vinegar and set aside.

▷ Melt margarine in a skillet over medium-high heat; add onions. Cook, stirring frequently, until golden brown, 2 to 3 minutes. Add wine and garlic powder; cook until most of the liquid evaporates, 6 to 8 minutes.

▷ Add berry purée and cook, stirring occasionally, until reduced by half, about 6 to 8 minutes. Stir in syrup mixture; serve warm or cold.

NUTRITIONAL INFO PER SERVING: Calories 22mg, Fat 1mg (Saturated Fat 0mg), Cholesterol 0mg, Carbohydrates 3mg (Fiber 1mg, Sugar 2mg), Sodium 1mg

COMMENTS:

1 *Because sugar substitutes differ from sugar in sweetness, the amount needed depends on the sweetener used:*
Sherried Raisin Sauce:
   Splenda or sugar - ½ *cup*
   Fructose - ⅓ *cup*
Blackberry Wine Sauce:
   Splenda or sugar - ¼ *cup*
   Fructose - 3 tablespoons
   For additional info, see
Sweeteners, *page 37*

2 *To reduce saturated fat, use trans-free margarine. Since it contains sodium (90mg per tablespoon), it will increase the sodium per serving to 10mg per serving in the* SHERRIED RAISIN SAUCE *and 8mg in the* BLACKBERRY WINE SAUCE.

3 *Fresh or frozen berries may be used.*

TOTAL SODIUM AND FAT PER INGREDIENT

Sodium:
Sherried Raisin Sauce:
Sodium:
   ¾ c raisins - 12mg
   1½ T cornstarch - 1mg
   ¼ t cloves - 1mg
   ½ c sherry - 11mg
Fat (Sat Fat):
   1 T NSA margarine - 8mg (2mg)
   or NSA butter - 12mg (8mg)

Blackberry Wine Sauce:
Sodium:
   2 c blackberries - 1mg
   ¼ c vinegar - 1mg
   ¼ c onions - 2mg
   ¼ c red wine - 3mg
Fat (Sat Fat):
   2 c blackberries - 1mg (0mg)
   1 T NSA margarine - 8mg (2mg)
   or NSA butter - 12mg (8mg)

BLENDER HOLLANDAISE

Sodium Per Serving – 22mg   Makes about 1 cup

This lightened-up hollandaise is simply divine; pour over asparagus, fish, or eggs. This does not hold very well, so make just before ready to serve.

1 egg

2 egg yolks

Juice of ½ lemon (about 1½ tablespoons)

1½ teaspoons Dijon-style mustard

⅛ teaspoon low-salt Worcester-shire sauce

⅛ teaspoon cayenne pepper or hot pepper sauce, such as *Tabasco*

¼ cup unsalted margarine or butter, melted[1]

▸ Place eggs, lemon juice, and Worcestershire in an electric blender; while motor is running, slowly add margarine until sauce is thick and creamy. Serve immediately.

NUTRITIONAL INFO PER ¼ CUP: Calories 120mg, Fat 12mg (Saturated Fat 3mg), Cholesterol 158mg, Carbohydrates 1mg (Fiber 0mg, Sugar 0mg), Sodium 22mg

VARIATIONS

ORANGE HOLLANDAISE SAUCE

Instead of lemon juice, add the juice of half an orange (about 3 tablespoons).

NUTRITIONAL INFO PER ¼ CUP: Calories 124mg, Fat 12mg (Saturated Fat 3mg), Cholesterol 158mg, Carbohydrates 2mg (Fiber 0mg, Sugar 1mg), Sodium 22mg

BERNAISE SAUCE

Omit lemon juice, cayenne, and Worcestershire. Instead, in a saucepan over medium heat, add ¼ cup wine vinegar, ¼ cup white wine, 1 finely minced shallot, 1 tablespoon minced fresh tarragon or chervil (or 1 teaspoon dried), ⅛ teaspoon ground black pepper, and ⅛ teaspoon onion powder. Cook, stirring frequently, until reduced to 2 tablespoons. Strain through a fine-meshed sieve and add to eggs in blender; slowly add margarine as directed.

NOTE: This is delicious served over asparagus, grilled meats, and with artichokes.

NUTRITIONAL INFO PER ¼ CUP: Calories 124mg, Fat 12mg (Saturated Fat 3mg), Cholesterol 158mg, Carbohydrates 2mg (Fiber 0mg, Sugar 1mg), Sodium 22mg

TOTAL SODIUM AND FAT PER INGREDIENT

Sodium:
1 egg - 70mg
2 egg yolks - 16mg
1½ t Dijon mustard - 180mg
⅛ t LS Worcestershire - 3mg
Fat (Sat Fat):
1 egg - 5mg (2mg)
2 egg yolks - 9mg (3mg)
¼ c NSA margarine - 32mg (6mg)
  or NSA butter - 48mg (32mg)

DESSERTS AND SWEETS

COMMENTS:

1 *If purchasing a prepared crust, look for shells with 55mg or less sodium per serving. See* RESOURCES, *page 272, for low-salt brands.*

2 *Because sugar substitutes differ from sugar in sweetness, the amount needed depends on the sweetener used:*

Splenda or sugar - 1 cup
Fructose - ¾ cup
For additional information, see Sweeteners, *page 37.*

3 *Even though egg substitutes have more sodium than eggs (115mg versus 70mg per large egg), most brands have very little or no fat. To keep fat and sodium to a minimum, use a combination of eggs and egg substitute. See* Eggs and Egg Substitutes, *page 38, for a comparison of fat and sodium in eggs and egg substitutes.*

PUMPKIN PIE WITH AMARETTO CREME

Sodium Per Serving – 62mg   Serves 8

A traditional pumpkin pie has about 349mg sodium per serving. Mine has been lightened up—both in fat and sodium. But you won't miss either, as you enjoy this creamy, spicy traditional favorite. Top with AMARETTO CREME *for a fine ending to any holiday dinner.*

1 BASIC PIE CRUST *(page 229)* **or unbaked pie shell**[1]
1 (15-ounce) can pumpkin
1 cup lowfat sour cream
¾–1 cup sugar substitute or sugar[2]
2 eggs, beaten, or ½ cup egg substitute[3]

¼ cup lowfat milk or half-and-half
1 teaspoon vanilla extract
1 teaspoon ground cinnamon
½ teaspoon ground ginger
½ teaspoon ground nutmeg
1½ cups AMARETTO CREME *(recipe follows)*

▷ Preheat oven to 350°F (180°C). Adjust oven shelf to lowest level.

▷ Prick crust with a fork; line bottom of shell with aluminum foil. Pour pie weights into the pie shell to hold its shape while baking (for info on pie weights, see COOKING TIP, page 247). Bake for 5 minutes in a preheated oven; remove weights and bake 5 minutes more. Remove shell from oven and let cool slightly. *NOTE: If using a refrigerated or frozen pie shell, this step is not necessary.*

▷ Meanwhile, in a large bowl, mix together all ingredients and pour into prepared crust.

▷ Place pie on the lowest oven shelf; bake for about 1 hour. Pie is ready when it no longer wiggles when pan is shaken. Remove and let cool. *NOTE: Pie will continue to cook as it cools; cracking indicates pie has cooked too long.*

NUTRITIONAL INFO PER SERVING: Calories 284mg, Fat 15mg (Saturated Fat 5mg), Cholesterol 62mg, Carbohydrates 31mg (Fiber 3mg, Sugar 6mg), Sodium 62mg (92mg with store-bought shell)

TOTAL SODIUM AND FAT PER INGREDIENT

Sodium:
1 BASIC PIE CRUST - 159mg
  or store-bought - 400mg
15 oz pumpkin - 25mg
1 c LF sour cream - 160mg
2 eggs - 140mg
  or ½ c egg substitute - 200mg
¼ c LF milk - 27mg
  or half-and-half - 25mg
1 t cinnamon - 1mg
½ t ginger - 1mg
Fat (Sat Fat):
1 BASIC PIE CRUST - 66mg (12mg)
  or store-bought - 56mg (16mg)
15 oz pumpkin - 4mg (0mg)
1 c LF sour cream - 27mg (16mg)
2 eggs - 10mg (3mg)
  or ½ c egg substitute - 0mg
¼ c LF milk - 1mg (1mg)
  or half-and-half - 7mg (4mg)

VARIATION

BRANDIED PUMPKIN PIE

Add ¼ cup brandy or cognac to the pumpkin mixture before pouring into the pie crust. Omit the AMARETTO CREME and top with lowfat whipped topping or ice cream.

NUTRITIONAL INFO PER SERVING: Calories 262mg, Fat 13mg (Saturated Fat 4mg), Cholesterol 62mg, Carbohydrates 26mg (Fiber 3mg, Sugar 3mg), Sodium 61mg (92mg with store-bought shell)

AMARETTO CREME

Sodium Per Serving – 0mg   Serves 8

This yummy topping is also good on bread pudding, fruit compote, or peach tart.

1½ cups frozen lowfat whipped toppping, thawed

1–1½ tablespoons amaretto or other almond-flavored liqueur

▸ Mix together the whipped topping and amaretto. Serve with the pie.

NUTRITIONAL INFO PER SERVING: Calories 39mg, Fat 2mg (Saturated Fat 2mg), Cholesterol 0mg, Carbohydrates 6mg (Fiber 0mg, Sugar 3mg), Sodium 0mg

ABSOLUTELY THE BEST BERRY PIE

Sodium Per Serving – 21mg   Serves 8

The secret to a great berry pie is that it have a fresh fruit taste that is not masked with a lot of sugar. The following recipe is a family favorite; use any fresh, frozen, or combination of berries that you wish.

1 BASIC PIE CRUST *(page 229)* **or unbaked pie shell[1]**

5 cups fresh or frozen berries (such as blackberries, blueberries, strawberries, raspberries, or any combination of these)

2–3 tablespoons cornstarch[2]

¼ teaspoon ground cinnamon

1 tablespoon lemon juice

⅔–1 cup sugar substitute or sugar[3]

½ teaspoon almond extract

▸ Preheat oven to 350°F (180°C). Adjust oven shelf to lowest level.

▸ Prick crust with a fork; line bottom of shell with aluminum foil. Pour pie weights into the pie shell to hold its shape while baking (for info on pie weights, *see* COOKING TIP, *page 247*). Bake for 5 minutes in a preheated oven; remove weights and bake 5 minutes more. Remove from oven and let cool slightly. *NOTE: If using a refrigerated or frozen pie shell, this step is not necessary.*

▸ In a large bowl, gently mix the berries with the cornstarch until well coated. If using frozen berries, allow fruit to stand 15 to 20 minutes until partially thawed.

▸ Add sugar substitute, lemon juice, almond extract, and cinnamon; gently toss until well mixed. Pour into prepared pie shell; place on lowest oven shelf and bake in a preheated oven for 40 to 45 minutes, until crust is golden brown. Remove and let cool before serving.

NUTRITIONAL INFO PER SERVING: Calories 207mg, Fat 8mg (Saturated Fat 2mg), Cholesterol 0mg, Carbohydrates 29mg (Fiber 4mg, Sugar 7mg), Sodium 21mg (51mg with store-bought shell)

COMMENTS:

1 *If purchasing a prepared crust, look for shells with 55mg or less sodium per serving (see RESOURCES, page 272).*

2 *When using frozen or overly juicy berries, use 3 tablespoons cornstarch.*

3 *Because sugar substitutes differ from sugar in sweetness, the amount needed depends on the sweetener used:*

  Splenda or sugar - 1 cup
  Fructose - ⅔ cup
  For additional information, see Sweeteners, *page 37.*

TOTAL SODIUM AND FAT PER INGREDIENT

Amaretto Creme:
Sodium:
  1 T amaretto - 1mg
Fat (Sat Fat):
  1½ c LF topping - 12mg (12mg)

Absolutely The Best Berry Pie:
Sodium:
  1 BASIC PIE CRUST - 159mg
    or store-bought - 400mg
  5 c blackberries - 5mg
  2 T cornstarch - 1mg
Fat (Sat Fat):
  1 BASIC PIE CRUST - 66mg (12mg)
    or store-bought - 56mg (16mg)

PECAN PIE WITH BOURBON CREME

Sodium Per Serving – 41mg	Serves 8

This great-tasting pie is made with maple syrup instead of corn syrup. Although rich and luscious, it is not too sweet. Topping this with the bourbon creme sends it over the top!

1 BASIC PIE CRUST *(page 229)* **or unbaked pie shell**

1½ cups pecan halves

⅔–1 cup sugar substitute or sugar[1]

3 tablespoons unsalted margarine or butter, at room temperature[2]

2 eggs, beaten, or ½ cup egg substitute[3]

½ cup maple syrup, preferably sugar free[4]

2 tablespoons strong coffee or espresso[5]

1 tablespoon molasses

1 tablespoon all-purpose flour

1 teaspoon vanilla extract

1½ cups BOURBON CREME *(recipe follows)*

▸ Preheat oven to 350°F (180°C).

▸ Place pecans in the bottom of an unbaked pie crust.

▸ In a large bowl, mix together the sweetener, margarine, egg substitute, maple syrup, coffee, molasses, flour, and vanilla; pour over the pecans.

▸ Bake in a preheated oven for 50 to 60 minutes, until a knife inserted in the center comes out clean. Remove and cool completely.

NUTRITIONAL INFO PER SERVING: Calories 382mg, Fat 27mg (Saturated Fat 5mg), Cholesterol 53mg, Carbohydrates 35mg (Fiber 3mg, Sugar 4mg), Sodium 41mg (72mg with store-bought shell)

BOURBON CREME

Sodium Per Serving – 0mg	Serves 8

This simple, yet delicious topping is also good on bread pudding, fruit compote, sweet potato pie, and apple tarts.

1½ cups frozen lowfat whipped topping, thawed

1–1½ tablespoons bourbon or whiskey

▸ Mix whipped topping with bourbon and serve with pie.

NUTRITIONAL INFO PER SERVING: Calories 36mg, Fat 2mg (Saturated Fat 2mg), Cholesterol 0mg, Carbohydrates 5mg (Fiber 0mg, Sugar 2mg), Sodium 0mg

BRANDIED APRICOT ALMOND TART

Sodium Per Serving – 50mg   Serves 8

This very rich tart recipe is from a friend from Seattle, who enjoyed a version of this at Place Pigalle in Pike Place Market. The combination of dried apricots and almonds is a wonderful treat for the palate.

- 1 BASIC PIE CRUST *(page 229)* **or unbaked pie shell**[1]
- 2 cups dried apricots, chopped
- ⅓ cup brandy or rum[2]
- 1 cup sliced almonds
- 3–4 tablespoons sugar substitute or sugar[3]

- ¼ cup unsalted margarine or butter, melted[4]
- ½ cup apricot preserves
- 3 eggs, slightly beaten, or ¾ cup egg substitute[5]
- ½ teaspoon almond extract

▶ Preheat oven to 350°F (180°C).

▶ Prick crust with a fork; line bottom of shell with aluminum foil. Pour pie weights into the pie shell to hold its shape while baking (for info on pie weights, *see* COOKING TIP, *page 247*). Bake for 5 minutes in a preheated oven; remove weights and bake 5 minutes more. Remove from oven and let cool slightly. *NOTE: If using a refrigerated or frozen pie shell, this step is not necessary.*

▶ Soak apricots in brandy for 15 to 20 minutes; drain, reserving liquid. Sprinkle apricots into prepared pie crust.

▶ In a bowl, mix together almonds, sweetener, margarine, apricot preserves, and reserved brandy; beat in eggs, one at a time, and almond extract. Pour batter over the apricots. Bake in a preheated oven for 1 hour, until almonds are golden brown. Let cool and serve with cream, if desired.

NUTRITIONAL INFO PER SERVING: Calories 465mg, Fat 23mg (Saturated Fat 4mg), Cholesterol 80mg, Carbohydrates 52mg (Fiber 5mg, Sugar 29mg), Sodium 50mg (80mg with store-bought shell)

COMMENTS:

1 *If purchasing a prepared crust, look for shells with 55mg or less sodium per serving (see* RESOURCES, *page 272).*

2 *For an alcohol-free tart, substitute 1 tablespoon brandy or rum extract for the liquor.*

3 *Because sugar substitutes differ from sugar in sweetness, the amount needed depends on the sweetener used:*
   Splenda or sugar - ¼ cup
   Fructose - 3 tablespoons
   For additional information, see Sweeteners, *page 37.*

4 *To reduce saturated fat, use trans free margarine. Since it contains sodium (90mg per tablespoon), it will increase the sodium per serving to 95mg.*
   To keep fat and sodium to a minimum, use a combination of trans free and unsalted.

5 *See* Eggs and Egg Substitutes, *page 38, for a comparison of fat and sodium in eggs and egg substitutes.*

TOTAL SODIUM AND FAT PER INGREDIENT

Sodium:
   1 BASIC PIE CRUST - 159mg
   or store-bought - 400mg
   2 c dried apricots - 26mg
   1 c almonds - 1mg
   3 eggs - 210mg
   or ¾ c egg substitute - 300mg
Fat (Sat Fat):
   1 BASIC PIE CRUST - 66mg (12mg)
   or store-bought - 56mg (16mg)
   2 c dried apricots -1mg (0mg)
   1 c almonds - 73mg (6mg)
   ¼ c NSA margarine - 32mg (6mg)
   or NSA butter - 48mg (32mg)
   3 eggs - 15mg (5mg)
   or ¾ c egg substitute - 0mg

LIGHT APPLE TART

Sodium Per Serving – 27mg   Serves 6

This light and refreshing tart is the perfect ending to a wonderful meal and is a great favorite whenever I entertain. The secret is using fructose, which keeps the taste of sugar to a minimum and allows the flavor of the apples to come through. Friends who have tried this using sugar, say it just doesn't taste quite the same.

1 BASIC PIE CRUST *(see pg 229)* **or unbaked pie shell**

3 apples (preferably 2 Fujis and 1 Braeburn), peeled and thinly sliced[1]

½–¾ cup sugar substitute or sugar[2]

1½ tablespoons all-purpose flour

¼ teaspoon ground cinnamon

2 tablespoons unsalted margarine or butter[3]

▸ Preheat oven to 425°F (220°C). Adjust oven shelf to lowest level.

▸ Place pie crust in a 9-inch tart pan with a removable base, pressing dough into the bottom and up the fluted sides of the pan.

▸ Arrange apple slices in a circular design. There will be 3 layers of alternating varieties (bottom and top are Fujis, middle layer is Braeburn slices).

▸ Mix together sweetener, flour, cinnamon, and margarine. If using a processor, pulse until well mixed; sprinkle evenly over the apples.

▸ Bake on the lowest oven rack for 40 to 45 minutes, until crust is golden brown. Remove and cool before serving.

NUTRITIONAL INFO PER SERVING: Calories 269mg, Fat 14mg (Saturated Fat 3mg), Cholesterol 0mg, Carbohydrates 34mg (Fiber 1mg, Sugar 7mg), Sodium 27mg (67mg with store-bought shell)

FOOD NOTE

ABOUT APPLES

Apples are high in fiber and potassium, have no fat, and are sodium free. They have many health benefits, including cancer prevention, cholesterol reduction, and reduced risk of stroke. There are over 2,500 varieties of apples, some of the most popular are: *Braeburn* (sweet-tart), *Fuji* (sweet), *Gala* (sweet), *Golden Delicious* (mellow-sweet), *Granny Smith* (tart), *McIntosh* (tart), and *Red Delicious* (sweet).

Selection: Should be firm, shiny, and free of blemishes.

Preparation: To minimize browning, prepare just before using, or to protect from browning, dip cut pieces into a solution of one part lemon juice and three parts water.

Storage: Keep in plastic bags in the refrigerator up to six weeks. Apples stored in fruit bowls do not stay crisp for very long.

FRESH STRAWBERRY TART

Sodium Per Serving – 29mg   Serves 6

This quick and easy tart makes the most beautiful presentation. Everyone wants to eat this first and save dinner for later. Use fresh strawberries for the best results.

1 BASIC PIE CRUST *(page 229)* **or unbaked pie shell**

Glaze:

1 cup fruit juice (such as apple, mixed berry, or cranberry/ raspberry)[2]

½–¾ cup sugar substitute or sugar[1]

2½ tablespoons cornstarch

5 cups fresh strawberries, halved

Frozen lowfat whipped topping (optional)

COMMENTS:

1 *Because sugar substitutes differ from sugar in sweetness, the amount needed depends on the sweetener used:*
Splenda or sugar - ¾ cup
Fructose - ½ cup
For additional information, see Sweeteners, *page 37.*

2 *If watching your sugar intake, use a diet fruit juice with no added sugar.*

▸ Preheat oven to 350°F (180°C).

▸ Prick crust with a fork; line bottom of shell with aluminum foil. Pour pie weights into the pie shell to hold its shape while baking (for info on pie weights, *see* COOKING TIP *below*). Bake for 20 minutes in a preheated oven; remove weights and bake 10 minutes more. Remove from oven and let cool slightly.

▸ *For the glaze:* In a small saucepan over medium-high heat, add fruit juice, sweetener, and cornstarch. Cook, stirring frequently, until glaze thickens to a syrupy consistency, about 5 minutes; remove and let cool slightly.

▸ Pour a few tablespoons glaze into the cooked pie crust to just cover the bottom of the shell. Arrange strawberries cut side down with the largest berries on the bottom and the smallest filling in the holes on top.

▸ Cover strawberries completely with remaining glaze; refrigerate for 2 to 3 hours. Serve with whipped topping, if desired.

NUTRITIONAL INFO PER SERVING: Calories 271mg, Fat 11mg (Saturated Fat 2mg), Cholesterol 0mg, Carbohydrates 39mg (Fiber 3mg, Sugar 10mg), Sodium 29mg (69mg with store-bought shell)

COOKING TIP

PIE WEIGHTS

Pie weights are reusable small ceramic or aluminum pellet-like weights used to keep an unfilled pie or tart crust from shrinking or forming bubbles during baking and are found in gourmet stores and some supermarkets. Another alternative, is using rice or beans, however, they have a short lifespan, as they may burn or become musty after repeated use.

For prebaked crust: Prick shell with a fork in several places. Line the pie shell with a piece of aluminum foil or parchment paper; pour in 1 to 2 cups pie weights. Bake in a preheated oven at 350°F (180°C) for 20 minutes; remove the weights and foil. Bake for 10 minutes more, until edges are golden brown.

For partially baked crust: If the pie has a filling that will be baked further, follow the prebaked crust directions above, except reduce baking time to 5 to 10 minutes then remove weights and foil; bake another 5 to 10 minutes before filling.

TOTAL SODIUM AND FAT PER INGREDIENT
Sodium:
1 BASIC PIE CRUST - 159mg
  or store-bought - 400mg
1 c fruit juice - 7mg
2½ T constarch - 1mg
5 c strawberries - 7mg
Fat (Sat Fat):
1 Basic Pie Crust - 66mg (12mg)
  or store-bought - 56mg (16mg)
5 c strawberries - 2mg (0mg)

CHOCOLATE DECADENCE TORTE

Sodium Per Serving – 9mg   Serves 16

Chocolate lovers beware, this torte may be addicting! This no-bake dessert is another of my most-requested recipes. Although it contains a lot of fat (mostly from the pecans), it is so rich that a little goes a long ways. Allow 4 hours for the torte to set up.

Crust:

2 cups ground dry roasted unsalted pecans[1]

½ teaspoon ground cinnamon

¼ cup unsalted margarine or butter, melted[2]

Filling:

½ cup unsalted margarine or butter, at room temperature[2]

⅓–½ cup sugar substitute or sugar[3]

2 eggs, or ½ cup egg substitute[4]

1 teaspoon vanilla extract

1 (12-ounce) package chocolate morsels, melted[5]

2 tablespoons frozen lowfat whipped topping, thawed

▷ *For the crust:* Mix together pecans, cinnamon, and margarine; press into bottom of springform pan. (The crust goes together quickly using a food processor. Place whole nuts and cinnamon in processor and pulse until nuts are finely ground; slowly add margarine. Proceed as directed.)

▷ *For the filling:* Combine margarine and sweetener; beat until light and fluffy. Mix in eggs, one at a time, and vanilla; beat 2 minutes. Mix in melted chocolate; fold in whipped topping. Pour into crust and refrigerate until firm, about 4 to 6 hours.

NUTRITIONAL INFO PER SERVING: Calories 370mg, Fat 34mg (Saturated Fat 7mg), Cholesterol 27mg, Carbohydrates 18mg (Fiber 4mg, Sugar 12mg), Sodium 9mg

---

COOKING TIP

MELTING CHOCOLATE

There are two ways to melt chocolate:

Microwave – Place in a microwave-safe container and microwave for 2 to 4 minutes at 50% power. Once chocolate appears shiny, remove and stir until completely melted.

Stove-top – Place chocolate in the top of double boiler over hot, near-boiling wate; stir until chocolate has melted.

CAKES AND CHEESECAKES

LEMON CURD-MASCARPONE CAKE

Sodium Per Serving – 53mg   Serves 12

This is my adaptation of a decadently rich, but light cake that appeared in **Bon Appetit**. *Although I've removed most of the sugar and sodium, it is still absolutely yummy. The best compliment came from a professional cake maker who asked for the recipe.*

Cake:
- **2 cups all-pupose flour[1]**
- **1½ tablespoons no-salt-added baking powder[2]**
- **½ cup (1 stick) unsalted margarine or butter, softened[3]**
- **1–1½ cups sugar substitute or sugar[4]**
- **2 eggs, or ½ cup egg substitute[5]**
- **1 cup lowfat milk**
- **1½ teaspoons vanilla extract**

Frosting and Filling:
- **12 ounces mascarpone[6]**
- **¼–⅓ cup sugar substitute[4]**
- **1½ cups LEMON CURD (page 266) or 1 (12-ounce) jar lemon curd, divided**
- **1 cup frozen lowfat whipped topping, thawed**
- **Sliced almonds (optional)**

▸ Preheat oven to 350°F (180°C). Lightly oil and flour the inside of two 8" round cake pans. *NOTE: Use light-colored pans, if possible. Darker pans absorb more heat and will cook too fast, oftentimes giving the cake a thicker, darker crust. If using darker pans, reduce the oven temperature to 325°F (160°C).*

▸ *For the cake:* Sift together the flour and baking powder; set aside.

In a large bowl, beat the margarine and sweetener together until light and creamy. Beat in the eggs, one at a time; add vanilla. Alternately mix in the flour mixture and milk, beating until smooth.

Pour into prepared cake pans; bake in a preheated oven for 35 to 40 minutes, until a toothpick inserted into the center of the cake comes out clean. Remove and let cool before frosting.

▸ *For the frosting:* Beat together mascarpone and sweetener until smooth, add ½ cup lemon curd; fold in whipped topping.

▸ *To assemble:* Place one cake layer on plate; spread with one-third of the mascarpone mixture. Top with remaining 1 cup lemon curd. Place the second cake layer on top; spread remaining frosting on sides and top of cake.

▸ Cover the sides of the cake with sliced almonds, leaving the top free of nuts (This takes a lots of time, but makes a gorgeous presenation.), or sprinkle almonds all over the cake. Refrigerate for several hours; bring to room temperature before serving.

NUTRITIONAL INFO PER SERVING: Calories 284mg, Fat 20mg (Saturated Fat 11mg), Cholesterol 113mg, Carbohydrates 23mg (Fiber 1mg, Sugar 3mg), Sodium 53mg

COMMENTS:

1 *A packaged cake mix may be used. Look for one with less than 100mg sodium per serving.*

2 *For information on no-salt-added baking powder, see* COMMENTS #1, *page 222.*

3 *To reduce saturated fat, use trans-free margarine. Since it contains sodium (90mg per tablespoon), it will increase the sodium per serving to 113mg.*

4 *Because sugar substitutes differ from sugar in sweetness, the amount needed depends on the sweetener used:*
Cake – Splenda or sugar - 1½ cups, Fructose - 1 cup
Frosting and Filling – Splenda or sugar - ⅓ cup, Fructose - ¼ cup
For additional information, see Sweeteners, *page 37.*

5 *See* Eggs and Egg Substitutes, *page 38, for a comparison of fat and sodium in eggs and egg substitutes.*

6 *Mascarpone is similar to cream cheese. Although low in sodium, it is high in fat.*

TOTAL SODIUM AND FAT PER INGREDIENT

Sodium:
2 c flour - 5mg
2 eggs - 140mg
  or ½ c egg substitute - 200mg
1 c LF milk - 115mg
12 oz mascarpone - 192mg
1½ c LEMON CURD - 188mg

Fat (Sat Fat):
2 c flour - 2mg (0mg)
½ c NSA margarine - 64mg (12mg)
  or NSA butter - 96mg (64mg)
2 eggs - 10mg (3mg)
  or ½ c egg substitute - 0mg
1 c LF milk - 5mg (2mg)
12 oz mascarpone - 166mg (84mg)
1 c whipped topping - 8mg (8mg)
1½ c LEMON CURD - 76mg (46mg)

CARROT CAKE

Sodium Per Serving – 22mg   Serves 12

This carrot cake is moist and full of flavor. No one will believe it's low in both salt and sugar.

1½ cups all-purpose flour

1½ teaspoons ground cinnamon

1 tablespoon no-salt-added baking powder[1]

½ teaspoon ground cloves

2 eggs, or ½ cup egg substitute[2]

⅔–1 cup sugar substitute or sugar[3]

⅔ cup vegetable or canola oil

1½ teaspoons vanilla extract

1½ cups grated carrots (about 2 medium)

¾ cup crushed pineapple, drained

⅓ cup unsweetened coconut (optional)[4]

½ cup walnuts, toasted and chopped[5]

CREAM CHEESE FROSTING (*page 267*)

▷ Preheat oven to 350°F (180°C). Lightly oil and flour the inside of a 13 x 9 x 2-inch rectangular baking dish, or two 9-inch cake pans. *NOTE: Use light-colored pans, if possible. Darker pans absorb more heat and will cook too fast, oftentimes giving the cake a thicker, darker crust. If using darker pans, reduce the oven temperature to 325°F (160°C).*

▷ Sift together the flour, cinnamon, baking powder, and cloves; set aside.

▷ In a large bowl, beat eggs, one at a time, with sweetener until smooth and creamy; slowly add oil, beating until well mixed. Stir in vanilla.

▷ Gradually add the flour mixture, beating until smooth; stir in carrots, pineapple, coconut, and walnuts.

▷ Pour into prepared baking dish or cake pans; bake in a preheated oven for 1 hour, or until a toothpick inserted into the center of the cake comes out clean. Remove and let cool before frosting.

NUTRITIONAL INFO PER SERVING WITHOUT FROSTING: Calories 298mg, Fat 23mg (Saturated Fat 6mg), Cholesterol 35mg, Carbohydrates 20mg (Fiber 3mg, Sugar 3mg), Sodium 22mg

POUND CAKE

Sodium Per Serving – 39mg   **Serves 14**

Pound cake is so versatile—it's good by itself, with a lemon glaze, or as a base for fresh fruit (such as strawberry shortcake). There are many recipes for pound cake that include baking powder and salt for leavening. This recipe has neither and gets its volume from the air that is beaten into the batter. It is important to have all the ingredients at room temperature which maximizes the amount of air that is beaten into the batter.

1½ cups (3 sticks) unsalted margarine or butter, softened[1]

2–3 cups sugar substitute or sugar[2]

6 eggs, or 1½ cups egg substitute[3]

1 tablespoon lemon extract

2 teaspoons vanilla extract

3 cups all-purpose flour

1 cup lowfat milk

▶ Preheat oven to 350°F (180°C). Lightly oil and flour the inside of a 9 x 5 x 3-inch loaf pan or bundt pan. *NOTE. Use light-colored pans, if possible. Darker pans absorb more heat and will cook too fast, oftentimes giving the cake a thicker, darker crust. If using darker pans, reduce the oven temperature to 325°F (160°C)*

▶ In a large bowl, beat the margarine and sweetener together until light and creamy; add eggs, one at a time, beating until smooth and creamy. Stir in lemon and vanilla extracts; alternately mix in flour and milk, stirring until well mixed.

▶ Pour into prepared pan; bake in a preheated oven for 1 hour and 15 minutes, or until a toothpick inserted in the center comes out clean. Remove and let cool.

NUTRITIONAL INFO PER SERVING: Calories 271mg, Fat 17mg (Saturated Fat 4mg), Cholesterol 92mg, Carbohydrates 24mg (Fiber 1mg, Sugar 1mg), Sodium 39mg

---

VARIATION

CREAM CHEESE POUND CAKE

Cream 8 ounces (1 cup) cream cheese with the margarine and sugar; proceed as directed.

NUTRITIONAL INFO PER SERVING: Calories 328mg, Fat 22mg (Saturated Fat 7mg), Cholesterol 110mg, Carbohydrates 25mg (Fiber 1mg, Sugar 1mg), Sodium 87mg

COMMENTS:

1 *To reduce saturated fat, use trans-free margarine. Since it contains sodium (90mg per tablespoon), it will increase the amount of sodium per serving by about 6mg per tablespoon.*

  To keep fat and sodium to a minimum, use a combination of trans-free and unsalted.

2 *Because sugar substitutes differ from sugar in sweetness, the amount needed depends on the sweetener used:*
  Splenda or sugar - 3 cups
  Fructose - 2 cups
  For additional information, see Sweeteners, page 37.

3 *Even though egg substitutes have more sodium than eggs (115mg versus 70mg per large egg), most brands have very little or no fat. To keep fat and sodium to a minimum, use a combination of eggs and egg substitute. See Eggs and Egg Substitutes, page 38, for a comparison of fat and sodium in eggs and egg substitutes.*

TOTAL SODIUM AND FAT PER INGREDIENT

Sodium:
  6 eggs - 420mg
    or 1½ c egg substitute - 600mg
  3 c flour - 8mg
  1 c LF milk - 115mg
Fat (Sat Fat):
  1½ c NSA margarine -
      192mg (36mg)
    or NSA butter - 288mg (192mg)
  6 eggs - 30mg (10mg)
    or 1½ c egg substitute - 0mg
  3 c flour - 4mg (1mg)
  1 c LF milk - 5mg (2mg)

SPONGE CAKE

Sodium Per Serving – 13mg   Serves 14

Of all the commercial cakes available, sponge cake has the least sodium, plus its low in fat. This is a basic sponge cake recipe with a hint of lemon, add a frosting of your choice or serve it with fresh fruit.

8 egg yolks

⅔–1 cup sugar substitute or sugar[1]

¼ cup water

1 teaspoon finely grated lemon peel, or ½ teaspoon lemon extract

2 teaspoons lemon juice

1 cup cake or all-purpose flour

2 egg whites

½ teaspoon cream of tartar

▹ Preheat oven to 350°F (180°C). Lightly oil and flour the inside of a 9x5x3-inch loaf or tube pan. *NOTE: Use light-colored pans, if possible. Darker pans absorb more heat and will cook too fast, oftentimes giving the cake a thicker, darker crust. If using darker pans, reduce the oven temperature to 325°F (160°C).*

▹ In a large bowl, beat egg yolks until thick and lemon colored. Gradually beat in the sweetener, mixing well between additions. Add water, lemon peel, and lemon juice; mix in flour.

▹ In another bowl, beat the egg whites and cream of tartar until stiff, but not dry; gently fold into the cake batter. Pour into prepared pan.

▹ Bake in a preheated oven for 1 hour or until a toothpick inserted into the center of the cake comes out clean; remove from oven and let cool.

NUTRITIONAL INFO PER SERVING: Calories 70mg, Fat 3mg (Saturated Fat 1mg), Cholesterol 120mg, Carbohydrates 8mg (Fiber 0mg, Sugar 0mg), Sodium 13mg

FOOD NOTE		

FLOUR COMPARISON

Most flours have very little sodium, except for self-rising flour, which has added leavening agents. The following is the sodium content per cup of several flours.

Cake flour 0mg	All-purpose flour 3mg	Soy flour..............11mg
Rice flour, white.......0mg	Rye flour....................1mg	Potato flour..........88mg
Rice flour, brown 13mg	Whole wheat flour 6mg	Self-rising flour....1,588mg

PUMPKIN CHEESECAKE

Sodium Per Serving – 123mg   Serves 16

This is a luscious, sugar-free cheesecake that is the perfect ending to a holiday dinner. Allow at least 5 hours for the cheesecake to set up before serving.

Crust:

1 cup coarsely ground low-salt ladyfingers, vanilla wafers, or shortbread cookies[1]

¼ cup coarsely ground almonds or pecans

⅓ cup unsalted margarine or butter, melted[2]

Filling:

8 ounces (1 cup) mascarpone[3]

1 cup (8 ounces) cream cheese[4]

1 cup (8 ounces) lowfat cream cheese or Neufchâtel[4]

⅔–1 cup sugar substitute or sugar[5]

3 eggs, lightly beaten, or ¾ cup egg substitute[6]

1 teaspoon vanilla extract

1 cup canned pumpkin

1 teaspoon ground cinnamon

¼ teaspoon ground nutmeg

⅛ teaspoon ground allspice

Topping:

1 cup frozen lowfat whipped topping, thawed

▷ Preheat oven to 350°F (180°C). Adjust oven rack to lowest position.

▷ *For crust:* In a food processor, mix together cookie crumbs, pecans, and melted margarine; press into bottom of springform pan. Bake in a preheated oven for 10 minutes; remove and let cool slightly.

▷ *For filling:* Cream together the mascarpone, cream cheeses, and sweetener; beat in eggs, one at a time. Add vanilla, pumpkin, and spices; pour into cookie crust.

▷ Bake on the lowest oven rack for 1 hour; turn off heat and let sit another 30 minutes. Remove from oven and let cool.

▷ Cover and refrigerate at least 5 hours or overnight. Remove springform rim and top cheesecake with whipped topping before serving.

NUTRITIONAL INFO PER SERVING: Calories 254mg, Fat 21mg (Saturated Fat 10mg), Cholesterol 89mg, Carbohydrates 12mg (Fiber 1mg, Sugar 7mg), Sodium 123mg

COMMENTS:

1 *Look for cookies with less than 25mg sodium per ounce.*

2 *To reduce saturated fat, use trans-free margarine. Since it contains sodium (90mg per tablespoon), it will increase the sodium per serving to 153mg.*

3 *Mascarpone is similar to cream cheese. Although low in sodium, it has a lot of fat.*

4 *To reduce fat and keep sodium to a minimum, combine regular cream cheese with lower fat brands. For a comparison of cream cheese varieties, see* FOOD NOTE, *page 42.*

5 *Because sugar substitutes differ from sugar in sweetness, the amount needed depends on the sweetener used:*
   Splenda or sugar = 1 cup
   Fructose - ⅔ cup
   For additional information, see Sweeteners, *page 37.*

6 *See* Eggs and Egg Substitutes, *page 38, for a comparison of fat and sodium in eggs and egg substitutes.*

TOTAL SODIUM AND FAT PER INGREDIENT

Sodium:
   1 c LS cookies - 40mg
   8 oz mascarpone - 128mg
   8 oz cream cheese - 671mg
   8 oz LF cream cheese - 904mg
   3 eggs - 210mg
      or ¾ c egg substitute - 300mg
   1 c pumpkin - 12mg
   1 t cinnamon - 1mg
Fat (Sat Fat):
   1 c LS cookies - 4mg (0mg)
   ¼ c almonds - 30mg (2mg)
   ⅓ c NSA margarine - 43mg (8mg)
      or NSA butter - 64mg (43mg)
   8 oz mascarpone - 104mg (56mg)
   8 oz cream cheese - 56mg (36mg)
   8 oz LF cheese - 56mg (32mg)
   3 eggs - 15mg (5mg)
      or ¾ c egg substitute - 0mg
   1 c pumpkin - 1mg (0mg)
   1 c whipped topping - 8mg (8mg)

COMMENTS:

1 To lower fat, use 2 additional whole graham crackers in place of the nuts.

2 To reduce saturated fat, use trans-free margarine. Since it contains sodium (90mg per tablespoon), it will raise the sodium per serving to 159mg.

3 Mascarpone, similar to cream cheese is low in sodium, but has a lot of fat.

4 See FOOD NOTE, *page 42, for a comparison of fat and sodium in cream cheese varieties.*

5 Because sugar substitutes differ from sugar in sweetness, the amount needed depends on the sweetener used:
Crust: *Splenda or sugar - 3 tsp*
   Fructose - 2 tsp
Filling: *Splenda or sugar - 1 cup, Fructose - ⅔ cup*
   For additional information, see Sweeteners, *page 37.*

6 See Eggs and Egg Substitutes, *page 38, for a comparison of fat and sodium in eggs and egg substitutes.*

TOTAL SODIUM AND FAT PER INGREDIENT

Sodium:
4 oz graham crackers - 340mg
8 oz mascarpone - 128mg
8 oz cream cheese - 520mg
8 o LF cream cheese - 1,080mg
¾ c LF sour cream - 102mg
3 eggs - 210mg
   or ¾ c egg substitute - 300mg
Fat (Sat Fat):
4 oz grahams - 20mg (4mg)
¼ c pecans - 29mg (2mg)
⅓ c NSA margarine - 43mg (8mg)
   or NSA butter - 64mg (43mg)
8 oz mascarpone - 104mg (56mg)
8 oz cream cheese - 79mg (50mg)
8 oz LF cheese - 56mg (16mg)
¾ c LF sour cream - 20mg (12mg)
3 eggs - 15mg (5mg)
   or ¾ c egg substitute - 0mg

CHEESECAKE WITH NORTHWEST BERRY SAUCE

Sodium Per Serving – 137mg   Serves 16

Most cheesecakes have loads of fat and sodium. Although lightened up, this adaptation is both rich and creamy, and paired with the berry sauce, makes a beautiful presentation. Prepare the day before to allow the cheesecake to set up.

Crust:
4 ounces lowfat graham crackers (about 8 crackers)
¼ cup pecans or walnuts[1]
⅓ cup unsalted margarine or butter, melted[2]
2–3 teaspoons sugar substitute or sugar
½ teaspoon ground cinnamon

Filling:
1 (8-ounce) package mascarpone[3]
1 (8-ounce) package cream cheese

1 (8-ounce) package lowfat cream cheese or Neufchâtel[4]
¾ cup lowfat sour cream
⅔–1 cup sugar substitute or sugar[5]
3 eggs, lightly beaten, or ¾ cup egg substitute[6]
1 teaspoon vanilla extract
½ teaspoon almond extract
1 teaspoon lemon juice

Topping:
NORTHWEST BERRY SAUCE *(page 268)*, **chilled**

▸ Preheat oven to 350°F (180°C).

▸ *For the crust:* In a food processor, grind up crackers and pecans. Add margarine, sweetener, and cinnamon; press into bottom of springform pan. Bake for 10 minutes; remove and let cool.

▸ *For the filling:* Cream together the mascarpone, cream cheeses, and sweetener. Beat in eggs, one at a time; mix in vanilla, almond extract, and lemon juice. Pour over cracker crust.

▸ Bake on the lowest oven rack in a preheated oven for 1 hour; turn off heat and let sit another 30 minutes. Remove from oven and let cool.

▸ Cover tightly and refrigerate at least 5 hours or overnight.

▸ *For the topping:* Remove springform rim; spread **NORTHWEST BERRY SAUCE** on top of cheesecake.

NUTRITIONAL INFO PER SERVING: Calories 227mg, Fat 21mg (Saturated Fat 10mg), Cholesterol 87mg, Carbohydrates 5mg (Fiber 0mg, Sugar 2mg), Sodium 137mg

CHOCOLATE CHIP CHEESECAKE

Sodium Per Serving – 141mg   Serves 16

This is a luscious, sugar-free cheesecake that is the perfect ending to a holiday dinner. Allow at least 5 hours for the cheesecake to set up before serving.

Crust:

1½ cups coarsely ground chocolate graham crackers (about 12 whole crackers)[1]

2 tablespoons sugar substitute or sugar

¼–⅓ cup unsalted margarine or butter, melted[2]

Filling:

1 cup (8 ounces) cream cheese[3]

1 cup (8 ounces) lowfat cream cheese[3]

1 cup (8 ounces) mascarpone[4]

⅔–1 cup sugar substitute or sugar[5]

3 eggs, lightly beaten, or ¾ cup egg substitute[6]

½ cup lowfat sour cream

1 teaspoon vanilla extract

1 (6-ounce) package chocolate chips (about 1 cup)

▷ Preheat oven to 350°F (180°C). Adjust oven rack to lowest position.

▷ *For the crust:* Mix together graham crumbs, sweetener, and melted margarine. Press into bottom of springform pan and bake in a preheated oven for 10 minutes. Remove from oven and let cool slightly.

▷ *For the filling:* Cream together the cream cheeses, mascarpone, and sweetener. Beat in eggs, one at a time, stir in sour cream and vanilla. Mix in chocolate chips; pour into cookie crust.

▷ Bake on the lowest rack in a preheated oven for 1 hour; turn off heat and let sit another 30 minutes. Remove from oven and let cool.

▷ Cover tightly and refrigerate at least 5 hours or overnight.

NUTRITIONAL INFO PER SERVING: Calories 261mg, Fat 22mg (Saturated Fat 12mg), Cholesterol 86mg, Carbohydrates 12mg (Fiber 1mg, Sugar 7mg), Sodium 141mg

COMMENTS:

1 *Graham crackers (about 12 crackers) mixed with ⅓ cup unsweetened cocoa powder or a ready-made chocolate cookie crust may be used.*

2 *To reduce saturated fat, use trans-free margarine. Since it contains sodium (90mg per tablespoon), it will raise the sodium per serving to 162mg.*

3 *For a comparison of fat and sodium among cream cheese varieties, see FOOD NOTE, page 42.*

4 *Mascarpone, similar to cream cheese, is low in sodium, but has lots of fat.*

5 *Because sugar substitues differ from sugar in sweetness, the amount needed depends on the sweetener used.*

  Splenda or sugar - 1 cup
  Fructose - ⅔ cup
  For additional information, see Sweeteners, page 37.

6 *See Eggs and Egg Substitutes, page 38, for a comparison of fat and sodium in eggs and egg substitutes.*

TOTAL SODIUM AND FAT PER INGREDIENT

Sodium:
  1 c cookies - 40mg
  8 oz mascarpone - 128mg
  8 oz cream cheese - 671mg
  8 oz LF cream cheese - 904mg
  3 eggs - 210mg
    or ¾ c egg substitute - 300mg
  ½ c LF sour cream - 68mg
Fat (Sat Fat):
  1 c cookies - 4mg (0mg)
  ¼ NSA margarine - 32mg (6mg)
    or NSA butter - 48mg (32mg)
  8 oz mascarpone - 104mg (56mg)
  8 oz cream cheese - 56mg (36mg)
  8 oz LF cheese - 56mg (32mg)
  3 eggs - 15mg (5mg)
    or ¾ c egg substitute - 0mg
  ½ c LF sour cream - 14mg (8mg)
  1 c chocolate chips - 48mg (30mg)

COMMENTS:

1 *Phyllo (also spelled fillo) dough is paper-thin pastry that is usually found in the frozen foods section of most supermarkets. Most often, several sheets are used to make strudel.*

To keep the dough from drying out, speed is essential; cover the sheets not being used with a damp towel.

2 *To ensure flakiness, each layer is usually brushed with melted butter. Using butter-flavored spray instead of the real thing, substantially reduces the fat and calories.*

3 *See* Sweeteners, *page 37, for the difference in sweetness of sugar and sugar substitutes.*

APPLE STRUDEL

Sodium Per Serving – 129mg   Makes 2 strudels / Serves 8–10

This is one of my husband's favorite desserts. This yummy strudel goes together quickly with packaged phyllo dough and is made even better with the cream cheese frosting. To insure flakiness, melted butter or margarine is usually brushed on each layer of the phyllo dough. Instead, I like to use butter spray, which gives a buttery taste to the strudel, but without the fat.

6 (13-inch by 9-inch) sheets phyllo dough[1]

Butter-flavored spray, or ¼ cup unsalted margarine or butter, melted[2]

2 apples, sliced (such as Braeburn or Fuji)

1–2 tablespoons sugar substitute or sugar[3]

½ teaspoon ground cinnamon

⅛ teaspoon ground nutmeg

⅓ cup chopped walnuts

¼ cup currants or raisins

1–1½ cups CREAM CHEESE FROSTING *(page 267)*

▷ Preheat oven to 350°F (180°C). Coat a baking sheet with nontick cooking spray.

▷ Place one piece of phyllo on work surface with the long side facing you; spray lightly with butter-flavored spray. Place a second sheet on top and spray again. Repeat with a third sheet.

▷ Spread half the apples in the center of the dough to within ½ inch of the edges. Evenly sprinkle one-half the sweetener, cinnamon, nutmeg, walnuts, and currants. Roll up jelly-roll style, tucking in sides.

▷ Repeat with remaining phyllo dough and ingredients, making a second strudel.

▷ Place strudels, seam side down, on prepared baking sheet. Spray the tops and sides with butter-flavored spray. Cut two or three 1-inch diagonal vents in the top of each strudel. Bake for 20 to 25 minutes, until golden brown. Remove and cool.

▷ Cover with CREAM CHEESE FROSTING and serve.

NUTRITIONAL INFO PER SERVING: Calories 200mg, Fat 15mg (Saturated Fat 5mg), Cholesterol 21mg, Carbohydrates 15mg (Fiber 2mg, Sugar 4mg), Sodium 129mg

TOTAL SODIUM AND FAT PER INGREDIENT

Sodium:
6 sheets phyllo dough - 551mg
10 butter sprays - 25mg
2 apples - 2mg
⅓ c walnuts - 3mg
1 c CHEESE FROSTING - 447mg
Fat (Sat Fat):
6 sheets phyllo - 7mg (2mg)
⅓ c walnuts - 56mg (5mg)
1 c CHEESE FROSTING - 53mg (33mg)

VARIATION

BERRY STRUDEL

Instead of apples, mix 2 cups blueberries or blackberries with 1 tablespoon cornstarch; proceed as directed.

NUTRITIONAL INFO PER SERVING: Calories 196mg, Fat 15mg (Saturated Fat 5mg), Cholesterol 21mg, Carbohydrates 15mg (Fiber 2mg, Sugar 4mg), Sodium 129mg

PEACH AND BLUEBERRY CRISP

Sodium Per Serving – 1mg   Serves 8

Peaches and blueberries go together so well. I'm sure you'll love this crisp that uses both these wonderful fruits. Either fresh or frozen fruit works well.

4 cups blueberries, fresh or frozen

2½ cups sliced peaches, fresh or frozen (about 2 large peaches)

3–4 tablespoons sugar substitute or sugar[1]

2 tablespoons cornstarch

½ teaspoon ground cinnamon

¼ teaspoon ground nutmeg

Topping:

¾ cup all-purpose flour

⅓ cup unsalted margarine or butter[2]

3–4 tablespoons sugar substitute or sugar[1]

1 teaspoon ground cinnamon

½ teaspoon ground allspice

½ cup chopped pecans or walnuts[3]

▶ Preheat oven to 350ºF (180ºC). Coat the inside of an 8-inch square baking dish with nonstick cooking spray.

▶ Combine berries, peaches, sweetener, cornstarch, cinnamon, and nutmeg. Pour into prepared baking dish. Cover with foil and bake in a preheated oven for about 1 hour, or until juices bubble. Remove from oven.

▶ *For the topping:* Meanwhile, mix together the topping ingredients:

In a food processor – Place flour, margarine, sweetener, cinnamon, and allspice in food processor; pulse until crumbly. Add nuts and pulse just enough times to incorporate the nuts.

By hand – Mix together flour, cinnamon, and allspice; set aside. Cream together the margarine and sweetener; add flour mixture; mixing well. Stir in nuts.

▶ Sprinkle topping evenly over the baked fruit; return to oven and bake, uncovered, for 30 minutes, or until the topping is golden brown. Cool slightly and serve.

NUTRITIONAL INFO PER SERVING: Calories 206mg, Fat 11mg (Saturated Fat 1mg), Cholesterol 0mg, Carbohydrates 28mg (Fiber 4mg, Sugar 12mg), Sodium 1mg

COMMENTS:

[1] *Because sugar substitutes differ from sugar in sweetness, the amount needed depends on the sweetener used:*

Splenda or sugar - 4 tbsp
Fructose - 3 tablespoons
For additional information, see Sweeteners, page 37.

[2] *To reduce saturated fat, use trans-free margarine. Since it contains sodium (90mg per tablespoon), increase the sodium per serving to 61mg.*

To keep fat and sodium to a minimum, use a combination of trans free and unsalted.

[3] *Toasted nuts will add more flavor (see COOKING TIP, page 90, for directions for several ways to toast nuts).*

TOTAL SODIUM AND FAT PER INGREDIENT

Sodium:
4 c blueberries - 6mg
2 T cornstarch - 2mg
3/4 c flour - 2mg
½ t cinnamon - 1mg
½ t allspice - 1mg

Fat (Sat Fat):
4 c blueberries - 2mg (0mg)
2½ c peaches - 1mg (0mg)
¾ c flour - 1mg (0mg)
⅓ c NSA margarine - 43mg (8mg)
   or NSA butter - 64mg (43mg)
½ c pecans - 39mg (3mg)
   or walnuts - 38mg (4mg)

1 *Because sugar substitutes differ from sugar in sweetness, the amount needed depends on the sweetener used:*

Splenda or sugar - 3 tbsp
Fructose - 2 tbsp
For additional information, see Sweeteners, *page 37.*

2 *Most packaged egg roll wrappers have up to 450mg sodium per wrap, but a few manufacturers offer low-salt wraps, such as* **Melissa's** *(9mg per wrap) and* **Dynasty** *(60mg per wrap). See* RESOURCES, *page 272, for additional info.*

APPLE TURNOVERS

Sodium Per Serving – 18mg   Serves 4

Once I discovered low-salt egg roll wrappers, I've found many uses for them, including these quick and delicious individual pies. Here are several of our favorite fillings, each makes four pies.

2 apples (such as Braeburn or Fuji), peeled and diced

2–3 tablespoons sugar substitute or sugar[1]

½ teaspoon ground cinnamon

4 EGG ROLL WRAPS *(page 229)* **or low-salt egg roll wrappers[2]**

Oil, for frying

▶ In a small saucepan over low heat, add apples, sweetener, and cinnamon. Cook, stirring frequently, until apples are soft, about 5 minutes; mash with a fork to make a thick applesauce. Divide mixture and spread on one side of wrappers; moisten edges with water. Fold on the diagonal, forming a triangle, and press edges together with a fork.

▶ Fry in oil over medium-high heat until golden brown, about 2 to 3 minutes per side; drain on paper towels. If desired, sprinkle with confectioner's sugar or finely ground sugar substitute. *NOTE: To grind, place sweetener in a blender or food processor and pulse until a fine powder.*

NUTRITIONAL INFO PER TURNOVER (WITHOUT OIL): Calories 167mg, Fat 1mg (Saturated Fat 0mg), Cholesterol 0mg, Carbohydrates 38mg (Fiber 3mg, Sugar 8mg), Sodium 18mg

APRICOT-PEACH TURNOVERS

Sodium Per Serving – 19mg   Serves 4

This is a quick to prepare turnover using dried fruit.

¼ cup chopped dried apricots

¼ cup chopped dried peaches

2–3 teaspoons sugar substitute or sugar[1]

4 EGG ROLL WRAPS *(page 229)* **or low-salt egg roll wrappers[2]**

Oil, for frying

▶ In a small saucepan over low heat, add apricots, peaches, sweetener, and enough water to cover the fruit. Cook, stirring frequently, until fruit is soft, about 5 minutes. Divide mixture and spread on one side of wrappers; moisten edges with water. Fold on the diagonal, forming a triangle, and press edges together with a fork.

▶ Fry in oil over medium-high heat until golden brown, about 2 to 3 minutes per side; drain on paper towels. If desired, sprinkle with confectioner's sugar or finely ground sugar substitute. *NOTE: To grind, place sweetener in a blender or food processor and pulse until a fine powder.*

NUTRITIONAL INFO PER TURNOVER (WITHOUT OIL): CCalories 174mg, Fat 0mg (Saturated Fat 0mg), Cholesterol 0mg, Carbohydrates 39mg (Fiber 2mg, Sugar 10mg), Sodium 19mg

TOTAL SODIUM AND FAT PER INGREDIENT

Apple Turnovers:
Sodium:
 2 apples - 2mg
 ½ t cinnamon - 1mg
 4 egg roll wraps - 68mg
Fat (Sat Fat):
 4 egg roll wraps - 1mg (0mg)

Apricot-Peach Turnovers:
Sodium:
 ¼ c dried apricots - 4mg
 ¼ c dried peaches - 3mg
 4 egg roll wraps - 68mg
Fat (Sat Fat):
 4 egg roll wraps - 1mg (0mg)

DRIED CHERRY-ALMOND TURNOVERS

Sodium Per Serving – 81mg   Serves 4

Here is another yummy turnover filled with cream cheese, nuts and dried fruit.

6 tablespoons (3 ounces) cream cheese[1]

2–3 teaspoons sugar substitute or sugar

¾ cup dried cherries or dried cranberries

2 tablespoons slivered almonds, chopped

4 low-salt egg roll wrappers or Egg Roll Wraps (page 229)[2]

Oil, for frying

▶ Mix together cream cheese and sweetener. Divide and spread on one side of each wrapper; top with cherries and almonds. Moisten wrapper edges with water; fold on the diagonal, forming a triangle, and press edges together with a fork.

▶ Fry in oil over medium-high heat until golden brown, about 2 to 3 minutes per side. Drain on paper towels. If desired, sprinkle with confectioner's sugar or finely ground sugar substitute. *NOTE: To grind, place sweetener in a blender or food processor and pulse until a fine powder.*

NUTRITIONAL INFO PER TURNOVER (WITHOUT OIL): Calories 307mg, Fat 12mg (Saturated Fat 5mg), Cholesterol 23mg, Carbohydrates 47mg (Fiber 3mg, Sugar 14mg), Sodium 81mg

CREAM CHEESE AND JAM TURNOVERS

Sodium Per Serving – 80mg   Serves 4

Here is another cream cheese-based turnover that is made with your favorite jam.

6 tablespoons (3 ounces) cream cheese[1]

¾ cup fruit preserves (such as apricot, raspberry, or strawberry)

4 low-salt egg roll wrappers or Egg Roll Wraps (page 229)[2]

Oil, for frying

▶ Evenly divided cream cheese and spread on one side of each wrapper; top with one-fourth the preserves. Moisten wrapper edges with water; fold on the diagonal, forming a triangle, and press edges together with a fork.

▶ Fry in oil over medium-high heat until golden brown, about 2 to 3 minutes per side; drain on paper towels. If desired, sprinkle with confectioner's sugar or finely ground sugar substitute. *NOTE: To grind, place sweetener in a blender or food processor and pulse until a fine powder.*

NUTRITIONAL INFO PER TURNOVER (WITHOUT OIL): Calories 324mg, Fat 9mg (Saturated Fat 5mg), Cholesterol 23mg, Carbohydrates 59mg (Fiber 1mg, Sugar 31mg), Sodium 80mg

COMMENTS:

1 *To reduce fat and keep sodium to a minimum, combine regular or whipped cream cheese with lower fat brands. For a comparison of cream cheese varieties, see* FOOD NOTE, *page 42.*

2 *See* COMMENTS #1, *page 258, for info on low-salt egg roll wrappers.*

TOTAL SODIUM AND FAT PER INGREDIENT

Dried Cherry-Almond Turnovers:
Sodium:
  3 oz cream cheese - 252mg
    or whipped cheese - 195mg
  ⅔ c dried cherries - 2mg
  4 egg roll wraps - 68mg
Fat (Sat Fat):
  3 oz cream cheese - 30mg (19mg)
  ⅔ c dried cherries - 1mg (0mg)
  2 T almonds - 14mg (1mg)
  4 egg roll wraps - 1mg (0mg)

Cream Cheese/Jam Turnovers:
Sodium:
  3 oz cream cheese - 252mg
    or whipped cheese - 195mg
  4 egg roll wraps - 68mg
Fat (Sat Fat):
  3 oz cream cheese - 30mg (19mg)
  4 egg roll wraps - 1mg (0mg)

COMMENTS:

1 *Because sugar substitutes differ from sugar in sweetness, the amount needed depends on the sweetener used:*

Crème Brûleé:

Splenda or sugar - ⅓ cup

Fructose - ¼ cup

Topping:

Splenda or sugar - ⅓ cup

Fructose - ¼ cup

For additional information, see Sweeteners, *page 37.*

2 *If using a vanilla bean, combine half-and-half, sweetener, and whole vanilla bean; cook, stirring frequently, until sweetener is dissolved, about 5 minutes. Remove from heat and split vanilla bean lengthwise; scrape out the seeds. Stir seeds into the warm half-and-half; proceed as directed. See* COOKING TIP, *page 261, for info on storing and using used beans.*

3 *Crème brûlée traditionally has a burnt sugar crust, however, if you want to lower the sugar content, it is just as delicious without it.*

CREME BRULEE

Sodium Per Serving – 38mg   Serves 6

No gourmet cookbook would be complete without a recipe for crème brûlée (or burnt creme). This luscious custard is the perfect ending to a special meal. Allow at least 3 hours before serving for custard to chill. You can also prepare the custard the day before, cover, and keep refrigerated until ready to serve.

2 cups half-and-half or light cream

¼–⅓ cup sugar substitute or sugar[1]

4 large egg yolks

1 teaspoon vanilla extract, or 1 vanilla bean[2]

4–6 teaspoons sugar substitute or sugar (optional)[3]

▸ Preheat oven to 300°F (150°C). Arrange six 6-ounce ramekins in a large roasting pan.

▸ In a saucepan over medium heat, add half-and-half and sweetener; cook, stirring frequently, until sweetener is dissolved, about 5 minutes. Remove from heat.

▸ In a medium bowl, beat egg yolks and vanilla; gradually add warm cream, stirring constantly.

▸ Fill ramekins equally with custard. Pour enough hot water into the roasting pan to come halfway up the sides of the ramekins. Bake in a preheated oven for 30 to 45 minutes, until custard is set. Remove and refrigerate at least 3 hours.

▸ Before serving, sprinkle sweetener over each custard, spreading evenly to the edges. Use a kitchen torch or place ramekins under a preheated broiler until sweetener has melted and browned, about 2 minutes.

NUTRITIONAL INFO PER SERVING: Calories 144mg, Fat 12mg (Saturated Fat 7mg), Cholesterol 170mg, Carbohydrates 4mg (Fiber 0mg, Sugar 0mg), Sodium 38mg

---

TOTAL SODIUM AND FAT PER INGREDIENT

Sodium:

2 c half-and-half - 198mg

or light cream - 192mg

4 egg yolks - 32mg

Fat (Sat Fat):

2 c half-and-half - 56mg (35mg)

or light cream - 96mg (64mg)

4 egg yolks - 18mg (6mg)

VARIATIONS

GRAND MARNIER BRULEE

Mix 2 tablespoons Grand Marnier or other orange-flavored liqueur with the yolks, before adding the warm cream; proceed as directed.

NUTRITIONAL INFO PER SERVING: Calories 161mg, Fat 12mg (Saturated Fat 7mg), Cholesterol 170mg, Carbohydrates 6mg (Fiber 0mg, Sugar 2mg), Sodium 39mg

BRANDIED MOCHA BRULEE

Add 1½ teaspoons instant coffee granules[1] and 1 tablespoon brandy to the simmering cream; whisk until coffee is dissolved. Proceed as directed.

NUTRITIONAL INFO PER SERVING: Calories 151mg, Fat 12mg (Saturated Fat 7mg), Cholesterol 170mg, Carbohydrates 4mg (Fiber 0mg, Sugar 0mg), Sodium 39mg

COMMENTS:

1 *I like to keep a jar of instant espresso on hand for recipes that call for coffee, as the flavor is a little stronger than regular instant coffee.*

FOOD NOTE

ABOUT VANILLA BEANS:

Vanilla beans come from the *vanilla planifolia* orchid and their flavor varies depending on where they are grown. The most commonly available beans are called Bourbon and come from Madagascar. Other varieties are Mexican (more mellow than Bourbon) and Tahitian (more aromatic, but less flavorful than Bourbon).

Preparation: Depending on how much flavor you want, either use the whole bean or just a portion. To get the most flavor, slice the bean lengthwise and place it in the liquid you are flavoring. You can also scrape the seeds from the bean and place both the bean and seeds in the liquid. If you find the little black seeds offensive, strain through a fine mesh sieve.

Useage: Vanilla beans can be reused several times (unless a bean with the seeds removed has been in hot cream, then there will be little flavor left). After using, rinse and dry the bean before storing (see below). Before throwing out spent beans, place them in a jar with sugar or coffee to add a hint of vanilla.

Storage: Beans will keep indefinitely in an airtight container in a cool, dark place, but may lose some flavor over time as they dry out. Discard any beans that are moldy.

COMMENTS:

1 *For an alcohol-free pudding, substitute 1–2 tablespoons rum or brandy extract for the whiskey.*

2 *Store-bought French bread averages about 173mg sodium per ounce. Even though I prefer French, any low-salt bread may be used, including cinnamon-raisin. If using the latter, omit the raisins and cinnamon in the recipe.*

3 *To reduce saturated fat, use trans-free margarine. Since it contains sodium (90mg per tablespoon), it will increase the sodium per serving to 113mg.*

4 *See Eggs and Egg Substitutes, page 37, for a comparison of eggs and egg substitutes.*

4 *Because sugar substitutes differ from sugar in sweetness, the amount needed depends on the sweetener used.*
Bread Pudding:
   Splenda or sugar - 1 cup
   Fructose - ⅔ cup
Whiskey Sauce:
   Splenda or sugar - ½ cup
   Fructose - 5 tablespoons
   For additional information, see Sweeteners, *page 37.*

TOTAL SODIUM AND FAT PER INGREDIENT

Sodium:
½ c raisins - 5mg
1 loaf FRENCH BREAD - 154mg
1½ c LF milk - 172mg
½ c half-and-half - 48mg
3 eggs + 1 yolk - 218mg
   or ¾ c egg substitute - 100mg

Fat (Sat Fat):
1 loaf FRENCH BREAD - 7mg (1mg)
1½ c LF milk - 7mg (3mg)
½ c half-and-half - 16mg (8mg)
⅓ c NSA margarine - 48mg (9mg)
   or NSA butter - 72mg (48mg)
3 eggs + 1 yolk - 17mg (5mg)
   or ¾ c egg substitute - 0mg
2 T whipped topping - 1mg (1mg)

BREAD PUDDING WITH WHISKEY SAUCE

Sodium Per Serving – 59mg   Serves 10–12

I love bread pudding, but it is usually full of fat, sugar and sodium. This lightened up version is so decadent, you'll never miss the bad stuff.

½ cup raisins or currants
¼ cup whiskey or bourbon[1]
1 loaf No Knead French Bread *(page 216)* **or low-salt bread, broken into pieces[2]**
1½ cups lowfat milk
½ cup half-and-half or light cream
2 tablespoons unsalted margarine or butter, melted[3]
3 eggs, or ¾ cup egg substitute[4]
1 egg yolk
⅔–1 cup sugar substitute or sugar[5]

1 teaspoon vanilla extract
¼ teaspoon ground cinnamon
⅛ teaspoon ground nutmeg

Whiskey Sauce:
¼ cup (½ stick) unsalted margarine or butter[3]
5–8 tablespoons sugar substitute or sugar[5]
2 tablespoons frozen lowfat whipped topping, thawed
2–4 tablespoons whiskey or bourbon[1]

▸ Preheat oven to 350ºF (180ºC). Coat the inside of 9x13-inch baking dish with nonstick cooking spray.

▸ Soak raisins in ¼ cup whiskey for 30 minutes.

▸ Place bread in a large bowl. In another bowl, mix together milk, half-and-half, 2 tablespoons margarine, eggs, sweetener, vanilla, cinnamon, and nutmeg; pour over bread. Stir in raisins and let sit for 15 to 20 minutes to allow the bread to absorb the whiskey mixture.

▸ Transfer to prepared baking dish; bake in a preheated oven for about 45 minutes, or until pudding is set and a knife inserted in the center comes out clean.

▸ *For the Whiskey Sauce:* Melt ¼ cup margarine in a saucepan over low heat; stir in sweetener, whipped topping, and whiskey. Heat through; serve pudding with warm sauce on top.

NUTRITIONAL INFO PER SERVING: Calories 244mg, Fat 9mg (Saturated Fat 3mg), Cholesterol 90mg, Carbohydrates 29mg (Fiber 1mg, Sugar 8mg), Sodium 59mg

FRUIT DESSERTS

ICE CREAM WITH BLUEBERRIES AND GRAND MARNIER

Sodium Per Serving – 52mg   Serves 4

This is a simple, yet elegant dessert and the added Grand Marnier is exquisite. For a beautiful presentation, place in a tall parfait or wine glass. If you want to jazz it up even more, add a little chocolate sauce or toasted pecans before serving.

1 cup fresh blueberries[1]

¼ cup Grand Marnier or other orange-flavored liqueur

4 scoops nonfat or lowfat vanilla ice cream or frozen yogurt

▸ Soak blueberries in Grand Marnier for 15 minutes or more.

▸ Place a scoop of ice cream in a glass goblet, top with one-fourth of the blueberries and Grand Marnier mixture. Serve with SHORTBREAD COOKIES (page 264), if desired.

NUTRITIONAL INFO PER SERVING: Calories 159mg, Fat 0mg (Saturated Fat 0mg), Cholesterol 0mg, Carbohydrates 27mg (Fiber 1mg, Sugar 11mg), Sodium 52mg

STRAWBERRY AND AMARETTO PARFAIT

Sodium Per Serving – 61mg   Serves 4

If you love strawberries and chocolate, you're going to enjoy this quick and delicious dessert.

4 scoops nonfat or lowfat vanilla ice cream or frozen yogurt

1 cup strawberries, hulled and sliced

4 tablespoons Amaretto or other almond-flavored liqueur[2]

4–8 tablespoons low-salt chocolate sauce[3]

Whipped cream (optional)

▸ Place a scoop of ice cream in a glass goblet; top with ¼ cup strawberries, 1 tablespoon Amaretto, and 1–2 tablespoons chocolate sauce. Top with whipped topping and serve.

NUTRITIONAL INFO PER SERVING: Calories 162mg, Fat 0mg (Saturated Fat 0mg), Cholesterol 0mg, Carbohydrates 28mg (Fiber 1mg, Sugar 12mg), Sodium 61mg

---

COMMENTS:

1 *Sliced strawberries or pears are also nice with Grand Marnier.*

2 *Amaretto also goes well with raspberries, blueberries, or sliced peaches.*

3 *Most chocolate sauce has added sodium (65mg per tablespoon) and fat. Two low-salt brands are* **Steel's** *(16mg) and* **Wax Orchards** *(40mg, and is also fat free). See RESOURCES, page 272 for more info.*

TOTAL SODIUM AND FAT PER INGREDIENT

Ice Cream with Berries:
Sodium:
  1 c blueberries - 1mg
  ¼ c Grand Marnier - 6mg
  4 scoops NF ice cream - 200mg
  or LF ice cream - 50mg

Strawberry/Amaretto Parfait:
Sodium:
  4 scoops NF ice cream - 200mg
  or LF ice cream - 4mg (2mg)
  1 c strawberries - 2mg
  4 T Amaretto - 6mg
  ½ c LS chocolate sauce - 35mg

COMMENTS:

1 *To reduce saturated fat, use trans-free margarine. Since it contains sodium (90mg per tablespoon), it will increase the sodium per cookie to 45mg.*

To keep fat and sodium to a minimum, use a combination of trans-free and unsalted.

2 *Because sugar substitutes differ from sugar in sweetness, the amount needed depends on the sweetener used.*

Splenda or sugar - ½ cup
Fructose - 5 tablespoons
For additional information, see Sweeteners, *page 37.*

SHORTBREAD COOKIES

Sodium Per Serving – 0mg   Makes 16 cookies

The secret to these tender, melt-in-your mouth cookies is not overworking the dough. To reduce the saturated fat, I use half butter and half margarine.

1 cup (2 sticks) unsalted margarine, butter, or a combination of each[1]

5–8 tablespoons sugar substitute or sugar[2]

2 teaspoons vanilla extract

2 cups all-purpose flour

▸ Preheat oven to 350°F (180°C).

▸ Cream together margarine, sweetener, and vanilla until light and fluffy; gradually add flour, mixing well, until it forms a soft dough. *NOTE: To make dough easier to handle, cover and refrigerate for 30 minutes.*

▸ Form into small balls, place on a baking sheet, 1 inch apart; flatten with a fork. Bake in a preheated oven for 15 to 20 minutes, or until lightly browned.

NUTRITIONAL INFO PER COOKIE: Calories 144mg, Fat 10mg (Saturated Fat 5mg), Cholesterol 16mg, Carbohydrates 12mg (Fiber 0mg, Sugar 0mg), Sodium 0mg

---

VARIATION

HAZELNUT SHORTBREAD COOKIES

Add ½ cup ground hazelnuts to the dough; proceed as directed.

NUTRITIONAL INFO PER COOKIE: Calories 159mg, Fat 12mg (Saturated Fat 5mg), Cholesterol 16mg, Carbohydrates 12mg (Fiber 1mg, Sugar 0mg), Sodium 0mg

---

TOTAL SODIUM AND FAT PER INGREDIENT
Sodium:
 2 c flour - 6mg
Fat (Sat Fat):
 ½ c NSA margarine - 64mg (12mg)
 ½ c NSA butter - 96mg (64mg)
 2 c flour - 2mg (0mg)

CHOCOLATE CHIP COOKIES

Sodium Per Serving – 3mg   Makes 4 dozen

These are some of the best low-salt cookies you'll ever eat . . . see if you don't agree.

½ cup (1 stick) unsalted margarine or butter[1]

1–1½ cups sugar substitute or sugar[2]

½ teaspoon vanilla extract

½ teaspoon almond extract

2 eggs, or ½ cup egg substitute[3]

2 cups all-purpose flour

2 teaspoons no-salt-added baking powder[4]

1 (6-ounce) package semi-sweet chocolate chips (about 1 cup)

½ cup chopped walnuts

▸ Preheat oven to 350°F (180°C).

▸ In a large bowl, beat the margarine, sweetener, vanilla, and almond extract until creamy; beat in eggs, one at a time.

▸ In another bowl, combine flour and baking powder; gradually add to the creamed mixture, mixing well after each addition. Gently stir in chocolate morsels and walnuts.

▸ Using a tablespoon, drop dough onto a baking sheet; bake in a preheated oven for 12 to 15 minutes, until golden brown.

NUTRITIONAL INFO PER COOKIE: Calories 67mg, Fat 4mg (Saturated Fat 1mg), Cholesterol 9mg, Carbohydrates 7mg (Fiber 1mg, Sugar 2mg), Sodium 3mg

NO-FLOUR PEANUT BUTTER COOKIES

Sodium Per Serving – 5mg   Makes 2 dozen

A similar version of this recipe is popping up all over, due to the popularity of low-carb foods. Not only are these low in carbs, but also low in sodium. If you like peanut butter, you'll love these tasty delights.

1 cup unsalted crunchy peanut butter

1 egg, or ¼ cup egg substitute[3]

⅔–1 cup sugar substitute or sugar[2]

1 teaspoon vanilla extract

▸ Preheat oven to 350°F (180°C).

▸ Mix together all ingredients. Drop by heaping teaspoons onto a baking sheet; flatten each cookie slightly with a fork.

▸ Bake in a preheated oven for 15 minutes, or until golden brown. *NOTE: Cookies will crisp up as they cool.*

NUTRITIONAL INFO PER COOKIE: Calories 72mg, Fat 6mg (Saturated Fat 1mg), Cholesterol 18mg, Carbohydrates 2mg (Fiber 1mg, Sugar 1mg), Sodium 5mg

---

COMMENTS:

1 *To reduce saturated fat, use trans-free margarine. Since it contains sodium (90mg per tablespoon), it will increase the sodium per serving to 15mg.*

2 *Because sugar substitutes differ from sugar in sweetness, the amount needed depends on the sweetener used.*
Chocolate Chip Cookies:
   Splenda / sugar - 1½ cups
   Fructose - 1 cup
No-Flour PB Cookies:
   Splenda or sugar - 1 cup
   Fructose - ⅔ cup
   For additional information,
see Sweeteners, *page 37.*

3 *See* Eggs and Egg Substitutes, *page 38, for a comparison of fat and sodium in eggs and egg substitutes.*

4 *For info on NSA baking powder, see* COMMENTS #1, *page 222.*

TOTAL SODIUM AND FAT PER INGREDIENT

Chocolate Chip Cookies:
Sodium:
  2 eggs - 140mg
    or ½ c egg substitute - 200mg
  2 c flour - 6mg
  ½ c walnuts - 4mg
Fat (Sat Fat):
  ½ c NSA margarine - 64mg (12mg)
    or NSA butter - 96mg (64mg)
  2 eggs - 10mg (3mg)
    or ½ c egg substitute - 0mg
  2 c flour - 2mg (0mg)
  1 c chocolate chips - 48mg (30mg)
  ½ c walnuts - 74mg (7mg)

No-Flour PB Cookies:
Sodium:
  1 c NSA peanut butter - 40mg
  1 egg - 70mg
    or ¼ egg substitute - 100mg
Fat (Sat Fat):
  1 c NSA PB - 128mg (24mg)
  1 egg - 5mg (2mg)
    or ¼ egg substitute - 0mg

COMMENTS:

1 *For those who are watching their egg intake and use egg substitutes, I've tried using them to make the curd, but the texture and consistency of the curd is unsatisfactory.*

2 *Because sugar substitutes differ from sugar in sweetness, the amount needed depends on the sweetener used:*

  Splenda or sugar - 1 cup
  Fructose - ⅔ cup

  For additional information, see Sweeteners, page 37.

3 *To reduce saturated fat, use trans-free margarine. Since it contains sodium (90mg per tablespoon), it will increase the sodium per serving to 43mg.*

LEMON CURD

Sodium Per Serving – 13mg   Makes about 2 cups

If you've never made lemon curd, you're in for a treat. It tastes similar to the filling in lemon meringue pie and is easy to make. Use it as a spread on breads and muffins, as a filling for lemon tarts, or between cake layers. This also makes a great hostess or Christmas gift, just ladle into decorative jars and seal (will keep for up to a week in the refrigerator).

4 teaspoons finely grated lemon peel, use the finest grate (about 4 lemons)

⅔ cup fresh lemon juice (about 4 lemons)

3 eggs[1]

⅔–1 cup sugar substitute or sugar[2]

⅓ cup unsalted butter or margine, melted[3]

▸ Place the lemon peel, lemon juice, eggs, and sweetener in a blender; whirl until well mixed. While blender is running, slowly add the melted butter.

▸ Pour into saucepan and cook over medium heat, stirring constantly, until it thickens to the consistency of pudding, about 5 minutes. Ladle into sterilized jars, screw on lids, and let cool. Keep refrigerated up to a week.

NUTRITIONAL INFO PER 2 TABLESPOONS: Calories 51mg, Fat 5mg (Saturated Fat 3mg), Cholesterol 51mg, Carbohydrates 1mg (Fiber 0mg, Sugar 0mg), Sodium 13mg

---

VARIATIONS

ORANGE CURD

Use orange instead of lemon for the peel and juice.

NUTRITIONAL INFO PER 2 TABLESPOONS: Calories 51mg, Fat 5mg (Saturated Fat 3mg), Cholesterol 51mg, Carbohydrates 1mg (Fiber 0mg, Sugar 0mg), Sodium 13mg

LIME CURD

Usc lime instead of lemon for the peel and juice.

NUTRITIONAL INFO PER 2 TABLESPOONS: Calories 51mg, Fat 5mg (Saturated Fat 3mg), Cholesterol 51mg, Carbohydrates 1mg (Fiber 0mg, Sugar 0mg), Sodium 13mg

TOTAL SODIUM AND FAT PER INGREDIENT

Sodium:
  ⅔ c lemon juice - 2mg
  3 eggs - 210mg
Fat (Sat Fat):
  3 eggs - 15mg (5mg)
  ⅓ c NSA butter- 64mg (43mg)
    or NSA margarine - 43mg (8mg)

GRANDMA'S ITALIAN FROSTING

Sodium Per Serving – 6mg   Makes 2 cups

Although high in fat, I must share my Italian grandmother's luscious frosting. It is absolutely the best . . . wonderfully creamy and not too sweet!

1 cup milk[1]

5 tablespoons all-purpose flour

½ cup (1 stick) unsalted butter or margarine, at room temperature[2]

½ cup shortening[3]

⅔–1 cup sugar substitute or sugar[4]

1 tablespoon vanilla extract

▶ In a small saucepan over medium heat, cook the milk and flour, stirring frequently, until a thick paste; remove and cool.

▶ In a bowl, cream together the butter, shortening, and sweetener; add the cooled flour mixture and beat until the consistency of whipped cream. Mix in vanilla and spread on cake; refrigerate until ready to use.

NUTRITIONAL INFO PER 2 TABLESPOONS: Calories 126mg, Fat 12mg (Saturated Fat 5mg), Cholesterol 17mg, Carbohydrates 5mg (Fiber 0mg, Sugar 1mg), Sodium 6mg

CREAM CHEESE FROSTING

Sodium Per Serving – 56mg   Makes 1½ cups

This creamy, slightly sweet frosting is delicious on streudels, turnovers, cinnamon rolls, and carrot cakes.

8 ounces (1 cup) cream cheese[5]

½–¾ cup sugar substitute or sugar[4]

1 teaspoon vanilla extract

▶ Mix cream cheeses and sweetener together until well blended and creamy; stir in vanilla. Spread on baked item; refrigerate until ready to use.

NUTRITIONAL INFO PER 2 TABLESPOONS: Calories 67mg, Fat 7mg (Saturated Fat 4mg), Cholesterol 21mg, Carbohydrates 1mg (Fiber 0mg, Sugar 0mg), Sodium 56mg

---

VARIATION

CHOCOLATE CREAM CHEESE FROSTING

Add 2 tablespoons chocolate sauce and refrigerate 15 minutes or more before using, to allow frosting to set up.

NUTRITIONAL INFO PER 2 TABLESPOONS: Calories 71mg, Fat 7mg (Saturated Fat 4mg), Cholesterol 21mg, Carbohydrates 2mg (Fiber 0mg, Sugar 1mg), Sodium 59mg

---

COMMENTS:

1 Lowfat or nonfat milk may be used, but it won't taste as rich.

2 While I think this tastes best with butter, trans-free or unsalted margarine may be used. If using trans-free, the sodium per serving will increase to 51mg.

3 Although many of you haven't used shortening for ages, in this case it's worth it.

4 Because sugar substitutes differ from sugar in sweetness, the amount needed depends on the sweetener used:

Grandma's Italian Frosting:
  Splenda or sugar - 1 cup
  Fructose - ⅔ cup
Cream Cheese Frosting:
  Splenda or sugar - ¾ cup
  Fructose - ½ cup
  For additional information, see Sweeteners, page 37.

5 To reduce fat and keep sodium to a minimum, combine regular or whipped cream cheese with lower fat brands. For a comparison of cream cheese varieties, see FOOD NOTE, page 43.

TOTAL SODIUM AND FAT PER INGREDIENT

Grandma's Italian Frosting:
Sodium:
  1 c milk - 98mg
Fat (Sat Fat):
  1 c milk - 8mg (5mg)
  ½ c NSA butter - 92mg (58mg)
    or NSA margarine - 64mg (12mg)
  ½ c shortening - 96mg (24mg)

Cream Cheese Frosting:
Sodium:
  8 oz cream cheese - 671mg
Fat (Sat Fat):
  8 oz cream cheese - 79mg (50mg)

NORTHWEST BERRY SAUCE

Sodium Per Serving – 0mg   Makes about 2 cups

This yummy sauce is the perfect topping for cheesecake, ice cream, or low-salt pound cake. For added interest, I add a little brandy.

2 cups fresh or frozen blueberries, raspberries, blackberries, or any combination of berries

3–4 tablespoons sugar substitute or sugar[1]

⅛ teaspoon ground cinnamon

Pinch freshly ground nutmeg

2 tablespoons brandy (optional)[2]

1 teaspoon cornstarch, mixed with 1 tablespoon water to make a paste

▷ In a small saucepan over medium heat, bring blueberries, sweetener, cinnamon, nutmeg, and brandy to a boil; cook, stirring constantly, until sweetener dissolves and juices from the berries release, 3 to 5 minutes.

▷ Slowly add cornstarch paste, stirring constantly, until desired consistency (sauce will thicken as it cools). Serve warm or cold.

NUTRITIONAL INFO PER 2 TABLESPOONS: Calories 18mg, Fat 0mg (Saturated Fat 0mg), Cholesterol 0mg, Carbohydrates 4mg (Fiber 1mg, Sugar 2mg), Sodium 0mg

APPENDIX

LOWEST SODIUM RECIPES

APPETIZERS
30mg or less:
Mushroom Pâté with Port and Almonds (p. 44) – 1mg
Stuffed Mushrooms (p. 46) – 2mg
Guacamole (p. 42) – 3mg
Crispy Pork and Shrimp Wontons (p. 52) – 11mg
Caramelized Onion Dip (p. 41) – 12mg
Spicy Roasted Red Pepper Hummus (p. 40) – 13mg
Cheesy Spinach Rolls (p. 49) – 16mg
Spinach and Feta Wontons (p. 51) – 21mg
Salmon Tortilla Roll-Ups (p. 48) – 24mg
Spicy and Cheesy Tortilla Swirls (p. 48) – 24mg
Spinach and Goat Cheese Rolls (p. 49) – 30mg

SOUPS
100mg or less:
Split Pea Soup (p. 64) – 41mg
Curried Yam and Apple Bisque (p. 55) – 45mg
Creamy Asparagus Soup (p. 54) – 50mg
Pumpkin Jalapeño Soup (p. 63) – 54mg
Mushroom Bisque with Brandy (p. 59) – 62mg
Minestrone (p. 65) – 66mg
Hearty Black Bean Soup (p. 69) – 67mg
Artichoke and Leek Soup (p. 56) – 79mg
Spicy Split Pea Soup (p. 64) – 80mg
Cream of Leek Soup (p. 61) – 81mg
Mushroom-Leek Soup (p. 61) – 82mg
Creamed Broccoli with Mandarin Orange (p. 57) – 83mg
Grandma's Lentil Soup (p. 66) – 96mg

SALADS
Side Salads - 50mg or less:
Grand Marnier Fruit Salad (p. 80) – 7mg
Four Bean Salad (p. 73) – 15mg
Fruit Salad w/Vanilla Yogurt (p. 80) – 17mg
Mixed Greens with Avocado and Orange (p. 84) – 20mg
Sweet and Sour Cole Slaw (p. 75) – 26mg
Spicy Cole Slaw (p. 75) – 27mg
Black Bean and Pepper Salad (p. 72) – 27mg
Bean, Pepper and Chèvre Salad (p. 72) – 37mg
German Potato Salad (p. 78) – 44mg
Warm Potato Salad (p. 78) – 44mg
Spinach, Dried Cranberries and Chèvre (p. 85) – 49mg

Main Course Salads - 50mg or less:
Avocado, Apple, Dates and Jicama Salad (p. 88) – 36mg
Chicken, Apple and Pecan Tossed Salad (p. 88) – 47mg

SALAD DRESSINGS
30mg or less:
Poppy Seed Dressing (p. 91) – 0mg
Orange Vinaigrette (p. 91) – 12mg
Caesar Dressing (p. 86) – 11mg
The Best Vinaigrette, p. 92 – 30mg
Raspberry Vinaigrette (p. 92) – 30mg

MAIN DISHES
Beef, Veal, Lamb and Pork – 90mg or less:
Pork Chops with Raspberry Sauce (p. 126) – 53mg
Rib-Eye Steak with Brandied Mushrooms (p. 120) – 66mg
Fruit Stuffed Pork Tenderloin (p. 127) – 70mg
Pan-Seared Steaks with Tarragon Sauce (p. 119) – 71mg
Veal Marsala (p. 124) – 78mg
Top Sirloin with Mustard Sauce (p. 121) – 83mg
Beef, Pork and Veal Meatloaf (p. 116) – 89mg

Fish and Seafood – 95mg or less:
Tuna in Marsala Sauce (p. 131) – 46mg
Broiled Salmon with Pesto (p. 134) – 89mg
Orange Roughy in Creamy Leek Sauce (p. 129) – 93mg
Horseradish Grilled Salmon (p. 133) – 94mg

Meatless – 90mg or less:
Creamy Mushroom Pasta (p. 152) – 35mg
Quick Pesto (p. 154) – 52mg
Sun-Dried Tomato Pesto (p. 154) – 71mg
Veggie Burgers (p. 143) – 85mg

Poultry – 95mg or less:
Chicken-Mushroom Stuffed Potatoes (p. 147) – 73mg
Fried Chicken (p. 96) – 77mg
Oven-Baked Chicken (p. 96) – 77mg
Fried Chicken with Country Gravy (p. 97) – 78mg
Yummy Turkey Tacos (p. 166) – 79mg
Chicken-Mushroom Alfredo (p. 152) – 80mg
Herb Roasted Game Hens (p. 118) – 84mg
Chicken Breasts with Shallot Sauce (p. 106) – 85mg
Marsala Chicken (p. 104) – 85mg
Chicken Piri Piri (p. 108) – 86mg
Chicken in Mushroom-Asparagus Sauce (p. 105) – 88mg
Roasted Game Hens with Orange Sauce (p. 118) – 88mg
Turkey Stroganoff (p. 112) – 91mg
Sweet and Sour Turkey Meatloaf (p. 116) – 91mg
Creamy Cheesy Chicken Stuffed Potatoes (p. 147) – 91mg
Chicken Paprika with Tomato Cream (p. 103) – 94mg
Chicken Pot Pie (p. 114) – 94mg
Chicken Tagine with Eggplant (p. 117) – 94mg
Mushroom Chicken Paprikash (p. 103) – 95mg

SIDE DISHES
25mg or less:

Caramelized Shallots and Asparagus (p. 171) – 3mg
Basic Steamed Rice (p. 195) – 6mg
Wild Mushroom and Walnut Sauté (p. 179) – 6mg
Wild Mushrooms in Madeira Sauce (p. 179) – 6mg
Asparagus with Tarragon Vinaigrette (p. 170) – 9mg
Green Beans/Leeks in Tarragon Sauce (p. 178) – 9mg
Succotash (p. 187) – 9mg
Dried Fruit and Curry Rice Dressing (p. 198) – 10mg
Green Beans in Shallot Sauce (p. 178) – 10mg
Baked French Fries (p. 187) – 11mg
Corn, Leek and Snap Pea Sauté (p. 176) – 11mg
Pan-Roasted Potatoes (p. 184) – 15mg
Quick Refried Beans (p. 192) – 17mg
Herbed Couscous (p. 194) – 17mg
Refried Black Beans (p. 192) – 17mg
Couscous with Apricots and Pine Nuts (p. 194) – 18mg
Creamy Tarragon Green Beans (p. 178) – 18mg
Rice Pilaf with Pecans and Currants (p. 196) – 18mg
Wild Rice and Cranberry Pilaf (p. 196) – 18mg

BREAKFAST
100mg or less:

Blueberry Pancakes (p. 209) – 80mg
Potato Pancakes (p. 209) – 31mg
Breakfast Tacos (p. 205) – 49mg
Potato Crusted Breakfast Pizza (p. 207) – 65mg
The Mixup (p 202) – 82mg

SANDWICHES AND WRAPS
200mg or less:

Veggie Sandwiches with Hummus (p. 212) – 109mg
Cream Cheese and Veggie Sandwich (p. 212) – 121mg
Sloppy Joes (p. 213) – 122mg
Tuna Sandwiches (p. 210) – 161mg
Open-Faced Avocado-Tuna Grill (p. 210) – 184mg
Curried Chicken Salad Sandwich (p. 211) – 184mg

ANYTIME QUICKIES
100mg or less:

Fresh Fruit Smoothie (p. 214) – 2mg
Yogurt Gruel with Granola and Nuts – 90mg

BREADS & BAKED GOODS
50mg or less:

Lemon Currant Scones (p. 224) – 15mg
Orange Currant Scones (p. 224) – 15mg
Blueberry Muffins (p. 225) – 17mg
Chocolate Chip Scones (p. 224) – 17mg
Rosemary Herb Bread (p. 217) – 18mg
No Knead French Bread (p. 216) – 19mg
Mango Bread (p 221) – 20mg
Poppy Seed Muffins with Lemon Glaze (p. 226) – 22mg
Jalapeño Cornbread (p. 222) – 24mg
Olive-Sage Bread (p. 218) – 24mg
Everyday Multigrain Bread (p 218) – 25mg
Cornbread (p. 222) – 31mg
Herbed Buttermilk Biscuits (p. 223) – 31mg
Quick Herbal Flatbread/Pizza Crust (p. 219) – 37mg
Cinnamon Buns (p. 22) – 49mg

CONDIMENTS, SAUCES AND OTHER BASICS
25mg or less:

Blackberry Wine Sauce (p 239) – 1mg
Cranberry-Orange Relish w/Grand Marnier (p 234) – 1mg
Mango Salsa (p. 235) – 2mg
Pineapple-Mango Salsa (p. 235) – 2mg
Sherried Raisin Sauce (p. 239) – 2mg
Mucho Caliente Fresh Tomato Salsa (p. 236) – 3mg
Black Bean-Mango Salsa (p. 235) – 4mg
Fresh Corn Relish (p. 234) – 5mg
Low-Sodium Pickles (p. 233) – 5mg
Basil Mayonnaise (p 231) – 8mg
Chili Sauce (p. 238) – 7mg
Egg Roll Wraps (p 229) – 11mg
Tex-Mex Hot Salsa (p. 236) – 11mg
Blender Mayonnaise (p 231) – 15mg
Chipotle Mayonnaise (p 231) – 18mg
Basic Pie Crust (p 229) – 20mg
Bernaise Sauce (p 240) – 22mg
Blender Hollandaise (p 240) – 22mg
Chicken or Beef Stock (p. 232) – 20mg
Orange Hollandaise (p 240) – 22mg

DESSERTS
25mg or less:

Shortbread Cookies (p. 264) – 0mg
Hazelnut Shortbread Cookies (p. 264) – 0mg
Peach and Blueberry Crisp (p. 257) – 1mg
Chocolate Chip Cookies (p. 265) – 3mg
No-Flour Peanut Butter Cookies (p. 265) – 5mg
Chocolate Decadence Torte (p. 248) – 9mg
Sponge Cake (p. 252) – 13mg
Apple Turnovers (p. 258) – 18mg
Apricot-Peach Turnovers (p. 258) – 19mg
Absolutely The Best Berry Pie (p. 243) – 21mg
Carrot Cake (p. 250) – 22mg

LOW-SODIUM FOOD RESOURCES

There is a wide selection of low-salt foods available in most supermarkets, health food stores, and online resources. Availability of products or variations in nutritional information may occur dependent upon geographic region, local suppliers, and production changes. The following is a partial listing of manufacturers and online grocers that offer low-salt products. For additional products and manufacturers, check the latest edition of the **Pocket Guide to Low Sodium Foods** or our website, **www.lowsaltfoods.com**.

NOTE: Unless otherwise specified, no endorsement is intended of companies and their products, nor is any adverse judgment implied for companies and products not mentioned.

LOW-SALT PRODUCTS

BY MANUFACTURER

The following brands are carried by many grocers. Also listed are the products they offer and some online sources *(see page 274 for online info)*.

Adios Carbs
LS, low carb tortillas
Available from LowCarbCutters

American Prairie
NSA beans

Athenos
Basil and Tomato Feta

Bearitos
NSA, lowfat refried beans
Available from The Better Health Store, Healthy Heart Market, SaltWatcher

Blazing Blends
NSA chile seasonings
Available from Blazing Blends

Colavita
Lower salt pasta sauce

Dynasty
LS egg roll wrappers

Eden Organic
NSA beans, tomatoes
Available from The Better Health Store, Healthy Heart Market, Mother Nature, SaltWatcher, Shop Natural, and Strictly Natural

Gwaltney
LS bacon
Available from Saltwatcher

Health Valley
NSA and LS vegetarian chili
Available from Health Valley and online grocers

Melissa's
LS egg roll wrappers
Available from Melissa's

Mojave
NSA taco seasoning

Morning Select
LS cream cheese

Pomi
NSA tomatoes

Natural Value
LS beans

S&W
LS tomatoes

Safeway Select
LS bacon
Available at Safeway stores

Santa Barbara
LS salsa

Steel's
NSA chutney and sauces
Available from eDiet Shop, eFood Pantry, and LowCarbCutters

The Spice Hunter
NSA chili powder
Available from Mother Nature

Vogue Cuisine
Chicken, onion, and vegetable base
Available from Vogue Cuisine

Walden Farms
LS low carb alfredo sauce
Available from Walden Farms and LowCarbCutters

Welshire Farms
LS bacon and uncured ham
Available from SaltWatcher

Westbrae Natural
LS beans
Available from The Better Health Store, Shop Natural, and Strictly Natural

BY FOOD TYPE

Listed below are some brands of low-salt foods used in many of *The Hasty Gourmet™* recipes.

Alfredo sauce
Walden Farms

Bacon

Bar-S	Oscar Meyer
Corn King	Smithfield's
Farmland	

Bouillon / Bases

Bernard	Featherweight
Diamond Crystal	Gourmet Award
Emes	

Bread

Alvarado St. Bakery	
Damascus	Giant
Ener-G	Nature's Path
Food for Life	Rudolph's
Freihofer	Vermont Bread Co
French Meadow	

Bread crumbs

4C	New World Foods
Ener-G	Taam
Edward & Sons	

Broth / Soup

Bernard	Hain
Campbell's	Shelton's
Croydon House	

Cheese

Alpine Lace	Le Chevrot
Bel Gioioso	Lucerne
Black Diamond	Miller's
Great Lakes	Mozzarella Co.
Helluva Good	Organic Valley
Hillandele Farms	Polly-O
Horizon Organic	Vermont

Chili powder (NSA)
The Spice Hunter

Chips

Bearitos	Naturally Preferred
Blue Farm	Padrinos
El Ranchero	Que Pasa
Jays	Snyders of Hanover
Kettle Chips	Utz

Egg roll/wonton wrappers

Azumaya	Melissa's
Dynasty	

Horseradish

Beano's	Heluva Good
Deaver	Inglehoffer
Boar's Head	

Hot Pepper Sauce

McIllhenny	Phamous Phloyd's
Mr. Spicy	Watkins

Ketchup

Estee	Hunt's
Featherwieght	Steel's
Hain	Tree of Life
Heniz	Westbrae Natural

Leavening agents (baking soda and yeast)

Ener-G	Featherweight

Margarine / Butter

Fleischman's	Promise

Mayonnaise

Arise	Hain
Featherweight	Saffola
Geffen	Spectrum

Mustards

Bee Maid	Haus Barkyte
Brad's	Hickory Farms
Cherchies	HoneyCup
East Shore	Plochman's
Featherweight	Temeraine
Grey Poupon (Honey Dijon)	
Hain	Westbrae Natural

Olives
Lindsay

Pasta sauce

Eden	Mother
Enrico's	Pomodor
Francesco Rinaldi	Savion
Manischewitz	Teresa's
Med-Diet	Tree of Life
Melissa's	Walnut Acres

Pesto

Candoni	Santini
Rising Sun Farms	

Peanut Butter

Adams	Kettle
Arrowhead Mills	Natural Value
Atkins	North Farm
Crazy Richard's	Peter Pan
Eastwind	Smucker's

Pickle Relish

B&G	Farman's
Cascadian Farm	Mt Olive
Claussen	

Pie crusts

Great Value	Pet-Ritz
Marie Callender's	

Pita/Pocket bread

Garden of Eatin'	Giant

Salsas

Cannon's	Hot Cha Cha
Dianaa's	Quinn's
Floribbean	Santa Barbara
Frog Ranch	Steel's
Garlic Survival	Tree of Life
Gloria's	

Sausage (lower salt)

Gerhard's	Johnsville

Seasonings

Bell's	McCormick
Cavender's	Mrs. Dash
Chef Paul Prudhomme	
Fortner's	The Spice Hunter
Graham Kerr's	Tone's

Soy Sauce (lower salt)

Angostura	Rice Road
House of Tsang	Yamasa

Tomato products

America's Choice	Hunt's
Bel Aire	La Squisita
Cento	Muir Glen
Contadina	Pomi
Del Monte	S&W
Eden	Tree of Life

Tortillas / Wraps

Adios Carbs	Pinata
Casa Fiesta	Tumaro's
Lavash	

Vegetable juices

Aylmer	RW Knudsen
Hunt's	V8

Worcestershire sauce

Angostura	Robbies
Life	

ONLINE MANUFACTURERS

Allen Canning Company
www.allencanning.com
(NSA vegetables)

Annie's Naturals
792 Foster Hill Rd.
North Calais, VT 05650
800.434.1234 or 802.456.8866
www.anniesnaturals.com
(LS salad dressings and BBQ sauce)

Blazing Blends
www.blazingblends.com
(salt-free spice blends and barbecue rubs)

Drew's Salad Dressings
926 Vermont Route 103
Chester, Vermont 05143
800-228-2980
www.chefdrew.com
(LS salad dressings and marinades)

Eden Foods, Inc.
701 Tecumseh Rd.
Clinton, MI 49236
888.424.EDEN
www.edenfoods.com
(LS canned beans and tomatoes)

Garden of Eatin'
800.434.4246
www.gardenofeatin.com
(LS chips and flour tortillas)

Gloria's Gourmet Foods
425 2nd St. Alley
Lake Oswego, OR 97034
800.782.5881 or 802.388.6581
www.gloriasgourmet.com
(LS salad dressings and fruit sauces)

N.K. Hurst Co.
P.O. Box 985
Indianapolis, IN 46206
800.426.2336 or 317.634.6425
www.nkhurst.com
(LS bean soup mixes)

Melissa's
P.O. 21127
Los Angeles, CA 90021
800.588.0151
www.melissas.com
(LS egg roll wrappers)

Mozzarella Company
800.798.2954 or 214.741.4072
www.mozzco.com
(several NSA and LS cheeses)

Mr. Spice c/o Lang Naturals
850 Aquidneck Ave.
Newport, RI 02842
800.SAUCE.IT or 401.848.7700
www.mrspice.com
(NSA sauces, also fat and sugar free)

Rising Sun Farms
5126 So. Pacific Hwy.
Phoenix, OR 97535-6606
800.888.0795 X-211
www.risingsunfarms.com
(LS cheese spreads)

Vogue Cuisine, Inc.
3710 Grand View Blvd.
Los Angeles, CA 90066
888.236.4144
www.voguecuisine.com
(lower sodium soup bases)

Walden Farms
800.229.1706
www.waldenfarms.com
(LS alfredo and chocolate sauce)

ONLINE GROCERY STORES

The Better Health Store
305 N. Clippert
Lansing, MI 48912
877.876.8247
www.thebetterhealthstore.com
(carries many low-sodium products)

DietaryShoppe.com
www.dietaryshoppe.com
(carries several low-sodium products)

eDiet Shop
P.O. Box 1037
Evanston, IL 60204-1397
800.325.5409 or 847.679.5409
www.edietshop.com
(carries several low-sodium products)

eFood Pantry
2520 S. Grand Ave. East
Springfield, IL 62703
800.238.8090
www.efoodpantry.com
(carries several low-sodium products)

Healthy Heart Market
800.753.0310
www.healthyheartmarket.com
(carries only low-sodium products)

www.mykoshermarket.com
(carries kosher foods, including several low-sodium products)

www.mothernature.com
(carries several low-sodium products)

www.netgrocer.com
(online grocer carrying many low-sodium products)

www.peapod.com
(regional online market carrying many low-sodium foods)

Salt Watcher Inc.
2002 Covert St.
Pittsburgh, PA 15210
412.882.0243
www.saltwatcher.com
(carries over 250 low-sodium products)

www.shoplowsodium.com
(carries many low-sodium products)

www.shopnatural.com
(carries several low-sodium products)

Strictly Natural, Inc.
31 Seabreeze Ave.
Thornhill, ON L4J 8R6 Canada
877.771.1230 or 905.771.0095
www.strictlynatural.com
(carries several low-sodium products)

WorldPantry.com, Inc.
1024 Illinois St.
San Francisco, CA 94107
866.972.6879 or 415.581.0067
www.worldpantry.com
(carries several low-sodium products)

THE DASH DIET

NHLBI Health Information Center
(Publication #01-4082)
P.O. Box 30105
Bethesda, MD 20824-0105
301.592.8573 or
240.629.3255 (TTY)
www.nhlbi.nih.gov

INDEX